NSE4 Study Guide Series
Book Two of Four

Introduction to Fortigate
Part-II Infrastructure
Fortinet Network Security Introduction

By Daniel Howard
NSE8 #003255

For any comments or recommendations, please email me directly at howardsinc@gmail.com

Introduction to Fortigate Part-II Infrastructure

Copyright © 2020 iFirewall LLC

Black and White Edition

ISBN: 9798621133221

Imprint: Independently published

Dedication

To my wonderful wife Samantha for all her love
and support throughout this project.

To my wonderful kid's Araya, Darwin, and Ryker for being awesome
and allowing daddy time to write this book!

To my buddy Freddy Smeltzer for all the proofreading work he helped me with
and also the lab guide within this book!

To the rest of my family, friends, and colleagues,
thanks for providing your support!

About the Author

Daniel Howard is an independent author and subject matter expert in many Fortinet technologies. He is only a few hundred to obtain the prestigious Fortinet Network Security Expert 8 certification, a grueling 2-day on-site lab examination. For the past decade, Daniel has worked in the carrier space, highly focused on consulting, managing, and maintaining Fortinet networks for Manage Security Service Providers (MSSPs). He has managed several carrier migration projects, deployments, provided technical training to customers, and served as a technical escalation point throughout his career. Daniel works at Fortinet as a Technical Account Manager to this day, consulting within the carrier space, and continues to assist various security engineering and operation teams.

To stay updated on my latest content, consider following my Facebook page, Amazon author page, or the Fortinet Press website.

https://www.facebook.com/fortinetpress/

https://www.amazon.com/Daniel-Howard/e/B08BS3B4NY

https://fortinetpress.com/

Enjoy!

Acknowledgments

This book took many, many hours of my life to write. I'm grateful that I've had awesome leadership and mentors throughout my career to help me get to this point to give back. I am certainly standing on the shoulders of giants. I appreciate all the feedback that has been provided. I want to stress that all the typos and errors that may have slipped into this book series are 100% my fault and have no reflection on Fortinet as a company and anyone who has helped me with this book's content. I am an independent author and publisher that writes during my free time when I'm not working as a Fortinet TAM or fulfilling my duties as a father and husband.

After I decided to publish Part-I of the series, I honestly had doubts if I would keep writing and complete the series because I did think many folks would be interested in the book; however, I was very wrong. A few months after I published Part-I, my book started selling around the world literally. I had folks from Germany, Denmark, France, Japan, and the UK purchasing Part-I. I also had many folks that contacted me asking when Part-II would be released. I could not believe it. As a whole, I appreciate the support and feedback of the entire community, and I want to thank you for the motivation to keep writing! And here we are, Part-II is complete.

I want to give special thanks to Mike Pruett with FortinetGURU for taking the time to review Part-I of the series on his YouTube channel. He is an awesome guy, and I love his passion for Fortinet technology!

I also want to give special thanks to my friend Freddy Smeltzer for providing a very robust GNS3 lab setup guide with FortiOS. I believe anyone that is just starting to learn Fortinet technologies would benefit greatly from this lab!

Network Security Expert 4 (NSE4) Exam

The NSE4 certification recognizes your ability to install and manage the day-to-day configuration, monitoring, and operation of a FortiGate device to support specific corporate network security policies.

<u>Who Should Attempt the NSE4 Certification?</u>

The NSE4 exam is designed for security professionals involved in the day-to-day management, implementation, and administration of a security infrastructure using FortiGate devices. The current cost to attempt the exam is $400.

<u>NSE4 Exam details</u>

As of December 2020, there are two NSE4 exams available through Pearson Vue testing, which are:

1) **NSE4_FGT-6.2**
    a. 70 Questions
    b. Two hours to complete
    c. Available in English and Japanese
    d. Registration end 4/30/2021
2) **NSE4_FGT-6.4**
    a. 60 Questions
    b. 105 minutes
    c. Available in English and Japanese
    d. No posted end date

The high-level domains of knowledge covered by the NSE4 exam are:

1) System and Hardware
2) Firewall and NAT
3) Authentication
4) Content Inspection
5) Routing and L2 Switching
6) VPN
7) Logging and Diagnostics

Part-I & Part-II of this NSE4 study guide focuses on infrastructure technologies related to FortiGate. For example, layer-2, layer-3, layer-4, VPNs, HA, logging, SD-WAN, and troubleshooting.

Table of Contents

Introduction to FortiGate Infrastructure Part-II

Part-II Infrastructure NSE4 Study Guide

- Part-II Introduction
- Chapter Overviews
- Lab Setup Guide

I troduction to FortiGate Infrastructure Part-II picks up right where Part-I left off with Chapter 5. Part-I of the series focused on taking someone with basic computer networking knowledge and bringing them up to speed with basic FortiGate functions. Part-II builds on all the basic concepts by stepping into more advanced technologies FortiOS has to offer.

The NSE4 blueprint topics are logically separated into two sections, Infrastructure and Security. The purpose of this segregation of material is to build your skillset up layer by layer because you will not be able to understand DPI Web Filtering without first understanding basic FortiOS routing and the Session table functions. A common misconception is that there are two exams for the NSE4; this is false. You only need to pass one test to become NSE4 certified.

The feedback I received back from Introduction to FortiGate Part-II was mostly positive. People from around the world reached out to me to discuss the book's content and ask questions. I really felt a lot of appreciation from certain folks. I could tell other folks that already have FortiGate experience was a little frustrated with the book because it was too basic. With Part-II of this NSE4 study guide series, I hope to satisfy both sides of people who already have some FortiGate experience but looking to increase their skillset and folks who are new to FortiGate that only have the knowledge provided in Part-I. I'm confident that even the most experienced FortiGate engineers will learn something new after reading this book. I'm also confident that I will not lose new folks as I walk through the various topics discussed in this book.

> *Infrastructure - The basic underlying framework or features of a system or organization.*

I recommended in Part-I of this NSE4 study guide series to have a lab because I feel like real hands-on experience is critical for understanding new technologies. I took this a step further in Part-II by providing detailed instructions on setting up a GNS3 lab with FortiOS VM. I urge you to take time and set up this lab before you start working your way through this book because as I discuss these various technologies, I hope you will be configuring FortiOS inline with me!

FortiOS is a fast-moving technology with constant updates and new features. Fortinet is one of the most innovative companies globally. It is honestly hard to keep up with all the changes, so I decided to base Part-II on 6.4, the latest MR. Once all books of this NSE4 study guide series are complete, one of my goals is to go back and upgrade all the content to the latest MR at that point in time. So as I release new books, they will be based on the latest MR regardless. With that being said, most folks do not run the latest MR in production; an N-1 method is more common. Essentially, this means operating one MR behind the latest. Using an N-1 MR method allows Fortinet to work major software defects out of new MR code bases. From what I've seen in my tenure working with Fortinet products and customers, a new MR production code base will not be deployed until at least the 4th patch within an MR. Note, this does not always hold true for engineering teams who aggressively certify Fortinet products to obtain the features they want for their deployments.

Infrastructure Part-II Chapter Overview

Part-II of the NSE4 study guide series has seven chapters and build off what you learned in Part-I. Here is the complete list of Chapters in this book:

Part-II Chapter 5 | VDOMs and Session Helpers

Chapter five starts off with reviewing Virtual Domains (VDOM) technology on FortiOS, a feature to segregate a single FortiGate into virtual firewalls. These virtual firewalls are autonomous from each other but share global settings. Chapter five also reviews Session Helper technology. Session Helpers are a new concept to many network engineers who only work with layer-2/layer-3 routers and switches. FortiGate is a stateful device, and therefore Sessions Helpers will always be a factor when working with protocols like FTP, SIP, or RTP.

Part-II Chapter 6 | High Availability (HA)

In chapter six, we begin our journey into FortiGate High Availability (HA) technologies. HA is a major item for modern networks accounting for hardware failures to maintain availability for countless network services. The argument is not if hardware will fail but when. FortiGate HA provides businesses the right tools to handle hardware failures gracefully.

Part-II Chapter 7 | Logging and Monitoring

In chapter seven, we step into the fundamental lifeline of any successful Security Operations Center (SoC), the log. FortiOS has robust logging around many different features. This chapter reviews how to configure logging and provides details around certain specific FortiOS logging features administrators need to account for. Lastly, in this chapter, various monitoring features are discussed. FortiGate provides many monitoring tools to gain insight into what is going on within your network.

Part-II Chapter 8 | IPsec VPN

Chapter eight might be my favorite chapter in Part-II of this NSE4 study series. I have always loved working with IPsec, and this chapter provided us the opportunity to deep dive into the technology. After reading this chapter and knowing true, you will be confident in how IPsec works and how to implement it on FortiGate!

Part-II Chapter 9 | SSL VPN

Chapter nine focuses on TLS technology and how FortiGate uses this technology to create SSL-VPN for remote users! By the end of this chapter, you will feel confident in how TLS works and how to configure and manage SSL-VPN features on FortiOS.

Part-II Chapter 10 | SD-WAN

Chapter ten is where we get to the good stuff, SD-WAN. Within this chapter, we unmask this magical technology that focuses on dynamic best path application routing. By the end of this chapter, you will have a great foundation in FortiOS SD-WAN to build on.

Part-II Chapter 11 | Diagnostics and Troubleshooting

Chapter eleven, the last chapter of the book we focus on troubleshooting methodologies. We walk through various troubleshooting steps and methods, starting with the FortiGate system health. This chapter also touches on troubleshooting methods for networking, VPNs, HA, and SD-WAN.

FortiOS Lab Setup Guide

Not everyone has the cash to spend on purchasing a lab FortiGate device, but this doesn't mean there are no other avenues to obtain hands-on experience!

The purpose of this lab setup guide is to provide you an environment to practice what is discussed throughout the course of this book. Fortinet allows individuals to download a trial version of the FortiGate VM; note that the temporary license is only valid for 15 days. In this section, we walk through the steps to implement a virtualized network with FortiOS at the center. Please note that this is not an all-inclusive guide, such topics as how to navigate GNS3 and how to disable Hyper-V are not included. If you are experiencing any issues with the platforms demonstrated in this guide, I would suggest visiting the vendor forums or documentation. We will be using the following products in this lab setup guide:

- VirtualBox version 6.1.14 – This is what we will use as our hypervisor. A hypervisor enables us to run multiple virtual machines on our physical host and share our host's resources. Please note that additional host configuration may be needed.
- GNS3 version 2.2.14 – This is what we will use as our network simulator. GNS3 comes fitted with many tools such as Wireshark and can be utilized with the GNS3 VM to provide faster appliance deployments.

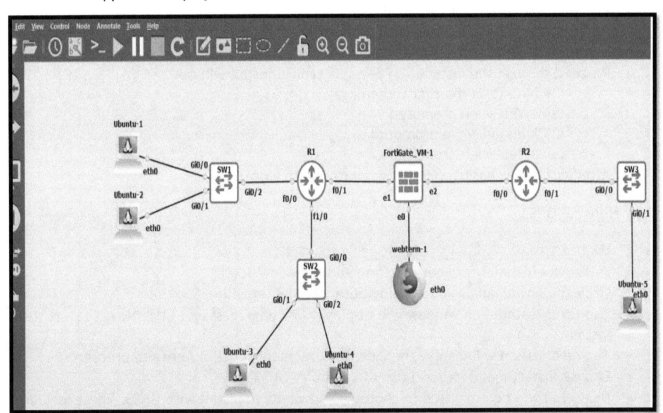

In addition to the platforms listed above, we will also be using several virtual machine images. This guide will document where to download these images and how to incorporate them into GNS3. We will be using the following software

- Cisco ISOv and Cisco ISOvl2 - These are the Cisco images we will use in the lab to simulate routers and switches. Cisco allows you to download these images, but you must purchase a Cisco VIRL license. There are other vendor router and switch images that are freely available to the public, as well.
- GNS3 VM version 2.2.14 - This is a Linux-based virtual machine that runs a GNS3 server; this allows us to run QEMU and KVM images from this server vs. our host machine. Windows host can have difficulties running KVM images.
- Fortinet VM64 KVM v6 build1778 - We will need to use the KVM version for this lab.
- Webterm - This is a GNS3 appliance that can be found from the GNS3 marketplace; it is free to use and will be our method to reach the FortiGate GUI.

Note the software versions for this lab because, as with any technology, things change. I believe this lab will continue to serve as a baseline and starting point for folks that wish to obtain hands-on experience with FortiOS.

Step 1: Install VirtualBox

- Visit ww.virtualbox.org
- Go to downloads and download the VirtualBox package for your platform.
- Run the VirtualBox .exe file.
- Proceed through the installation prompts typical install will be:
  - Click **Next** on the first three pages
  - Click **Yes** when prompted
  - Click **install** when prompted
  - Click **Yes** when prompted
- After VirtualBox has been installed, move on to step 2.

Step 2: Install GNS3

- Visit https://www.gns3.com/software/download
- Select the installer for your platform and click download.
- Once the download has been completed, run the .exe file.
- The GNS3 installation window will display a welcome message. Click **Next** to start the install.
- The next screen will display the License Agreement. Click, **I Agree** to proceed.
- Choose a start menu folder. I use the default "GNS3".
- Next, you will be prompted to choose components to install with GNS3. These include Wireshark, Dynamips, QEMU, and so on. I will keep the preselected defaults and click **Next**.

- Select an installation folder or keep the default and click **install.**
- During the installation phase, if you have selected any third-party tools during the "Choose Components" step, they will be installed now. You will be prompted to accept the license agreement of third-party tools. Npcap will prompt you for installation options; make sure the following are selected:
    - o Automatically start the Npcap driver at boot time
    - o Support loopback traffic ("Npcap Loopback Adapter" will be created)
    - o Support raw 802.11 traffic (and monitor mode) for wireless adapters
    - o Support 802.1Q VLAN tag when capturing and sending data
- Click **Next** to install Npcap, then click finished once Npcap has finished installing.
- After GNS3 finishes installing, click **Next,** and you will be offered a free license of Solarwinds Standard Toolset. This is not required for the Fortigate lab; you can either download it or select no and click **Next.**
- At this point, GNS3 will be installed on your system; click Finish to close the GNS3 installation wizard.

Step 3: Install GNS3 VM

Before moving to this stage, VirtualBox and GNS3 need to be installed on your PC. Please note that for best performance, GNS3 and GNS3 VM need to be running the same version. If you have downloaded GNS3 in the past but not the VM, you might need to update your current GNS3 install. In the example, GNS3 2.2.16 will need GNS3 VM version 2.2.16 for optimal performance.

- Navigate to https://www.gns3.com/software/download-vm. Click the download link beside VirtualBox.
- Once downloaded, you need to extract the compressed file to the folder of your choosing.
- Next, we will need to import the gns3 VM.ova image into VirtualBox.
    - o Open VirtualBox and select **New**
    - o Enter the following information:
        - ▪ Name: GNS3 VM
        - ▪ Type: Other
        - ▪ Version: Other/Unknown (64-bit)
    - o Click **Continue.**
    - o Select the amount of memory to assign to this VM (you want to remain with in the green area of the slider) and click **Continue.**
    - o VirtualBox will then prompt you for "Appliance to Import", select the gns vm.ova that we extracted earlier, and click **Continue.**
    - o Next, set the appliance settings as needed; the defaults in our case will be fine. Then select **Import.**
- Next (once the import completes), we will need to configure the network adaptor for both VirtualBox and the GNS3 VM.

- o Go to VirtualBox and select Preferences, then **Network**
- o Here select the **Host-only Networks** tab
- o Click the plus symbol on the right-hand-side and enter an IP and subnet mask for this adapter. You can use the automatically assigned IP from your system if you choose to do so, and click done once complete.
- o Next right click on the GNS3 VM and select **Settings**
- o Navigate to the **Network** menu and set Adapter 1 to **Enable** and attach it to **Host-only Adaptor**
- o Select **vboxnet0** from the dropdown menu and click **OK**

Step 4: Configure GNS3

In this step, we will be configuring GNS3 to use the GNS3 VM, and we will be importing appliances to run our Fortigate lab.

- • First, we will need to configure GNS3 to run using the GNS3 VM.
  - o Run GNS3 and the Setup Wizard should launch automatically; if not, click help from the GNS3 menu and click Setup Wizard.
  - o Select **Run modern IOS** and hit **NEXT.**
  - o On this screen, you will be prompted to configure the local server, choose 127.0.0.1 from the menu (port should be 3080 TCP), and hit **NEXT.**
  - o You will reach a screen that says "Local server status" with "Connection to local server successful" click **NEXT.** If you receive a warning that says "VirtualBox doesn't support nested virtualization", click **OK.**
  - o The next screen will display, "In order to run the GNS3 VM, you must first have VMware or VirtualBox installed, and the GNS3 VM.ova imported with one of these software". Select VirtualBox and select the name of the GNS3 VM that we configured in VirtualBox (it should be auto-detected, make sure the VM is running). Assign the desired amount of vCPU cores and RAM, then click **Next**
  - o The next page will display a summary. Click **Finish.**
  - o GNS3 should now be configured to run using the GNS3 VM

- • Next, we will need to import appliances to build our network topology. Remember that if you choose to use Cisco images, you will need a Cisco VIRL license (this method will work with other vendor images as well, some of these can be obtained for free from the vendor). I tend to use cisco-iosvl2 for network switches and cisco-iosv for network routers.
  - o From GNS3 main view, click **File** from the toolbar, then select **Import appliance.**
  - o Navigate to your **Downloads** folder (or destination where the images are stored) and click to open.
  - o You will be prompted with a screen that says, "Please choose a server type to install the appliance", make sure that you select "install the appliance on the GNS3 VM (recommended)" and click **Next.**

- o The next screen will display "Qemu settings", make sure that **/user/bin/qemu-system-x86_64** is selected and click **Next**.
- o The next screen will display the "Required Files", on this page, you will need to select the appliance version that you wish to install. The status bar will show "Missing files".
- o Select the version of the VM that you wish to install and click **Import**. (The import option assumes that you already have the necessary file downloaded if GNS3 is unable to locate the file select **download**. This will open a browser window with the associate website to download the file.)
- o After clicking **Import** (and after downloading the required file), a window will open, allowing you to browse to the file location of the image/virtual disk image for the device you are importing. Click **Open**.
- o Next, GNS3 will check the md5 checksum and file size versus the .gnsa template; if the values match gns3 will upload a copy of that file to the GNS3 VM.
- o In the "Required files" window, the status of the uploaded VM will change from "Missing" to "Ready to install". Select the version of the uploaded VM and click **Next**.
- o The next screen will display "Usage" and will display the default settings. Click **Finish**.
- o Finally, you will be prompted that the appliance has been successfully installed. Click **Ok** to exit.
- o You can now click the **Browse all Devices** options from the left menu pane to drag and drop the newly created appliance into your topology.
- Now we are ready to install the FortiGate KVM virtual firewall. As previously noted, you will need to visit the Fortinet support portal (https://support.fortinet.com) and register an account. You will navigate to **Downloads>VM Images>FortiGate** and select **KVM** as the platform, then just download the image.
  - o Once you have downloaded the FortiGate KVM image, the file will need to be extracted. Simply right-click on the .zip file and click extract. The extracted file will be fortios.qcow2 as this is a QEMU image.
  - o Next, open up GNS3 and navigate to **Edit>Preferences>QEMU>Qemu VMs** and click on **New**.
  - o The "New QEMU VM template" window will be displayed; go ahead and name your FortiGate VM and click **Next**.
  - o On this screen, you will need to assign RAM to the FortiGate; with the default 15-day license, a Fortinet VM only supports 1 CPU core and 1024 MB of RAM. Set the RAM to 1024 MB and click **Next**.
  - o This screen will ask you to select a console type; for this demonstration, we will select **Telnet** and click **Next**.
  - o This screen will ask you to "Please choose a base disk image for your virtual machine", this is the fortios.qcow2 image that we downloaded earlier. Click **Browse..** and navigate to the file location of the .qcow2 image. Click **Finish**.

o You can customize your FortiGate VM further by clicking **Edit** from the GNS3 toolbar then selecting **Preferences**. Navigate to **QEMU VMs** and select the FortiGate VM and select **Edit**. Here you can configure the network adapter count, as well as interface type etc.

Step 5: Base FortiGate Configuration

In this step, we will be doing a basic network configuration for the FortiGate VM as well as installing Webterm to provide a web browser to log into the FortiGate VM GUI.

- Now that you have successfully created the FortiGate appliance, let's put a basic configuration on the device so that we can access the web GUI.
  - o Click on all devices from the left GNS3 toolbar and select the FortiGate. Drag and drop the firewall into the GNS3 project area.
  - o Right-click on the FortiGate and click on the start option; this will boot the device and open a console window. If the console window does not open automatically, right-click on the device and select console.
  - o Once the device finishes booting, the console will prompt you to log in. The default username is admin, and the password is left blank.
  - o FortiOS will now prompt you to change the admin password, change the password, and remember the password as you will use it to log into the GUI.
  - o Now we will configure interface ethernet1/1 with an IP address and necessary services.
  - o Enter the following console commands:
    - config system interface
    - edit port1
    - set mode static
    - set ip 192.168.1.1 255.255.255.0
    - set allowaccess https http ping ssh
    - end
  - o At this point, you will be ready to install Webterm and access the web-based GUI.
- Webterm is a lightweight Linux-based docker container that includes a Firefox web browser; the following steps show how to download the appliance and install in GNS3.
  - o First, browse to https://www.gns3.com and select marketplace, and search the marketplace for webterm.
  - o Click the download button for webterm.
  - o Once the download finishes, open up GNS3 and select **file>import appliance>** and select the webterm.gns3a image from your downloads folder and click open.
  - o Select to install the appliance on the GNS3 VM and click **Next**.
  - o Click **Finish** on the next screen, and Webterm will now be available to use in GNS3.

- Now we will configure Webterm with an IP address and connect the Webterm docker to our FortiGate firewall.
  - Click on all devices from the left GNS3 toolbar, drag and drop Webterm into the GNS3 project window.
  - Right-click on Webterm and select start, then double click on the device to bring up the TightVNC Viewer window.
  - A Firefox browser window will be displayed by default; minimize this window.
  - Left-click inside the TightVNC Viewer window to display a list of options and select **Terminal**. This action will open a Linux shell.
  - Enter the following commands to set the network for the Webterm docker. Please note that the IP address you assign Webterm will need to be in the same subnet as the recently created FortiGate VM.
    - ifconfig eth0 192.168.1.50 netmask 255.255.255.0 up
    - route add default gw 192.168.1.1
    - echo "nameserver 1.1.1.1" > /etc/resolv.conf
    - to verify type ifconfig

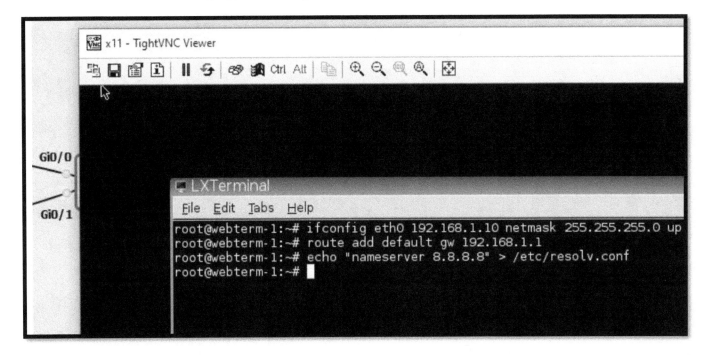

- Next, we will need to connect the Webterm docker container to the FortiGate VM via ethernet and log into the FortiGate http GUI.
  - From the GNS3 left toolbar, click add a link.
  - Click on the Webterm docker and select eth0.
  - Now click on the FortiGate VM and select eth0. Please note that in the above steps, we configured port1 on the FortiGate CLI; there is a naming offset in GNS3. **port1 = eth0.**

- o Now click on Webterm to open the TightVNC Viewer. Mozilla Firefox should be displayed by default; if it is not, left-click and select **Applications>Mozilla Firefox.**
- o Type http://192.168.1.1 and hit **enter.**
- o You will reach the GUI login landing page, enter admin as the username and enter the password you configured in the FortiGate CLI earlier.
- o At this point, you can now configure the FortiGate from the GUI and practice different scenarios in a lab setting.

Lab Setup Summary

Alright, folks, that's it! At this point, you should have a fully operational FortiOS lab! Nice work! Now we are ready to start working our way through chapter five! Let's get to it!

NSE4 Blueprint Topics Covered

Chapter 5 | Session Helpers and VDOMs

- Define and Describe Session Helpers
- Configure Session Helpers
- Understand and Configure ALG
- Define and describe VDOMs
- Understand Management VDOM
- Understand VDOM Administrators
- Configure multiple VDOMs
- understand and configure Inter-vdom link
- limit resource allocated to VDOMs
- Inter-VDOM Link Hardware Acceleration
- VDOM Diagnostics

In this chapter, we are going to focus on Session Helpers and VDOMs. We are going to review details on how to configure and manage both technologies on FortiOS. I will show you how to limit VDOM resources, so a single VDOM does not take all the CPU and memory from all the others. Also, we get a chance to discuss what Inter-VDOM links are. Sometimes it is necessary to route between VDOMs, and this is the feature we use.

The other topic we cover in this chapter is something called *Session Helpers*. This technology is required for some protocols that need special assistance in certain NAT'ing situations to be functional when passing through stateful firewalls like FortiGate. We will go over another feature called Application Layer Gateway or ALG, which is essentially a Session Helper. We will go into detail on what ALG is and discuss how and when to use it!

Session Helpers

Let me start by saying, if you are working with a Session Helper, it is most likely not a good day because you only need to engage this configuration if something is broken or if you are performing certification testing in a lab and something is not working quite right.

Many application protocols require a Session Helper. The fundamental reason they are required is because FortiOS maintains Session Entries for all allowed traffic and expects certain traffic back with the associated layer-3/layer-4 parameters for said Session Entry. Remember, an SNAT/DNAT Session Entry is built off the NAT IP, the original source port, destination port, and IP values.

These protocols that require Session Helpers leave FortiGate using one source port, and return traffic may be using a different port than the one it left on. This is because, at the application layer, a source port was shared with the other side of the network-based application. The application uses the port/IP shared via the application layer instead of the header source TCP/IP port or IP it came in on.

This might sound odd, and you might be wondering why the application would do this. Well, at the beginning of computer networking technologies, these applications were not designed to deal with NAT or stateful devices. When the Internet first started to gain traction, there were only routers and switches devices that dealt with mostly layer-2 and layer-3 header information. A basic router only cares about looking up the destination IP address in an IP packet, so it knows which interface to forward the packet out. Once the packet is forwarded, the device did not create any Session Entry or keep any metadata about the packet. Therefore, when these applications were first written, they didn't have issues because the older routers were stateless devices.

Many RFC standards have been revised to account for NAT and stateful devices now, and a lot of the time, you need to disable session helpers because the newer version of the application now accounts for NAT and stateful firewalls like FortiGate and having the Session Helper enabled actually breaks the communication sometimes.

As you could see, if applications accounted for stateful devices and NAT from the beginning of the Internet, we would never have needed Session Helpers to be created in the first place. And the solution can now break the application. It is a case-by-case basis if a Session Helper is required. You find out quickly when an application does not work.

A Session Helper looks inside the application-level data and pulls out the port and IP address the return traffic will use. FortiOS creates an Expected Session Entry, or FortiOS can actually modify the application-level data within some protocols like SIP to account for the correct egress port number or IP NAT address.

I've spent many hours of my life troubleshooting Session Helpers and trying to figure out if it was required to be enabled or disabled or if they were actually solving the problem or creating the problem. There is a lot of trial and error with session helpers because most of the time, systems administrators responsible for the applications do not know what RFC the application conforms to or what version the application is, so it's really guesswork. That being said, working with applications that are affected by Session Helpers can be more of an art than a science.

Session Helpers on FortiOS

The first thing to review is where to find all the session helpers on FortiOS. In the CLI, navigate via:

```
config system session-helper
    ..
    edit 9
        set name ftp
        set protocol 6
        set port 21
```

```
    next
..
end
```

These are the default values, and no way do you need to remember all of these. We are only going to talk about the most popular Session Helpers. The first is SIP Session Helper, a module to handle the Session Initiation Protocol (SIP) and RTP traffic.

<u>SIP Session Helper</u>

SIP Session Helper dynamically inspect SIP 5060 traffic and, if required, opens pinhole sessions for voice (RTP) traffic. Like I said before, the reason for this is because SIP communicates ports for RTP voice data (Real-Time Protocol) within the application layer SIP message headers, and FortiOS needs to be aware of these ports to allow return traffic back through the firewall, and essentially there must be a Session Entry waiting to accept the traffic which we call a 'pinhole'. Also, when NAT'ing occurs in some cases, it is required to translate the SIP application data IP's to reflect the real public IP address on the egress interface and not a private one. The NSE7 goes over these topics in detail.

On 6.4 FortiOS, SIP Helper is disabled by default and must be explicitly enabled. These settings are located via CLI:

```
NSE4-PASS # config system settings
NSE4-PASS (settings) # set default-voip-alg-mode
proxy-based           Use a default proxy-based VoIP ALG.
kernel-helper-based   Use the SIP session helper.

NSE4-PASS (settings) # show ful | grep sip
    set sip-helper enable
```

Note here that the **kernel-helper-based** setting means FortiOS uses SIP Session Helper, and **proxy-based** means FortiOS uses SIP ALG. Lastly, the **sip-helper** setting must be toggled to be enabled.

Next, to disable SIP Session Helper, it must be disabled in the CLI under *'config system settings'* and then the SIP entry under *'config system session-helper'* must be deleted as well.

```
NSE4-PASS (settings) # show ful | grep sip
    set sip-helper disable
NSE4-PASS #   config system session-helper
NSE4-PASS (session-helper) # edit 13
NSE4-PASS (13) # show
config system session-helper
    edit 13
        set name sip
        set protocol 17
        set port 5060
```

```
    next
end
NSE4-PASS (13) # next
NSE4-PASS (session-helper) # delete 13
```

Lastly, I provide a list of debug commands for SIP Helper for your notes.

```
#diagnose sys sip
#diagnose sys sip dialog list
#diagnose sys sip mapping list
#diagnose sys sip status
```

SIP Application Layer Gateway

ALG stands for Application Layer Gateway and provides the same base functions for SIP and RTP as the SIP Session Helper module and more. In most cases, you would want to use SIP ALG if pinholes are a factor. SIP ALG provides additional protection from various SIP attacks. You can also use this feature for SIP rate limiting, syntax checking of SIP and SDP message contents, and lastly, provide more detailed log messages. As of 6.4 FortiOS, by default, all SIP traffic is processed by SIP ALG.

ALG provides more granular control on things like pinhole creation. Administrators can choose not to create pinhole Session Entries for things like RTP. ALG could be disabled; the below CLI commands would be used to accomplish this. Firstly is to create a VoIP Profile and apply to Firewall Policy Entry:

```
config voip profile
edit Voip_Profile
config sip
set status disable
end

NSE4-PASS #config firewall policy
NSE4-PASS(policy) # edit 0
NSE4-PASS (0) # set action accept
NSE4-PASS (0) # set utm-status enable
NSE4-PASS (0) # set voip-profile Voip_Profile
```

As you can see, we had to disable ALG in a VoiP profile explicitly and then apply the profile to a Firewall Policy Entry that accepts the SIP traffic. There are many more features on SIP ALG, and unfortunately, these details are not covered in the NSE4, so for more detailed information on SIP ALG, checkout:

https://pub.kb.fortinet.com/ksmcontent/Fortinet-Public/current/FortiGate_6_0/fortigate-sip-603.pdf

FTP Session Helper

The next Session Helper module I am going to cover in this chapter is for FTP. FTP utilizes two ports for communication, which are 21 and 20 TCP. Port 21 is used for the initial connection setup, and 20 is used for the actual data transfer. FTP must use Session Helper because it negotiates its data ports by using two different methods over the application layer on port 21, and FortiOS needs to know about the ports negotiated so a pinhole session entry can be allocated for the data traffic. Pinhole sessions are also called expected sessions.

The two types of FTP are called Active and Passive. The Active FTP method is where the FTP client sends the FTP server the PORT command over port 21. The client then sends its IP address and source port value. Then the server initiates a connection for the data transfer connection back to the client on the specified open port. If this FTP client is communicating behind a FortiGate without a session helper configured, then that initial server-side TCP SYN packet for the data connection is drop if there is not an explicit WAN->LAN port forward configured. For the Active method, the FTP Session Helper parses out the client source port value, which is conveyed through the application layer, and dynamically inserts a new session entry so that the server TCP SYN packet is allowed through.

For the Passive FTP method, the client initiates the data connection using the PASV FTP command over TCP port 21. This command tells the FTP server to open a port locally and then communicates to the client what port to connect to for the TCP data connection. Then the client initiates the data connection. This method is used to bypass network firewall issues for the client-side but could cause issues on the server-side because of the same logic.

As you can see, ports are being negotiated behind the scenes over port TCP 21 that FortiGate would not know about if it was not for the Session Helper feature. The FTP Session Helper on FortiGate is enabled by default.

```
FGT# show system session-helper | grep ftp -f
config system session-helper
..
    edit 9
        set name ftp <---
        set protocol 6
        set port 21
    next
..
```

To explicitly disable a Session Helper, the following commands could be used.

```
FGT# config firewall service custom
FGT(custom)#edit Helper-disable
FGT(Helper-disable)# set tcp-portrange 21
FGT(Helper-disable)# set helper disable
FGT(Helper-disable)# end
```

Time to look at the DNS session helper.

<u>DNS Session Helper</u>

Before moving onto the VDOM NSE4 topics, I want to take a little time to review the DNS Session Helper. Check out the below CLI output:

```
30E-B-231 (global) # show sys session-helper | grep dns -f
config system session-helper
    edit 14
        set name dns-udp <---
        set protocol 17
        set port 53
    next
end
```

The purpose of the DNS session helper is for DNS translation, which was created to modify DNS replay from a DNS server. Details can be found in this KB:

https://kb.fortinet.com/kb/documentLink.do?externalID=FD34099

The reason I bring this up is that having a Session Helper engaged for traffic accepted by the Session Table prevents ASIC offload in general. Meaning, as of 6.4 MR and below, DNS traffic is not offloaded because of the DNS Session Helper is enabled by default. If your environment has a high volume of DNS traffic and does not use DNS translation, you may want to consider deleting the DNS session helper to optimize traffic flow.

This brings us to the end of our Session Helper NSE4 topics; coming up are VDOMs!

Virtual Domains

The first question to ask is, what is a Virtual Domain (VDOM) on FortiGate?. A VDOM is a virtual firewall context that logically separates a single FortiGate platform into different virtual firewalls. For example, each VDOM contains its own Routing Table, Policy Tables, UTM Profiles, Policy Objects like Address Objects, and VPN's. One reason we would want this feature would be to set up a multitenant environment. Meaning multiple enterprise customers using the same physical FortiGate platform. VDOM's provide the granularity to accommodate each environment's needs and keep settings completely separate from each other. See *Image 5.1* for a visual.

Image 5.1 – VDOM Example

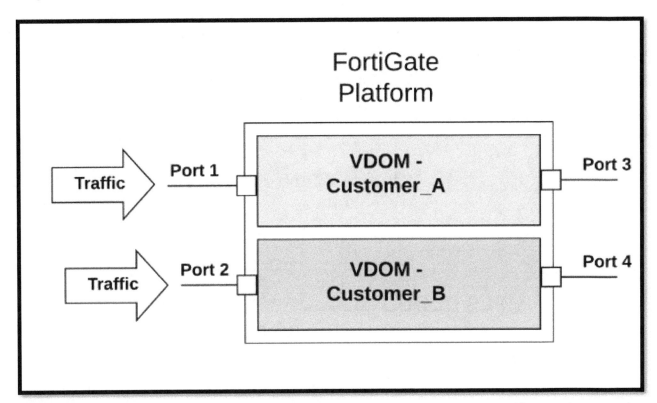

Interfaces are tagged with a VDOM value. These labels steer ingress traffic to the associated VDOM context, and each packet is processed by that VDOM, just like it was a standalone FortiGate. In the above example, Port 1 and Port 3 are tagged with the value Customer_A which is, of course, the Customer_A VDOM. VDOM's can only route traffic through interfaces associated with its context. For example, Customer_A VDOM has no clue what settings or ARP entries are associated with Port 4, because Port 4 is tagged with Customer_B value. Note, VDOM's can be associated with virtual interfaces like VLANs as well and are not constrained to only physical interfaces. VLAN interfaces can be associated with a different VDOM than its parent interface.

Note, VDOM's have independent settings for many things, but they share common global settings. For example, all the settings under **'config system global'** will be applied to all VDOMs on FortiGate. So tread lightly when making global changes!

By default, a FortiGate platform comes with ten available VDOMs. This value can be increased depending on the FortiGate model by purchasing additional VDOM licenses; talk to your sales folks.

VDOM Use Case

A common use case for FortiGate VDOM's is for carrier MSSPs environment. Many carriers integrate FortiGate VDOM technology into their enterprise customers' MPLS cloud or SD-WAN networks. All enterprise customers that share the MPLS cloud also share a single datacenter firewall (Cloud firewall), which would most likely be a higher-end FortiGate platform like a 5001E, 6500F, or 3700E, which can obtain the highest throughput within the FortiGate product suite. See Image 5.2 for a visual of a high-level architecture of an MPLS cloud integrated with FortiGate VDOMs. The General logic goes:

MPLS-Site → MPLS-CLOUD → VLAN Trunk Inside → FGT-VDOM → VLAN Trunk Outside

Image 5. 2 – VDOM Use Case

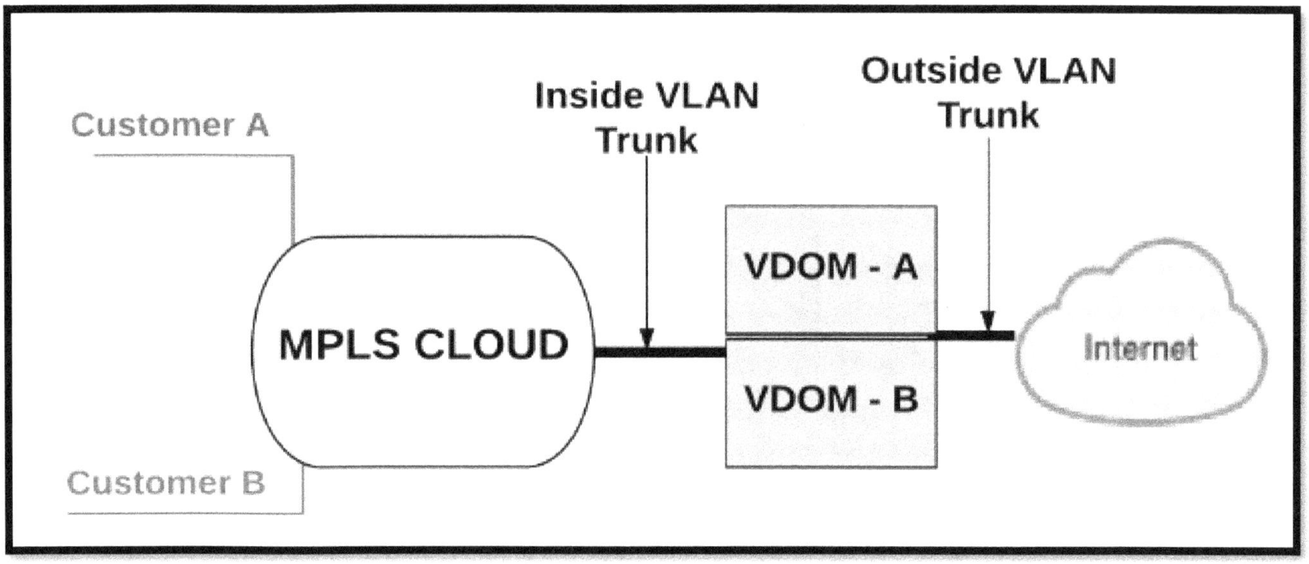

VDOM Management traffic and FortiGuard Updates

Another caveat when you start working with multiple VDOM's is that by default, the root VDOM is the management VDOM, and the Management VDOM is used to obtain UTM updates for AV/IPS, etc. and to perform Web Filter queries. Note, each VDOM does not store local UTM databases. Essentially, be sure the root VDOM has access to the FortiGuard Distribution Network (FDN), or else you're going to have problems.

The root VDOM needs to resolve DNS for FDN services and have network reachability to these domains. A good test is to ping these FQDN's from root VDOM CLI, which will test layer-3 reachability and DNS functionality:

```
# exec ping service.fortiguard.net
# exec ping update.fortiguard.net
# exec ping securewf.fortiguard.net
```

Here is a complete list of FortiGuard URLs:

https://docs.fortinet.com/document/fortigate/6.4.0/ports-and-protocols/622145/anycast-and-unicast-services

Next, it is important to know that the Management VDOM also is responsible for NTP, SNMP, DNS Filtering, logging, and any system-related service. Long story short, make sure your root VDOM, by default, has access to the Internet and a good DNS resource. You will know very quickly if it does not!

Enabling VDOM Mode and Overview

To enable VDOM's on a FortiGate 6.0 and below, we must turn on the feature in the CLI via:

```
NSE4-PASS # conf system global
NSE4-PASS (global) # set vdom-admin enable
NSE4-PASS (global) # end
You will be logged out for the operation to take effect
Do you want to continue? (y/n)
```

To enable VDOM's on FortiGate 6.2 an higher, the CLI syntax is a little different; see CLI output below:

```
NSE4-PASS # conf system global
NSE4-PASS (global) #
NSE4-PASS (global) # set vdom-mode multi-vdom
NSE4-PASS (global) # end
```

The reason for this change was to add the option 'set vdom-mode **split-vdom,**' which essentially splits and locks FortiGate into two VDOMs, a Management and a Traffic VDOM. This feature was created to accommodate Security Fabric while FortiOS is using VDOMs. Moving on, once you log back in, your GUI and CLI will be a little different post VDOM enablement. The left GUI windowpane now has a drop-down to select a VDOM to work in. See *image 5.3*, and now there is a global context and a root context. Any changes made in the Global context affects the entire device, and changes in root VDOM are isolated to only that context. As you add more VDOM's to the device, this list increases. Note, the CLI structure changes some as well once VDOM's are enabled.

Image 5.3 – GUI Enabled VDOM

```
NSE4-PASS # config global                // item 1
NSE4-PASS (global) # config system global  // item 2
NSE4-PASS (global) # end
NSE4-PASS (global) # end
NSE4-PASS # config vdom                  // item 3
NSE4-PASS (vdom) # edit                  // item 4
<vdom>    Virtual Domain Name
root
NSE4-PASS (vdom) # edit root
current vf=root:0
NSE4-PASS (root) #                       // item 5
```

Take a moment to review the new CLI structure.

I'll start with *item 1*; when you first log into FortiGate, you are in the base context, meaning outside of VDOM and Global context. From here, we can pivot into either Global or a VDOM. To pivot into the global context, issue the 'config global' at the base, and you see the command prompt change and inserts **(global),** which indicates we are now operating at the global level. Next, see *Item 2* line in CLI above, the command '**config system global**', this command descends us into the global settings table, from here, you can start making changes. Remember, it is a two-step process to be able to modify the global config table in VDOM mode. Next, see *item 3* CLI line, from the base context to access a VDOM context issue the **config vdom** command. From here, we can select a VDOM to work in using the '**edit**' command and then selecting a

VDOM. Lastly, see *item 5,* the command prompt now indicates we have entered the root vdom by inserting **(root)** as an indicator.

Creating New VDOM

FortiOS makes creating a new VDOM very easy. See CLI output below:

```
NSE4-PASS (root) # next                    //item 1
NSE4-PASS (vdom) # edit Sales_VDOM         //item 2
current vf=Sales_VDOM:3                     //item 3
NSE4-PASS (Sales_VDOM) #                    //item 4
```

Take a moment to review the CLI output.

> *Be careful not to typo VDOM names when attempt to select them with the Edit command. This will cause FortiOS to create a new VDOM. Tab is your friend!*

The first command issued is the 'next' command, which simply takes you back one configuration level to the VDOM selection table. Item 2, we issue the 'edit Sales_VDOM' command. Since Sales_VDOM does not exist in the table, then the '*edit*' command creates a brand new VDOM names 'Sales_VDOM'. This process takes a few seconds because FortiOS is running scripts in the background creating the VDOM default objects, but once complete, the CLI presents current vf=Sales_VDOM:3 and pivot the CLI to the newly created (Sales_VDOM) context. Note, the **3** within Sales_VDOM:**3,** this is an index value and is referenced throughout FortiOS and debug commands.

Mapping Interfaces to VDOMs

Currently, the Sales_VDOM cannot except network traffic because there are no virtual or physical interfaces mapped to the context, but we can change this; see CLI output below:

```
NSE4-PASS (Sales_VDOM) # config sys int
NSE4-PASS (interface) # edit internal5
NSE4-PASS (internal5) # show
config system interface
    edit "internal5"
        set vdom "root"
        set type physical
        set snmp-index 11
    next
end
NSE4-PASS (internal5) # set vdom Sales_VDOM        //item 1
NSE4-PASS (internal5) # show
```

```
config system interface
    edit "internal5"
        set vdom "Sales_VDOM"
        set type physical
        set snmp-index 11
    next
end
```

The same command 'set vdom' is used to map a VDOM to virtual interfaces as well.

In this CLI output, we first descend into the interface context internal5, and once there, we issue the 'set vdom Sales_VDOM' command, which effectively maps this interface to the Sales_VDOM context. Meaning, all traffic that ingresses internal5 will be processed by all logic stored within Sales_VDOM. This VDOM has its own independent ARP Cache, Routing Table, and Policies. From a layer-2 a layer-3 perspective, Sales_VDOM only has visibility to internal5.

VDOM Administrators

Now that we know the purpose of VDOMs and a little bit about them, now let's talk about managing them. Each VDOM can have one or more Administrators configured to manage it. These VDOM Administrators are restricted to accessing only their VDOM. They cannot manage settings at the global level or any other VDOM, which is useful in an enterprise network when

Image 5.4 – VDOM Admin Configuration

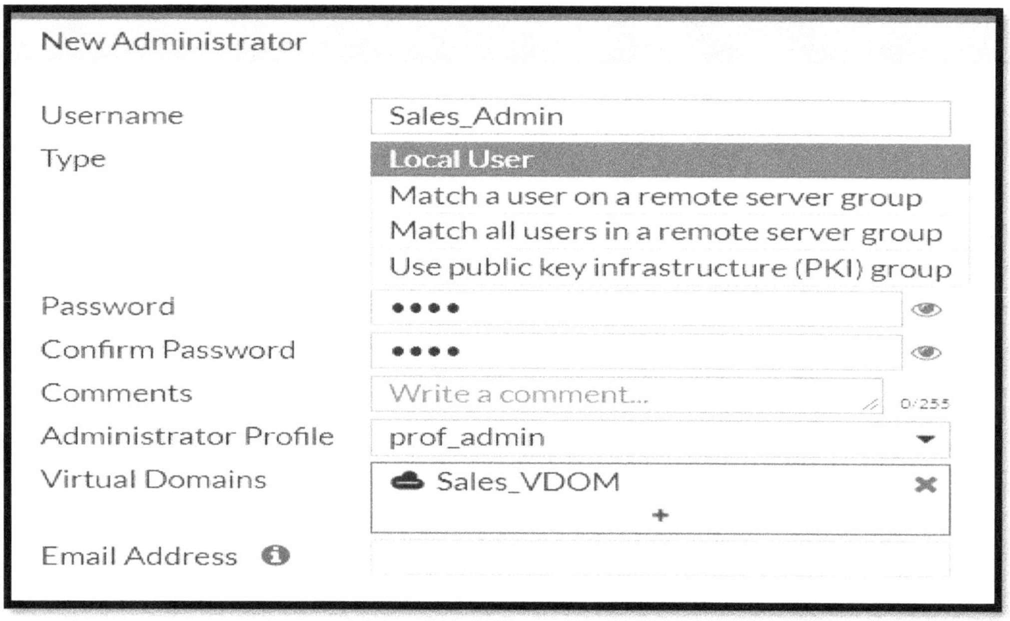

certain Network Administrators are responsible for certain parts of the network. To configure a VDOM admin in the GUI, go to Global Context - '**System -> Administrators -> Create New**' .

It is required to specify **prof_admin** profile for the *Administrator Profile*. This provides Virtual Domain options right below where the newly created Sales_VDOM is referenced. This effectively restricts the Sales_Admin to the Sales_VDOM post login. Remember, the prof_admin does not have access to the global context; only the super_admin profile can access the global context and all VDOM's on FortiGate. Also note, prof_admin can have access to multiple VDOMs.

<u>VDOM Modes</u>

VDOM can be configured in different operational modes. The options are:

1) Operational Mode: NAT or Transparent
2) Inspection Mode: Flow-Based or Proxy
3) NGFW Mode: Profile-based or Policy-based

The first mode to discuss is Operational Mode. Each VDOM can act as a layer-2 or a layer-3 firewall per NAT or Transparent configuration. To modify this config, goto the vdom settings in the CLI via:

```
NSE4-PASS # conf vdom
NSE4-PASS (vdom) # edit root
current vf=root:0
NSE4-PASS (root) # config system settings
NSE4-PASS (settings) # set opmode ?
nat               Change to NAT mode.
transparent       Change to transparent mode.
```

Next, *Inspection Mode* for a VDOM can be set in the CLI via:

```
NSE4-PASS # config vdom
NSE4-PASS (vdom) # edit Sales_VDOM
NSE4-PASS (root) # config system settings
NSE4-PASS (settings) # set inspection-mode proxy
```

Lastly, you can set the *ngfw-mode* setting to be *policy-based* from *profile-based* via cli:

```
0: config vdom
0: edit Sales_VDOM
0: config system settings
0: set inspection-mode flow
0: set ngfw-mode policy-based
0: set ssl-ssh-profile "certificate-inspection"
0: end
0: end
```

When setting a VDOM ngfw-mode to *Policy-Based,* the inspection mode must be *Flow-based,* and an SSL inspection profile must be selected, which is used for the entire VDOM. In the previous example, the **"certificate-inspection"** is the SSL inspection profile used.

Inter -VDOM Links

An Inter-VDOM link is a feature that allows VDOM's within FortiOS to communicate with one another. What I mean by this is, an Inter -VDOM link is a virtual Ethernet or PPP segment that binds two VDOM's together with virtual interfaces. This could be required due to specific routing requirements since each VDOM has its own routing table and assigned interfaces. See image 5.5.

Image 5.5 – Inter VDOM Link

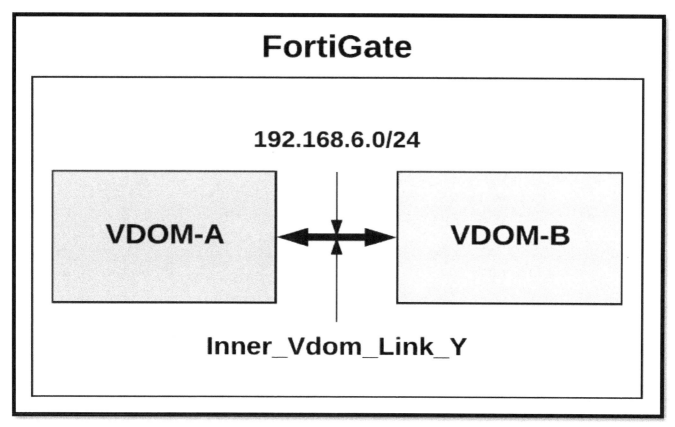

In this example, there is VDOM-A and VDOM-B with an Inter-VDOM link of 'Inter _Vdom_Link_7'. This link has a subnet assigned of 192.168.6.0/24. We could configure VDOM-A to be 192.168.6.1 and VDOM-B to be 192.168.6.2 and route traffic between them. Note, just like every other interface on FortiGate, this requires a Firewall Policy Entry to allow the traffic.

Next, let's go over this configuration. The first thing to configure is the actual virtual segment and map it to the VDOMs. See CLI output:

```
config global
config system vdom-link
    edit "Vdom_Link_Y"
        set type ethernet
    next
end
```

by issuing the *edit* command, an Inter-VDOM link named *Vdom_Link_Y is created*. On the backend, this generates standalone virtual interfaces that are associated with each other. These interfaces are differentiated by a 0 and 1 being appended to the name of the Inter-VDOM link. In this example, the name of our virtual interfaces would be:

1) Vdom_Link_Y**0**
2) Vdom_Link_Y**1**

Next, map these newly created interfaces to the VDOMs, VDOM-A, and VDOM-B, respectively. Let's do that real quick; see CLI output below:

```
NSE4-PASS (Vdom_Link_Y0) # show

config system interface
    edit "Vdom_Link_Y0"
        set vdom "VDOM-A"
        set ip 192.168.6.1 255.255.255.0
        set allowaccess ping
        set type vdom-link
        set snmp-index 20
        set macaddr 62:b9:c4:bd:17:d5
    next
end
NSE4-PASS (Vdom_Link_Y0) # next
NSE4-PASS (interface) # edit Vdom_Link_Y1
NSE4-PASS (Vdom_Link_Y1) # show
config system interface
    edit "Vdom_Link_Y1"
        set vdom "VDOM-B"
        set ip 192.168.6.2 255.255.255.0
        set allowaccess ping
        set type vdom-link
        set snmp-index 21
        set macaddr 66:b6:85:c7:6b:ac
    next
end
```

Once we have the Inter-VDOM links configured and mapped to their respective VDOM, for traffic to pass between VDOMs, a Policy and Routing statement(s) must be configured for **each** VDOM participating in the Inter-VDOM link. Think of this virtual interface, just like any other FortiOS interface. Reference Policy and Routing chapters in Part-I if needed.

Image 5.6 – GUI Inter-VDOM Link

Lastly, I want to mention it is not required to have an IP on an Inter-VDOM link if you are just routing traffic between the VDOMs. Your static route gateway address would be just all zero's (0.0.0.0/0) pointing to an Inter-VDOM link interface in this case. One reason you require an IP address on Inter-VDOM link interfaces is if you wish to perform SNAT or DNAT on traffic passing the virtual link. There are also other reasons to give your Inter-VDOM link interfaces an IP address, for example, if you wish to have admin access or run a routing protocol on the virtual link.

<u>Inter-VDOM Link Hardware Acceleration</u>

We have discussed offloading network traffic to specialized ASIC chips on FortiGate. For Inter-VDOM links, it is also possible to offload network traffic; however, we must use the preconfigured or 'built-in' Inter-VDOM interfaces. FortiGate platforms that have NP4 or NP6 chipsets have these special Inter-VDOM interfaces. The name of these magical special Inter-VDOM link interfaces built to offload traffic between VDOMs are:

npu0_vlink
- npu0_vlink0
- npu0_vlink1

npu1_vlink
- npu1_vlink0
- npu1_vlink1

by default, these interfaces are mapped to the root VDOM. The reason I listed two Inter-VDOM links is because most many FortiGate platforms have two NP6 chipsets. These two chipsets are bound to different physical interfaces, and also each is bound to their virtual Inter-VDOM link interfaces. For completeness, Inter-VDOM links that are created through additional configuration are not offloaded to the Network Process ASIC chipsets.

Inter-VDOM Links Transparent vs. NAT mode

Inter-VDOM links can be bound to VDOMs running Transparent mode. The catch here is that you cannot have two VDOM with each running Transparent mode share an Inter-VDOM link with each other. To have a Transparent mode VDOM bound to an Inter-VDOM link, the VDOM on the other side must be running in NAT mode. To configure a NAT VDOM to Transparent VDOM via Inner-VDOM link, the below CLI settings can be used:

```
config global
config system vdom-link
edit vdom-link_
set type ethernet
end
config system interface
edit vdom-link_0
set vdom NAT-MODE
set ip 192.168.100.1
next
edit vdom-link_1
set vdom Transparent-MODE
end
```

A few specific settings to take note of are, the NAT VDOM must be configured with an IP address. Also, the Inter-VDOM link itself must use type **ethernet.** There should be no IP address configured on the Transparent side of the Inner-VDOM link.

Lastly, note a VDOM can have more than one Inter-VDOM link. So you can imagine how one could create many different virtual topologies using NAT mode and Transparent mode VDOMs.

Fortinet documentation for NAT to Transparent mode Inter-VDOM links:

https://docs.fortinet.com/document/fortigate/6.0.0/handbook/199083/inter-vdom-routing

Limit VDOM Resources

When you have hundreds of VDOMs on a multitenant device, a major concern is letting one customer overrun the entire device; this is a bad day. To prevent this from happening, Fortinet has provided features to limit VDOM resources. The first place I want to draw your attention to is the GUI via 'Global > System > VDOM' windowpane. See image 5.7. Here we can see what VDOM's are using what resources. In this image, we can gather only the root VDOM utilized, which is using 12% CPU and 22% total memory.

Image 5. 7 – VDOM Resource Utilization

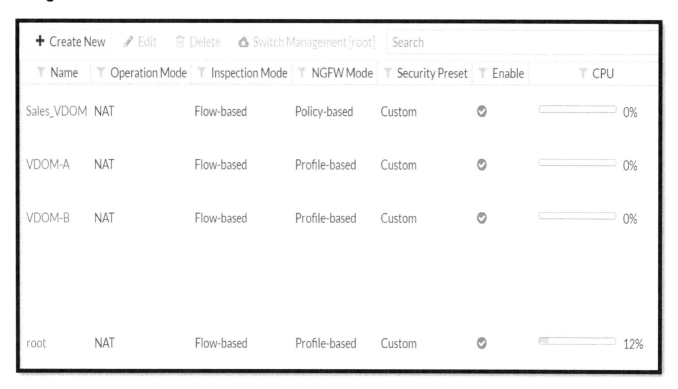

Name	Operation Mode	Inspection Mode	NGFW Mode	Security Preset	Enable	CPU
Sales_VDOM	NAT	Flow-based	Policy-based	Custom	✓	0%
VDOM-A	NAT	Flow-based	Profile-based	Custom	✓	0%
VDOM-B	NAT	Flow-based	Profile-based	Custom	✓	0%
root	NAT	Flow-based	Profile-based	Custom	✓	12%

Also, I want to point out that this provides information on the VDOM Operation Mode, Inspection Mode, and NGFW Mode. Next, if a VDOM is selected on this page, your screen pivots into a new Windowpane where resources can be limited on a per VDOM basis. See image 5.8 on the next page.

Image 5.8 – VDOM Resource Configuration Page

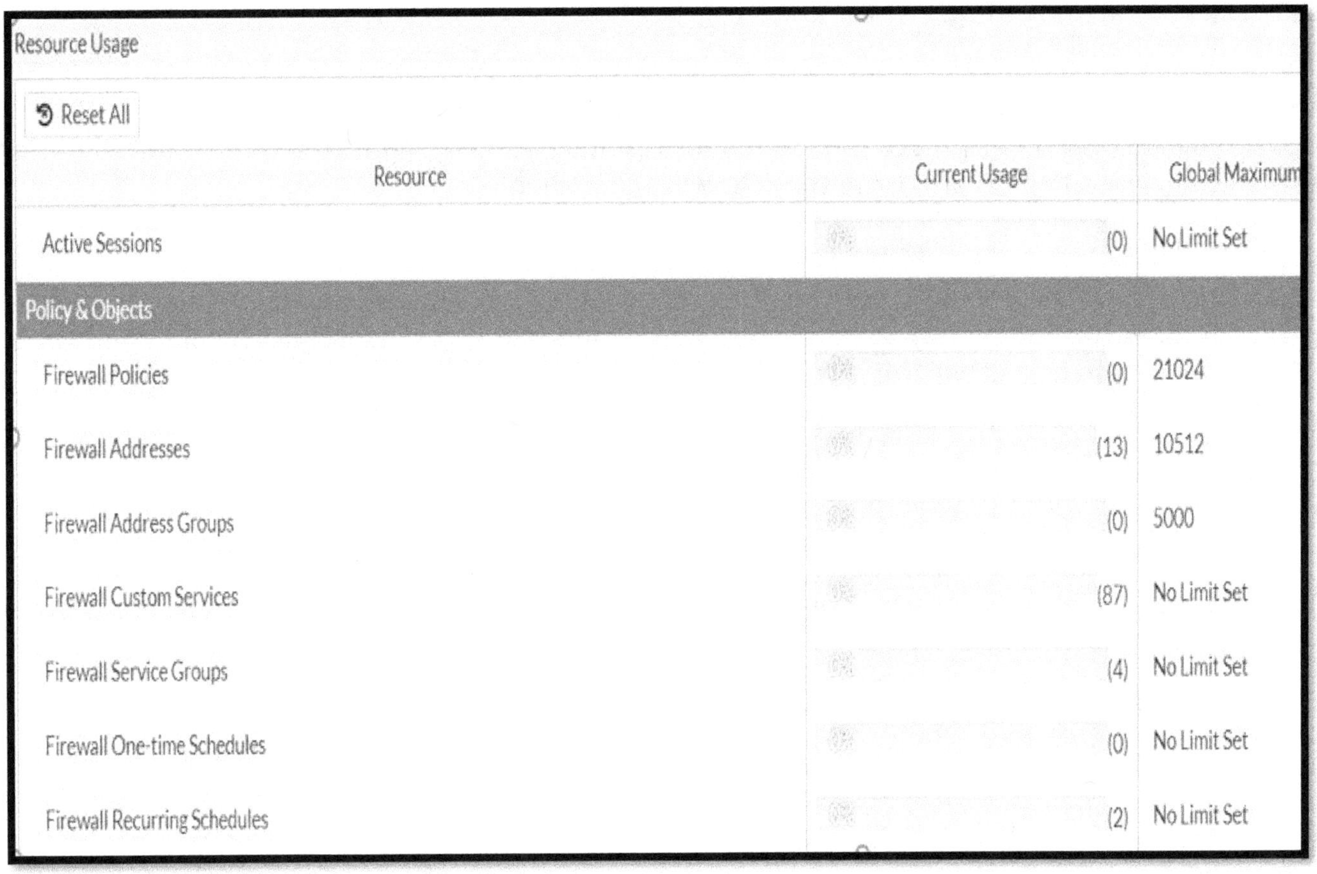

Resource Usage		
↻ Reset All		
Resource	**Current Usage**	**Global Maximum**
Active Sessions	(0)	No Limit Set
Policy & Objects		
Firewall Policies	(0)	21024
Firewall Addresses	(13)	10512
Firewall Address Groups	(0)	5000
Firewall Custom Services	(87)	No Limit Set
Firewall Service Groups	(4)	No Limit Set
Firewall One-time Schedules	(0)	No Limit Set
Firewall Recurring Schedules	(2)	No Limit Set

Here you can see things like active sessions, various Firewall objects configured, and what the global max is for each object. One of the most critical configurations on this GUI page is to limit Active Sessions by specifying a number under *Guaranteed*. This is so if a customer is under a DoS attack, the entire device will not be affected. Also, for you engineers out there, you can be sure that every VDOM is allocated a certain amount of resources like VPNs, Users, Objects ..etc., in a fair manner so that one VDOM does not use all available resources on the platform. Global limits can be set for things like sessions and policies as well.

VDOM License

The last thing I'm going to discuss in this chapter is the VDOM license model. By default, most FortiGate platforms come with a max of 10 VDOMs (I believe 30E's are 5). You can add VDOM's to each platform by purchasing additional licenses. You can check the device current 'Max number of virtual domains' via the output of *get sys status*:

```
NSE4-PASS # get sys status
......
Current virtual domain: root
```

Max number of virtual domains: 10
Virtual domains status: 4 in NAT mode, 0 in TP mode
Virtual domain configuration: enable
…….. .

VDOM licenses are sold in increments from resellers, and yes, these licenses can be stacked. Once you receive a certificate file from your reseller, you will receive a license key. Next on FortiGate, go to the CLI and issue the following command:

execute upd-vd-license <license key>

Applying a VDOM license does not require a reboot. Note, in High Available environments, each unit requires the same level of VDOM licenses. In my role as a Technical Account Manager at Fortinet, I've had to have this conversation many times, informing my customers about this detail for HA to work properly. Once again, each unit <u>must</u> have the same amount of licenses within a HA cluster.

<u>VDOM Diagnostics</u>

There are a few diagnostic commands you can store away in your notebook when troubleshooting VDOMs. Here are a few I've used in my experience. The first is:

```
30E-A (global) # diagnose sys vd stats
root      cpu:19% mem:38%
VDOM-TEST       cpu:1%  mem:0%
```

This command is handy when trying to see which VDOM on your platform is using the most CPU and memory. The next command is useful for displaying how many objects each VDOM is limited to.

```
30E-A (global) # diagnose sys vdom-property
Resource for vdom VDOM-TEST: Current, Guaranteed, Maximum
session: 0, 0, 0
ipsec-phase1: 0, 0, 0
ipsec-phase2: 0, 0, 0
ipsec-phase1-interface: 0, 0, 0
ipsec-phase2-interface: 0, 0, 0
dialup-tunnel: 0, 0, 0
firewall-policy (IPv4, IPv6, policy46, policy64, DoS-policy4, DoS-policy6,
multicast): 0, 0, 0
firewall-address (IPv4, IPv6, multicast): 21, 0, 0
firewall-addrgrp (IPv4, IPv6): 2, 0, 0
custom-service: 87, 0, 0
service-group: 4, 0, 0
onetime-schedule: 0, 0, 0
recurring-schedule: 3, 0, 0
user: 0, 0, 0
```

```
user-group: 0, 0, 0
sslvpn: 0, 0, 0
There are no workers, make sure the requested module is enabled.
proxy: 0, 0, 0
log-disk-quota: 0, 0, 0
```

The last command I want to mention here is:

```
30E-A (global) # diagnose sys vd list
system fib version=32
list virtual firewall info:
….
name=VDOM-TEST/VDOM-TEST index=3 enabled fib_ver=4 use=47 rt_num=0 asym_rt=0
sip_helper=0, sip_nat_trace=1, mc_fwd=0, mc_ttl_nc=0, tpmc_sk_pl=0
ecmp=source-ip-based, ecmp6=source-ip-based asym_rt6=0 rt6_num=9
strict_src_check=0 dns_log=1 ses_num=0 ses6_num=0 pkt_num=6
        tree_flag=1 tree6_flag=1 nataf=0 traffic_log=1 extended_traffic_log=0
svc_depth=2
        log_neigh=0, deny_tcp_with_icmp=0 ses_denied_traffic=no
tcp_no_syn_check=0 central_nat=0 policy_mode_ngfw=0 block_land_attack=0
link_check_local_in=0
        fw_session_hairpin=no  keep-PRP-trailer=0 auxiliary_ses=0
        ipv4_rate=0, ipv6_rate=0, mcast6-PMTU=0, allow_linkdown_path=0
        per_policy_disclaimer=0
        mode=standalone ha_state=work prio=0 vid=0
vf_count=5 vfe_count=0
…..
```

This command will provide a quick snap of what features are being used on a per vdom basis. This wraps up chapter 5! Check out the chapter summary and those end of chapter questions!

Summary

Chapter five is under the belt! Great job! This chapter was more or less a miscellaneous chapter following Part-I of this NSE4 study guide series. In this chapter, we covered the FortiOS Session Helpers and VDOMs. In short, Session Helpers proactively open expected sessions for certain protocols like FTP, SIP, and RTP. A VDOM is a method to virtualize multiple firewalls on a single platform.

We started this chapter by reviewing Sessions Helpers and how they are used to perform SNAT or DNAT within the application layer of some protocols. Also, this feature is used to insert expected sessions into the FortiOS Session Table for return traffic.

We moved to the Virtual Domains topic or VDOMs, and we reviewed how VDOM's are essentially a virtual firewall within FortiOS. All VDOM's share the same global settings. We discussed how to configure new VDOMs and map interfaces to them.

Next, we discussed how to create VDOM admins and assign permissions to them. We also went over VDOM modes, which can be either NAT or Transparent mode. Next, we went over Inter-VDOM links. We reviewed how to configure these virtual links and details around using them to route traffic between VDOMs.

Lastly, we discussed how to limit VDOM resources on FortiOS, so one VDOM does not take all the resources on a platform, and what debugs we can run to view this information on FortiOS. It's time to test your newly found knowledge! Move on to the end of chapter questions, good luck!

Chapter Five Review Questions

1. For 6.4 FortiOS, SIP Helper is disabled, and ALG is used by default.
    a. True
    b. False

2. SIP Helper provides the same base functions for SIP as the Application Layer Gateway module, but SIP Helper provides SIP security features as well.
    a. True
    b. False

3. What is the default management VDOM?
    a. mgmt
    b. management
    c. root-mgmt
    d. root

4. What is one reason the management VDOM is important?
    a. This is the only VDOM that provides management protocol access.
    b. This is the only VDOM that can run UTM features
    c. This is the only VDOM that communicates to FortiGuard for updates.
    d. Every VDOM can be configured to be a management VDOM.

5. In a VDOM environment, which VDOM does FortiOS system DNS traffic spawn from?
    a. From the local VDOM from where the request originated.
    b. Local system DNS spawns from the management VDOM only.
    c. All local out traffic originates from the root VDOM.
    d. You must enable DNS lookup settings on a per VDOM basis.

6. The management VDOM is always root and cannot be changed.
    a. True
    b. False

7. A Physical interface associated virtual interfaces must reside in the same VDOM.
    a. True
    b. False

8. A Transparent Mode VDOM can only create an inter-vdom link with a NAT Mode VDOM.
    a. True
    b. False

9. An Inter-VDOM link must have an IP address configured for both sides of the virtual interface.
    a. True
    b. False

10. VDOM's share a pool of global resources that are distributed evenly depending on how many VDOM's are created.
    a. True
    b. False

11. FortiGuard Web Rating queries are only performed by the management VDOM.
    a. True
    b. False

12. What VDOM debug command will show how much CPU and memory each VDOM is using?
    a. diagnose sys vd stats
    b. diagnose sys vd list
    c. diagnose sys vdom-property
    d. get vd system resources

Chapter 6 | High Availability

NSE4 Blueprint Topics Covered

- Identify Different Operation HA Modes
- Config HA
- Understand HA Election Process
- Identify primary secondary units
- Debug HA sync
- Configure Session sync
- HA failover types
- Identify how HA modes pass traffic
- Configure and understand Virtual Clustering
- Verify HA operations
- Upgrade HA firmware
- FortiGate Clustering Protocol
- HA Clustering Requirements
- Understand Virtual Clustering
- HA Diagnostics

Rundancy, redundancy, and redundancy, that's the name of the game for this chapter. All modern computer network requirements include inline or geo-redundant devices to account for device failure. It's not the question <u>if</u> hardware will fail, but <u>when</u> hardware will fail. Fortinet has created a couple of solutions for FortiGate redundancy. The technology this chapter mostly covers is called FortiGate Clustering Protocol (FGCP) High Availability or FGCP HA for short. In this chapter, we have the opportunity to go over some different HA methods FortiGate has to offer! We will also dive into the details on how FortiGate FGCP HA technology works behind the scenes in parallel with overall cluster operations. We also get the chance to touch on HA traffic flow, and I will explain what happens during a hardware failure within HA clusters.

By the end of this chapter, you should have confidence in what HA methods are available and how to configure and troubleshoot these methods. You will also understand how the FGCP HA synchronization process works regarding static FortiOS configuration and dynamic data like sessions. You will also understand Virtual Cluster with VDOMs. Lastly, in this chapter, I will discuss how to create a HA health baseline and how to troubleshoot HA issues when they arise.

Alright, that's enough chit'-chat, let's go ahead and dive into the nuts and bolts of FortiGate High Availability!

High Availability Overview

High Availability was created to deal with hardware failures. Many technologies have been created to account for failures like these. The reason behind all these efforts is up-time. In today's computer networks, businesses cannot afford downtime, and FortiOS around the world support business-critical applications, and when these applications are unavailable, this can cost companies tens or hundreds of thousands of dollars per hour, maybe more. With potential losses like these, companies are pouring money into network redundancy, which includes FortiGate firewalls.

I already mentioned two types of redundancy, inline HA or geo-redundant (or out of line). Let's talk a little more about these two methods.

<u>HA Inline Method</u>

When I say, 'inline' what I mean is a HA environment within a single hot site or another way to put it is, the path that egress and ingress network traffic is actively taking to the Internet or other private remote sites. See image 6.1:

Image 6.1 – Site 'A' Inline FortiGate 'A'

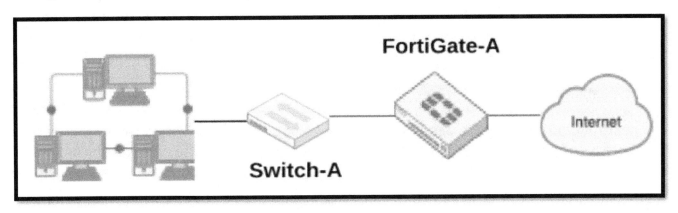

Here is an example of FortiGate-A acting as an 'inline' firewall for Site-A. If FortiGate-A has a hardware failure, then Site-A has no network base connectivity to the Internet until FortiGate-A is replaced with known-good hardware once more. This type of topology is where FortiGate FGCP High Availability (HA) comes into play using Active-Passive mode or Active-Active mode.

HA allows network engineers to place a backup standby (or active) firewall that is a mirror replica of the Master Active FortiGate. So when the active firewall fails, then the backup steps

Image 6.2 – Inline HA FortiGate setup

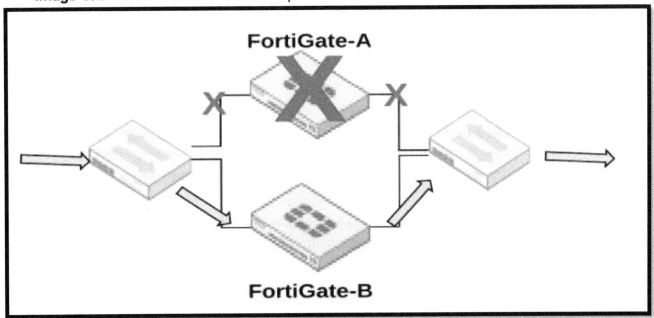

in and takes its place. The reason this is possible is that the active FortiGate pushes all its configuration and dynamic information like sessions to the backup unit(s). Per Image 6.2, you can see, network-based traffic is redirected to the Standby FortiGate if FortiGate-A fails. This creates inline redundancy. This example would be called Active-Passive HA, meaning one FortiGate handles traffic while the passive FortiGate monitors the health of the active FortiGate and takes on the Master role if a hardware failure is detected. Later in the chapter, we will discuss how the standby unit detects hardware failures and how HA data is handled within the HA cluster. A FortiGate HA Active-Passive cluster can be viewed as a single FortiGate essentially. The Fortinet proprietary protocol used to manage the cluster is called FortiGate Cluster Protocol (FGCP); we discuss this protocol in more detail throughout the chapter.

High Availability Geo-Redundant Method

The next method to discuss is Geo Redundant HA or out of line HA. This is where the standby FortiGate is not physically near or even talking with the active unit. Also, the standby unit might know nothing about the status of the active unit. In this method, the related FortiGate configurations are controlled by a central management device called FortiManager that can replicate configurations using something called Policy packages.

When using this method, if a failure occurs on the active FortiGate, then IP routing is used to swing traffic over to the hot standby environment. Most of the time, BGP is used for this type of redundancy or some load-balancers. But essentially, FortiGate plays a very small role in the HA setup here other than being ready to accept new network traffic. Fortinet has developed a Distributed HA Clusters method where FGCP supports autonomous HA clusters installed in geographically separated locations. These clusters could be in different buildings or across the country from each other.

A FortiGate HA protocol that could be used here to synchronize only session data and not the configuration is the protocol *FortiGate Session Life Support Protocol* (FGSP), which is usually used in conjunction with external load balancers. At this point, we should have a general understanding of what FortiGate HA is and why we need it.

HA Operational Modes

I wanted to clarify here; I will only be discussing the FortiGate Cluster Protocol (FGCP) operational modes. FGCP is the protocol responsible for the HA communication in FortiGate and is what this chapter mostly covers. The other Fortinet HA technologies are VRRP, FGSP, SLBC, and ELBC. I will not be going over these technologies in this chapter.

There are two HA operational modes for FGCP Active-Passive (A-P) and Active-Active (A-A). Note, FortiGate operating in NAT or Transparent mode can both form an FGCP HA cluster.

HA Active-Passive

We touched on this method in the prior example. Essentially, once a HA Cluster is established, only one FortiGate processes traffic; this unit is called the Master. All other units are passively standing by waiting for the Master to have a hardware failure and become the Master of the cluster themself and process network connections. We discuss in detail the HA failover process and what events take place later in the chapter. Note that FGCP supports FortiGate clusters of two, three, or four units. The units not actively processing traffic are subordinate units (or slaves), which are synchronized with the primary unit.

HA Active-Active

When an HA cluster using Active-Active mode, this means all units in the cluster actively participating in the processing of network traffic and UTM security inspection. There is still only one Master of a cluster, which plays an important role. The Master in an A-A cluster receives all network traffic initially and is responsible for distributing traffic to other Slave units. Just like in A-P mode, when the Master fails, a slave unit is promoted to Master and then handles distributing network connections among any Slave unit(s). This method is also referred to as HA load balancing. Firewall Policies that do not contain UTM profiles are not load-balanced and are processed by the primary unit when using the FGCP HA A-A method. Traffic load balancing is configurable in the HA settings.

HA Traffic Flow

This section discusses how traffic flows through the different HA clusters modes and how MAC addresses are used to make FortiGate Clustering work.

HA Virtual MAC

Once you configure FortiGate to be in a HA Cluster, FGCP generates and assigns virtual MAC addresses for each interface. These Virtual MAC addresses are what make seamless HA failover possible. The reason we need virtual MAC addresses is because all NIC MAC addresses should be globally unique, and devices should not be able to share MAC addresses. However, in HA Clustering, it is required for all devices to share related interface MAC address information. So when a failure occurs, all other network devices would view the newly elected Master unit as the same device and would see the same IP and MAC address. If the MAC address did have to change post failover, this would cause a delay in network traffic because all devices on the same LAN would require to relearn the new MAC addresses, and this would take time and would not be a seamless failover transition.

For NAT Mode, a different virtual MAC (vMAC) is assigned to each primary units' interfaces and subinterfaces; VLANs are assigned the same virtual MAC as the parent interfaces. LAG and

Redundant Interfaces are assigned the virtual MAC of the first physical Interface in the aggregate bundle.

For Transparent Mode, FGCP assigns a virtual MAC for the primary unit's management IP address. Note you can connect to this management IP from any physical interface.

Virtual MAC Construction

A virtual MAC (vMAC) is generated base on the following algorithm:

00-09-0f-09-<group-id >-(<vcluster_integer> + <idx>)

The first part of a FortiGate HA virtual MAC (vMAC), is **00-09-0f-09,** and to obtain the other four MAC hex characters for the vMAC, the HA Group ID setting is referenced, and the last two hex characters are generated from the virtual cluster-ID and interface index value. I touch more on virtual clusters shortly. The group-id is configured during the initial HA configuration on FortiGate. See CLI output:

```
VM-A (ha) # show
config system ha
    set group-id 99
    set mode a-p
    set override disable
end
```

Under config system ha, is where the group-id is configured and, in this case, is 99. So 99 would be converted to hex, which would be 63 (binary 0110 0011). In this case, I am not using Virtual Clustering, which is a method to have some VDOM's to be primary and accept traffic on slave FortiGate within a cluster and other primary VDOM's to accept traffic on the Master to load balance traffic. We touch on this more later in the chapter.

Next, let's take a closer look at our MAC addresses after we configure the HA settings:

```
30E-B (global) # show sys ha
config system ha
    set group-id 99
    set group-name "HA-Cluster-1"
    set mode a-p
    set password …
    set hbdev "lan2" 0
    set override disable
    set monitor "wan"
end
30E-B (global) # diagnose hardware deviceinfo nic wan
..
System_Device_Name      wan
Current_HWaddr          00:09:0f:09:63:00
Permanent_HWaddr        04:d5:90:9d:9b:b9
```

..
..

In the output above, you can see that 63 has indeed been placed in the next hex fields because our group-id is 99 in this case. The reason that the last hex values are 00, is because the wan interface on this device index value is 0, and we do not have Virtual Clustering enabled. The last values are calculated via (<vcluster_integer> + <idx>). The vcluster_integer value is 0 for Virtual Cluster 1, and for Virtual Cluster 2, the value is 0x80; in older firmware versions, the value was 20. Hence the virtual MAC may change via upgrade. Once you add these values to the interface index value, then you receive the last hex values for the virtual MAC address used in FGCP HA.

Note, the Permanent_HWaddr cannot be changed, and the Current_HWaddr represents the HA virtual MAC. Remember that between MR upgrades, index values can change; therefore, the Virtual MAC may change.

If two independent FGCP HA Clusters are sharing same LAN segment, then be sure each cluster group-id's are unique else a MAC address conflict will occur

---

HA A-P Traffic Flow

NAT Mode FortiOS, working in A-P HA Mode, network traffic is only sent to the Master unit because it is the only unit that responses to broadcast, ARP, and the Virtual MAC addresses for the cluster. Meaning, ARP packets broadcasted to both Master and Slave devices asking for the MAC address for IP X; only the Master responds. Therefore, the switch handling the layer-2 ARP traffic builds a MAC address table entry that binds the vMAC to the interface facing the Master FortiGate. I will walk through the flow of events within Image 6.3

A device is asking for the MAC address of 192.168.1.1, which, as we know now, is a Virtual MAC. In A-P mode, only the Master responds with the vMAC, and the Slave device does nothing. All subsequent packets follow the same path until hardware failure occurs.

In the case of FortiOS running Transparent mode, A-P HA Virtual MACs are not directly involved in the layer-2 communication. With TP mode, the Master unit again takes responsibility when layer-2 communication is received and performs all MAC address table lookups and forwarding functions. The Slave device does not respond to transmissions. For the TP FortiGate's management IP, a Gratuitous ARP is sent to the neighboring devices to update their MAC table with a vMAC for the clusters' management IP address. A Gratuitous ARP is an unsolicited ARP packet sent into the network for the sole purpose of a device to announce its self onto a network. So all devices on the LAN can adjust their MAC tables to account for the newly received MAC address.

Image 6.3 – vMAC Master Reply Only

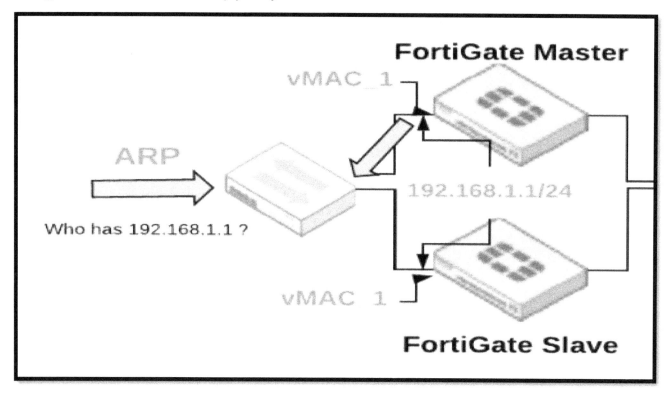

HA A-A Traffic Flow

FGCP Active-Active (A-A) is where all units in the cluster actively participate in the processing of networking traffic and security functions. The Master of the cluster is responsible for distributing traffic to slave members. This traffic flow is a bit more complicated than the A-P traffic flow. We will go through an example on FortiOS NAT Mode using FGCP A-A; see Image 6.4. In this example, we have two FortiGate's; the top one is the Master and the bottom of the Slave. Both units have their Port-1 Interface connected to the same LAN segment. Both units share the same IP that is used as a gateway for the LAN. Both units share a Virtual MAC address for Port-1. The difference here, and what you should notice, is I've referenced the Physical MAC address for each unit. The globally unique MAC for each unit's Port-1 interfaces is listed, which I have denoted as Physical MAC_1, for Master and Physical MAC_2 for Slave.

FortiGate HA Cluster with ha-mgmt-interfaces and ha-direct configured can forward logs direct out the local mgmt. interface independently

Image 6.4 – NAT Mode FGCP A-A Traffic Flow

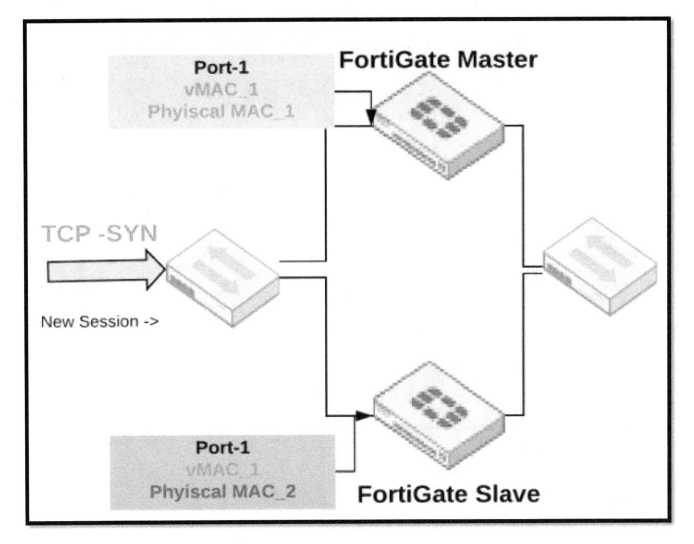

In Image 6.4, A TCP packet with the SYN flag set is sent to the cluster with a MAC address destination of Virtual MAC **vMAC_1** in which the switch forwards to the Master Unit because, in A-A, the Master is still the only unit that responds to the vMAC's for a cluster. At this point, the Master determines the Slave FortiGate should handle this new session in the HA cluster. The Master then creates a Session Table Entry to track the load-balanced sessions and then forwards the ethernet frame back out Port-1 with the destination ethernet address being the physical MAC address of Port-1 on the Slave FortiGate and the source Ethernet MAC address is the physical MAC address of the Master FortiGate. Next, the Slave FortiGate does two things; first, it forwards the TCP SYN packet egress to its destination; the second thing is the Slave FortiGate responds to the initial client's TCP SYN request with a TCP SYN/ACK. See image 6.5 for reference.

Image 6.5 – FortiOS NAT A-A Packet Flow 2

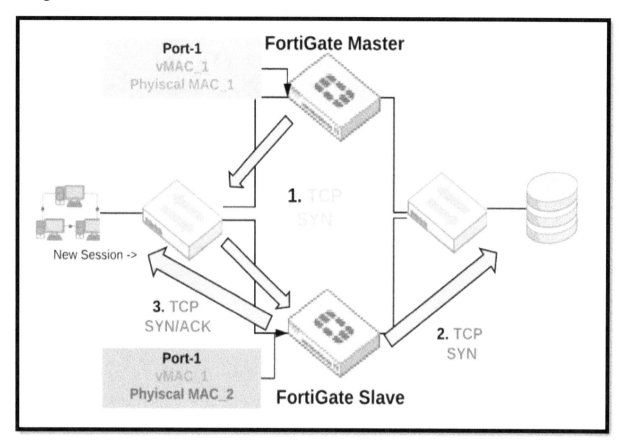

Let's recap on this:

1) The client sends TCP SYN Packet to FortiGate Cluster
   a. Source MAC: Original Client's MAC
   b. Destination MAC: Port-1 Cluster vMAC
2) Master creates a session to track load balanced session
3) Master forwards frame back out Port-1
   a. Source MAC: Physical Master MAC Port-1
   b. Destination MAC: Physical Slave MAC Port-1
4) Slave forwards TCP SYN connection via egress toward final IP destination
   a. Source MAC: Physical Slave MAC Outside Port
   b. Destination MAC: Local MAC of gateway IP
5) Slave responds to original clients TCP SYN connection with TCP SYN/ACK.
   a. Source MAC: Physical Slave MAC Port-1
   b. Destination MAC: Original client's MAC address

Next, the server response is handled in the same manner except on the flip side of the cluster, which is most of the time, the untrusted side or public side of the FortiGate. Let's go through this example of the server response. See image 6.6:

Image 6.6 – FortiOS NAT A-P Response Flow

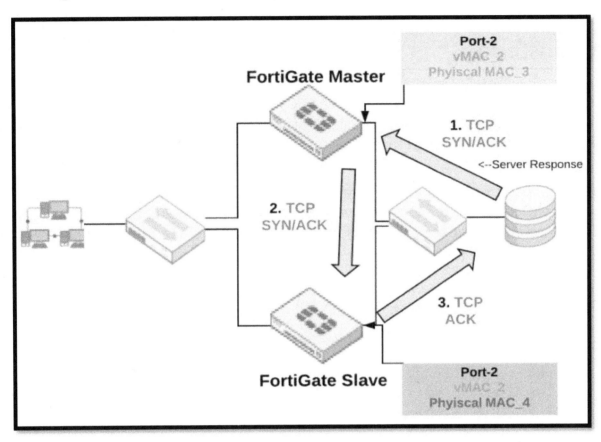

1) The server responds with TCP SYN/ACK to the FortiGate cluster vMAC_2 for outside Port-2
   a. Destination MAC: Master Port-2 vMAC_2
   b. Source MAC: Local gateway device MAC
2) FortiGate Master maps the response to an active session and finds FortiGate Slave is handling sessions.
3) Fortigate Master forwards ethernet frame to Slave unit.
   a. Source MAC: Master Port-2 Physical MAC_3
   b. Destination MAC: Slave Port-2 Physical MAC_4
4) Fortigate Slave response to the server with TCP ACK to complete the three-way handshake.
   a. Source MAC: Slave Port-2 Physical MAC_3
   b. Destination MAC: Local gateway device MAC

Note, the goal of FGCP is not to conserve bandwidth but to share CPU and memory resource load for security processing across the HA cluster. Lastly, regarding A-A load balancing, not all traffic is load-balanced by default; only traffic accepted by policies that require <u>Proxy Based</u> security processing can be sent to Slave unit(s); however, this can be changed in the CLI under #config system ha via load-balance-all setting.

Virtual Clustering

Virtual Clustering is the concept of having Active VDOMs and passive VDOMs. This method allows us to place VDOM's that are actively processing traffic on a FortiGate acting as a Slave device and is another method to share resources across an FGCP HA cluster. This is called VDOM partitioning and can only be used with HA FGCP A-P mode. VDOM's must be enabled as well.

This method supports up to four FortiGates per HA Cluster. However, only two FortiGates actively pass traffic; the third and fours FortiGate members are standby only. When Virtual Clustering is enabled, then two virtual clusters are created, one and two. To enable virtual clusters, use the below CLI commands:

```
Master#
#config global
#config system ha
..
#set vcluster2 enable
#config secondary-vcluster
#set vdom Sales Engineering
#set priority 50
..
#end
#end

Slave#
#config global
#config system ha
#config secondary-vcluster
#set priority 200
#end
```

The Slave backup unit <u>priority</u> setting under *secondary-vcluster* will need to be higher if it's required to accept traffic for VDOMs placed within virtual cluster two (secondary-vcluster). You can think of the HA cluster splitting into the two independent environments for VDOMs. When you use the command 'config secondary-vcluster', this allows you to, firstly, set the priority on the physical device for the second cluster. The rule is, the high the priority is preferred. What this means is any VDOM's associated with the virtual cluster two follow this preference. For example, if the slave FortiGate unit has its virtual cluster two (secondary-vcluster) set to a higher priority, then any VDOMs configured under `config secondary-vcluster` is processed by Slave FortiGate. Let's look at an example; see Image 6.7:

In this example, Virtual Cluster two (secondary-vcluster) is configured with a priority of 100 on the Master device and configured with a 200 value on the Slave device. We also associated Sales VDOM to the Secondary vCluster this, in turn, makes the FortiGate Slave device the primary for VDOM Sales.

Image 6.7 – vCluster diagram

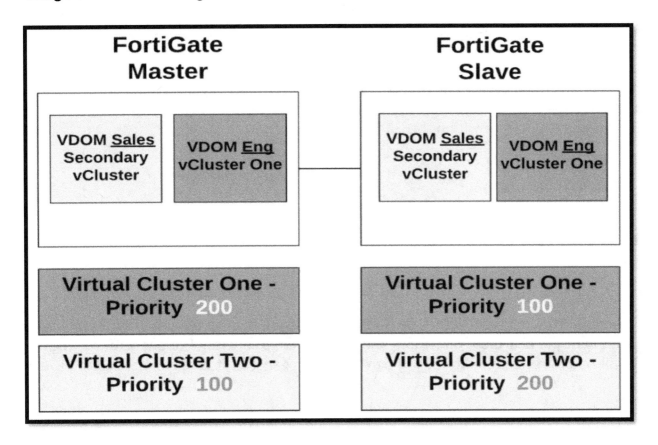

This wraps up VDOM virtual cluster in FGCP HA. In the next section, we are going to jump into HA operations.

HA Cluster Operations

We are making significant progress in the HA department! In this section, we go into the details of FGCP and look at what's under-the-hood. I'm going to talk more about heartbeat interfaces and their purpose. We also discuss Monitored Ports and how they work in line with cluster failover functions.

I am sure you are wondering at this point how the Master FortiGate is selected within a HA Cluster, which is a significant topic and is called the HA Election Process. We will be discussing this in-depth later in this section. Also, we go over various tasks the Master FortiGate is responsible for and what task the Slave is responsible for.

Lastly, in this section, we will go over an in-depth cluster failover process and discuss things like what can trigger HA failover and what occurs post failover.

Heartbeat Interface

The first thing on the docket to discuss is Heartbeat interfaces, which is a keystone to HA FGCP operations, and one of the most important FGCP HA functions is the Heartbeat interface(s) (HB). This interface is dedicated to communication with other cluster members. What I mean when I say *communication*, this interface is used for heartbeat packets and unit synchronization by default. FGCP sends HB packets constantly as a keep-alive mechanism; if the Master or Slave unit fails to receive these keep-alive frames from each other, then the peer is declared dead. The HB Interface is declared within the HA config under:

```
30E-B (ha) # show
config system ha
..
    set hbdev "lan2" 0
..
end
```

In this example, the heartbeat interface is lan2. The reason for the zero after lan2 is because you can set multiple heartbeat interfaces and assign them priorities. The one with the highest priority will be active, and the lower will be standby. In general, it is recommended to have at

Image 6. 8 – Heartbeat interface diagram

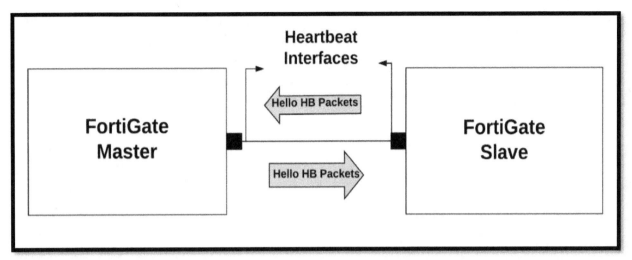

least two heartbeat interfaces to account for NIC failure. If you want to set lan3 as a heartbeat interface but only as a backup encase lan2 fails, then the config would be:

```
config system ha
..
    set hbdev "lan2" 100 "lan3" 50
..
end
```

Next, by default, an HB packet is sent every 2 seconds, and peer(s) are declared dead if six HB packets are missed, meaning a failover occurs at 12 seconds of missed HB packets. The following CLI options configure these settings:

```
30E-B (ha) # show ful | grep hb
    set hb-interval 2
    set hb-lost-threshold 6
end
```

If only two Fortigate units in a HA cluster, then the HB interfaces should be directly connected if possible. The reason for this is to eliminate the factor of a switch issue or network congestion issues between heartbeat (HB) interfaces because HB packets must be exchanged between units, else like I said, cluster members would declare each other as dead an try to become the primary unit, which is very bad.

FGCP assigns HB interfaces an IP; the IP addresses assigned are static and do not change regardless of HA role. The IP assigned is within the 169.254.0.0/24 subnet, yes this is the APIPA range and would be assigned to host that are unable to access a DHCP server and should be non-routable over the Internet.

FGCP assigns the HB virtual IP address based on the FortiGate serial number, all serial numbers in the cluster are indexed, and the unit with the highest serial number receives 169.254.0.1, and the second-highest receives 169.254.0.2, and so on. The only time an HB virtual IP address might change is when a unit leaves the cluster and rejoins. The reasons HB virtual IP's are needed are to distinguish individual cluster members and push certain configuration or dynamic data updates.

Not only are the HB interfaces assigned a unique virtual IP address for sync and heartbeat packets, but they also use a particular ethernet type. Here is the list of FGCP HA EtherTypes and their function:

1) EtherType 0x8890 – NAT Mode Heartbeat packets
    a. Used to detect other cluster members and to detect peer unit's operational status. Used as a keep-alive function.
    b. Under `config system ha`, this EtherType can be modified with the "`set ha-eth-type`" command
2) EtherType 0x8891 – Transparent Mode Heartbeat
    a. Used to detect other cluster members and to detect peer unit's operational status in TP Mode. Used as a keep-alive function.
    b. Under `config system ha`, this EtherType can be modified with the "`set hc-eth-type`" command
3) EtherType 0x8892 – Session Synchronization
    a. In FGCP HA configuration, there is an option to dedicate certain interfaces for Session Synchronization only; Sync packets are tagged with EtherType 0x8892.
    b. Sync ports can be configured via:


```
#config system ha
#set session-sync-dev lan1 lan2
#end
```


4) EtherType 0x8893 – Telnet Sessions
    a. Telnet sessions are used to synchronize the cluster configurations
    b. FGCP also provides the ability to telnet to peer cluster members using the command # `exec ha manage`
    c. Under `config system ha`, this EtherType can be modified with the "`set l2-eth-type`" command.

Note, if routers or switches are used to carry FGCP HA traffic, then it must support these EtherTypes or support unknown EtherTypes, this covers the basics for FGCP HA Heartbeat interfaces and communication. Next, let's talk a little about HA security.

HA heartbeat encryption and authentication

You might be thinking, is FortiGate sending FGCP HA traffic in clear text? And the answer is yes, it is by default. Features have been added to provide FGCP HA Heartbeat traffic encryption and authentication services. To enable these settings, use the below commands:

```
#config system ha
#set authentication enable
#set encryption enable
#end
```

Lastly, here note that FGCP HA authentication and encryption uses AES-128 for encryption and SHA1 for authentication.

Monitored Interface

The goal of FGCP HA is redundancy and to account for network equipment failure. The logic is simple if a path becomes unusable for whatever reason, then FortiOS performs a cluster failover and promotes the backup Slave unit to the active FortiGate. Now the question is, how does FGCP determine if a network path is unusable? One method is Monitored interfaces. Part of the HA configuration is to declare Monitored Interface. This interface is special because FGCP actively monitors the declared interfaces for UP/UP status. Meaning, administratively up, and layer-1 signaling is up. If a Monitored interface(s) go into a downed state, then this triggers a cluster failover, and this is because Monitored interfaces are a part of the Fortigate FGCP HA Cluster Master election process. The logic goes, which cluster has the most 'UP' Monitored Interfaces become the Master. There are some conditions for a Monitored interface failure to trigger a failover. We discuss this in the next section, but for now, just know it is part of the puzzle.

In general, you only want to mark interfaces actively processing network traffic or high priority interfaces as Monitored Interfaces. Do not configure all possible interfaces to be Monitored; this would not be good practice. Next, do not set the Heartbeat interfaces also to be a Monitored interface because this makes no sense if you think about it. If an HB interface goes down, then this triggers a cluster failover because of the loss of HB packets between cluster members.

The following configuration declares the Monitored Interface(s) for the FGCP HA Cluster.

30E-B (ha) # show

config system ha

…

    set monitor "wan" "lan1"

end

The Monitored Interface is an especially important part of the FGCP configuration and, if used correctly, can save your network from downtime. The next item we are going to discuss is the FGCP HA Cluster Master Election process

FGCP Master Election Process

So we have discussed many things around FGCP HA so far. At this point, you might be wondering how in the world a FortiGate is declared Master of a HA cluster. That being said, two different logic trees are used to declare a Master unit. The settings from which these two logic trees stem from are:

1) override enable
2) override disable

Before we jump into the different logic structures, let us discuss this setting and how it affects the cluster. The setting is called *override* and can be found via cli:

```
#config system ha
..
    #set override disable    //or enable
    #set priority 200

..
#end
```

The override setting relates to the priority setting. When this setting is enabled, then the cluster member with the highest priority always takes the Master role if the number of up Monitored Interfaces are even. Yes, that is correct. Monitored Interfaces take precedence over the priority setting.

Now think about this and the behavior this would cause for the HA cluster. For example, if override was enabled and the Master FortiGate had Monitored interface(s) continually going up and down (flapping) due to an upstream switch issue. Every time the Monitored Interface goes down, the cluster would failover, and the Slave would become the Master, and the former Master would become the Slave. Now once the Monitored Interfaces come back up, since override enabled is used, the Slave again takes the Master role since it has even number UP Monitored Interfaces and the highest priority configured. Situations like this cause havoc on networks, and everyone will notice.

Next, if you set *override disable,* then the priority matters less. Now the HA Uptime value takes precedence over HA Priority. Now when a failover occurs, the former Master does not attempt to take back the primary role because of a high priority value. Most carriers operate with override disable because they need to control when failures occur and schedule maintenance windows for the procedure.

So we have discussed Monitored Interfaces, Priority, and HA Uptime. I want to take a moment to clarify HA Uptime. When an FGCP cluster is created, all units that join the cluster count how long they have been apart of a cluster. This variable is fed into HA cluster uptime for each unit. There must be at least three hundred seconds (5 minutes) variance between the unit's cluster uptime for this attribute to be referenced for the HA Master election process.

There is a difference between system uptime and cluster uptime. FGCP HA elections are based on cluster uptime.

```
30E-A (ha) # show ful | grep dif
    set ha-uptime-diff-margin 300
```

To find the cluster uptime for all units in the cluster, run the debug command below:

30E-A (global) # **diagnose sys ha dump-by vcluster**

<hatalk>   HA information.

vcluster_nr=1 vcluster_0:

...

omitted

...

    mondev: wan(prio=50,is_aggr=0,status=1)

    'FGT30Exxxxxxxx': ha_prio/o=1/1, link_failure=0, pingsvr_failure=0, flag=0x00000000, uptime/reset_cnt=**0**/1

    'FGT30Eyyyyyyyy': ha_prio/o=0/0, link_failure=0, pingsvr_failure=0, flag=0x00000001, uptime/reset_cnt=**26006**/0

Find line *uptime/reset_cnt=0/1* in the above output. The first 0 is uptime, and the FortiGate with a 0 in this field means this unit has a lower (less preferred) HA Uptime value. The Master unit in the cluster has an uptime of 26006. This HA Uptime value is measure in $1/10^{th}$ of seconds. So to make FortiGate FGT30Exxxxxxxx the new Master of the cluster, we would need to reset the HA Cluster Uptime on the current Master. We can do this via debug command:

30E-B (global) # diagnose sys ha reset-uptime

Note, this logs you out because a HA failover was triggered. Log back in, and run the vcluster command again:

```
30E-B (global) # diagnose sys ha dump-by vcluster
<hatalk>              HA information. vcluster_nr=1
vcluster_0:
```

...

omitted

...

```
    mondev: wan(prio=50,is_aggr=0,status=1)

        'FGT30Exxxxxxxx'': ha_prio/o=0/0, link_failure=0, pingsvr_failure=0,
flag=0x00000001, uptime/reset_cnt=635/1
        ' FGT30Eyyyyyyyy': ha_prio/o=1/1, link_failure=0, pingsvr_failure=0,
flag=0x00000000, uptime/reset_cnt=0/1
```

The value cnt=635 denotes the cluster Uptime. For completion, the second value in this same field:

uptime/reset_cnt=0/**1**

The one (1) here represents how many times the "diagnose sys ha reset-uptime" has been run on the unit. To recap here, we have discussed Priority, HA cluster Uptime, and Monitored Interfaces to be considered in the Master election process. The last attribute used to determine the HA Master, and very last in the order of logic, is the unit serial number. Here is a quick flow of each logic tree. With override enabled, the Master unit is select with the following logic.

HA Override Enabled

1) Monitored Interfaces
   a. FGCP firstly compares which FortiGate has the most Monitored Interfaces with the status of UP. The higher number wins.
2) HA Priority
   a. If Monitored Interfaces are even between cluster members, then FGCP selects the Master unit by comparing the HA Priority values of each unit. The highest value wins.
3) HA Up Time
   a. If, for some reason, the HA Priority is even between cluster units, then the HA Uptime value is used to select the cluster Master. The highest HA Uptime value is

preferred. The variance must be great than 5 minutes by default to be considered by FGCP.

4) <u>FortiGate Serial Number</u>
   a. The last variable used to select the Master cluster unit is the FortiGate serial number. The highest wins. I have never seen this value actually used to select the Master unit in a production network in my years working with HA. I believe this is just a catch-all, just in the small chance all the prior criteria are even.

Next, let us review the FGCP logic on how the Master unit is selected when override is set to disabled.

Override Disable

1) <u>Monitored Interfaces</u>
   a. Just like before, FGCP firstly compares which FortiGate has the most Monitored Interfaces with the status of UP. The higher number wins.
2) <u>HA Up Time</u>
   a. This is where things change; next, the HA Uptime value is used to select the cluster Master. The highest HA Uptime value is preferred.
3) <u>HA Priority</u>
   a. If Monitored Interfaces are even between cluster units and HA Uptime does not have a variance of 5 minutes, THEN FGCP will determine the Master unit by comparing the HA Priority values; the highest HA Priority is preferred.
4) <u>FortiGate Serial Number</u>
   a. and again, the last variable used to select the Master cluster unit is the FortiGate serial number. The highest wins.

Note, this is the election logic if remote link monitor is not used. Remote link monitor can trigger failovers before any other condition is evaluated.

That wraps how FGCP selects the Master unit for an HA cluster. The likelihood of seeing a question on the election process on the NSE4 exam is high, so take some time to know this.

Lastly, I want to clarify. The election process is always happening on FortiOS. It does not just occur when the units are configured for HA, and that is it. The FGCP Master selection process is perpetual, and the above logic is constantly used to find which unit should be the cluster Master. In the next section, we go over the different types of failover methods available for FGCP HA.

HA Failover Types

We have already discussed many things around FCGP like interface roles, how the Master unit is select, and HA traffic flow. This section goes into some details around what triggers an FGCP HA cluster failover and the different types.

Device Failover

The first type of failover is a Device Failover. If the Master unit stops sending heartbeat packets to the Slave units and the HB loss threshold is hit, then the Slave device declares the Master as dead and proactively assume the Master role of the cluster.

> *For HA failover testing be sure to physically unplug the cable because interface status down command will be replicated to other cluster members*

Interface Monitor Failover

An Interface Monitor failover is when a configured Monitored Interface on the Master FortiGate unit goes down for whatever reason, FGCP triggers the election process, and the cluster elects a new Master unit. Remember, the unit with the most Monitored Interface in the UP state is elected Master.

SSD Failure

FGCP can be configured to trigger a failover based on SSD failure. To enable this setting then to issue the below command:

```
config system ha
    set ssd-failover enable
end
```

Remote Link Failover

I first worked with this feature in 2016, and at that point in time, there was not a lot of documentation around how this was supposed to work. At that time, it was just me adjusting settings at random, attempting to recreate an issue. Since then, there has been a lot more information provided to the public around the functionality of the Remote Link Failover feature! Also, Fortinet development teams have put a lot of effort into enriching the feature.

So what is it? Remote Link Failover is a method to failover an FGCP HA cluster using a probe to check for good and bad network paths. Meaning, the Master can send out a continuous ping to a known good IP. If pings fail to return, then a failover can occur to the Slave unit. This method detects failures of up or downstream routers and switches that are not directly connected to FortiGate. See Image 6.9:

Image 6.9 – Remote Link Monitor HA Example

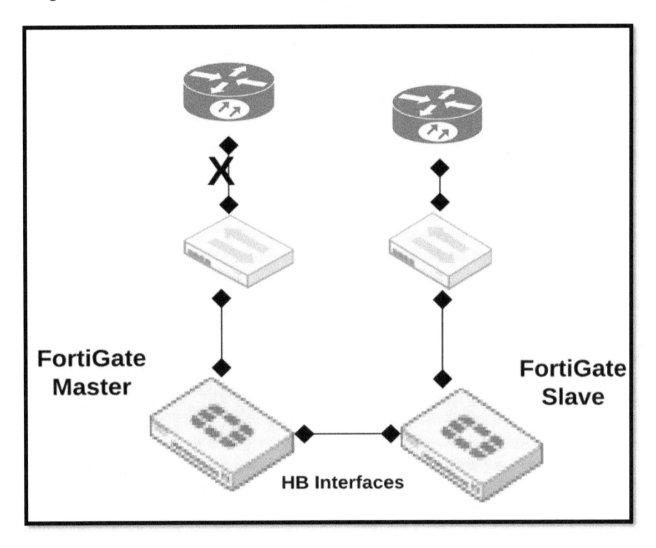

In this example, Master and Slave units are connected to independent switches and a pair of routers running on the north side of the topology. This is where Remote Link Monitor comes into play. By just monitoring the local interfaces on FortiGate, if the interface between the Master's switch and router goes down, this would not trigger a HA failover because the directly connected link would stay up and, therefore, the Monitored Interface on the Master unit would stay up as well and this would essentially black hole traffic. However, if a ping monitor were configured to ping the next-hop router, then FortiGate could detect if the path is good or not.

When configuring the ping monitor, be sure the remote monitored IP makes sense. Do not choose an IP that would be unreachable post failover because once a new Master is selected and the same IP is unreachable, and this could trigger another failover, a flip-flop essentially. Here is the remote link monitor HA CLI configuration is:

```
config system link-monitor
edit Remote-Link-Mon
set srcintf wan1
set server 192.168.10.10
set gateway-ip 192.168.10.1
set protocol ping
set ha-priority 13
set interval 1000
set failtime 5
end
..
config system ha
...
set pingserver-monitor-interface wan1
set pingserver-failover-threshold 13
set pingserver-slave-force-reset enable
set pingserver-flip-timeout 6
...
end
```

Take a moment to review. Note, the *pingserver-** HA settings will synchronize across a cluster.

To configure a remote link monitor for HA failover, the first object to configure is the actual link-monitor. The object is named **Remote-Link-Mon**; the object is configured to send ICMP packets to 192.168.10.10 sourcing wan1 interface with the gateway of 192.168.10.1. The *ha-priority* value of 13 relates to a new variable in FGCP called pingsvr_failure_value. The following config setting to review is *pingserver-failover-threshold*, which marks the pingsvr_failure_value value that triggers a HA failover. Since the threshold is configured to be 13 and if this link monitor dies, then this would meet the threshold value, which would cause the cluster to failover Note; this makes it possible to set multiple link-monitor and require more than one to fail to trigger a failover. To find the *pingsvr_failure_value* threshold value, goto the debug output below and find the *ha_prio* field:

*The counter variable **pingsvr_failure_value** related to remote link failure was once referenced as the GLOBAL PENALTY, the debug fields show **ha_prio***

```
30E-A (global) # get sys ha status
PINGSVR stats:
    FGT30Eyyyyyyyyyyy(updated 2 seconds ago):
        wan: physical/1000auto, up, rx-
bytes/packets/dropped/errors=271054675/935185/0/0, tx=214777919/665610/0/0
        pingsvr: state=down(since 2020/08/29 06:47:18), server=192.168.10.10,
ha_prio=13
    FGT30Exxxxxxxxxxx(updated 2 seconds ago):
        wan: physical/1000auto, up, rx-
bytes/packets/dropped/errors=17555893/111492/0/0, tx=12312268/33480/0/0
        pingsvr: state=N/A(since 2020/08/28 18:09:48), server=192.168.10.10,
ha_prio=13
```

In the above output, you can see both Master and Slave devices have a pingsvr_failure_value value of 13, and this is because I kept the remote link-monitor in a failed state post failover and did not use the *pingserver-slave-force-reset* command, which would have reset the *pingsvr_failure_value* value post failover once the *pingserver-flip-timeout* value expired. Note, the slave device cannot send out probe packets; only the Master can.

Next, within the *Remote-Link-Mon* object, the interval 1000 means link-monitor sends a ping probe every 1 second since this value is in milliseconds, and the failtime of 5, means 5 ping probes must fail to mark the interface as down. Meaning, in this example, it would take 5 seconds for link-monitor to put wan1 in a failed state, but only if 192.168.10.10 became unreachable.

Next, let's review the HA configuration. The *pingserver-monitor-interface* will most likely match the link-monitor srcintf wan1 so to be related, in this case. The pingserver-failover-threshold setting relates to the ha-priority field under link-monitor. The logic goes, if link-monitor fails, the ha-priority value is added to the pingsvr_failure_value counter, the pingserver-failover-threshold sets the threshold of when this counter triggers a failover. This counter value is paired with the amount of UP monitored Interfaces.

..

```
FGT30Exxxxxxxxxx is selected as the Master because it has the least value 0 of
link-failure + pingsvr-failure.
```
..

FortiOS counts the Failed Monitored Interfaces and Link Monitor failure together. These two values are then compared between cluster members, and the unit with the lowest combine value becomes Master.

The next setting to discuss is *pingserver-slave-force-reset*. When this setting is enabled, after a failover occurs, the newly promoted Master clears the *pingsvr_failure_value* value on the Slave device only <u>after the</u> *pingserver-flip-timeout* threshold is met of 6 minutes (default is 60).

Meaning, after a failover occurs, after 6 minutes, the newly selected Slave unit has an opportunity to take back the Master role since the current Master clears its pingsvr_failure_value. So now, if the remote link monitor is still in a failed state, a failover will most likely occur again.

I want to talk more about *pingserver-flip-timeout*. You can think of this timer as a freeze period for Remote Link Monitor failover. But once this timer expires, the newly promoted Master resets the Slave pingsvr_failure_value value back to 0, so now they are even. Now think about this, if the cluster uses override enable, and that Slave unit has a higher priority, then the Slave wastes no time taking back the Master role regardless of link monitor state. The flip timeout value can be found in the following debug command:

```
30E-B (global) # diagnose sys ha dump-by vcluster
<hatalk>             HA information.

vcluster_nr=1
vcluster_0: start_time=1598713025(2020-08-29 07:57:05),
state/o/chg_time=2(work)/3(standby)/1598829763(2020-08-30 16:22:43)
         pingsvr_flip_timeout/expire=360s/345s
```

One more scenario to think about, what if override is disabled, and pingsvr_failure_value value is set back to 0 for the Slave unit, and the link monitor probe is still in a dead state. The condition here would also trigger a failover because the *pingsvr_failure_value* value would increment to meet the threshold for a HA failover after the flip timer expires. Therefore, the remote monitored IP should be reachable post failover. Fortinet did place a command to manually reset the *pingsvr_failure_value* value back to 0 on a Slave device. This command might be needed if *pingserver-slave-force-reset setting* was configured to be disabled.

```
30E-B (global) # diagnose sys ha pingsvr-slave-force-reset
pingsvr_failure_value is reset from 13 to 0 for FGT30Exxxxxxx in vcluster 0
<hatalk>             HA information.
```

To summarize these commands:
1) pingserver-monitor-interface "wan"
   a. The interface related to link-monitor for HA failover
2) pingserver-failover-threshold 13
   a. The threshold value for ha-priority in link-monitor configuration
3) set pingserver-slave-force-reset enable
   a. Post Remote Link Monitor failover after the flip timeout expires, this setting resets the Slave unit *pingsvr_failure_value* value back to 0
4) set pingserver-flip-timeout 6

    a. The freeze period in minutes for Master to ignore Remote Link Monitor and hold off on resetting Slaves *pingsvr_failure_value* value.

Lastly, to check the status of a link monitor probe the follow debug command is available, here is an example of a probe that is alive and one that is state die:

```
30E-A (root) # diagnose sys link-monitor status
Link Monitor: test, Status: alive, Server num(1), Flags=0x1 init, Create
time: Fri Aug 28 16:02:14 2020
Source interface: wan (4)
Gateway: 192.168.209.62
Interval: 1000 ms
  Peer: 192.168.209.62(192.168.209.62)
        Source IP(192.168.209.1)
        Route: 192.168.209.1->192.168.209.62/32, gwy(192.168.209.1)
        protocol: ping, state: alive
                Latency(Min/Max/Avg): 0.485/0.611/0.522 ms
                Jitter(Min/Max/Avg): 0.000/0.126/0.030
                Packet lost: 0.000%
                Number of out-of-sequence packets: 0
                Fail Times(0/1)
                Packet sent: 8, received: 8, Sequence(sent/rcvd/exp): 9/9/10

30E-B (root) # diagnose sys link-monitor status
Link Monitor: test, Status: die, Server num(1), Flags=0x1 init, Create time:
Fri Aug 28 16:13:18 2020
Source interface: wan (4)
Gateway: 192.168.209.62
Interval: 1000 ms
  Peer: 2.2.2.2(2.2.2.2)
        Source IP(192.168.209.1)
        Route: 192.168.209.1->2.2.2.2/32, gwy(192.168.209.62)
        protocol: ping, state: die
                Packet lost: 100.000%
                Number of out-of-sequence packets: 0
                Recovery times(0/5) Fail Times(0/1)
                Packet sent: 18, received: 0, Sequence(sent/rcvd/exp): 19/0/0
```

This wraps up Remote Link Monitor for HA failover. The next item to discuss in this section is a feature called Link Fail Signal.

Link Fail Signal

Post HA cluster failover, one of the most important functions is for the connected switch to update their MAC to interface mappings with the vMAC for cluster connected interfaces. We already know post failover, the newly promoted Master unit will announce itself onto the LAN by sending a GARP, and this should update any switches on the LAN, and should cause traffic to be switched to the newly prompted Master. However, there is another command we can use here just in case the GARP does not make it to the former master switch or if GARP is ignored, and that is Link Fail Signal. Once enabled, upon monitored interface failure, FortiGate will then proceed to shut down all interfaces except HB interfaces for one second. In theory, this should cause any connected devices to flush any MAC's associated with the former Master device. The command to implement this behavior is found in the CLI via:

```
config system ha
set link-failed-signal enable
end
```

Session pickup and failover

Something new we have not discussed yet is Session Pickup. Session pickup is a feature within FGCP running in A-P mode that allows the Master unit to push all active sessions to Slave units. In case of failure, the Slave unit will already know about all the active sessions and will not have to relearn network traffic, which would take time and cost downtime. Essentially, if Session Pickup is enabled, then active sessions are not required to restart. The CLI setting for this feature is found via:

```
30E-B (global) # conf sys ha
..
set session-pickup disable
..
```

There is much more to cover on session sync, which we will touch on later in this chapter.

Secondary FortiGate Failure

The last type of failure of Secondary or Slave unit failure if the cluster is running in A-P mode, this would be the least impactful type of failure because the Master unit continues to process traffic. This failure is detected by the heartbeat loss threshold being met on the Master unit. One thing to note here, to detect this type of failure, be sure to have a monitoring solution of Syslog or SNMP so this can be detected and resolved.

In the next section, we cover in-depth HA synchronization for configuration and dynamic data synchronization. We have a lot to cover, so let's get to it!

HA Synchronization Operations

One of the primary functions of FGCP is to take FortiOS static configuration and take active sessions or dynamic data like DHCP and push this information to Slave units. HA Synchronization is an ongoing operation since things are always being updated on FortiOS, either new config or new active sessions. It is important to know how this works to have expectations of behavior during various HA events. We are going to talk about static configuration synchronization first.

HA Complete Configuration Sync

When an FGCP HA cluster is configured, and once all the units decide who the Master is, the next operation is configuration sync. This process begins with all units within a cluster generating a configuration checksum, a hash. The Slave units send their config file hash to the Master unit. The Master then compares them to see if they match. If the hashes do not match, then the configuration synchronization process begins.

Image 6.10 – CSUM Compare Config Sync

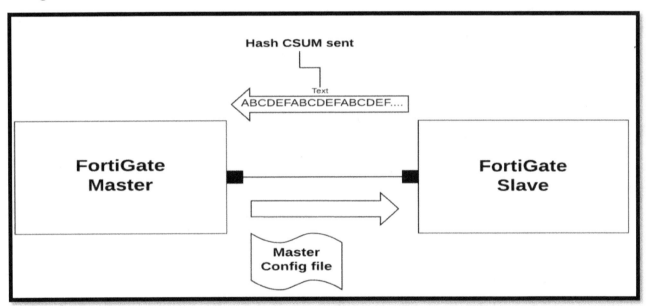

The initial config sync starts with the Master pushing its complete configuration to the secondary(s) Slave FortiGates. Slave FortiGate processes this config file and provision the configuration internally. This is a full configuration synchronization. By default, FGCP checks every 60 seconds that the config hash values match for each unit in the cluster. If a Slave unit becomes out of sync, the hash value is then checked every 15 seconds, and after five checks, a complete re-synchronization is performed.

HA Incremental Synchronization Overview

Once the initial complete configuration synchronization is performed, then subsequent updates are incremental. Incremental synchronization would be things like new Firewall Policies or Address Objects. Every time an administrator makes changes to the Master unit, the configuration will be pushed to the Slave unit.

Note that incremental updates also include dynamic data like active Session Entries, IPsec SA's, routing table, and DHCP leases as just an example.

Objects not Synchronized Overview

Not all configuration objects are synchronized across the cluster because some device settings must be per unit. Here is a list of items not synced to other cluster members.

1) HA config settings
   a. config system ha, <u>most</u> settings are not synced across other cluster members and is a per-device configuration.
2) Hostname
   a. Every host in a cluster is a special little butterfly with there own hostname.
3) HA Reserved Management interface
   a. This is something we have not touched on yet in this chapter, but this interface can be configured for induvial cluster management used for SNMP polling, for example. The route associated with the *Reserved Management interface* is not synced as well
4) Licenses
   a. Sorry but true, you must buy two of everything!! No freebies here; for a cluster to be functional, all licenses must be the same on each unit.
5) UTM Cache data
   a. various cached UTM data for Web filtering, Email filtering, etc.. are not synced between members.

UTM Database Synchronization

The Master FortiGate within a cluster is responsible for all UTM updates and FortiGuard communication. For example, when the AV/IPS databases are downloaded from FDN, the Master pushes this update to all Slave units.

Note, if your HA cluster shows 'out-of-sync' then check your UTM database and be sure they are the same version.

Session Table Synchronization Overview

Like I mentioned before, FGCP can be configured to synchronize sessions. All synchronization activity occurs over the HA heartbeat link using TCP/703 and UDP/703 packets. In A-P mode, All TCP and IPsec sessions can be synchronized to Slave units except sessions that are being handled by a proxy-based security profile. TCP and IPsec session sync is enabled via:

```
config system ha
set session-pickup enable
end
```

FGCP synchronizes IKEv1 Security Associations (SAs) between Slave units within clusters. Hence, if a failover occurs, IKE is not required to establish new SAs. IKEv2 synchronizes the IKE and ISAKMP SAs from the Master to the Slave unit(s). However, for IKEv2, FGCP cannot use the IKE SA to send/receive IKE traffic because these messages include a sequence number in every IKE message and would require synchronizing every message to Slave units to keep in sequence. So instead, FGCP synchronizes IKEv2 Message ID's which allows the re-negotiate send/receive message ID counter after failover, which allows IKE SA to remain up instead of re-negotiating the tunnel in full, so time is still saved. I know we have not discussed IPsec yet; we go into these terms in our IPsec chapter.

Next, UDP and ICMP are stateless protocols; however, there is still a Session Entry for each connection on FortiOS. These Session can indeed be synchronized as well with the following CLI command:

```
config system ha
set session-pickup enable
set session-pickup-connectionless enable
end
```

The last session sync option to talk about multicast. Multicast Session Entries can be synchronized across cluster members by using the following CLI command:

```
#config system ha
#set multicast-ttl <5 - 3600 sec>
#end
```

The second argument is to tell FortiOS how long to keep Multicast routes in the Slave unit(s) routing table. The lower the value here, the more often multicast routes are synced to Slave(s).

Session Pick-up Delay

Session pickup delay is an option that reduces the number of sessions that are synced across a cluster. The command to configure this can be found in the CLI via:

```
#config sys ha
#set session-pickup-delay-enable
#end
```

Once *session-pickup* is enabled, when a Session is created, it is pushed to the Slave unit(s), even very short-lived sessions. To prevent short-lived sessions from being synced across a cluster, the pickup delay setting must be enabled. Once configured, FortiOS only pushes sessions to the Slave unit(s) only if the session has remained active for more than 30 seconds.

Session Synchronization review

I've covered the main objectives of the NSE4 exam in these past sections regarding FGCP HA Session synchronization. However, I want you to know there are many caveats for Session sync in general. Each protocol is different, and each has its own unique challenges. In this section, I want to give a short and sweet list of what types of Sessions are pushed to the Slave units and some corner cases. Full disclosure, I do not expect you to memorize this entire list. This list is just for reference and for you to notes. Essentially, you need to test your HA failover solution and make sure it works how you want it for your network!

1) Most TCP sessions are synchronized across an HA cluster
   a. Only TCP sessions that are not scanned by AV, Web Filter, Spam Filter, Content archived, SIP TCP, SCCP.
2) SIP Session Failover
   a. if session pickup is enabled, FGCP supports the UDP SIP session failover for HA A-P Mode only. All active SIP calls with setup complete and RTP flows established are maintained, and calls will continue.
3) Multicast Sessions supported
4) IPv6, NAT64, and NAT66 supported
5) Sessions using Proxy-based security profiles are not supported with session sync.
6) Sessions using Flow-based security profiles are supported with session sync. However, the active sessions are no longer actively inspected by security profile functions.
7) If both Proxy and Flow-based security profiles are applied to a policy, these sessions do not sync with slave units.
8) Sessions for SIMPLE, SCCP signal sessions are not supported
9) Sessions that are accepted by security policies containing VIPs or virtual servers with SSL offloading or HTTP multiplexing enabled are not supported
10) Explicit web proxy, explicit FTP proxy, WCCP, WAN optimization, and Web Caching sessions are not supported.
11) SSL VPN is partly supported, only authentication failover is supported for SSL VPN web mode sessions. Not support for SSL VPN tunnels.
12) PPTP and L2TP sessions are not supported.
13) IPsec VPN SA's IKEv1 sessions sync is supported
14) WAN Optimization sessions are not supported.

Wow! What a long boring list. The moral of the story here is to test your HA solution before you put it into production. Let's move on! Next, we talk about route synchronization.

<u>FGCP Route Table Synchronization</u>

The Master unit keeps all Slave units kernel routing table up-to-date with itself with the latest routing information. The Forward Information Base (FIB) routing information on the Master unit is push to all Slave units within a cluster. This is important because, after a failover, the newly promoted Master can continue to forward traffic without the lag time of having to relearn routing information.

The FIB can be found with #get router info kernel. Routes found via #get router info routing-table all, are not synced. These are high-level configurable routes used to populate the FIB. Post failure, a newly promoted Master must rebuild its routing table from static routes and any

The output of #get router info routing-table all – is expected to be empty on Slave units. Only FIB is synchronized across HA cluster.

dynamic routing protocols. While this happens, FortiOS continues to forward traffic via kernel routes received from FGCP before failover. FortiOS provides a few commands that can be used to change how FIB routes are shared between units. These commands can be found in the CLI under #config system ha :

```
30E-B (ha) # show ful | grep route
    set route-ttl 10
    set route-wait 0
    set route-hold 10
```

The first setting to discuss is *route-ttl*. So you know now that the Master unit actively pushes its FIB to all cluster members but not the routing table. Remember, the routing table is used to build the FIB. Now, when a failure over occurs, the newly promoted Master will indeed build its own routing table, but this takes time to gather all the routing data from the network if we are dealing with routing protocols. So while the newly prompted Master builds its routing table, traffic is forwarded with the FGCP HA FIB route information. The route-ttl field controls how long the FIB routes stay active on the newly promoted Master; by default, it is ten seconds. So essentially, FortiGate has ten seconds to completely rebuild its routing table before the

It is expected for the Slave routing engine to only start after a failover and once the unit become the Master of a cluster

provided FIB routes are flushed. The newly generated routing table is used to rebuild the FIB with its information. Suppose FortiGate has an exceptionally large routing table running many routing protocols. In that case, you may need to increase the route-ttl timer to give FortiGate more time to rebuild its route table.

Note that routing protocol-specific settings (BGP/OSPF) help with a smooth routing failover; however, we don't cover those in this chapter.

The next setting to discuss is *route-hold*. This setting controls how long the Master waits between sending routing updates to other members in the cluster. By default, this value is 10 seconds. Once again, if dealing with a large routing table, you may consider increasing this value or even dedicating an interface to FGCP synchronization so as not to disrupt heartbeat traffic.

The last setting to discuss here is *route-wait*. Every time a routing table update occurs, the Slave unit is updated as well by default. This feature was created to account for link flapping, which could generate a lot of unwanted updates within the cluster. To enable this setting, specify the route-wait setting an argument that specifies the number of seconds between updates. For example, wait 30 seconds between updates the command would be:

```
config system ha
    set route-wait 30
```

That wraps up our routing FCGP HA synchronization section. At this point, you should understand how FortiOS failover works regarding route synchronization across an HA cluster and how FortiGate continues to forward traffic before its routing table is built post failover. In the next section, we cover FGCP HA cluster management.

HA Cluster Management

We already discussed in chapter one how to manage a standalone FortiGate. Most basic principles still apply in an FGCP HA environment, but there are some special things to consider. In-band management, the same method still applies; the production interfaces are also used for management access. However, this will always take you to the Master FortiGate unit within a cluster. Sometimes it is required to set up things like SNMP monitoring on induvial cluster units, so how do we accomplish this? The solution is Reserved HA Management Interface. This special interface is available in NAT and Transparent modes. The function of this interface, once configured, is to allow users or applications to communicate directly to the GUI or CLI interfaces of any cluster member. Since the reserved interface is unique between cluster members, the configuration for this interface is not synced from the Master device. Each interface IP address can be unique as well. To configure this on a cluster member, you can use the CLI via:

```
30E-B# config global
30E-B (global) # config system ha
..
set ha-mgmt-status enable
    config ha-mgmt-interfaces
        edit 1
            set interface "lan3"
            set gateway 192.168.209.62
        next
    end
..
```

The above configuration marks lan3 as a Reserved HA Management Interface on 30E-B FortiGate. As you can see, a gateway is set here as well. At this point, we could navigate to lan3 Interface in the CLI and configure a unique IP that would not sync across the cluster.

Next, there is a method to manage Slave cluster members from the master unit, as well. The method to perform this is found in the CLI via:

```
30E-B (global) # execute ha manage
<id>     please input peer box index.
<0>      Subsidary unit FGT30Eyyyyyyyyy
30E-B (global) # execute ha manage 0 admin
Warning: Permanently added '169.254.0.1' (ED25519) to the list of known
hosts.
30E-A #exit
..
```

The base command is #execute ha manage; the first argument is the index value of the cluster member to manage, which can be found via questions mark output '?' this must be referenced along with an admin username on 6.2+. Once the password is entered, access is granted to the Slave members' CLI interface. To leave this context, issue the 'exit' command. That covers FGCP HA Cluster management; the next topic we cover in this chapter is upgrading firmware!

HA Firmware Upgrade

Inherently, upgrading a HA cluster is different than just upgrading a single standalone FortiGate. The reason for this is because more than one FortiGate must be upgraded. After all, for FGCP HA synchronization to occur, all cluster members must be on the same firmware versions. There are two methods to upgrade an HA cluster:

1) uninterruptable upgrade which the default
2) uninterruptable upgrade disabled

The default upgrade method is 'uninterruptable upgrade' enabled. The expected behavior is once you upload new firmware to the Master unit, the Master then pushes the image to all Slave devices, and the Slave (s) is upgraded first:

```
Slave-FGT (global) #
Firmware upgrade in progress ...
Done.
The system is going down NOW !!

Please stand by while rebooting the system.
Restarting system.

Slave-FGT (global) # Get image from ha master OK.
Check image OK.
Please wait for system to restart.
```

Next, if an uninterruptable upgrade is disabled, once the firmware is uploaded to the Master, the Master pushes the image out to all Slave units, and the firmware upgrade process simultaneously occurs only the Master and all other Slave units. Note, firmware only needs to be uploaded to the Master unit.

Now that we have covered the basic FGCP HA theory, we can jump into the configuration piece of the puzzle and clarify any gaps in your understanding of FGCP works.

HA Cluster configuration

Now is the time we start to make things happen with FortiGate using FGCP HA technology; this is the section where everything comes together, a very cool moment! First, I am going to present an FGCP HA topology, and then we are going to create a HA cluster with our fresh factory defaulted FortiGate's! And Lastly, we verify the cluster synchronization and perform a failover. Here we go! The topology we are going to create is seen in Image 6.11:

Image 6.11 – Basic FGCP HA Topology

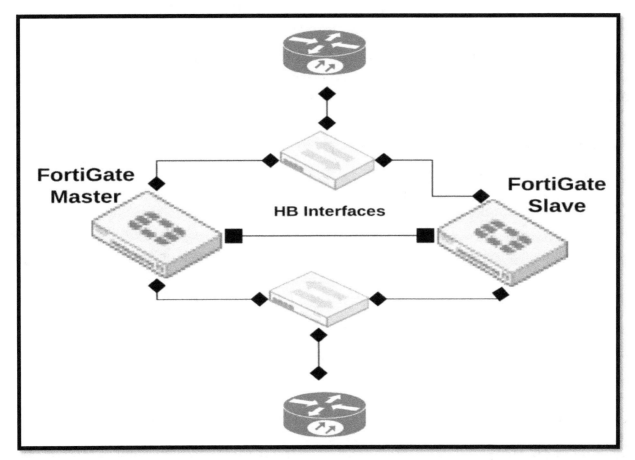

Image 6.11, is your basic FGCP HA topology; above and below the FortiGate's in the diagram are the North and South switches and routers, respectfully. The south side is the inside LAN network, and the north is the outside WAN network. Note, there are many HA topologies; we could easily add more switches and routers to each side; we could also add more FortiGate's to the FGCP HA cluster. Lastly, we could create an entirely separate FGCP HA cluster in a separate geographic location and have the two clusters talk to each other about session information, which could be used as a hot disaster recovery (DR) site. This chapter does not go into these details or topologies.

Before we start configuring our FortiGate, a few prerequisites are needed before we form an FGCP HA cluster. For a cluster to form, the following must be the same between devices:

1) Firmware
2) Operating Mode (NAT or Transparent)
3) Hard drive type and settings
4) Licenses (VDOM, FortiGuard, FortiClioud ..etc)
5) Hardware platform and VM license type
6) Related interfaces connected to related broadcast domains
   a. For example, if port1 on Master is connected to the LAN switch, then port1 on Slave should be connected to the LAN switch. This is so the vMAC and policies make sense to the LAN if a failure occurs.

These are the high-level requirements before an FGCP HA cluster can form. Before creating an FGCP HA cluster, all interfaces should be configured with a static IP address. However, once a HA cluster is formed, DHCP/PPPoE addressing can be used.

The first step in the configuration is to set unique hostnames for each unit. This could be done via console or SSH.

```
FGT1 (global) # set hostname 30E-A
..
FGT2 (global) # set hostname 30E-A
..
```

Next, we need to navigate in the cli via #config sys ha, and provide each unit unique HA settings and remember most settings in this configuration section do not sync across the cluster, nor does the hostname. Here is the configuration for the first FortiGate 30E-A:

```
30E-A (ha) # show
config system ha
    set group-id 99
    set group-name "HA-Cluster-1"
    set mode a-p
    set password NotAStrongPassword123
    set hbdev "lan2" 0
    set override disable
    set priority 200
    set monitor "wan" "lan3"
end
```

Next, we will configure the 30E-B unit HA settings with the same method.

```
30E-B (global) # show sys ha
config system ha
    set group-id 99
    set group-name "HA-Cluster-1"
    set mode a-p
```

```
     set password NotAStrongPassword123
     set hbdev "lan2" 0
     set override disable
     set priority 100
     set monitor "wan" "lan3"
end
```

Find the HA configuration of group-id 99. I mentioned before; this ID must match for all cluster members, and this value is also used to generate the vMAC addresses for the HA cluster. Next, the setting group-name is how the HA cluster is viewed when communicating with other Fortinet devices like FortiManager or FortiAnalyzer. The group-name must match. I've seen issues in carrier environments when this value is not unique, so if your managing many HA clusters, give them a unique group-name to avoid future issues. Next is the HA mode setting, which in this case, we are using Active-Passive mode (a-p). Next is the HA password, which is NotAStrongPassword123. The next configuration is *hbdev*; this value is the heartbeat interface, which is lan2. The override is set to disable, meaning the unit with the highest priority will not always take the master role. Next is priority setting, which relates to the override setting, the cluster unit with the highest priority when override is set to enable will be Master only if every member has an even number of UP Monitored Interfaces. Lastly, the Monitored Interfaces are wan, and lan3; if these interfaces go down, then a HA failover will be triggered.

Next, before we cable our Heartbeat interfaces (lan2) to each other. Be sure we meet our requirements for HA; first issue the #get sys status:

```
30E-B (global) # get sys status
Version: FortiGate-30E v6.2.5,build1142,200819 (GA)
Virus-DB: 1.00000(2018-04-09 18:07)
Extended DB: 1.00000(2018-04-09 18:07)
IPS-DB: 6.00741(2015-12-01 02:30)
IPS-ETDB: 0.00000(2001-01-01 00:00)
APP-DB: 6.00741(2015-12-01 02:30)
INDUSTRIAL-DB: 6.00741(2015-12-01 02:30)
Serial-Number: FGT30Eyyyyyyyy
Botnet DB: 1.00000(2012-05-28 22:51)
BIOS version: 05000016
System Part-Number: P17455-05
Log hard disk: Not available
Hostname: 30E-B
Operation Mode: NAT
Current virtual domain: root
Max number of virtual domains: 5
Virtual domains status: 1 in NAT mode, 0 in TP mode
Virtual domain configuration: multiple
FIPS-CC mode: disable
Current HA mode: standalone
Branch point: 1142
```

```
Release Version Information: GA
System time: Thu Aug 27 11:54:48 2020
```

Next, run the same command on 30E-A.

```
30E-A (global) # get sys status
Version: FortiGate-30E v6.2.5,build1142,200819 (GA)
Virus-DB: 1.00000(2018-04-09 18:07)
Extended DB: 1.00000(2018-04-09 18:07)
IPS-DB: 6.00741(2015-12-01 02:30)
IPS-ETDB: 0.00000(2001-01-01 00:00)
APP-DB: 6.00741(2015-12-01 02:30)
INDUSTRIAL-DB: 6.00741(2015-12-01 02:30)
Serial-Number: FGT30Exxxxxxxxx
Botnet DB: 1.00000(2012-05-28 22:51)
BIOS version: 05000016
System Part-Number: P17455-05
Log hard disk: Not available
Hostname: 30E-A
Operation Mode: NAT
Current virtual domain: root
Max number of virtual domains: 5
Virtual domains status: 1 in NAT mode, 0 in TP mode
Virtual domain configuration: multiple
FIPS-CC mode: disable
Current HA mode: standalone
Branch point: 1142
Release Version Information: GA
System time: Thu Aug 27 12:00:46 2020
```

Take some time to analyze the output. The question is, will these units be able to form an FGCP HA cluster? Starting at the top, the first value to notice is:

```
v6.2.5,build1142
```

Here we can confirm that our FortiGate units are indeed running the same firmware. Note here the build number -> 1142. If you recall, in chapter one, we went over this, all GA releases have a build number, and they should always stay consistent. However, 99.99% percent of the time, a GA release will always have the same build number, but it is worth checking to be sure the build number matches because this is what truly matters. A reason this might change would be maybe if a major flaw is found within GA release, and the code base is withdrawn and then published again with a fix, but this would be rare. The next items to check are:

```
BIOS version: 05000016
System Part-Number: P17455-05
Log hard disk: Not available
```

These values here are important as well for a HA FCGP cluster to synchronize correctly. Even though these units are both 30E FortiGate's, don't assume they have the exact same hardware. Most of the time, when new platform lines are releases (E's series), there are generations released in sequence. Sometimes flaws are found in hardware, maybe in driver chipsets, disk, or memory, and a different hardware component is select to correct the problem. When this occurs, the System Part-Number value will change; the Part-Number is what confirms the FortiGates are the exact same hardware. Next, Log Disk should be the same and the same configuration, for example, the same partitions. The disk can be checked with the following command:

```
# diagnose hardware deviceinfo disk

Disk SYSTEM(boot)               14.9GiB      type: SSD [ATA 16GB SATA Flash]
dev: /dev/sda
  partition          247.0MiB, 188.0MiB free  mounted: N  label:  dev:
/dev/sda1(boot) start: 1
  partition          247.0MiB, 181.0MiB free  mounted: Y  label:  dev:
/dev/sda2(boot) start: 524289
  partition ref:   3 14.2GiB,  14.1GiB free  mounted: Y  label:  dev:
/dev/sda3 start: 1048577

Disk HDD          ref:  16 111.8GiB    type: SSD [ATA D2CSTK251M3T-012]
dev: /dev/sdb
  partition ref:  17 110.0GiB, 109.5GiB free  mounted: Y  label:
LOGUSEDX3CEB909F dev: /dev/sdb1 start: 2048

Total available disks: 2
Max SSD disks: 1  Available storage disks: 1
```

In this output, you should notice the partitions, SSD type, log disk, Disk HDD type, and related partitions all must be the same for all cluster members. The next line to review is the UTM databases.

```
..

Virus-DB: 1.00000(2018-04-09 18:07)
Extended DB: 1.00000(2018-04-09 18:07)

..
```

The UTM databases do not have to match before cluster sync. If there is a mismatch between DB versions, wait 5-10 minutes after you attempt to form a cluster, then double-check the Master can reach FortiGuard servers for updates and issue the command:

```
#exec update-now
```

This command forces an update, and the cluster UTM DB's should sync if licensed properly. The next lines to look at is:

```
Operation Mode: NAT
Current virtual domain: root
Max number of virtual domains: 5
Virtual domains status: 1 in NAT mode, 0 in TP mode
Virtual domain configuration: multiple
FIPS-CC mode: disable
```

All these values must match between units; they must have the same operation mode, VDOM or not, max number or VDOMs (license), and FIPS-CC mode status. Alright, so everything looks good here; note I only have static IP's on the interfaces. We are ready to form our HA cluster! The next step here is to cable each unit's heartbeat interface, and once that is complete, the magic will happen! If you wish to watch the process, there are a few debug commands to show this output:

```
diag debug reset
diag debug enable
diagnose debug console timestamp enable
diag debug application hasync -1
diag debug application hatalk -1
```

Let's take a snippet of this output while the HA cluster is forming.

```
30E-B (global) # 2020-08-27 12:53:53 <hasync> reap child: pid=625, status=0
2020-08-27 12:53:53 <hatalk> vcluster_0: ha_prio=1(slave),
state/chg_time/now=3(standby)/1598557771/1598558033
2020-08-27 12:53:57 slave's configuration is not in sync with master's,
sequence:0
2020-08-27 12:54:03 <hasync> reap child: pid=630, status=0
2020-08-27 12:54:04 <hatalk> vcluster_0: ha_prio=1(slave),
state/chg_time/now=3(standby)/1598557771/1598558044
```

```
2020-08-27 12:54:12 slave's configuration is not in sync with master's,
sequence:1
```

Give the cluster 1-2 minutes to synchronize initially, maybe longer depending on configuration size. To check the status of the cluster, run below CLI debug command:

```
30E-B (global) # get sys ha status
HA Health Status: OK
Model: FortiGate-30E
Mode: HA A-P
Group: 99
Debug: 0
Cluster Uptime: 4 days 7:12:48
Cluster state change time: N/A
Master selected using:
    <2020/08/27 12:59:01> FGT30Eyyyyyyyyyy is selected as the master because
it has the largest value of uptime.
    <2020/08/27 12:49:31> FGT30Exxxxxxxxxx is selected as the master because
it has the largest value of uptime.
    <2020/08/27 12:47:51> FGT30Eyyyyyyyyyy is selected as the master because
it's the only member in the cluster.
ses_pickup: disable
override: disable
Configuration Status:
    FGT30Eyyyyyyyyyy(updated 0 seconds ago): in-sync
    FGT30Exxxxxxxxxx(updated 3 seconds ago): in-sync
System Usage stats:
    FGT30Eyyyyyyyyyy(updated 0 seconds ago):
        sessions=18, average-cpu-user/nice/system/idle=0%/0%/0%/100%,
memory=44%
    FGT30Exxxxxxxxxx(updated 3 seconds ago):
        sessions=1, average-cpu-user/nice/system/idle=0%/0%/0%/100%,
memory=44%
HBDEV stats:
    FGT30Eyyyyyyyyyy(updated 0 seconds ago):
        lan2: physical/1000full, up, rx-
bytes/packets/dropped/errors=11502648/16609/0/0, tx=3775808/11537/0/0
    FGT30Exxxxxxxxxx(updated 3 seconds ago):
        lan2: physical/1000full, up, rx-
bytes/packets/dropped/errors=244302717/891671/0/0, tx=240241684/716138/0/0
MONDEV stats:
    FGT30Eyyyyyyyyyy(updated 0 seconds ago):
```

```
        wan: physical/1000auto, up, rx-
bytes/packets/dropped/errors=2155069/8611/0/0, tx=4129429/7039/0/0
   FGT30Exxxxxxxxxx(updated 3 seconds ago):
        wan: physical/1000auto, up, rx-
bytes/packets/dropped/errors=160158650/600465/0/0, tx=151342559/426618/0/0
Master: 30E-B            , FGT30Eyyyyyyyyyy, HA cluster index = 1
Slave : 30E-A            , FGT30Exxxxxxxxxx, HA cluster index = 0
number of vcluster: 1
vcluster 1: work 169.254.0.2
Master: FGT30Eyyyyyyyyyy, HA operating index = 0
Slave : FGT30Exxxxxxxxxx, HA operating index = 1
```

Take some time to step through the above output.

This command is the most basic HA troubleshooting command; if you don't know any other HA troubleshooting commands, know this one and the output by heart. This output provides high-level details on the cluster and its operational status. Within this output, you can determine which member is the current Master. Also, you can find statistics on packet drops on interfaces.

Once the cluster is in sync, we can now proceed to cable "wan" interface of both Master and Slave to the north switch and "lan3" of both units to the south switch. At this point, we can continue to IP the lan3 and wan interfaces. We know now that the Master unit takes ownership of these IP's using a vMAC unless a failure occurs, and then the Slave would then be prompted to Master. At this point, any configuration performed on the Master is replicated to the Slave device.

This section covers the HA configuration; at this point, you should understand how FGCP works and how to configure it. The next section goes over HA diagnostics and troubleshooting.

HA Diagnostics

From time to time, you may run into issues with FGCP HA cluster synchronization issues. There are some tools available when a sync issue occurs.

When I first started working as a Fortinet carrier TAM, the first 2-3 months, all I worked on was HA issues. They are not fun. The reason these cases are high priority is that if a failure did occur on the Master, the configuration on the Slave units cannot be validated to work as the Master unit. Most HA issues stem from a CSUM mismatch. In this section, the goal is to give you a general idea of troubleshooting HA issues. The first thing we are going to discuss is gathering an HA baseline for the cluster.

HA Health Baseline

A baseline is a point of reference to be called 'normal' or what is expected. It is harder to call out anomalies if there is nothing to compare to. The best HA command on FortiGate to obtain a quick snapshot of the HA status is the one we ran in the prior section:

```
# get sys ha status
```

This output tells you if your cluster is in sync and who the Master is, which are two critical pieces of information. To find if cluster members are in sync and who is Master can be found in the debug output below:

```
..

Configuration Status:
    FGT30Eyyyyyyyyyy(updated 0 seconds ago): in-sync
    FGT30Exxxxxxxxxx(updated 3 seconds ago): in-sync

..

Cluster state change time: N/A
Master selected using:
    <2020/08/27 12:59:01> FGT30Eyyyyyyyyyy is selected as the Master because
it has the largest value of uptime.
    <2020/08/27 12:49:31> FGT30Exxxxxxxxxx is selected as the Master because
it has the largest value of uptime.
    <2020/08/27 12:47:51> FGT30Eyyyyyyyyyy is selected as the Master because
it's the only member in the cluster.

..
```

Within this output, we can see the cluster is in sync, and the Master unit is FGT30Eyyyyyyyyyy, and it was select because it has the largest uptime value. We can also gather interface statistics like errors or dropped packets.

```
..

HBDEV stats:
    FGT30Eyyyyyyyyyy(updated 0 seconds ago):
        lan2: physical/1000full, up, rx-
bytes/packets/dropped/errors=11502648/16609/0/0, tx=3775808/11537/0/0
    FGT30Exxxxxxxxxx(updated 3 seconds ago):
        lan2: physical/1000full, up, rx-
bytes/packets/dropped/errors=244302717/891671/0/0, tx=240241684/716138/0/0

..
```

Packet drop stats could be useful if the cluster keeps losing heartbeat packets with other members, which could point to a bad cable or congestion on the HB network. If this output shows that the cluster members are not in-sync, this means we need to dig deeper to see where the mismatch is. The command to show cluster hash values is:

```
30E-B (global) # diagnose sys ha checksum cluster

================== FGT30Exxxxxxxxx ==================

is_manage_master()=1, is_root_master()=1
debugzone
global: 60 8a 27 2c 28 49 1d fe 5b 8d 90 91 ef 70 4a b5
root: b1 a2 b8 35 42 82 35 af 89 62 3e 28 1d cf 47 95
all: 99 7c c5 64 a6 e0 42 9a df aa 5d 66 79 65 c5 c2

checksum
global: 60 8a 27 2c 28 49 1d fe 5b 8d 90 91 ef 70 4a b5
root: b1 a2 b8 35 42 82 35 af 89 62 3e 28 1d cf 47 95
all: 99 7c c5 64 a6 e0 42 9a df aa 5d 66 79 65 c5 c2

================== FGT30Eyyyyyyyyyy ==================

is_manage_master()=0, is_root_master()=0
debugzone
global: 60 8a 27 2c 28 49 1d fe 5b 8d 90 91 ef 70 4a b5
root: b1 a2 b8 35 42 82 35 af 89 62 3e 28 1d cf 47 95
all: 99 7c c5 64 a6 e0 42 9a df aa 5d 66 79 65 c5 c2

checksum
global: 60 8a 27 2c 28 49 1d fe 5b 8d 90 91 ef 70 4a b5
root: b1 a2 b8 35 42 82 35 af 89 62 3e 28 1d cf 47 95
all: 99 7c c5 64 a6 e0 42 9a df aa 5d 66 79 65 c5 c2
```

This output shows hash values for all VDOM's, global and all. Comparing hash values could be helpful to point out specific sync issues with a certain VDOM by comparing mismatched hash values. A method to re-sync the FGCP cluster is using the recalculate hash command:

```
30E-B (global) # diagnose sys ha checksum recalculate
<Enter> or <global/vdom-name>    <Enter> to re-calculate all checksums, or
global/vdom-name to re-calculate global or a specific vdom HA checksum.

30E-B (global) # diagnose sys ha recalculate-extfile-signature
          HA sync information.
hasync recalculating signatures for all external files ... Done.
```

The recalculate command, if no argument is provided, then a recalculation is performed for all VDOMs and global as well. The next command recalculates the hash value for external files. External files are things like the UTM database synced across the cluster. The next command to know about is:

```
30E-B (global) # diagnose sys ha hadiff status
pid: 0
state: idle
vdom:
log: enabled
max-sync-turns: 3
max-unsync-wait: 5
sync-failure: 0
master-lastcsum: c7 eb 90 0d 7a 4f 74 a0 a0 25 fd 39 fd 90 e1 03
```

This command will show the Master csum; run this command on all backup units to see if hash matches. Idle means nothing to do, if you see this on a Slave unit that is out of sync, this is not desirable, and in this case, you would have to manually trigger a synchronization. This command can be run on the Slave unit(s) as well:

```
#diagnose sys ha hadiff status | grep state
state: get-csum <------ Slave waiting on response from Master
```

If the output shows 'get-csum' for a long period, then the Slave may be stuck at the get-csum state, and at this point, I would recommend scheduling a maintenance window and kill the two FGCP daemons on Master and Slave units. The expected behavior, whenever you kill a daemon, is for it just to restart. Be careful killing daemon on production devices, and I would get Fortinet TAC approval before doing this as well. The two HA daemons are:

```
hasync
hatalk
```

To Kill a daemon, first find the process ID:

```
#diag sys top
Run Time:  0 days, 1 hours and 49 minutes
0U, 0N, 0S, 100I, 0WA, 0HI, 0SI, 0ST; 1008T, 554F
        newcli      906      R       0.4      0.7
        hatalk      460      S <     0.4      0.7
```

In this case, the hatalk process ID (PID) is 460. So to kill the daemon, the command would be:

```
#diagnose sys kill 11 460
```

The 11 value generates an entry in the crashlog, which could be useful to Fortinet's development team regarding software fixes. Here is a crashlog example snippet:

```
26: 2020-08-27 14:21:50 Signal <11> was sent to process <00460> by user
<admin>
27: 2020-08-27 14:21:50 <00460> firmware FortiGate-30E
v6.2.5,build1142b1142,200819 (GA) (Release)
28: 2020-08-27 14:21:50 <00460> application hatalk
29: 2020-08-27 14:21:50 <00460> *** signal 11 (Segmentation fault) received
***

..
```

The last command to discuss is to review HA sync packets. Sync packet debug can be accomplished with the below sniffer command that looks for ethernet frames with EtherType of 0x8892

`#diagnose sniffer packet any 'ether proto 0x8892' 4`

Here is an example output:

```
30E-B (root) # diagnose sniffer packet any 'ether proto 0x8892' 4
interfaces=[any]
filters=[ether proto 0x8892]
1.102634 lan2 in Ether type 0x8892 printer hasn't been added to sniffer.
1.488612 lan2 in Ether type 0x8892 printer hasn't been added to sniffer.
```

These are synchronization packets, nothing to do with a printer. This sniffer command allows you to view sync packets transferring the HB interface or explicitly configured sync interface(s).

In my experience in troubleshooting HA synchronization issues, sometimes the easiest way to fix the problem is to perform a config backup on Master, modify the config with the Slave specific config settings, disconnect the Slave and restore the configuration, and re-connect the Slave HB interfaces back to the Master. This method has worked for me in the past. Before implementing this procedure on a production network, I recommend submitting a TAC case for guidance. The last thing we are going to talk about in this section is HA Split-brain.

HA Split Brain

HA split-brain is worth a mention and is something that will take down your network if it happens. The FGCP HA split-brain condition is when something happens to the heartbeat cable(s) or interfaces that cause the Master and Slave units to mark the other as dead because they stopped receiving heartbeats. When this occurs, all cluster units will attempt to take the Master role. When this happens, a vMAC conflict occurs on the connected LAN, and traffic will stop being processed. When a HA cluster is in this state, you must take down all units, but one until the heartbeat interface issue can be resolved, and this is why it is so important to have redundant heartbeat interfaces to avoid this condition.

This brings us to the end of the diagnostic troubleshooting sections of FGCP HA and the end of Chapter 6. The information provided here is only the tip of the iceberg when it comes to HA. If you are interested in digging further into FortiGate HA technologies. The NSE7 material goes over more complex HA topologies and troubleshooting methods.

Chapter Summary

I'll try not to be too 'redundant'... explaining the redundancy we covered in this chapter. Sorry, I have to slip in dad jokes here in there! But yes, this chapter was all about FGCP HA, which is the technology Fortinet created to account for hardware failures and react to such situations by having a hot standby or active unit available!

We spoke about two redundancy methods in this chapter, which are *inline*, which is a HA FGCP cluster within a single site or LAN network, and geo-redundancy, where devices are placed geographically in separate locations and routing is used to swing traffic to the various locations based on specified conditions. Note, the inline and geo-redundancy can be combined with HA FGCP.

Next, we cover the two FGCP HA operational modes Active-Passive (A-P) and Active-Active (A-A). A-P method is where only one FortiGate handled production traffic, and the Slave device(s) monitor the Master unit for hardware failure. A-A is where the Slave device(s) actively participate in the traffic processing, and the cluster effectively load-balance the traffic.

FGCP HA traffic flow for A-P, only the Master handles traffic, and with A-A, the Master will distribute some sessions to Slave units. Virtual MAC's are used by the cluster to assume related MAC addresses in case of failure. In A-A, the Master uses the physical MAC of Slave unit(s) to load balance traffic.

Virtual Clustering is where certain VDOM's can be placed on a Slave device and is considered the primary VDOM that will actively process traffic, which is a load balancing method.

We reviewed FGCP HA operations. The Heartbeat (HB) interfaces are used to send keep-alive messages between cluster members. If HB packets hit the loss threshold, then a cluster failover will occur. There are several methods where failover can be triggered; for example, link monitor failover, SSD failure, and monitor interface failure. Session synchronization can be used to create a smooth transition post failover so sessions can stay active on Slave unit(s).

The HA Master performs a complete configuration synchronization during the initial cluster setup and then only performs incremental updates. The hostname and most HA settings for cluster units are not synchronized. The Master synchronizes its FIB to Slave units to account for the lag time of the Slave units to rebuild their own routing-table post failover event. Uninterruptable upgrade method will first upgrade the Slave unit(s) and then the Master unit. If disabled, all units will upgrade at the same time, which causes downtime.

Lastly, in this chapter, we covered some basic HA diagnostics troubleshooting steps. The Master unit creates a config CSUM and shares it with Slave members; if no match, then the sync process will start. There are many HA debug commands we can use to fix HA sync problems. HA, split-brain is when the heartbeat link goes down or becomes degraded, and HB packets are lost between units causing every unit to think the other is dead and attempts to take the Master role, which causes a vMAC conflict on the LAN.

That wraps up chapter six! Now it is time to test your knowledge with the end of chapter questions!

End of Chapter Six Questions

1. What is the FGCP HA Virtual MAC OUI?
    a. 09-09-0f-09
    b. 0f-09-0f-09
    c. 00-09-0f-0f
    d. 00-09-0f-09

2. How is the Virtual MAC extension identifier (the second half) created?
    a. created with arbitrary numbers
    b. created from the hash value from the cluster name
    c. created from group-id, virtual cluster number, and interface index value
    d. created from group-id and cluster index values.

3. What is Virtual Clustering?
    a. When you have multiple FGCP HA instances geographically separated
    b. Is when the Master load-balances traffic to Slave units
    c. Is when primary VDOMs actively pass traffic on Master and Slave units.
    d. Is when virtual cluster index values are shared across FGCP

4. What is not the purpose of Heartbeat interfaces?
    a. Used as a keep-alive mechanism between cluster members
    b. Used to synchronize dynamic data by default
    c. Uses UDP to encapsulate heartbeat packets
    d. Uses different EtherTypes to identify different FGCP communication

5. Monitored Interfaces are used to detect heartbeat failures.
    a. True
    b. False

6. With Override Enable, what is the Master election process?
    a. Monitored Interfaces UP > Cluster uptime value > Priority > Serial Number
    b. Monitored Interfaces UP > Priority > Cluster uptime value > Serial Number
    c. Cluster uptime value > Monitored Interfaces UP > Priority > Serial Number
    d. Priority > Cluster uptime value > Monitored Interfaces UP > Serial Number

7. With Override Disable, what is the Master election process?
    a. Monitored Interfaces UP > Cluster uptime value > Priority > Serial Number
    b. Monitored Interfaces UP > Priority > Cluster uptime value > Serial Number
    c. Cluster uptime value > Monitored Interfaces UP > Priority > Serial Number
    d. Priority > Cluster uptime value > Monitored Interfaces UP > Serial Number

8. SSD failure can trigger cluster failover
    a. True
    b. False

9. By default, FGCP checks every 30 seconds that the config hash values match for each unit in the cluster.
    a. True
    b. False

10. If a Slave unit becomes out of sync, the hash value is then checked every 15 seconds, and after five checks a complete re-synchronization is performed
    a. True
    b. False

11. What MAC address is used in A-A when the Master forward packet to the Slave unit?
    a. Master tunnels packets through HB interface for Slave to process
    b. Master forwards frame to Slave using unique vMAC address for Slave unit.
    c. Master forwards frame to Slave using the Slaves physical MAC address
    d. Master cannot forward packets to Slave units in A-A mode.

12. The Master unit will synchronize what routing information to Slave units?
    a. Forwarding Information Base
    b. The routing table configuration
    c. static routes
    d. No route information is shared in FGCP

13. The full HA configuration is synchronized between units.
    a. True
    b. False

14. Split Brain HA issue is when:
    a. the Master device fails, and Slave is prompted to Master

b. the Slave device fails only

c. multiple devices within a cluster attempt to take on the Master role

d. multiple devices within a cluster forward traffic to the Master unit only

15. What command enables session synchronization within a cluster?
   a. set sess-sync enable
   b. set session-pickup enable
   c. set sync-pickup enable
   d. set sync-session enable

16. What command will trigger a failover for FGCP with override disable?
   a. exec ha system failover
   b. diagnose ha system failover
   c. diagnose sys ha reset-uptime
   d. diagnose ha manage 0 admin

17. What command will provide cluster csum?
   a. diagnose sys checksum cluster
   b. diagnose ha checksum cluster
   c. diagnose sys ha checksum cluster
   d. diagnose sys ha csum cluster

18. What HA debug command will show cluster high-level status?
   a. exec sys ha status
   b. get sys ha status
   c. get sys ha cluster
   d. diagnose sys ha stats

19. What command will calculate a new csum for a cluster?
   a. diagnose ha checksum recalculate
   b. diagnose sys ha checksum recalculate
   c. diagnose sys ha recalculate
   d. diagnose sys ha csum recalculate

20. What are the two FGCP daemons that run in the background on FortiOS
   a. fgcpd and syncd
   b. fgcpd and hasync

     c. hatalk and fgcpd
     d. hatalk and hasync

Chapter 7 | Logging and Monitoring

NSE4 Blueprint Topics Covered

- Log basics
- Describe performance and logging
- Identify local log storage
- configure logging
- Understand disk allocation
- Identify External log storage
- Configure log backups
- configure alert email and threat weight
- configure remote logging
- understand log transmission
- configure reliable logging and OFTPS
- understand miglogd
- Understand FortiView

Logs can be used for many things: auditing, security issues, system performance stats, or policy enforcement. The reason I placed logging within the Infrastructure book and not the Security FortiOS books is that inherently a log does not perform a security function by itself on FortiOS. External tools like a SIEM or FortiAnalyzer must be used with various logs to create a security function for log entries. The focus of this chapter is logging from the perspective of FortiOS. The first question to ask, what is a log? A log is the metadata generated around an event or condition. FortiOS has many different log types generated from various processes.

Logs are essential to network operations and come with many responsibilities. One of the most important ones is not to lose your logs! This could happen due to hardware failure, misconfiguration, or security breach, etc. Many compliance standards require companies to maintain certain log retention, or else your organization could get their compliance state revoked.

Some FortiGate platforms come with a large enough disk to store logs locally. There are a few settings to consider when going with this option. In general, it is best practice to send logs to a dedicated device to store logs because, as you may know, logs can take up a lot of disk space. When I worked for a carrier MSSP, the SIEM we had was receiving around 30,000 events per second (EPS), which is a lot of data to deal with for any system. I've seen Carrier-grade FortiAnalyzer devices handled between 3,000 – 7,000 Events Per Seconds (EPS). With a log volume this high, it would not be feasible to log to a local disk. This would just run FortiGate into the ground, and it would log itself to death, which I have seen many times.

It is crucial to understand log retention and disk allocation, which we discuss in this chapter. I also talk about the logging daemon, and we get a chance to look under the hood and view some different configuration options within this daemon. The last topics covered in this chapter are Log View, FortiView, and the alert email feature. After this chapter, you should be confident in FortiOS logging and monitoring features and what they have to offer for your environment! Let's get to it!

Log Basics

Logging is essentially the act of tracking and recording process executions. Let's face it, without logs and debugs, we would have no clue what computers are doing and why they are doing it. FortiOS generates metadata around many different types of events and writes this data into log messages. Logs can be generated from network traffic that records basic IP information for a session. Logs can also be security-related and can provide insight around various UTM features. Once the metadata is gathered from a process execution, the metadata is packed up and transmitted in a known format to be stored somewhere, either locally or on a remote device. When I say 'known format,' of course, I mean RFC standard. Also, the receiving device can be programmed to receive certain Syslog data and make use of this data, for example, a FortiAnalyzer. FortiGate 6.4 supports the following Syslog RFCs:

1) RFC 5424: The Syslog Protocol
2) RFC 5425: Transport Layer Security (TLS) Transport Mapping for Syslog

A common location for logs to be stored in a Fortinet network is on a FortiAnalyzer (FAZ), which is a log aggregator. Meaning, a FAZ can run reports by querying its local database to answer questions like, which one of my users is on Facebook the most? Questions like this are answered by analyzing logs stored on the FAZ local database and rendering all the data into a single report or search result. Also, A FAZ can handle long term log storage for many Fortinet products if sized correctly. We touch more on FAZ through this chapter.

Syslog is a format that conforms to industry standards and contains many key pair values. For example, a timestamp field within a Syslog message would look something like "localtime=11:22:33". This key pair has a tree-like structure because different message types have specific key pair values. Meaning a HA event is not going to have Web Filtering related messages. It would have specific data around why HA generated an event; maybe a failover occurs, so a log message was recorded. We can answer many questions about our network when reviewing Syslog messages. One of the main problems with the log message is there are so many! Without tools like searchable databases and SIEM devices, log messages are not really feasible to work with on a large scale. In the next section, we walk through the process of FortiOS, generating a log message.

> *timestamps are important, be sure FortiOS has the correct time via NTP.*
>
> *NSE4-PASS (global) # diagnose sys ntp status*
>
> *NSE4-PASS (global) # execute time*

There are many stages in the life of a packet where a log message can be generated. Some logs can be generated from packets dropped at the local-In policy or others at the transit firewall policies. Some FortiOS settings would even log implicit deny traffic and many other odd types of network traffic; the following CLI output has a few examples of the FortiOS available log settings:

```
30E-B (root) # config log setting
30E-B (setting) # show ful
config log setting
    set resolve-ip disable
    set resolve-port enable
    set log-user-in-upper disable
    set fwpolicy-implicit-log disable
    set fwpolicy6-implicit-log disable
    set log-invalid-packet disable
    set local-in-allow disable
    set local-in-deny-unicast disable
    set local-in-deny-broadcast disable
    set local-out disable
    set daemon-log disable
    set neighbor-event disable
    set brief-traffic-format disable
    set user-anonymize disable
    set expolicy-implicit-log disable
    set log-policy-comment disable
    set log-policy-name disable
    set faz-override disable
    set syslog-override disable
end
```

Take a moment to review these unique log settings here.

All these settings could be configured on a per-VDOM basis. Note, be careful turning these additional features on because if there is odd behavior that generates a lot of network traffic, then this could run the FortiOS logging daemon miglogd into the ground and drain all the bandwidth from your network with logs!

As FortiGate accepts traffic via firewall policies and routes traffic accordingly, behind the scenes FortiOS is activity recording this process into log messages to give us insight into what it did with the data and why. Depending on configuration settings, FortiOS writes log message locally or generate network packets and send log messages to a remote device(s). The high-level purpose of logs is to help monitor network traffic, identify problems, and obtain baselines for starters. Here is an example of a FortiOS log message in full:

..

```
date=2020-08-31 time=15:8:10 idseq=241147566572961832 itime=2020-08-31
17:37:35 euid=1032 epid=1048 dsteuid=3 dstepid=101 type=utm subtype=app-ctrl
level=information action=pass sessionid=10009 policyid=1 srcip=10.1.1.1
dstip=2.2.2.2 srcport=10019 dstport=20 proto=6 vrf=32 logid=1059028704
service=tcp/20 user=user group=group eventtime=1598914090052034450
filesize=2345 incidentserialno=0 direction=incoming appid=38473
srcintfrole=undefined dstintfrole=undefined appcat=Video/Audio
app=Vimeo_Video.Play filename=Vimeo Demo hostname=www.vimeo.com
eventtype=signature clouduser=video-watcher@yahoo.com cloudaction=others
srcintf=lan
dstintf=lan2 tz=-0700 devid=FGT30Exxxxxxx vd=root dtime=2020-08-31 15:48:10
itime_t=1598920655 devname=HA-Cluster-1_FGT30
..
```

This was a test log generated by running the following CLI command:

`#diagnose log test`

Take a moment to review this log message and generate some questions. Note, this is one entry. Could you imagine if there were hundreds of thousands or millions of log messages like this one? It would be too much data to go through manually. This is where products like FAZ come into play that parses out these log messages and inserts them into searchable database tables. The next item I want to cover with you is the FortiOS log types and subtypes.

For details on every log field see :
https://fortinetweb.s3.amazonaws.com/docs.fortinet.com/v2/attachments/be3d0
e3d-4b62-11e9-94bf-00505692583a/FortiOS_6.2.0_Log_Reference.pdf

Log Types and Subtype

On FortiGate, there are three different types of log messages. These top-level types are then subdivided into subtypes. The top-level log message Types are:
1) **Traffic** log type
   a. Records network traffic flow data
2) **Event** log type
   a. Records system-level information like HA events.
3) **Security**(**utm**) log type
   a. Records security events like IPS or AV matches.

If you review the log message's output on the prior page, we can see that the log type is *type=utm*, and the subtype is *subtype=app-ctrl*, which is short for application control. Next, is to review all the Subtype log messages on FortiOS See table 7.1.

To debug logging on FortiOS run the follow CLI command:

 # diagnose debug application miglogd -1

Table 7.1 – Log Types and Subtypes

Traffic log	**Event** log	**Security** log
Forward	Endpoint Control	Application Control
Local	High Availability	Antivirus
Sniffer	System	Data Leak Prevention
Multicast	User	Web Application Firewall
	Wireless	Anomaly (DoS)
	WAD (proxy)	IPS
	VPN	Web Filter
	Router	Anti-Spam (email)
	Compliance-check	DNS
	Security-audit	VOIP

Take a few moments to review the FortiOS log subtypes.

Traffic log, subtype Forward is a log message generated by processed transit traffic that is either excepted or rejected by a firewall policy. We go over some firewall policy options to modify this behavior. Next, the Local subtype is a log message that contains information about traffic destined for the FortiGate itself, which could be a management connection. The last type here, the Sniffer subtype, contains information around the traffic processed by the one-arm sniffer feature. We have not discussed this feature, but essentially this is a method to mirror traffic to another port on FortiGate, which could be further analyzed by 3rd party security appliances. Lastly is the subtype multicast is to log events around multicast traffic.

The Event type log, subtype Endpoint Control, are log messages generated when FortiGate interacts with FortiClient. FortiClient can join FortiOS in the Security Fabric and maintain a telemetry connection. Next is the High Availability subtype, I've already used an example in this chapter of HA generating log messages, but a common message that HA generates is when a failover occurs, which could be caused by the heartbeat failure threshold being met. Next, System subtype log messages are generated from things like admin logins or FortiGuard updates. The User subtype is generated when a user authenticates to a firewall policy. Next is the Wireless subtype, I know we have not discussed FortiGate wireless technology yet, but certain FortiGate platforms have built-in WiFi or can manage FortiAP via CAPWAP. These platforms with built-in WiFi are called FortiWifi and not FortiGate. The Router subtype log stems from routing protocols like BGP or OSPF. VPN subtype logs are generated from events like IPsec tunnels going up or down or SSLVPN login failures. The wad subtype logs are generated by the Web Proxy, which records events related to processing web requests.

Security Log (type=utm), subtype Application Control records message around using App-control features, which is used to identify what applications are running on the network or used for application routing. The subtype Antivirus records events around the UTM feature AV, and when active in a firewall policy, log messages are generated when AV matches occur or other events around AV. The next subtype is Data Link Prevention or DLP. DLP is used to look for things like credit card numbers or social security numbers within documents that attempt to leave the network; if a match occurs, then a log is generated. The Anti-Spam subtype relates to the email filter UTM feature, and if detection occurs, then the event is logged. Web Filter subtype records activity related to the HTTP(s) traffic flowing through a policy with Web Filter enabled. The next subtype is Intrusion Prevention System (IPS), which relates to the UTM IPS features, which would log things like IPS matches. IPS blocks known malicious exploits. The next subtype is Anomaly, which relates to FortiOS DoS policy features and logs messages around matches in the DoS policy. The last security subtype is the Web Application Firewall (WAF), which has specific signatures to protect against things like HTTP(s) attacks or SQL injections; logs are generated if a match occurs.

Note, some subtype log messages have an 'eventtype' that will further clarify the reason for the log message creation. For example:

```
type="utm" subtype="virus" eventtype="infected" level="warning"
```

The *eventtype* here further clarifies why the AV on FortiOS generated this log message, and in this case, an infected file was caught! For a full comprehensive log message reference guide for 6.4 FortiOS, see the following link:

http://docs.fortinet.com/document/fortigate/6.4.0/fortios-log-message-reference/524940/introduction

Log Severity Level

The next piece of the puzzle is log severity. I remember questions like this being on my CCNA exam for cisco. Essentially, each log message is indexed and given a priority level that maps to 8 different possible values. The values are 0-7, with 0 being the most critical log message and 7 being the least critical. Table 7.2 outlines these levels of criticality for log messages.

FortiOS stores all log messages equal to or exceeding the log severity level selected.

Table 7.2 – *Log Severity Levels*

Levels	Details
0 - Emergency	System unstable
1 - Alert	Immediate action required
2 - Critical	Functionality effected
3 - Error	An error exists that can affect functionality
4 - Warning	Functionality could be affected
5 - Notification	Information about normal events
6 - Information	General System information
7 - Debug	Diagnostic information for investigating issues

Take a moment to review the above table.

To configure various log levels on FortiOS, the following CLI commands can be used:

```
NSE4-PASS (global) # conf log fortianlyzer filter
NSE4-PASS (filter) # set severity ?
emergency        Emergency level.
```

alert	Alert level.
critical	Critical level.
error	Error level.
warning	Warning level.
notification	Notification level.
information	Information level.
debug	Debug level.

This configuration means events marked with a certain log severity level or higher generates a log message. This is a method to lower your log volume if needed. For example, if you only care about the emergency and alert severity level, you would configure the alert severity. The next thing we need to review is the log message layout.

Log Message Layout

A log message has two major parts, a header, and a body. A header contains fields that exist in all log types. For example, the date, time, logic, type, subtype, and level are all fields in the header. The body contains fields that may only exist for specific *eventtype* of log messages. Let us look at a webfilter log example:

Header:

```
date=2020-08-31 time=17:38:09 idseq=2411475665572961859 bid=600033 dvid=1035
itime=1598920688 euid=1032 epid=101 dsteuid=3 dstepid=101 logver=602051142
type="utm" subtype="webfilter" level="warning"
```

Body:

```
action="blocked" sessionid=30001 policyid=1 srcip=1.1.1.1 dstip=2.2.2.2
srcport=30001 dstport=20 proto=6 cat=26 logid="0316013056" service="HTTP"
user="user" group="group" eventtime=1598920689288812050 sentbyte=0 rcvdbyte=0
craction=4194304 crscore=30 crlevel="high" srcintfrole="undefined"
dstintfrole="undefined" direction="N/A" method="ip" reqtype="direct"
url="http://www.abcd.com/ww.abcd.com" hostname="www.abcd.com"
catdesc="Malicious Websites" eventtype="ftgd_blk" srcintf="lan"
dstintf="lan2" msg="URL belongs to a denied category in policy" tz="-0700"
devid="FGT30Exxxxxxxx" vd="root" devname="HA-Cluster-1_FGT30E"
```

In the body portion of the message, we can gather, this connection was blocked because Web Filter determined this domain to be malicious. We can gather what policy, source/destination IP's and ports used in the Session Entry. When using 3rd party log aggregation solutions, it is critical to understand the log format. FAZ will know the format of each log by default.

It is not feasible to memorize every log message format and the variables in each field. When testing FortiOS logging to SIEM solutions or event handlers, the easiest method to generate the log you want is by performing the action on FortiGate. If you want your SIEM to know when the FortiGate IPS sensor is being triggered by source IP X, then point your pen-testing software to route through FortiGate IPS policy and review the IPS log messages that are generated. You could also test things like HA failover, gather these log messages, and then write rules around them. This is important because log format can change between MR versions; know your FortiOS code version message format, and account for changes.

Log ID numbers

Every log message has a log id field, logid=1059028704. The first two digits represent the Log Type. Traffic log *logid* begins with "00" and Event log *logid* begins with "01". Next, the second two digits represent the subtype; for example, if VPN was the Subtype, then the second two digits within the *logid* would be "01" and so the first four digits for this log would be "0101". I am talking about this because sometimes it is useful to know this id field to make it easier to create rules on 3rd party SIEM devices. For a full list of *logid* definitions, see the following link:

https://docs.fortinet.com/document/fortigate/6.2.0/fortios-log-message-reference/656858/log-id-definitions

The next item to discuss in this section is how logging could impact performance.

Performance Impact

At the beginning of the chapter, I mentioned that I've worked in environments that generate high log volume. Most carriers I've worked with generate between 3,000 – 7,000 EPS per FAZ platforms, maybe more. I've seen 10Gbps fiber connections dedicated to only log messages. So you can now see how logs can degrade the network and degrade the transit network, but generating logs can also degrade FortiGate's performance. I've worked a few cases where miglogd was being over-utilized. The rule of thumb, the more logs generated, the more resources this cost FortiGate regarding CPU, memory, and possibly disk space. On FortiOS CLI, performance statistic logging can be enabled.

```
#config sys glo
#set sys-perf-log-interval 5
#end
                    - Time in minutes between updates of performance
statistics logging. (1 - 15 min, default = 5, 0 = disabled).
```

This setting is used to keep an eye on FortiGate system health for things like CPU, Memory, and Sessions in which log messages are sent containing this data. The next topic I want to cover is log management.

Log Management

There are two major questions to answer to obtain good log management and logging "Best Practices". Firstly, how many logs does your device need to ingest? How many logs is

FortiGate(s) generating? Granted, these are loaded questions. We could look at log EPS (Events Per Seconds) or events per day, but the bigger question is, how do we determine how many events per day a FortiGate is sending? To obtain details about the log rate on FortiGate, run the below commands:

```
30E-B (global) # diagnose test application miglogd 6
mem=228, disk=0, alert=0, alarm=0, sys=0, faz=829, faz-cloud=0, webt=0,
fds=480
interface-missed=282
Queues in all miglogds: cur:0  total-so-far:70178
global log dev statistics:
faz 0: sent=829, failed=0, cached=0, dropped=0 , relayed=136987


30E-B (global) # diagnose test application miglogd 4
..
faz
traffic: logs=87 len=57024, Sun=0 Mon=58 Tue=29 Wed=0 Thu=0 Fri=0 Sat=0
compressed=36401
event: logs=656 len=274557, Sun=0 Mon=172 Tue=484 Wed=0 Thu=0 Fri=0 Sat=0
compressed=230113
virus: logs=12 len=6729, Sun=0 Mon=8 Tue=4 Wed=0 Thu=0 Fri=0 Sat=0 compressed=4762
..
```

You might notice no output explicitly says "remote logging rate" or something like that, which would be nice when sizing your logging solution. There are commands on FortiAnalyzer that shows the log rate for FortiGate. So to find our EPS or events per day on FortiGate, we need to first look at the output of 'sent=829' (taken from the first command). This value is how many logs total have been sent to FAZ, 829. You can go to FAZ and add the total Traffic/Security/Event log types, and they should add up to 829. The next command shows the amount of compressed data sent to FAZ via *compressed=36401*; this means FortiGate sent 36.401 Kilobytes worth of <u>Traffic</u> logs to FAZ in this case. All the line items under the *faz* section of the "**diagnose test application miglogd 4**" command needs to be added together (traffic, event, virus..etc.). Note the total in this output:

1) Total logs sent to FAZ: 829
2) Total data sent to FAZ: traffic+event+virus compressed= 271.276 Kilobytes

I used traffic, event, and virus line items from the debug output only as examples. All must be added together to obtain the total data sent.

Next, divide these totals over the period of time you tested. For example, if this was output from only one hour, then we would divide these totals by 3,600 because that is how many seconds are in an hour.

829/3600 = 0.23 EPS

271.276/3600 = 0.075 Kilobytes sent per second

Note, this is my lab environment, which does not generate a lot of log data. However, the method would remain the same. I would recommend looking at your log EPS and data sent over the course of a week or so.

Now with these values, I can start planning how much storage I need and what FAZ platform/VM would work for my ESP rate. First, let's do the storage requirements:

0.075*86000= 6,450 KB per day

6,450 * 365 = 2,354,250 KB = 2.35 GB per year

So with my lab environment, in theory, if I do not change anything with my environment regarding the logging and traffic being processed, then I would need 2.35 GB per year worth of storage to hold my log data. Note, for a FAZ, this only accounts for the Archive database and not the Analytics database, which I will touch on in just a second.

Next, let us look at the EPS; this is a little more straight forward. The FAZ sizing guides provide max values for the EPS. Find the most recent FAZ datasheet online and cross-reference your EPS value with the '*Analytic Sustained Rate (logs/sec)*' line items for the various platforms. Once you find one that fits your EPS needs, then check to make sure it has enough data storage to accommodate your log retention.

Log retention is how long you intend to keep your logs. This would be something specific to your organization, and any compliance standards the organization may fall under. Note on FAZ, as I said before, there are Analytics log data and Archive Log data. Analytics data is essentially raw logs that have been parse and inserted into various SQL tables to be used for reporting or log searching, which I refer to as the FAZ SQL DB. Archive data are the raw log message that is compressed on FAZ used to build the FAZ SQL DB. We must account for both entities regarding sizing.

Here is another method to obtain storage requirements. See the below formula's:

```
Log_Rate = X EPS

Analytic Size Storage=(Log_Rate * Analytic Log Size * 86400) * Analytic period

Archive Size Storage=(Log_Rate * Archive Log Size * 86400) * Archive Period
```

Note, an average indexed log is 400 bytes, and an average compressed log is 50 bytes. This can be referenced in the above formula. The last thing to do is add the Analytic Size Storage + Archive Size Storage = Total Storage required. I would add <u>at least</u> 20% to the Total Storage required value to account for 'anomalies.'

At the beginning of the chapter, I said the question, "how much log traffic does a FortiGate generate?" is a loaded question; let me explain that. You can think of FortiGate as having five different logging levels. These levels all depend on what features you decide to use in your environment. Here is the short and sweet of it:

1) Firewall only logging
   a. FortiGate is only being used as a packet filter firewall for layers 3 and 4.
2) Firewall + VPN logging
   a. IPsec/SSL is being used
3) Firewall + VPN + Flow UTM logging
   a. Certain Flow UTM features are also being used
4) Firewall + VPN + Proxy UTM logging
   a. Proxy UTM features are also being used
5) Firewall + VPN + Proxy UTM + Flow UTM + FSSO logging

These are not official logging levels. This is just an example to show you the more features you turn on, and the more traffic that is being processed, then the more logs FortiGate generates. So if you decide to turn on UTM and implement FSSO in the middle of the year (after you sized your FAZ), then it is possible for you to run out of storage space on your FAZ. This is why I said calculate log requirements with your production configuration using live traffic, if possible.

Image 7.1 – FortiAnalyzer Security Fabric Page GUI

Security Fabric Settings	
FortiAnalyzer Logging	
IP address	192.168.209.160 Test Connectivity
Logging to ADOM	root
Storage usage	0% 85.39 MiB / 50.00 GiB
Analytics usage	0% 82.98 MiB / 35.00 GiB (Number of days stored: 2/60)
Archive usage	0% 2.41 MiB / 15.00 GiB (Number of days stored: 2/365)
Upload option	Real Time Every Minute Every 5 Minutes
Allow access to FortiGate REST API	
Verify FortiAnalyzer certificate	

Honestly, sizing FAZ platform(s) correctly can be more of an art than a science. When reviewing the FAZ datasheets, the last thing to note here is that the number shown is from a lab environment and is what that platform can do in theory.

I will stop myself from going down a rabbit hole by talking about data retention policy methods on FAZ because this book is on FortiOS. The last thing I want to show you on FortiGate regarding FAZ is the Security Fabric FortiAnalyzer GUI page. This page has a lot of great information that can tell you how much Analytic and Archive storage has been used on FAZ. See Image 7.1 on the prior page. Next, we go over the log settings in a Firewall Policy Entry.

Firewall Policy Log Settings

FortiGate provides many options when it comes to logging, and a Firewall Policy Entry has three settings regarding when and if log messages are generated, which are:

1) Disabled
   a. No logs generated by traffic accepted by policy regardless
2) Security Events (utm)
   a. If enabled, then the policy generates Security and Traffic logs. Logs are only be generated if a security event is triggered by a UTM profile, causing a traffic log to be generated for the same Session Entry.
3) All Sessions (all)
   a. Regardless if network traffic triggers a security event, a traffic log is generated for all Session Entries created for the policy that allowed the traffic.

See image 7.2 for GUI configuration, and the CLI configuration is found via:

> *If you are not receiving the expected log messages, check this setting first.*

```
30E-B (root) # config firewall policy
30E-B (1) # set logtraffic
all       Log all sessions accepted or denied by this policy.
utm       Log traffic that has a security profile applied to it.
disable   Disable all logging for this policy
```

Image 7.2 – Policy Logging Options

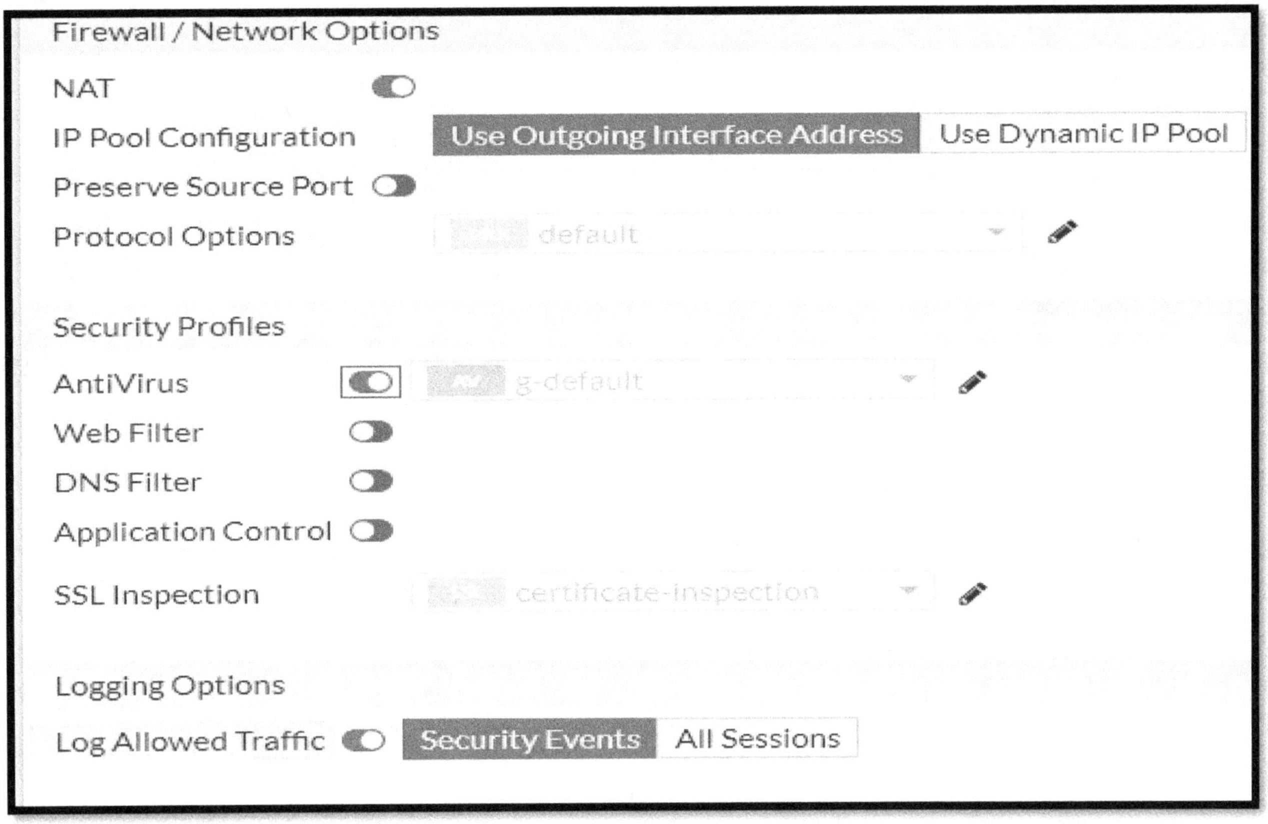

UTM Extended Logging

UTM Extended Logging is a feature to add HTTP header information to the 'rawdata=' field when HTTP traffic is denied. The following UTM profiles can have extended logging enabled – antivirus, application, DLP, IPS, WAF, and Web Filter. The 'set extended-log' setting is found under each UTM profile configuration. The header information that is added is to each log message is:

1) Method
2) X-Forwarded-For
3) Request-Content-Type | Response-Content-Type
4) Referer
5) User-Agent

Note that if reliable logging to Syslog servers, then the rawdata field's value can be a max of 20KB. When logging to FAZ or disk, then the max value is 2KB, and any data beyond this is cut off. Next, there is an additional option under Web Filter profiles "set web-extended-all-action-log enable" if this setting is enabled, then all allowed traffic would have HTTP header information added to generated log messages. This wraps up extended UTM logging; the next topic to cover is logging local on FortiGate.

Local Logging

In general, logging locally on FortiGate is a bad idea. You want to avoid using the local disk on FortiGate platforms to store logs long term. This is a good way to end the life of the hardware prematurely. I am not saying you can't do it, or there are not situations where it is required, but just be mindful.

Just like FAZ, FortiOS has a local SQL database that is built from raw log messages, and this database could be used for various tasks like generating reports or log viewing.

Enable Local Logging

Local logging can be enabled from the CLI or the GUI via Log & Report > Log Settings. CLI options below and see Image 7.3 for the GUI on how to enable local logging.

```
FGT3HDxxxxxxx (setting) # show ful
config log disk setting
    set status enable
    set ips-archive enable
    set max-policy-packet-capture-size 100
    set log-quota 0
    set dlp-archive-quota 0
    set report-quota 0
    set maximum-log-age 7
    set upload disable
    set full-first-warning-threshold 75
    set full-second-warning-threshold 90
    set full-final-warning-threshold 95
    set max-log-file-size 20
    set roll-schedule daily
    set roll-time 00:00
    set diskfull overwrite
```

end

Image 7.3 – GUI Log Settings

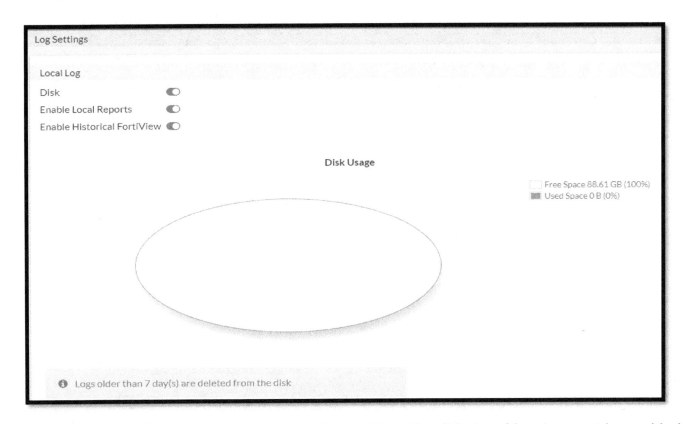

By default, logs older than seven days are deleted from the disk. Local logging must be enabled for data to appear on FortiView for realtime (now), but historical log information can be pulled from FortiCloud or FortiAnalyzer. Next, to enable local reports, this is configurable under Log Settings GUI as well. Note, FortiOS reserves 25% of disk space for system-level operations and to account for quota overflow. The CLI command to view space used on the hard disk is:

```
FGT3HDxxxxxxxx # diagnose sys logdisk usage
Total HD usage: 608MB/118145MB
Total HD logging space: 88608MB
HD logging space usage for vdom "root": 0MB/88608MB
```

The default behavior, when the FortiGate disk is full, is to overwrite the oldest log message. This can be changed in the CLI via:

```
config log disk setting
..
#set diskfull [overwrite | nolog]
..
```

If the *nolog* option is selected, then FortiGate stops logging to disk once full. The next options to discuss are:

```
    set full-first-warning-threshold 75
    set full-second-warning-threshold 90
    set full-final-warning-threshold 95
```

These settings control when warning messages are trigger regarding utilized space on the local disk. By default, the first warning will trigger when the disk reaches 75% of max capacity, the second at 90%, and the last one at 95%. This can be changed if needed. Before we move on to the next section, I want to cover a few more settings under # config log disk setting. First, take a look at all the settings with quota in the name.

```
config log disk setting
..
    set log-quota 0
    set dlp-archive-quota 0
    set report-quota 0
..
end
```

FortiGate platforms with disk are not hot swappable like RAID arrays. If disk goes bad, then the entire platform must be replaced.

A quota here is how many MB are allocated for each type of function that needs disk storage space to operate, which are logs, DLP, and reports. By default, there are no quota's and FortiOS will start overriding the oldest entries at 75% of usage. I would recommend placing quotas for anything that is stored on the local disk to increase performance and extend the overall life of the hardware. Most FortiGate's with disk come with an SSD (solid-state disk), and these disks have a certain read/write per cell. This is also called a "program/erase" (P/E) count. Essentially, once the disk becomes full, and FortiOS starts overwriting the oldest data this will start generating a very high PE count until the SSD is unusable. Once this happens, it's RMA time and possible downtime.

The next thing to discuss here is log rolling. Logs are placed into a file on the local disk. This is a flat-file. The act of 'rolling' means taking that flat-file and compress it using a compression method like bzip, gzip, or tar; there are many compression methods out there. The setting max-log-file-size is the maximum size FortiOS allows the flat log file to grow before compressing it. The rolling schedule means, if the flat-file size does not hit the max-log-file-size threshold, regardless, roll the file at the specified time. The term 'rolling' is not really intuitive, but it means compressing. On FAZ, there are options to roll and then upload files to a remote FTP server for long term storage. FortiGate has these options as well.

Lastly, here are some good disk debug commands to put in the note book:

```
FGT3HDxxxxxxxx # fnsysctl df -h
```

Filesystem	Size	Used	Available	Use%	Mounted on
none	6.1G	29.1M	6.0G	0%	/tmp
none	6.1G	764.0K	6.1G	0%	/dev/shm
none	6.1G	26.0M	6.0G	0%	/dev/cmdb
/dev/sda2	247.9M	66.2M	168.8M	28%	/data
/dev/sda3	14.1G	38.0M	13.4G	0%	/data2
/dev/sdb1	110.0G	580.3M	103.8G	1%	/var/log

```
FGT3HDxxxxxxxxxx # diagnose hardware deviceinfo disk
FGT3HDxxxxxxxx #  get hardware  status
Model name: FortiGate-300D
ASIC version: CP8
ASIC SRAM: 64M
CPU: Intel(R) Core(TM) i3-3220 CPU @ 3.30GHz
Number of CPUs: 4
RAM: 7996 MB
Compact Flash: 15331 MB /dev/sda
Hard disk: 114473 MB /dev/sdb
USB Flash: not available
Network Card chipset: Intel(R) Gigabit Ethernet Network Driver (rev.0003)

Network Card chipset: FortiASIC NP6 Adapter (rev.)
```

If you know your platform has a disk, but these commands don't show it, format device via clean install tftp new image and run HQIP. May need to RMA unit.

This covers our local logging section. The moral of the story, use a remote logging solution if all possible.

Log Data Backup

So if you do not have a backup for your log files and a failure occurs, this could be a resume' generating event 😊 . There is a saying in Information Technology; when everything is working, no one thanks you, but when something goes wrong.. it's all your fault. Having backups of your data will either make you the hero or.. 'just that guy', don't be that guy. In this section, I go into details about log rolling, uploading, and downloading.

FortiOS Log Rolling, downloading and Uploading

Log rolling is essentially compressing a flat-file. The purpose of this is to save storage space. The default max log file size to the rolling threshold is 20 MB's. Rolling can also be performed at a scheduled time, even if the max log file size threshold is not met. The upload log options for FortiGate platforms that have disk can be found via:

```
FGT3HDxxxxxxxxxxx (setting) # show ful | grep upload
    set upload enable
    set upload-destination ftp-server
    set uploadport 21
    set uploadpass Password123
    set uploaddir '/tmp/FGT1/'
    set uploadtype traffic event virus webfilter IPS emailfilter dlp-archive
anomaly voip dlp app-ctrl waf dns ssh ssl cifs
    set uploadsched disable
    set uploadtime 00:00
    set upload-delete-files enable
    set uploadip 192.168.160.1
    set uploaduser FTP-USER
```

The above configuration allows you to upload logs to an FTP server. You must provide parameters specific to your FTP servers, like Port, Username/password, IP address, and directory. There are also parameters to schedule uploads on a regular basis.

Next, FortiOS provides a feature to download logs from the GUI. This can be accomplished in the upper left-hand corner of the Log & Report Menus. See the image below:

Image 7.4 – Download Icon

Remote Logging

We already spoke about FortiAnalyzer (FAZ), which is one of Fortinet's remote logging solutions. In this section, we go over a few others out there that Fortinet offers.

<u>FortiCloud</u>

Image 7.4 – FortiCloud Services

FortiGate Analytics & Management	No Subscription	With Subscription
Traffic and application visibility	✓	✓
Hosted log retention	7 days	1 year
Cloud provisioning	✓	✓
Reporting	✓	✓
Customized log retention		✓
Config Management	3 times	unlimited

The first item to discuss is FortiCloud. FortiCloud can perform many functions, and a logging solution is one of them. FortiCloud is ideal for small to medium businesses essentially. Once you

Check FortiGate connection to FortiCloud:

 # diagnose test application miglogd 20

 # diagnose test application forticldd 1

 # diagnose test application dnsproxy 7

create an account at support.fortinet.com, you can use these same credentials to access FortiCloud at forticloud.com. See Image 7.4 for details on FortiCloud services.

Image 7.5 – FortiCloud Interface

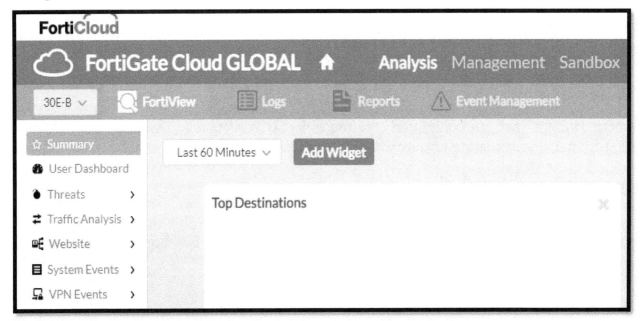

As you can see, FortiCloud, by default, only keeps your logs for 7 days, which is fine if you have no log retention requirements. Aside from the logging solution FortiCloud provides, here you could also have central management, event management, AV sandboxing, and various other services. See Image 7.5 for a quick snapshot of the interface. The next logging solution is to touch on is FortiSIEM.

FortiSIEM

I pretty much refer to a SIEM as a four-letter word. All SIEM platforms I have interacted with have been fairly complex, but at the end of the day, a SIEM is the heart of any SoC and is where all the event correlation occurs and is the central point for an enterprise's log messages. The end goal of a SIEM is to detect anomalies by referencing various log messages that could point to a security incident in which an SoC Analyst would investigate.

I've had the opportunity to work with FortiSIEM, and the first thing I noticed was it's way more intuitive than other SIEM products I've worked within the past. I could write another book on this product easily. FortiSIEM is a feature-rich product that does many things and could be used as a sole remote logging solution. The next remote logging option is generic Syslog.

Syslog

I worked in an environment once where we literally used a flat Syslog file with raw log messages inserted into it. You had to perform a lot of 'Ctrl+F' to find anything useful. It was hard to use. Most organizations use Syslog servers for long-term storage and compliance. Products like the FortiAnalyzer can organize logs into a searchable manner that is intuitive to use. Note, you can configure FortiGate to send multiple streams of logs to many Syslog servers. To configure this, go to the CLI via:

```
NSE4-PASS (global) # config log syslog
syslogd      Configure first syslog device.
syslogd2     Configure second syslog device.
syslogd3     Configure third syslog device.
syslogd4     Configure fourth syslog device.
```

The more streams that are configured, the more FortiGate is taxed. The last remote logging solution to touch on is remote logging GUI configuration.

GUI Remote Logging Settings

To configure FAZ remote logging on FortiGate is straight forward. This configuration option is found in the GUI; if VDOMs are enabled, go to Global context > Log & Report > Log Settings, and

Image 7.6 – GUI log settings

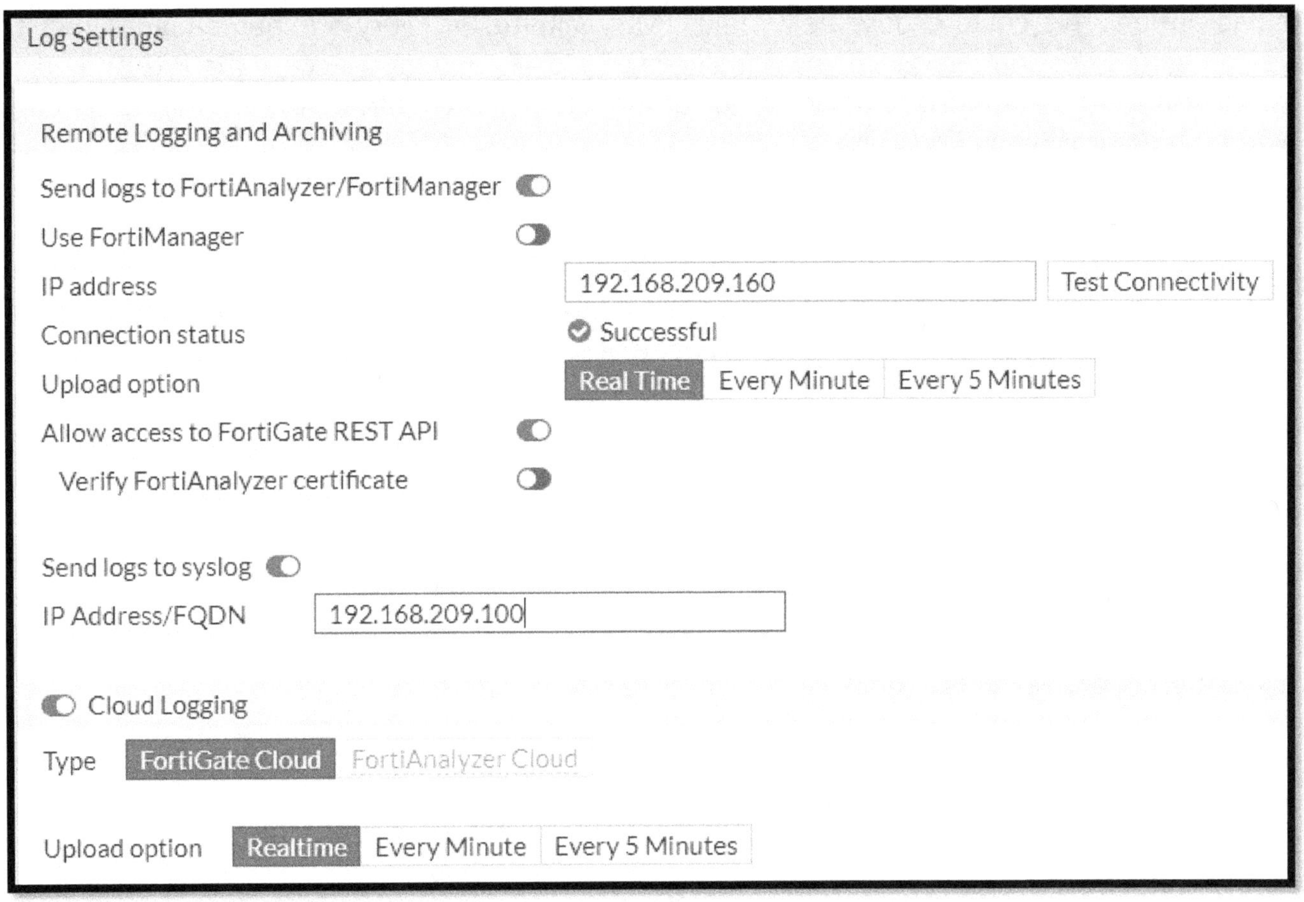

you should see something like Image 7.6. You can test the FAZ connection by clicking the "Test Connectivity" button, which should show a Successful response if FortiGate is authorized on FAZ. Also, there is a CLI command to test this connection and provides more details:

```
30E-B (global) # exec log fortianalyzer test-connectivity
FortiAnalyzer Host Name: FAZVM64
FortiAnalyzer Adom Name: root
FortiGate Device ID: FGT30Exxxxxxxxxxxx
Registration: registered
Connection: allow
Adom Disk Space (Used/Allocated): 85184512B/53687091200B
Analytics Usage (Used/Allocated): 84594688B/37580963840B
Analytics Usage (Data Policy Days Actual/Configured): 2/60 Days
Archive Usage (Used/Allocated): 589824B/16106127360B
Archive Usage (Data Policy Days Actual/Configured): 2/365 Days
Log: Tx & Rx (2 logs received since 15:16:07 09/02/20)
IPS Packet Log: Tx & Rx
Content Archive: Tx & Rx
Quarantine: Tx & Rx
```

Next, in Image 7.6, A FortiGate configured to send logs to FAZ at 192.168.209.160 and send logs to the Syslog server at 192.168.209.100 and lastly send logs to FortiCloud. Note, there are upload options, we could choose Real-Time, Every Minute, or Every 5 minutes upload logs to the configured destination. Once you point logs to FAZ IP, you must access the FAZ and go to Device Manager > Unauthorized devices and authorized the FortiGate. Below are the CLI settings for this configuration on FortiGate:

```
30E-B (setting) # show
config log fortianalyzer setting
    set status enable
    set server "192.168.209.160"
    set certificate-verification disable
    set upload-option realtime
end
```

Each remote logging FortiAnalyzer setting has specific filter options. Meaning, you can pick what information you wish to send to FAZ. Here are the options:

```
30E-B (filter) # show ful
config log fortianalyzer filter
    set severity information
    set forward-traffic enable
    set local-traffic enable
    set multicast-traffic enable
    set sniffer-traffic enable
    set Anomaly enable
    set voip enable
    set dlp-archive enable
    set filter ''
    set filter-type include
end
```

The next topic to discuss is the remote logging store and upload feature.

Store and Upload Feature

FortiGate platforms with hard drives have a store and upload option, and this is used to reserve bandwidth at the right time. For example, if you do not want FortiGate to send log messages during peak business hours, and in this case, you can configure FGT to upload logs during off-hours. To configuration this, go to the CLI via:

```
FGT3HD3xxxxxxxxxx # config log fortianalyzer setting
FGT3HDxxxxxxxxxxx (setting) # set upload-option ?
store-and-upload    Log to hard disk and then upload to FortiAnalyzer.
```

Once the store-and-upload option is set, then the following settings are made available to schedule the upload time:

```
..
    set upload-option store-and-upload
    set upload-interval daily
    set upload-time 00:59
..
```

FortiAnalyzer Temporarily Unavailable

So what happens if FAZ becomes unavailable? At that point in time, FortiGate starts caching log messages. The miglogd daemon is used to cache these logs. To find details around this, run the following CLI debug:

```
30E-B (global) # diagnose test application miglogd 6
mem=247, disk=0, alert=0, alarm=0, sys=0, faz=2116, faz-cloud=0, webt=0,
fds=594
interface-missed=296
Queues in all miglogds: cur:178  total-so-far:130675
global log dev statistics:
faz 0: sent=2002, failed=0, cached=114, dropped=0 , relayed=433691
Num of REST URLs: 15
```

Here we can see there are 114 cached logs and 2002 sent with non-dropped so far. Once FAZ becomes available again, FortiGate then forward buffered logs. FortiGate platforms with disk can be configured to buffer logs on local disk via cli:

```
#config system global
#set faz-disk-buffer-size 500 // This is in MB's
#end
```

To debug the log disk buffer, FortiOS has the following cli command:

```
# diagnose test application miglogd 41
..
VDOM:root
Queue for: global-faz

    memory queue:
        num:0 size:0(0MB) max:101906636(97MB) logs:0

    disk max queue size:500MB total:0MB
..
```

The last command to note here is:

30E-B (global) # **diagnose log kernel-stats**

fgtlog: 1

fgtlog 0: total-log=4513, failed-log=0 log-in-queue=0

..

With this command, we can see if the queue is full, then the failed-log value increases, which indicates dropped logs. Also, here we can see how many logs are currently in the queue, which is none. If you ever believe you are missing logs or not receiving logs, check FortiGate using these commands to investigate further. Our next topic we are going to discuss is sending logs from the VDOM level.

VDOM Remote Logging

As you should know, all system-level traffic uses the root (management) VDOM for communication, which includes logging by default. Back in the day, when I worked at an MSSP running FortiGate 4.3 GA code base, our customers would sometimes ask to receive Syslog from their cloud firewall. They did not know anything about VDOMs; they just wanted their Syslog to be fed into whatever 3rd party device for whatever reason. Well, this was a problem because, at that point in time, FortiGate could not send Syslog data out on the VDOM level. So we had to come up with a workaround to accomplish this, and how we did this was we created an inter-vdom link per customer and used a host route for their Syslog IP from the root VDOM to Customer VDOM. This was a hack, to be honest. Now we have the option to send logs on a per VDOM level! To configure this, go to the CLI via:

```
NSE4-PASS (VDOM-A) # config log fortianalyzer override-setting
NSE4-PASS (override-setting) # show
config log fortianalyzer override-setting
    set override enable
    set status enable
    set server "192.168.209.161"
end
```

Where was this command 6 years ago! Now logs generated from VDOM-A are locally sourced and log messages reference the VDOM-A routing table.

Log Encryption Transmission

FortiGate allows log messages to be sent in an encrypted manner using TLS/SSL communication, which is enabled by default in 6.4 GA.

30E-B (setting) # show ful

config log fortianalyzer setting

..

   set enc-algorithm high

   set ssl-min-proto-version default

..

The TLS/SSL creates a tunnel for the OFTP (Optimized Fabric Transfer Protocol) connection. We discuss this protocol soon.

<u>Reliable Logging</u>

The next item to discuss is reliable logging, which allows FortiGate to send log messages using TCP instead of UDP. Inherently, TCP guarantees packet delivery with ACK response messages. The drawback here is that this could slow log transmissions when compared to UDP. If reliable logging is enabled for Syslog, then the default port used is 601 TCP. The last topic to discuss in this section is OFTPs.

<u>OFTPs Logging</u>

Optimized Fabric Transfer Protocol over SSL (OFTPs) is a Fortinet proprietary protocol used between FortiGate and FortiAnalyzer/FortiManager, and the purpose of this protocol is to synchronize information between the devices or carry log transmission. There are two main functions for OFTP:

1) Bi-directional connectivity checking and health checks, quarantine access, file transfer, and log display from FortiGate. These functions use TCP port 514
   a. File transfers can happen for things like IPS archives.
2) Log Transmissions
   a. If 'reliable' is <u>enabled,</u> then TCP port 514 is used
      i. required to send encrypted logs to FAZ
   b. if 'reliable' is <u>disabled,</u> then UDP port 514 is used

This section wraps up the remote logging section. In the next section, we focus on finding information in log messages using features like FortiView!

Syslog reliable logging uses the following standards:

(global) # conf log syslogd setting

*legacy-reliable   - syslogging by RFC **3195** (Reliable Delivery for Syslog).*

*reliable   - by RFC **6587** (Transmission of Syslog Messages over TCP).*

FortiView, Log Searching, and Monitoring

This section walks through many items located within the Log & Report GUI dropdown section, FortiView, and some alerting features! First up, Log & Report section!

<u>GUI Log & Report</u>

The Log & Report section of FortiOS has many tools to investigate what type of traffic FortiGate is processing and possible concerns on the network. See Image 7.7:

Image 7.7 – Log & Report Menu

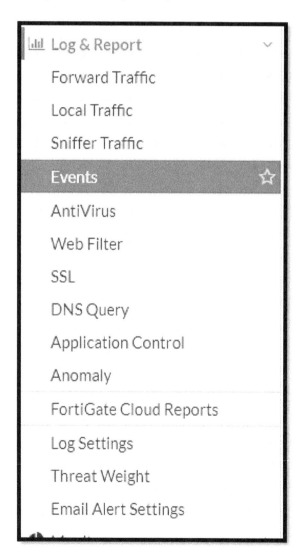

The first item to review here is the Forward Traffic menu, which renders log messages into a viewable manner for us to see, located via Log & Report > Forward Traffic. When troubleshooting transit traffic issues, this is a great location to start. The first question to ask, do you see the interesting traffic within the log message? If so, then was it allowed or blocked by a firewall policy? Which one? As you can see, you can quickly isolate policy handling the traffic flow.

Image 7.8 – Forward Traffic GUI

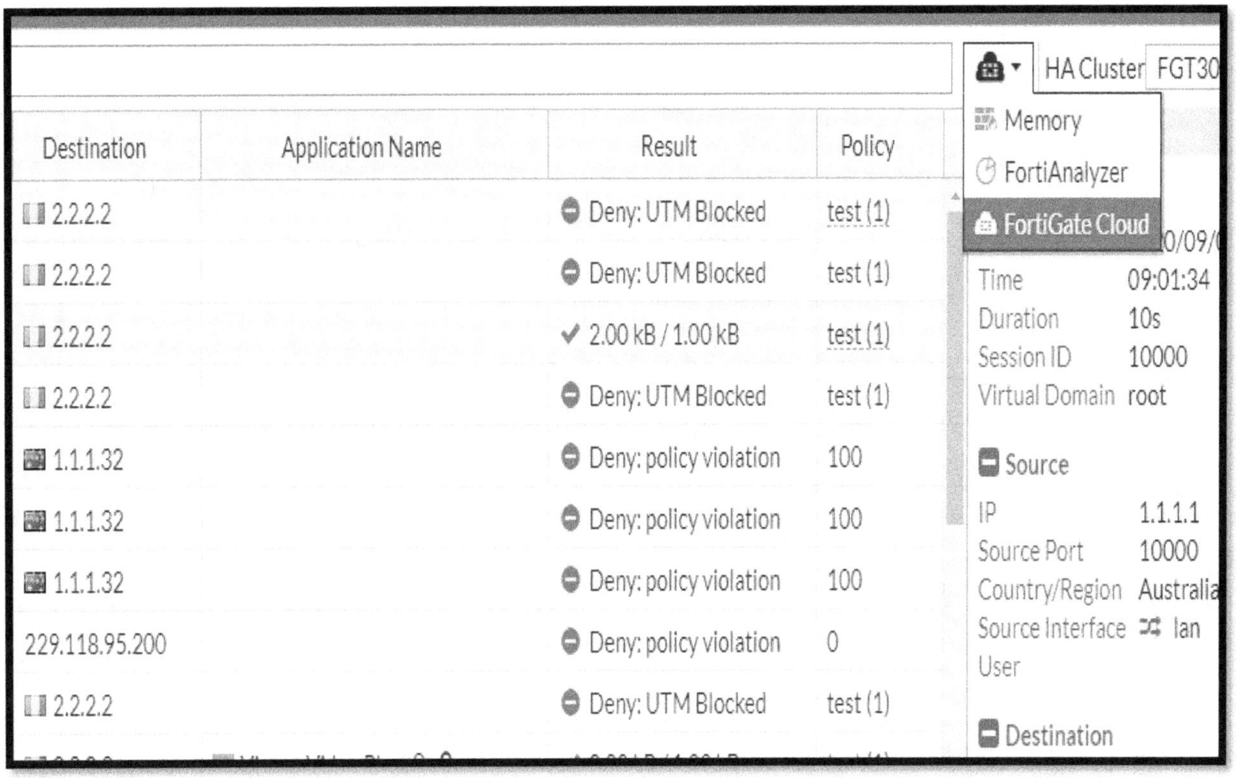

Within Image 7.8, I want you to notice the current dropdown selection. Notice you have three choices of where you want to display logs from Local Memory, FAZ, or FortiCloud. This is a handy feature. On the right side of the image has a windowpane that holds all the forward traffic detail that provides specific information around the session. The next menu is Local Traffic, and this page uses the same method to display logs and provides detailed information around local-in traffic. The Events menu allows the same options regarding where logs are pulled from. The Event subtypes available here are System, Router, VPN, User, Endpoint, HA, WiFi, FortiExtender, and SDN Connector. See Image 7.9 on the next page for details.

Logs for Antivirus, Web Filter, SSL, DNS Query, Application Control, and Anomaly (DoS) are also available under this menu. One more thing I want to mention in this section is the filter feature. Note, any log message field is searchable. The nice thing about the GUI filter is that once you select an attribute to filter on like destination, then the next section auto-populates with results of what is currently found in your logs. See Image 7.10 for details. This is why it is important to

Image 7.9 – Event Menu GUI

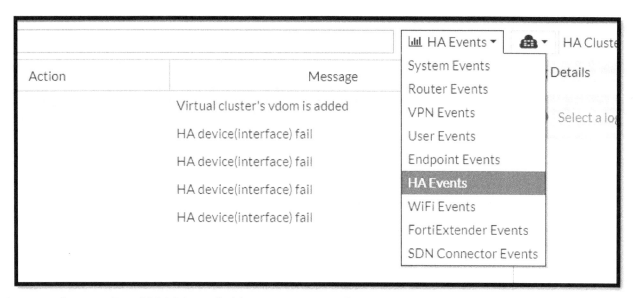

have at least a FortiOS VM available, so you can play around with all these features and see just how intuitive it is for yourself.

The image below provides an example of filtering for the IP address of 1.1.1.32. Note, this did auto-populate. The next thing I want to mention is that some administrators do not always have access to the GUI. So log searching using this method would not be possible. However, in situations like this, there are methods to search through logs using the CLI. A little bit more

Image 7.10 – GUI Log Filter Feature

difficult but still effective. The method is to apply a filter of what you want to find and then execute the display command. See below CLI output:

```
FGT3HDxxxxxxxxxxxxx # execute log filter
category          Category.
device            Device to get log from.
dump              Dump current filter settings.
field             Filter by field.
free-style        Filter by free-style expression.
```

```
ha-member          HA member.
max-checklines     Maximum number of lines to check.
reset              Reset filter.
start-line         Start line to display.
view-lines         Lines per view.
FGT3HDxxxxxxxxxxxxxxx # execute log filter category
Available categories:
 0: traffic
 1: event
 2: utm-virus
 3: utm-webfilter
 4: utm-ips
 5: utm-emailfilter
 7: utm-anomaly
 8: utm-voip
 9: utm-dlp
10: utm-app-ctrl
12: utm-waf
15: utm-dns
16: utm-ssh
17: utm-ssl
18: utm-cifs
19: utm-file-filter
FGT3HDxxxxxxxxxxx # execute log filter dump
category: event
device: disk
start-line: 6
view-lines: 5
max-checklines: 0
HA member:
Filter:
Oftp search string:
FGT3HD3915807098 # execute log display
5394 logs found.
5 logs returned.
..
6: date=2020-09-02 time=16:10:12 logid="0100020027" type="event"
subtype="system" level="information" vd="root" eventtime=1599091812608607508
tz="-0700" logdesc="Outdated report files deleted" msg="Delete 4 old report
files"
..
```

As you can see, the filter here can become very granular so to isolate the exact type of logs you require. This wraps up log searching on FortiGate; the log search features overall are wonderful to have and very intuitive to use. Go here first (or FAZ) when investigating your network. The next thing I want to discuss is a caveat that might be useful in your environment.

Hiding Usernames

Fortinet knows organizations are required to comply with many different types of standards, and this is why there is an option to hide usernames within log messages. This can be configured in the CLI via:

```
30E-B (root) # conf log setting
30E-B (setting) # set user-anonymize
enable     Enable anonymizing user names in log messages.
disable    Disable anonymizing user names in log messages.
```

Note, log messages insert 'anonymous' within the 'user' field for all log types that have this field. Moving on! the next topic I want to cover with you is UUID log matching.

UUID Log Matching

Every Firewall Policy has a UUID, which is an arbitrary value generated to identify Firewall Policy Entries uniquely. The UUID is automatically randomly generated upon policy creation and cannot be configured. One cool feature on FortiOS is the ability to search this value to find what logs have been accepted by a certain policy. To quickly search for traffic that has been accepted by a policy, right-click a Firewall Policy Entry and on the context menu, select "Show Matching Logs" this takes you to the Forward Traffic page with the select Firewall Policy Entry UUID.

Image 7.11 - Forward Traffic UUID Search

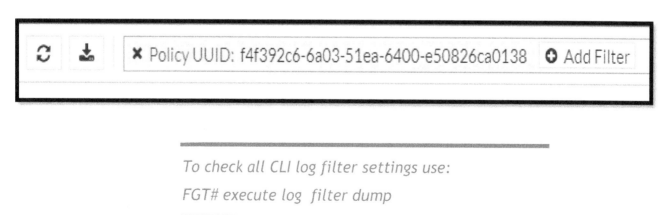

To check all CLI log filter settings use:

FGT# execute log filter dump

Image 7.12 – Show Matching Logs UUID

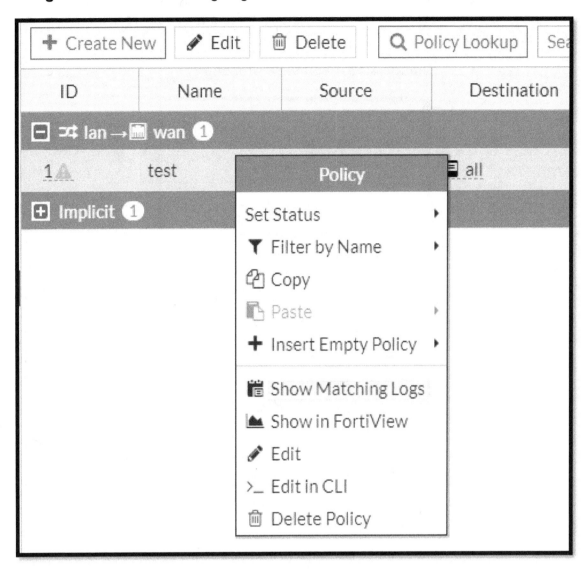

That's it for UUID logs; the next item in this section to discuss is FortiView.

FortiView

I touched on FortiView a little bit in chapter one. The main difference between FortiView and the various log views is the enrichment of the data. FortiView provides context to the logs. For example, FortiView provides basic application log information but provides the risk of the application and the sent/received bytes for the application. Also, FortiView provides more security-related data around sessions. For example, you can find information about viruses, malicious websites visited, or compromised hosts. The best part of FortiView, in my honest opinion, is the drill-down feature. Essentially once you find what you are looking for, you can easily right-click the entry and select 'Drill Down,' More specific information around the connection is provided, which is an excellent feature for a Security Analyst. Also, FortiView provides a nice compact view of all the applications running through the network, which is great for auditing purposes.

Image 7.13 – FortiView Dropdown

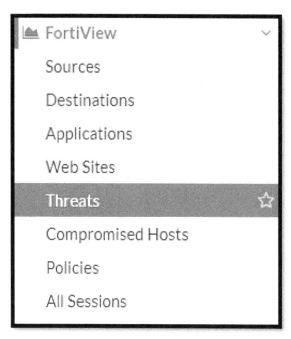

As I said, the best part of FortiView is the context around the data provided. You can easily see which host has the most Session Entries on your device or which host has been exhibiting malicious activity.

Image 7.14 – FortiView Threats Drill Down

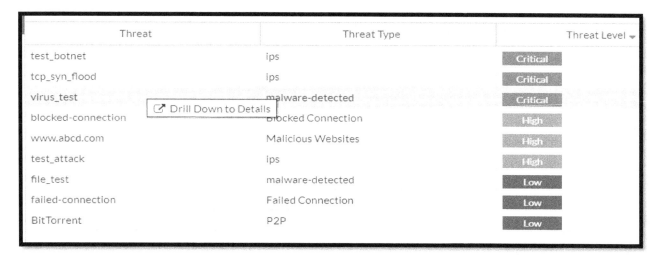

Threat	Threat Type	Threat Level ▾
test_botnet	ips	Critical
tcp_syn_flood	ips	Critical
virus_test	malware-detected	Critical
blocked-connection	Blocked Connection	High
www.abcd.com	Malicious Websites	High
test_attack	ips	High
file_test	malware-detected	Low
failed-connection	Failed Connection	Low
BitTorrent	P2P	Low

Image 7.14 gives more details about what types of threats FortiView can show you. Everything from AV detections to bit torrent connections. The next question to answer is, how are we alerted when FortiGate detects anomalies in the network? Well, most of the time, this is where a SIEM, SNMP, or event handler on FAZ comes into play for larger networks, but for smaller networks, FortiGate provides a built-in email alerting, which is a nice convenience; we go over this next.

<u>Config Alert Email</u>

To configure email alerting on FortiGate, you require an SMTP server to relay your email. You could set up an open-source SMTP server like PostFix or use a free relay server like google.

Image 7.15 – Email Alert Settings

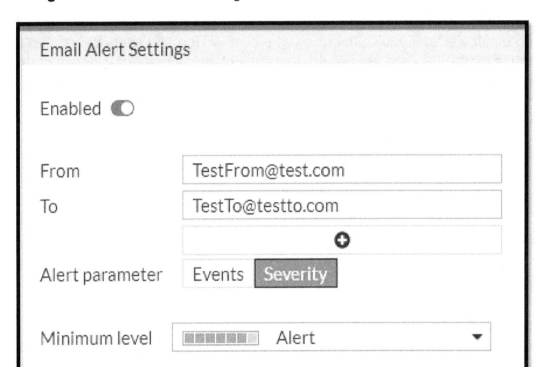

I want you to note in Image 7.15 that an email alert can be sent by log Severity level or from an Event like AV match. Here is an example configuration:

```
NSE4-PASS (email-server) # show
path=system, objname=email-server, tablename=(null), size=360
config system email-server
    set server "smtp-relay.example.com"
    set authenticate enable
    set username "username_here"
    set password Password123
end
```

These settings are system-level settings found in the global context. This can also be configured in the GUI via Global > Advanced > Email Service. Next, is the configuration for the VDOM your working with, which is:

```
config alertemail setting
    set username "test@test.com"
    set mailto1 "admim_email@company123.com"
    set IPS-logs enable
    set antivirus-logs enable
    set webfilter-logs enable
    set violation-traffic-logs enable
end
```

This configuration sends emails to admim_email@company123.com with source test@test.com. To send a test email using the following CLI command:

```
#diagnose log alertmail test
```

That wraps up email alerts. if you're not using your own SMTP relay, every vendor has their own requirements for mail relay, and you would need to look at their specific documentation. The last thing we need to cover in this section is Threat Weight.

Configure Threat Weight

You might have noticed in the FortiView Image 7.14, (2 pages back) there are threat weight scores for each event. FortiGate has default threat values for various events, but these threat values might not match your needs for your network. So in corner cases where you need to

Image 7.16 – Threat Weight

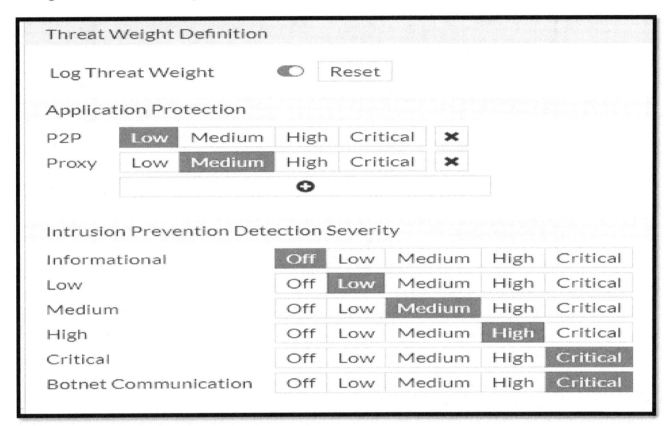

tweak these, there are options to do so. For example, if your organization focuses heavily on email traffic, then you could go into this section and any alert for email related activity you could set to critical, which makes it easy to categorize log messages. To adjust these values, in the GUI, navigate to VDOM > Log & Report > Threat Weight. When various security UTM actions are taken on FortiOS, and a log message is generated, within a 'type=utm' log message, there are two fields these settings relate to, which are:

```
score=30 crlevel="high"
```

crlevel maps to the Client Reputation Level. The options for this field are - Off, Low, Medium, High, and Critical, and each level has a numeric value assigned called a Client Reputation Score, *(score)*. These values are used in report functions on FAZ to show risky clients. Note, these scores can be adjusted.

Image 7 17

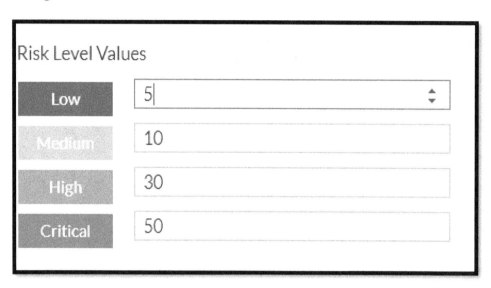

We cover many search features FortiOS has to offer in this section. The best advice I can give around this topic is to take time to review the various FortiView menu's and log monitoring menus. You will be surprised by the insight you can gain into your network.

This completes our journey for chapter 7! Nice work; next is our chapter summary and then some end of chapter questions!

End of Chapter 7 Summary

Logging and Monitoring, not the most glamorous topic to discuss, but no doubt, it's a particularly important subject. Without logs, IT professionals would be in the dark regarding what's going on in the network. Logs messages are essentially metadata generated by various types of process executions. The miglogd process is responsible for handling all log functions on FortiOS. On FortiOS, there are three Types of log messages which are Traffic, Event, and Security. Each log Type branches off into many different subtypes. These subtypes have specific fields related to that specific process that generated the log message. For example, FortiOS could generate a log Type Security, Subtype Antivirus, and it contains a message field stating that a virus was detected!

We discussed how high log volume generation could potentially impact the performance of FortiGate and the surrounding network. FortiGate can use a few different upload methods, which are Real-Time, Every Minute, Every 5 Minutes. Also, FortiGate has a scheduled upload option to only upload logs to a remote device(s) during off-hours, so not to affect production traffic.

Log management involves correctly sizing log storage and planning for log retention, and having log backups. There are two databases on FortiAnalyzer that need to be accounted for, the Analytical database, which is referenced by many functions on FAZ to organize logs into a viewable manner, and the Archive database, which holds the raw log data used to build the Analytical database.

We reviewed local logging and how this could impact FortiGate hardware long term, and how it is best practice to store logs on a remote device. FortiView and the log view on FortiGate can query FortiAnalyzer and FortiCloud logs to be rendered locally in the GUI.

Fortinet offers a few remote logging solutions, with the most popular one being FortiAnalyer. However, there are other solutions like FortiCloud and FortiSIEM. Lastly, 3rd party Syslog servers can be used as well.

If FortiAnalyzer is unreachable, then FortiGate caches logs locally until FortiAnalyzer becomes available again. There are a few debug commands that can display how many logs have been cached and sent.

Optimized Fabric Transfer Protocol over SSL (OFTPs) is a Fortinet proprietary protocol used between FortiGate and FortiAnalyzer/FortiManager, and the purpose of this protocol is to synchronize information between the devices or handle log transmissions. OFTP communications can be encrypted using SSL/TLS, making it OFTPs. FortiGate can send logs using UDP or TCP, which is called reliable logging.

FortiOS provides many features to make sense of log messages like FortiView or Log view. FortiView enriches log data and provides context around specific events. Log view allows you to look at different log Types from FortiGate GUI. There are also methods to view raw logs from the CLI.

Lastly, email alerts can be triggered by various log messages to notify administrators when certain events occur on FortiGate. This covers Chapter 7 summary; your one step closer to obtaining your NSE4 certification! Next, challenge yourself by answering the end of chapter questions!

End of Chapter Questions

1) What are the Types of log message FortiOS can generate?
    a. Forward, Security, and Event
    b. Traffic, Authentication, and Security
    c. Traffic, Security, and Event
    d. Security, Forward, and Event

2) How many log Severity levels are there?
    a. 4
    b. 5
    c. 7
    d. 8

3) How to enable VDOM remote logging?
    a. Logs are sourced from the VDOM they are generated by default
    b. You must use the override command under remote logging settings at the VDOM level
    c. An inter-vdom link is automatically created on FortiOS to route traffic to the correct VDOM
    d. This is not possible, all log traffic sources from the management VDOM only

4) What is Reliable Logging?
    a. This does not exist on FortiOS
    b. Is a proprietary protocol used by FortiGate
    c. Remote logging will use TCP
    d. Remote logging will use UDP

5) What is OFTPs?
    a. Open File Transfer Protocol Over SSL
    b. Opensource File Trivial Protocol Over SSL
    c. Optimized Fabric Transfer Protocol over SSL
    d. Open Fabric Transfer Protocol over SSL

6) What is OFTPs used for?
    a. So administrators can upload config files to FortiGate
    b. Provides communication between FortiGate and FortiAnalyzer/FortiManager

    c. To provide a standard log format

    d. To backup config files to the local workstation.

7) What does FortiGate do if FAZ is unavailable?

    a. All logs are lost if FAZ is unavailable

    b. FortiGate will log to disk by default

    c. FortiGate will send logs to FortiCloud if FAZ is unavailable

    d. FortiGate will cache logs locally until FAZ comes back online.

8) What command will show cached logs on FortiGate

    a. FortiGate cannot cache logs

    b. diagnose test application miglogd 3

    c. diagnose test application miglogd 2

    d. diagnose test application miglogd 6

9) What command will test the FAZ connection?

    a. diag log faz test

    b. diag log fortianalyzer test-connectivity

    c. exec log fortianalyzer test-connectivity

    d. exec fortianalyzer test-connectivity

10) Threat Weight cannot be changed on FortiOS

    a. True

    b. False

11) What is log rolling?

    a. When logs are sent to the remote logging device

    b. When logs are sent to local disk

    c. When the log file is compressed

    d. When the log file is overwritten

12) What are to major parts of a FortiOS log message?

    a. Top and bottom

    b. Type and Subtype

    c. Header and Footer

    d. Body and Header

13) What is a method to obtain HTTP header data within the UTM log message?
   a. HTTP Logging
   b. UTM metric logging
   c. Extended Logging
   d. L7-defaults-enable command

14) What command will provide diagnostic output for the local disk?
   a. diagnose sys logdisk usage
   b. diagnose sys logdisk usage 6
   c. diagnose logdisk usage 1 0
   d. diagnose sys logdisk

15) What is the default port and protocol for Syslog traffic on FortiOS?
   a. TCP 601
   b. UDP 601
   c. UDP 514
   d. TCP 514

Chapter 8 | IPsec

NSE4 Blueprint Topics Covered

- Understand IPsec and IKE fundamentals
- Understand Phase 1 and Phase 2
- Understand route-based VPN
- ESP Encapsulation
- Understand Security Associations
- IPsec Topologies
- Configure Site-to-site VPN
- Configure Hub-and-Spoke VPN
- Phase-2 best practice
- Configure Remote Access VPN
- Understand ASIC offload with VPN
- Configure redundant VPNs
- VPN best practices
- Verify IPsec VPN
- Understand Dial-up VPN

One of my favorite technologies to work with is IPsec, and when I was employed as a Network Analyst, I worked with the technology daily. To this very day, my job is to support large IPsec deployments for carriers. If you want to be a good FortiGate firewall engineer, then IPsec is one of those technologies you must know by heart. Many topics fall under IPsec, and I plan to cover many of them in this chapter. The goal of this chapter is to teach you IPsec from the ground up. So if you know nothing about IPsec, this is a perfect chapter for you. By the end of the chapter, we will be configuring IPsec tunnels between FortiGate's and routing traffic between them. We are also going to be performing various IPsec debugging and verification on these tunnels.

We start off this chapter by going over IPsec fundamentals, including going over things IKEv1, ISAKMP, Oakley group, and SKEME. We discuss the different phases of the IPsec VPN establishment. I'm going to discuss the difference between Transport Mode and Tunnel mode IPsec. We also discuss the difference between Oakley Aggressive mode and Main Mode. I talk about ESP encapsulation and how Security Associations secure packets. Next, we discuss how NAT-T is used with IPsec. I go over different IPsec topologies like Site-to-Site and Dial-up. We go through deployment examples of dynamic IPsec tunnels between FortiGate's and also between FortiGate and FortiClient.

Once we lay a strong foundation of IPsec theory, then I begin to explain how FortiGate uses the IPsec framework. I explain the other required configurations like policies and routing statements to obtain end to end connectivity. Next, I go over a few different IPsec architectures, including Auto-Discovery VPN (ADVPN), in this chapter.

This might be one of the most technical chapters yet in this NSE4 study guide series. If you know nothing around IPsec and all these terms are just letters, that is ok. It better sometimes to start with a clean slate than to unlearn things. If you are reasonably strong in IPsec, I still recommend reading the theory portion of this chapter because it is always nice to have a refresher.

I can't stress it enough; IPsec is a critical subject to understand. I say this because if you do not have a strong foundation in IPsec technologies, then FortiGate SDWAN will make no sense to you because SDWAN relies on IPsec tunnels heavily in general SDWAN design.

Alright folks, it's time to take this chapter head-on! I hope you are as excited as I am to begin! Let's get started.

IPsec Theory Fundamentals

In the first section, we are going to step through vendor-independent IPsec fundamentals. Note, IPsec is a large subject, and this section focuses on IPsec theory regarding the most common FortiGate use cases aligned with NSE4 topic goals. This chapter is not meant to cover IPsec comprehensively regarding all possible uses and options. The scope of the fundamentals here is angled tightly around how you will most likely use IPsec when working with FortiGate's. That being said, if you already know IPsec theory but just want to know how FortiGate uses IPsec, then skip to the "FortiGate IPsec Implementation" section.

The first questions to ask here are, what is IPsec? And why do we need it? Well, IPsec is an open standard framework that can house many different types of protocols and functions. The purpose of using the IPsec framework is to create a secure private channel(s) between two devices that have never communicated before over the public Internet. By using IPsec across the public Internet for communication between devices, we can accomplish origin authenticity, confidentiality, and Integrity.

A common use case for IPsec is when it is used to create an encrypted tunnel between two private LANs geographically separated. Most of the time, the LAN gateway device is used to terminate the IPsec tunnel; this is where transit data enters and exits the encrypted tunnel. Sometimes a single organization manages both sides of the tunnel, but sometimes, the other side is managed by a separate entity. Meaning, you are required to work with someone you

Image 8.1 – Site to Site IPec Tunnel

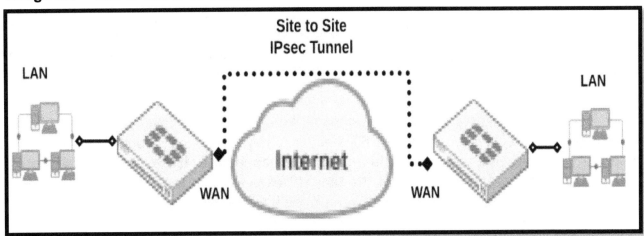

never spoke with before to build an IPsec tunnel between your organizations and route traffic through it. See Image 8.1.

Here we see the most basic common usage of IPsec, A Site-to-Site encrypted tunnel. In this example, IPsec could allow the clients within each LAN to communicate with each other using only their private IP addresses. The external WAN interface is used most of the time to terminate the IPsec connection. When I say 'terminate,' I mean this is where the encryption and decryption occur. FortiGate can also be a transit device for encrypted IPsec traffic, and the tunnel terminates elsewhere.

When I first started working with IPsec, I liked to think of the two IPsec termination points as just being directly connected. They are essentially, just not in a physical sense but a logical one. I'm sure you are wondering at this point how exactly this secure communication is accomplished. In the next sections, we start looking at the various protocols used in the IPsec framework.

IPsec Protocol Suite

When I am talking about IPsec on the job (or working on it), I am bad about referencing IPsec and all its functions as just *IPsec*. This is technically wrong, it's just lingo. In reality, there is a whole suite of functions and protocols used for one effort to obtain IPsec's purpose, which is to create a secure tunnel for data to pass through. The first item I want to talk about is header data added to an '*IPsec packet.*'

IPsec Encapsulation

The first protocol I want to touch on within the IPsec protocol suite is the Encapsulating Security Payload (ESP). ESP is its own IP protocol and is assigned IP protocol 50, making it a transport protocol like UDP or TCP, which are maintained by the Internet Assigned Number Authority (IANA). ESP is defined within RFC 4303 https://tools.ietf.org/html/rfc4303. Remember that IP protocol values are referenced in the IPv4/IPv6 header, so the receiving device knows the offset regarding how to parse the header and payload information.

IPsec has two modes: Transport Mode (Authentication Header) and Tunnel mode (Encapsulating Security Payload). Since I've worked with FortiGate firewalls, I've only worked with Encapsulating Security Payload (ESP) Tunnel mode. FortiGate can support AH for Phase-2, which I will not be covering in this chapter.

ESP encapsulates packets starting with the original IP header. So the Layer-3 header and above is encapsulated and encrypted. After the ESP header, a new IP header is applied and is used for transportation between IPsec peers. Within this newly applied IPv4/IPv6 header, the protocol value field is 50, indicating ESP. Most of the time, IPsec peers' public IPs are in the source and destination IP fields. NAT is permitted between IPsec peers, which we will discuss later in this chapter.

Image 8. 2 –Encapsulating Security Payload Structure

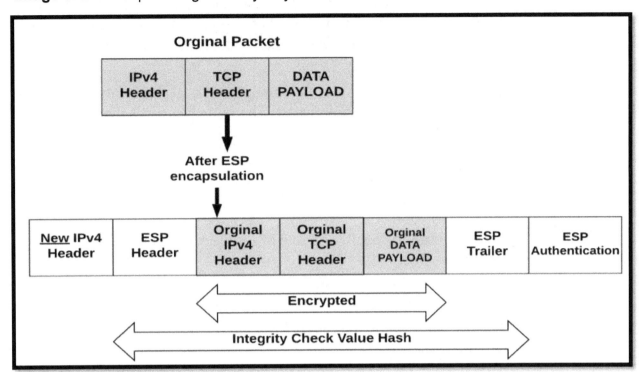

Take a look at Image 8.2; this provides a visual of the ESP packet structure. The original IPv4 header, TCP header, and data payload are encrypted. Next, an ESP Header and Trailer are generated and placed at the beginning and end of the encrypted payload, respectively. Next, an Integrity Check Value (ICV) hash function is calculated from the newly generated ESP Header, ESP Trailer, and original packet data. This hash is then encrypted, which turns the hash string into a Message Authentication Code (HMAC), which is used by the receiving IPsec peer to ensure ESP message integrity and authenticity. We break down the details of this process later in the chapter.

Now you know the high level of how ESP wraps itself around a packet to protect it; however, we still need to review what lies within the ESP header and trailer! These fields are critical, and I will be referencing them throughout this chapter. First, let's talk about the ESP header fields, which are:

1) Security Parameters Index (SPI) field - 32 bits
   a. The SPI is an arbitrary value generated but is very important. SPI is used so the receiving system can map ESP packets to the correct Security Associate (SA). For now, think of a SA as an IPsec instance, and if multiple IPsec instances (site-to-site tunnels) are built off of a single interface, then the SPI would be what directs the ESP packet to the correct instance. You can think of the SPI value performing the same function as TCP/UDP port number do for applications. We talk more about SA soon.
2) Sequence Number field - 32 bits

a. ESP packets are given sequence numbers to protect again replay attacks. Essentially, FortiOS expects certain sequence numbers to be received within a sliding window range, and if an ESP packet sequence number falls outside the window range, then ESP packets are discards. I discuss Anti-Replay later in this chapter.

That's it for the ESP header! Next, in terms of bits, would be the payload. After the payload (original IPv4, TCP, and data payload) is the ESP trailer. The following fields live within the ESP trailer.

1) Padding (0-255 octets)
   a. This field is used to extend the payload data size to a size that fits the encryption algorithm cipher block size used within the SA.
2) Pad Length field – 8 bit
   a. This 8-bit field is used to specify the size of the prior Padding field.
3) Next Header field – 8 bit
   a. This field is used to specify the type of IP protocol contained in the encrypted payload. A value of 4 indicates an IPv4 header, and a value of 41 indicates the value of an IPv6 header. A value of 6 indicates TCP. The value of 59 means no next header.
4) Integrity Check Value field (ICV)
   a. a variable-length field that holds the Hashed Message Authentication Code or HMAC, which is generated by encrypting the output hash function from the ESP header, Payload, and ESP trailer fields.

The HMAC value used in the ICV was a bit confusing for me when I first started studying IPsec, hence why I am clarifying here. Once the original packet is encrypted, and the ESP header and trailer are generated, a hash is created. This hash is then encrypted using the SA encryption algorithm and shared secret key (we talk about keys soon), which means for the receiving IPsec peer to make sense of the hash value, the receiver must first decrypt the ICV before a hash can be extracted and used to compare it to a newly generated hash calculated from the data received. Firstly, this says two things: I can indeed decrypt the hash meaning my IPsec peer sent this ESP packet, and two, when I compare the decrypted hash value, it matches my local hash calculation, which means the data here is good with no corruption.

The other IPsec encapsulation method to mention here is called an Authentication Header (AH), which is assigned protocol 51. AH is not widely used, and I've never used it in a production network. Know that AH does not apply encryption services to packets.

This wraps up IPsec encapsulation protocols. Now that we have the ESP packet structure down, it's time to dive deeper into how IPsec peers actually establish secure tunnels, which points us to Security Associations (SAs).

Security Association (SA)

A Security Association (SA) is a group of security parameters that each IPsec peer agrees upon and uses to obtain confidentially, integrity, and authenticity for network communication, in short. Before we talk about how SAs are agreed upon and negotiated, I believe you need to know what objects a SA holds and why. The main items within a SA are:

1) Security Protocol
   a. ESP or AH
2) Encryption Method
3) Hashing Method
4) Authentication Type
   a. Type of authentication used, Pre-shared Key, Public Key or Signature
5) Diffie-Hellman Group
   a. DH Group
6) Lifetime
   a. How long a SA is valid

Since agreeing on SA's is critical for IPsec to function and to obtain secure communication, I want to step through each of these items in more detail.

The first SA component is the Security Protocol; when working on FortiOS, this will most likely be Tunnel mode, which uses ESP. Next, the Security Protocol is bound together with a specific encryption algorithm and hash algorithm, which are also referred to as a Transform-Set. Transform-Sets are predefined sets of algorithms to perform security services on a packet. Remember, before I mentioned, original packets are encrypted, and ESP packets are authenticated by each side of the IPsec VPN tunnel; this requires both peers to agree on an encryption algorithm, hash algorithm, and Security Protocol (ESP/AH). A Transform-set would look something like this:

1) ESP_AES128_SHA
2) ESP_AES256_SHA256
3) AH_3DEC_MD5

If I chose Transform-set #1 above, then this tells the remote IPsec peer, I want to use ESP IP protocol and encrypt our packets with AES-128 bit and use SHA-1 as our hash function.

The next item within a SA is the Authentication type; this defines what method the IPsec peers use to authentication each other. FortiGate offers two types of authentication for IKEv1, which are PSK (Pre-Shared Key) or certificates.

The next part of the SA is the Diffie-Hellman (DH) group. The purpose of DH in IPsec is to generate and share pseudo-random number (Nonce) values using a secure method over an insecure channel between two devices that have never communicated before. Each IPsec peer Nonce value is used with the Authentication value (PSK/Certificate) to generate an agreed-upon shared secret key. The DH algorithm is fascinating, but unfortunately, the details of the DH algorithm is also beyond the scope of this book, but I highly recommend you check it out for yourself! For the purpose of the NSE4 exam and IPsec, just know DH is used between IPsec peers to agree on a shared secret key privately.

The last item I want to touch on here is the <u>Lifetime</u> value with an SA's. This is how long a shared secret key is valid for securing communication between IPsec peers before it must be recalculated. I will talk more about how session keys are generated later in the chapter. For now, I want to recap on what we know.

We know that IPsec uses security protocols ESP and AH; we will only be discussing ESP in this book. We know about the structure of ESP fields and what their purpose is. We know that an SA is a set of algorithms and values that each IPsec peer agrees upon and is used to obtain confidentially, integrity, and authenticity for secure network communication. Before we move on to Internet Key Exchange, I want to provide a method to remember the required parameters of an SA. It is an acronym called HAGEL (pronounced *haggle)*, which stands for:

1) **H**ash
   a. SHA-1, SHA-256, MD5 etc..
2) **A**uthentication
   a. PSK or certificates
3) **G**roup
   a. DH Group value 1,2,5 ..etc
4) **E**ncryption
   a. DES, 3DES, AES, AES256 etc..
5) **L**ifetime
   a. time session keys are valid

When building an IPsec VPN, you need to know these items along with the IPsec Peer IP address. As I said before, IPsec is a framework that houses many protocols to be used for one overall purpose, secure communication. You can think of the IPsec SA as a box for many different security protocols that can be easily swapped in or out. Check out Image 8.3.

Have you ever seen that game that toddlers play where they have various block shapes that must match the correct hole? Well, you can think of IPsec SA as having the same concept. The IPsec framework allows you to switch out and use different security protocols. IPsec peers could agree on a wide variety of combinations; they just need to match. We could use AES-128 with SHA-1 or 3DES with MD5; as long as both peers agree on the security algorithms in play, then

Image 8.3 – IPsec SA Framework

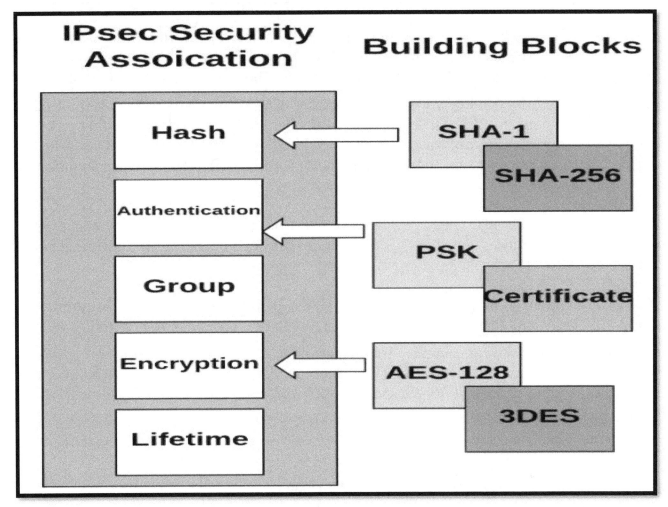

the IPsec tunnel will work. However, you should consider using more robust encryption and hashing algorithms to obtain a better overall security posture.

The last thing I want to mention on SA's before we move on are the three elements that uniquely identify a SA within the Security Association Database. These identifiers are:

1) The security protocol (AH or ESP)
    a. IPSEC Security Protocol Identifier
2) The destination IP address
3) The Security Parameter Index (SPI)

Right now, this is just arbitrary information for you to know in which I will be referencing later in the chapter.

This section wraps up the IPsec encapsulations and the Security Association overview section. In the next section, we start talking about Internet Key Exchange version One (IKEv1) and its role in the IPsec protocol suite.

Internet Key Exchange Version One

Internet Key Exchange Version One (IKEv1) is a hybrid protocol used within the IPsec protocol suite to set up, create, and negotiate Security Associations. The reason IKE is called a hybrid protocol is that it delegates a lot of work to subprotocols. The subprotocols that IKEv1 uses are:

1) Internet Security and Key Management Protocol (ISAKMP)
   a. Defined in RFC 2409, "   ISAKMP ([MSST98]) provides a framework for authentication and key exchange but does not define them. ISAKMP is designed to be key exchange independent; that is, it is designed to support man different key exchanges."
2) Oakley
   a. Defined in RFC 2409, "Oakley ([Orm96]) describes a series of key exchanges-- called "modes"-- and details the services provided by each (e.g., perfect forward secrecy for keys, identity protection, and authentication)."
3) SKEME
   a. Defined in RFC 2409, "   SKEME ([SKEME]) describes a versatile key exchange technique that provides anonymity, reputability, and quick key refreshment."

Note here within RFC 2409 for context, "This document describes a protocol using part of Oakley and part of SKEME in conjunction with ISAKMP to obtain authenticated keying material for use with ISAKMP, and for other security associations such as AH and ESP for the IETF IPsec DOI."

When in doubt, read the RFC. The only problem with RFC documents is that they are not always easy to understand and they are more or less wrote for programmers to understand. The first thing I want to do is to explain ISAKMP, Oakley, and SKEME in plain English.

The first item to cover, ISAKMP. The purpose of ISAKMP is to negotiate, establish, modify, and delete Security Associations (SA's). This protocol defines the procedure, and packet format to accomplish this, which is called ISAKMP Payload Type, meaning ISAKMP marks the contents of its packet. Another responsibility of ISAKMP is to specify the packet format, which is called an ISAKMP payload, for transferring keying and authentication data. In other words, ISAKMP defines an agreed-upon format framework to transfer key'ing data, authentication data, and SA information. ISAKMP focuses on the details of managing SA items, for example, the negotiating method, modifying method, and deleting method for SA's. ISAKMP is not directly involved in secret key creations but serves as a transportation mechanism between IPsec peers to come up with an agreed-upon secret key used to seed encryption, authentication, and integrity of ESP packets. ISAKMP labels each IPsec peer as an Initiator and Responder. The initiator is who begins the communication, and the Responder is the one who reacts to the initial communication request. Also, ISAKMP defines phases between IPsec exchanges, which are Phase One and Phase Two. We go into detail around these two phases later in the chapter.

The next item to cover is OAKLEY. The purpose of OAKLEY is to provide IPsec a way to create agreed-upon secret keying material between IPsec peers. This 'material' is then used to come up with secret keys. The basic mechanism for this key exchange is the Diffie-Hellman algorithm. The Diffie-Hellman key exchange algorithm provides mechanisms that allow two parties to agree on a shared value without requiring encryption. This shared value can then be used to seed subsequent IPsec data encryption for ESP packets. ISAKMP provides the transport container for the Diffie-Hellman process essentially. OAKLEY defines modes of different exchanges, while ISAKMP defines the phases. We go over the different Modes or methods of key exchanges later in the chapter.

The last item here to touch on is SKEME, which provides mechanisms for IPsec to exchange and use public-key encryption. SKEME has a fast re-keying mechanism that is used for authentication within IPsec. This wraps up the subprotocols that IKEv1 interacts with. In the next section, we put together everything that we have learned so far, and we go over the Phase-1 and Phase-2 IPsec peering process.

IPsec Phase-1

At this point, we have gathered enough concepts around IPsec to talk about Phase-1 and Phase-2. Phase-1 is where two IPsec devices use ISAKMP to establish a secure, authenticated channel that is used for the management and maintenance of the IPsec tunnel. ISAKMP Phase-1 has its own SA, and either OAKLEY Main Mode or Aggressive Mode is used to accomplish the Phase-1 exchange. Note that these *Modes* are only used in Phase-1. As discussed, ISAKMP is transportation for the key exchange. Note that ISAKMP uses UDP on port 500 by default, and ESP does not use UDP but uses IP protocol 50. In this section, I will only be discussing Phase-1 using PSK authentication method to keep things simple. The first Oakley mode to review is Main Mode.

ISAKMP Main Mode

Main Mode is called Identify Protection Exchange because IPeer authentication hash and identities are encrypted. The goal of Main Mode is to separate the SA proposal exchange from the key exchange and authentication process. In turn, this is meant to provide identity protection. Main Mode has six message exchanges total. See Image 8.4: Let's go ahead and step through Image 8.4 together, and I'll break down each message sent. Note that three unique

Image 8.4 – Phase-1 Main Mode Exchange

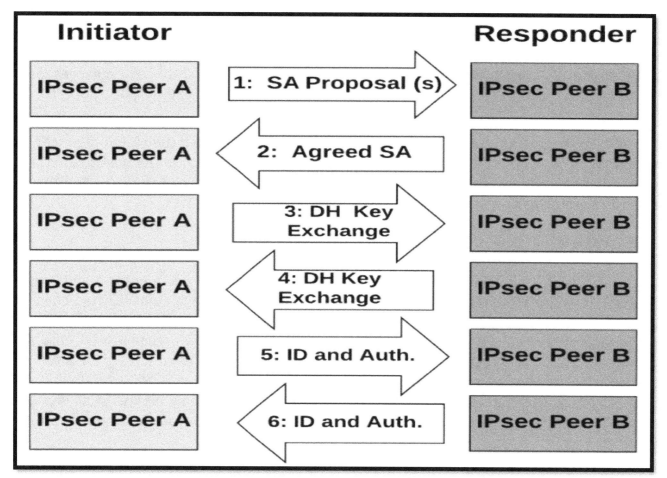

keys are generated during Phase-1, which are used to seed various other security functions; in RFC 2409, these keys are labeled, SKEYID_d, SKEYID_a, and SKEYID_e.

Image 8.5 – Message One Main Mode Phase-1

```
Transform number: 1
Transform ID: KEY_IKE (1)
⊞ Transform IKE Attribute Type (t=1,l=2) Encryption-Algorithm : AES-CBC
⊞ Transform IKE Attribute Type (t=14,l=2) Key-Length : 256
⊞ Transform IKE Attribute Type (t=2,l=2) Hash-Algorithm : SHA2-512
⊞ Transform IKE Attribute Type (t=4,l=2) Group-Description : 2048-bit MODP
⊞ Transform IKE Attribute Type (t=3,l=2) Authentication-Method : PSK
⊞ Transform IKE Attribute Type (t=11,l=2) Life-Type : Seconds
⊞ Transform IKE Attribute Type (t=12,l=4) Life-Duration : 86400
```

1) The Initiator begins the communication by sending an ISAKMP packet using UDP port 500 with the *Type Payload: Security Association* (which is a subtype of ISAKMP message). This first message contains all the possible SA's that the initiator conforms to. See Image 8.5, which is a Wireshark snippet output of message one.

2) Message two is from the Responder and is to inform the Initiator that it selected and agrees upon an SA that was purposed. So now, each IPsec peer knows what security algorithms and methods are used to create secure communication channel(s) between the two points.

3) Message three is the beginning of the Diffie-Hellman key exchange. This exchange is carried in ISAKMP Payload Type Key Exchange. Remember, on the backend this function is governed by the Oakley standard. The Initiator sends it DH Public Key (Nonce value) to the remote IPsec peer, which is used with a DH Private Key. The DH Public and Private Keys are seeds for the method to create an agreed-upon secret key and a unique authentication string, by using the PSK (in this case) and other unique attributes of the communication. The DH *secret key* is then used to seed the encryption process and HMAC (Hash Message Authentication Code) for each ESP packet later on.

4) Message four, the Responder sends the Initiator its DH Public key (nonce value)

5) Message five, at this point, both IPsec peers have calculated an agreed-upon DH secret key, which is used to encrypt and create an authentication hash (HMAC). Remember, HMAC is a hash value that is encrypted with the secret key using encryption and hash values selected in the agreed-upon SA. This ISAKMP Payload Type is Identification and is used to transport the HMAC string used for authentication that only the other peer can decrypt and should be able to create the same unique calculated hash value. This variable is called HASH_I in RFC 2409. Also, the source IP of the IPsec peer is sent as the peer *Identifier* value most of the time, but other *Identifier* values can be used as well, like FQDN. The ID here is used by the Responder as part of the authentication process for the Initiator peer. The *Identifier* value can be one of many types, but the host and subnet ID values are the most common. So the two critical encrypted items sent are:
     i. Authentication Hash
     ii. IPsec peer identification

6) Suppose the Responder was able to decrypt the previous message and was able to generate the same unique hash value locally, and it matches what was received. In that case, the Initiator IPsec peer is authentication, and the Responder repeats the process by sending the Initiator an encrypted, unique authentication string, and the Initiator must do the same. This authentication variable sent by the Responder is called HASH_R in RFC 2409. If the Initiator decrypts the message ok and matches the provided unique string value, then the Responder is authenticated by the Initiator, and Phase-1 is complete.

Ok, great, once Phase-1 using Main Mode is complete, this means that the IPsec peers have agreed on a shared SA for ISAKMP management traffic and also agree on the secret key value generated by combining DH key exchange method results with the PSK (authentication method) (and other unique attributes for the connect) which in turn is used to authenticate the IPsec peers to each other.

If you care exactly how the Initiator and Responder calculate authentication values on the backend, then here is the algorithm provided by RFC 2409, the below variables are defined in the RFC (Ctrl+f is your friend 😊):

..

HASH_I = prf(SKEYID, g^xi | g^xr | CKY-I | CKY-R | SAi_b | IDii_b)

HASH_R = prf(SKEYID, g^xr | g^xi | CKY-R | CKY-I | SAi_b | IDir_b)

..

It is not a requirement to know this algorithm calculation for any Fortinet certification (not yet!).

ISAKMP Aggressive Mode

Alright, we discussed Phase-1 using Main Mode, which protects the authentication hash and IPsec peer identity. Next, it is time to discuss Phase-1 using *Aggressive Mode,* which does not separate out the ISAKMP exchanged parameters, and therefore, the hash authentication and peer identity are not encrypted. Aggressive Mode uses only three messages to complete the Phase-1 exchange. Take a look at Image 8.6 on the next page.

Let's go through the messages sent in Aggressive Mode for Phase-1. The first thing to note is that all these messages are sent unencrypted.

1) The first message the Initiator sends is the SA proposal(s), DH public key and nonce data, and also the Identity of the IPsec peer, which is its IP address most the time.
2) The Responder receives the message and matches a SA proposal within its own configuration. Next, the DH public key and nonce is used to create a secret key internally. An Authentication Hash is generated but NOT encrypted. This is because Initiator does not have the Responders DH Public Key and nonce data to generate the shared secret key.
3) Once the agreed SA, DH public key, and the nonce are received from the Responder, the Initiator will then generate the shared secret key. Next, this information will be used against the Authentication Hash to validate the IPsec peer. If no issues with validation, then Initiator will then generate its own authentication Hash and send back to the responder. The Responder will validate the Authentication Hash, and if good, then Phase-1 is complete.

You might be asking yourself why we need an Aggressive Mode Phase-1? Aggressive Mode is usually required when the Initiator has a dynamic IP (unknown IP)or is an endpoint using remote

Image 8.6 – Aggressive Mode Phase-1

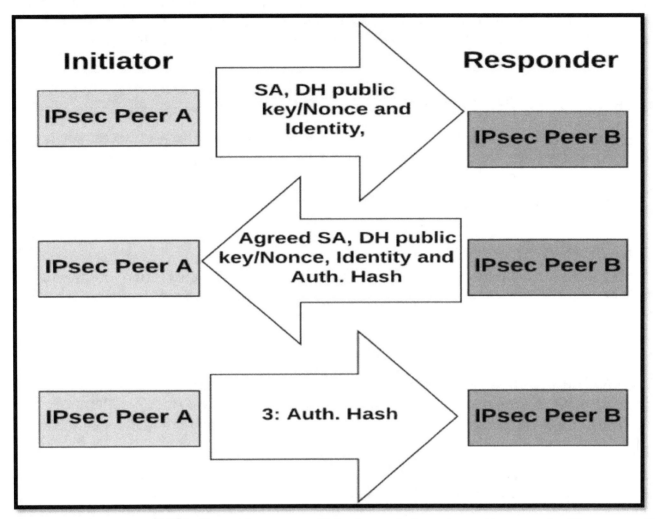

access or Dial-up IPsec VPN. Since the source IP is dynamic in nature, the remote IPsec peer IP address can not be statically assigned in the IPsec configuration locally, and therefore identification verification cannot occur using IPsec peer IP address.

RFC 2409:

> "When using pre-shared key authentication with Main Mode, the key can
>
> only be identified by the IP address of the peers since HASH_I must
>
> be computed before the initiator has processed IDir. Aggressive Mode
>
> allows for a wider range of identifiers of the pre-shared secret to
>
> be used."

With Fortigate, there are options to configure Local_IDs to separate Dial-up VPNs that share a single interface and/or local gateway IP, which could then be given different firewall policy access.

At this point, you should understand that Phase-1 is either accomplished using Main Mode or Aggressive Mode. That ISAKMP establishes its own SA to manage the IPsec VPN. Before we move on into our Phase-2 discussion, I want to touch on the Session keys that are generated out of Phase-1. Phase-2 would make more sense if we had a stronger handle on the key generation and what various keys are used within IPsec.

<u>Session Keys Generation Details</u>

I'm going to reference RFC 2409 in this section. Remember, the DH shared secret key is one of the seed values to create the following Session Keys. The variables I'm going to be referencing are:

- Encryption Key = SKEYID_e
- Authentication Key = SKEYID_a
- Derivative Key = SKEYID_d

First, the Encryption Key is used by ISAKMP for symmetric encryption of overall IPsec management traffic. This key is used in Phase-1 Main Mode to protect Authentication Hash and IPsec peer identity. If no PFS, this key is also be used in Phase-2. For example, if the SA contained AES256, then the Encryption key value would be used by AES256 as a seed value to encrypt the payload within ESP packets sent to the remote IPsec peer.

Next, Authentication Key is used by ISAKMP to create the authentication hash or HMAC. Any future ISAKMP information exchanges like rekeying, dead-peer-detection (DPD), or Modify messages ..etc., will be authenticated using HMAC generated using the Authentication Key.

Next, the Derivative Key is given to IPsec since IPsec cannot create its own key(s). The Derivative Key is then used in the creation of the Phase-2 encryption key(s), which are defined in the RFC as *KEYMAT,* which I will be referring to as Phase-2 Session Keys.

We are now ready for our Phase-2 discussion. Full disclosure here, you do not need to know all the details around key generation and DH to work with IPsec. Before we jump into configuring FortiGate to work with IPsec, I'll give a rundown of what you need to know. Me personally, I need to understand the low-level details of certain technologies for me to feel comfortable working with it, but again this is not required to manage IPsec technology in general.

IPsec Phase-2

The purpose of IPsec Phase-2 is to separate out secure communication for ISAKMP management traffic and *transit* data traffic (ESP). Transit traffic being normal user traffic that is being encrypted with IPsec services. Most of the time, IPsec is transparent to the end-users, and they have no idea their traffic is being secured by an IPsec. They just know when they connect to a VPN, they can get to internal company resources or to the company intranet.

Phase-2 works in the same manner as Phase-1 regarding the creations and negotiation of SA's. A big difference is that Phase-2 requires two SA's, one for inbound traffic and one for outbound traffic. Each SA is given an SPI as an identifier. Also, a single Phase-1 tunnel can support multiple Phase-2 child tunnels. Image 8.7 provides a nice visual.

Image 8.7 – IPsec Phase-2 Diagram

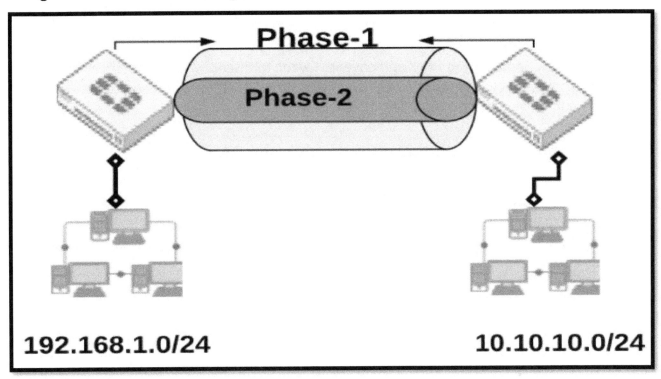

Each FortiGate authenticates itself to the other during the IPsec Phase-1 process. Next, once Phase-2 is established, client machines on LAN 192.168.1.0/24 (left side) and 10.10.10.0/24 (right side) would be able to communicate with each other over the public Internet using only private IP space. The IPsec VPN interface can be viewed as a logical interface and requires the same policies and routing statements for traffic to pass through FortiGate. The next question to ask, what is the process of establishing the IPsec Phase-2?

Time to run through a scenario. For example, the two FortiGate's in Image 8.7 just established their Phase-1 over the public internet. Meaning one SA is protecting ISAKMP communication. The next set of communication to take place is called Quick Mode (phase2). In Quick Mode, three messages are exchanged between the IPsec peers. Within these messages, two SA's are established, which are used for IPsec (transit traffic encryption). Note, these messages are protected with ISAKMP's Phase-1 SA. Let's take a look at the Quick Mode message exchange.

1) The first Quick Mode message is sent from the Initiator and contains:
   a. Authentication Hash, SA Proposal, DH Nonce, and source/destination Identification Payloads

2) If Initiators Authentication Hash is verified and approved, then the Responder will pick a SA from proposals that matches a local configuration. In message two, the Responder sends back:
   a. Agreed SA, Responders Authentication Hash, DH Nonce, and source/destination Identification Payloads.
3) Once the Initiator receives Message 2 from the Responder, it verifies the Authentication Hash; if good, then it will send one last message as an acknowledgment that Phase-2 is complete. This message contains one more Authentication Hash seeded with the Responder DH Nonce value as proof of authenticity.

Phase-2 has a few additional options and caveats I want to discuss with you before we move on. The first item being how we choose what traffic is allowed within the IPsec tunnel (Phase-2). This moves our conversation to Quick Mode Selectors.

Quick Mode Selectors

The first thing to discuss within these Phase-2 messages, which I believe is one of the more important values, are the "source/destination Identification Payloads" the way this is worded doesn't really make sense, but it is technically accurate. The purpose of the Phase-2 creation is to carry or be a means of transport for other hosts within a protected network that may need to use the IPsec VPN. FortiGate defines these hosts within the Phase-2 configuration as Quick Mode *Selectors*. This is one term that doesn't stay the same when working with various vendors.

Image 8.8 – Quick Mode Selector Diagram

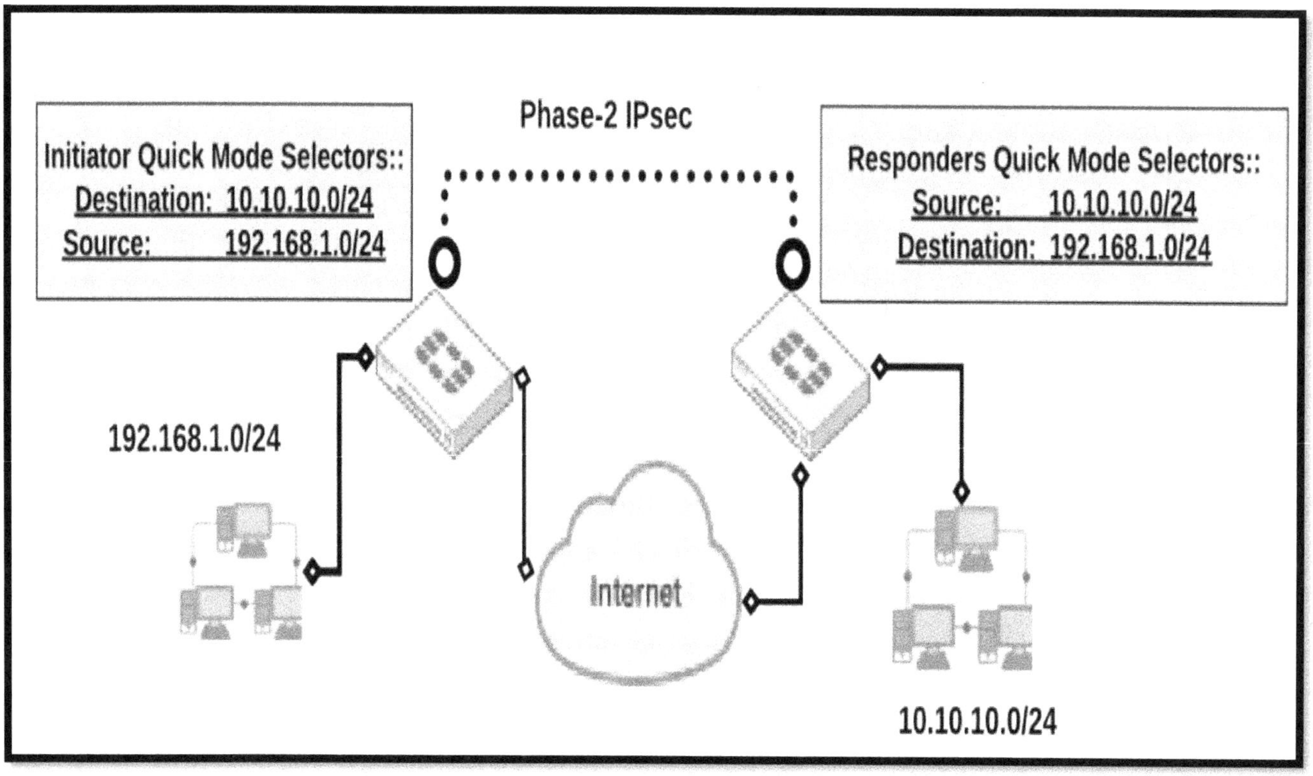

Cisco calls this Phase-2 values *Interesting Traffic* and other vendors *Encryption Domains*, but at the end of the day, the RFC calls these values: "4.6.2.1 Identification Type Values" per RFC 2407.

Since this is a FortiGate book, I will be using the term *Quick Mode Selectors (Selectors)*. These Selectors define what traffic can enter the Phase-2 IPsec tunnel. Most of the time, the source and destination values are IPv4 or IPv6 subnet. For example, if my Selectors were defined as Source=192.168.1.0/24 and Destination=10.10.10.0/24 on the Initiator IPsec peer, then the Responder IPsec peer must have inverted Selector values of Source=10.10.10.0/24 and Destination=192.168.1.0/04. You can think of these values as the gates for the Phase-2 access. These phase-2 attributes are a common reason IPsec Phase-2 does not establish, which is called a Selector mismatch. As stated before, you can have multiple Phase-2 built upon a single Phase-1, meaning there can be multiple Selector source and destination pairings. We will be configuration Fortigate IPsec Selectors later in the chapter. The next item I want to touch on is the Phase-2 key exchange and how we can apply an additional layer of security.

Perfect Forward Secrecy

Perfect Forward Secrecy (PFS) is an option during the Phase-2 to provide an additional layer of security. The high level is that during the Phase-2 setup, DH runs again so to generate fresh keys to be used for the bi-directional Quick Mode SA's. Hence, the key for Phase-1 ISAKMP SA is different from the child Phase-2 SA's. The reason behind this is to account for the Phase-1 secret key becoming compromised, and so PFS would prevent the Child SA' from becoming compromised as well. RFC, 2409 states:

" If PFS is desired and KE payloads were exchanged, the new keying

material is defined as

KEYMAT = prf(SKEYID_d, g(qm)^xy | protocol | SPI | Ni_b | Nr_b)"

When PFS is enabled, this requires Quick Mode to perform a new DH Key Exchange during Phase-2 tunnel negotiation or whenever the Phase-2 key Lifetime expires. The next item I want to cover with you is Key Lifetime.

Key Lifetime

Lifetime values are configured for Phase-1 and Phase-2. This means that the secret keys generated are only used for a certain amount of time, data transfer, or both. Most of the IPsec VPNs I've worked on, use the time *lifetime* value to set the threshold when a new shared secret key should be generated by Oakley by performing an additional DH exchange.

You might be asking yourself why it is required for keys to change once generated. The reason behind this is because, over time, the DH shared secret Key can be compromised. The workaround for this is to keep changing the keys, which in theory would require the attacker to keep having to compromise new keys, which would make it less feasible for the attacker to be successful. The rule is, the larger the DH Group, the more secure the Key Exchange method. This is beyond the scope of this book because there are entire books written on encryption theory, which I would highly recommend reading; it really is amazing what can be accomplished with computing. The next Phase-2 option I want to discuss is XAuth.

Extended Authentication XAuth

Extended Authentication is commonly referenced as XAuth. I'll be honest, and this is not technically Phase-2 (Quick Mode); however, it is not technically Phase-1 either. XAuth could be viewed as the 1.5 Phase. The most common use case for XAuth is to force Dial-up IPsec users to provide their credentials before being allowed access to the VPN. There are four message types used in the XAuth exchange, which are:

1) ISAKMP_CFG_REQUEST
   a. It is sent from IPsec Gateway to the client requesting authentication.
2) ISAKMP_CFG_REPLY
   a. The Client replies with credentials (Username/password)
3) ISAKMP_CFG_SET
   a. IPsec Gateway sends authentication success or failure
4) ISAKMP_CFG_ACK
   a. The client replies with acknowledgment of success or failure

The fact that the client requires Phase-1 authentication (PSK) and then must supply a username and password makes IPsec remote access Dial-up deployments two-factor authentication by nature.

We step through FortiGate Dial-up IPsec client XAuth configuration later in this chapter. The next IPsec features I want to discuss is also related to remote client IPsec users and that is Network Address Translation Traversal (NAT-T)

Network Address Translation Traversal (NAT-T)

It is common for IPsec Dial-up clients to be assigned a private IP because they are most likely operating within a private LAN environment. This means when the client attempts to access the IPsec VPN gateway, its source IP address is translated to a public. A standard was created to deal with situations like this, which is outlined in RFC 3947.

IPsec peers actually *detect* if NAT-T is required during the Phase-1 negotiation process. This is accomplished by IPsec peers sending ISAKMP Payload type NAT Discovery; this method involves hashing the client's source IP and port numbers and comparing it to hash values of IP and port within the received IP header.

"The NAT-D payloads are included in the third and fourth packets of

   Main Mode, and in the second and third packets in the Aggressive

   Mode." *RFC 3947*

Once ISAKMP detects remote IPsec peer is behind a NAT device, all further IPsec traffic (ESP, ISAKMP ..etc.) is encapsulated with a UDP header marked with port 4500. So note, if NAT occurs for the ISAKMP Phase-1 setup, then port 4500 UDP is used.

This wraps of NAT-T for the NSE4 certification, the next IPsec feature I need to discuss with you is a mechanism for IPsec peers to use to detect reachability issues.

Image 8.9 - NAT-T UDP Port 4500

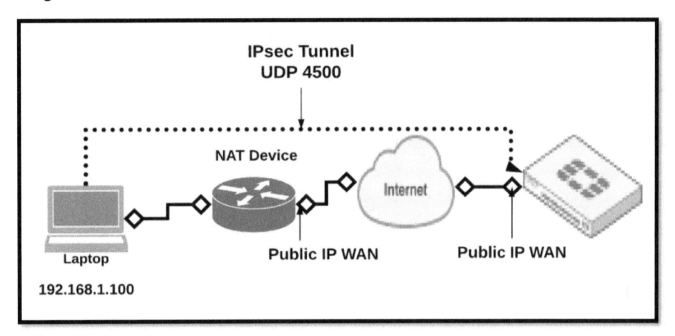

Dead Peer Detection

It never a good day when your FortiGate is sending ESP packets to an IPsec peer that is either down or no longer reachable because of network-related issues, and to prevent situations like this from happening, a standard was drafted, RFC 3706, and the feature is called Dead Peer Detection (DPD).

DPD is essentially a keep-alive option that can be used between IPsec peers. ISAKMP carries the DPD mechanisms with Payload Type Notify. The content of the message is R-U-THERE, and the reply is R-U-THERE-ACK. FortiGate has a few vendor-specific features regarding DPD, which we will discuss later in the configuration section. Here is an example DPD debug:

```
ike 0: IKEv1 exchange=Informational
id=72c77916b78ad434/233942a79c1b9053:678f3e95 len=92
ike 0: in 6..D6F0F75F79C8F4
ike 0:FGT-B_IPsec:623: dec 7…..7D361E67532A2E707
ike 0:FGT-B_IPsec:623: notify msg received: R-U-THERE-ACK
```

There are two more IPsec features to discuss before we move into the IPsec Topologies section and that is IKE Mode Config and Anti-Replay

IKE Mode Config

IKE Mode Config is the ISAKMP configuration method for Dial-Up IPsec clients and is also a Client to Server Type of Architecture. The IPsec Gateway must be configured as an IKE Mode Config

Image 8.10 – IKE Mode Config Message Exchange

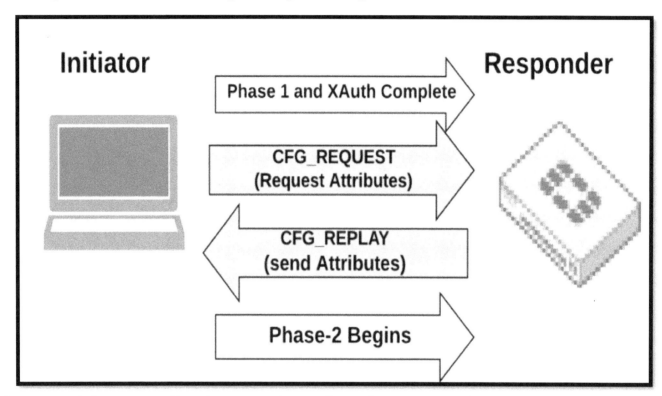

Server, and the remote IPsec host must be configured as an IKE Mode Config Client. This is how clients obtain things like the IP Address, DNS, WINS, and DNS suffix to be used when a host sends ESP packets to IPsec Gateway.

If IKE Mode config is not used, then it is possible to use DHCP or L2TP over IPsec to assign remote clients to host configuration parameters. And lastly, RADIUS can be used to assign end clients IP information by using a field in RADIUS called the Framed-IP-Address.

The last thing I want to touch on in this section is, if the DNS suffix is not provided and only an internal DNS IP, then the end host needs to use the FQDN of the destination host. This method is outlined via https://tools.ietf.org/id/draft-dukes-ike-mode-cfg-02.txt. The last item for

Be sure to account for routing when assigning an IP range for remote IPsec clients to us on the IPsec tunnel

IPsec Theory before we jump into IPsec Topologies is Anti-Replay, where we discuss how FortiGate protects against this type of attack.

Anti-Replay Protection

Anti-Replay is a security feature within IPsec that is meant to prevent DoS attacks. Let's first see how an IPsec DoS attack could occur. See Image 8.11 on the next page.

Since ESP packets transverse the public internet, it could be possible that somewhere between the IPsec peers ESP packets could be captured. Of course, the ESP packets are encrypted and can only be unlocked with the secret key with the known encryption algorithm, but even if an attacker doesn't have this information, they could still damage your network operations. They could do this by generating many copies of the captured ESP packets and sending them onward

> *FortiGate HA failover could cause issues with ESP sequence numbers and may be required to bounce VPN to re-sync sequence numbers.*

to their intended destination. In the scenario within Image 8.1 on the next page, the ESP packets are destined for an internal File Server. Take a moment to review.

Depending on the volume of the duplicated ESP packets', this could bring down the File server completely because it is too busy trying to process bogus packets instead of serving real clients, and this is where Anti-Replay protection comes in. How it works is that every ESP packet is given a sequence number, and this value is incremented by 1 for each ESP packet generated. Next, FortiGate has a feature to keep track of these sequence numbers and expects them to fall into a known range. This is called the sequence number range sliding window. Any sequence numbers that fall outside of this range are discarded. The FortiGate configuration details of Anti-Replay are discussed in the configuration section of the chapter. Note that IPsec log messages are generated if ESP packets are dropped due to the Anti-Replay protection, and the log contains the message "Invalid ESP packet detected (replayed packet)."

This wraps up Anti-Replay and also IPsec theory! At this point, you should feel good about how IPsec works and understand the various sub-protocols and processes that are used. In the next section, we discuss the different IPsec topologies and some use cases with each one.

Image 8. 11 - Anti Replay Diagram

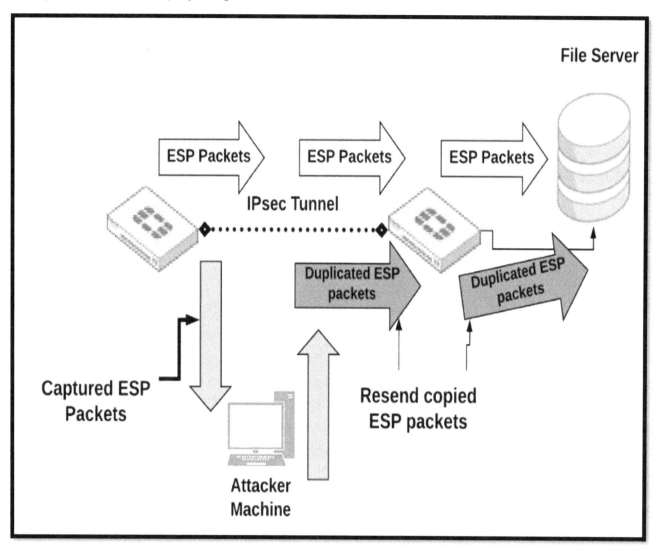

IPsec Topologies

Since we now know how IPsec functions at a low level, in this section, we focus on how we can use IPsec on a high level to secure communication in different types of use cases. We will go over some caveats for each IPsec topology. The first one to discuss is the site to site IPsec deployment.

Site-To-Site IPsec Topology

One of the most basic implementations of IPsec is the Site to Site tunnel. This is when two IPsec peers with static Public IP addresses assigned to their WAN interfaces exchange secure communication with each other. With this type of topology, the IPsec peers form a Phase-1 tunnel and then a Phase-2 tunnel for the internal LAN devices to use. Each LAN network should have a unique subnet just like any other internal LAN because LAN devices will use the remote LAN's private IP space to communicate. Sometimes this is not possible, and a NAT'ed VPN must

Image 8.12 - Site-to-Site IPsec Topology

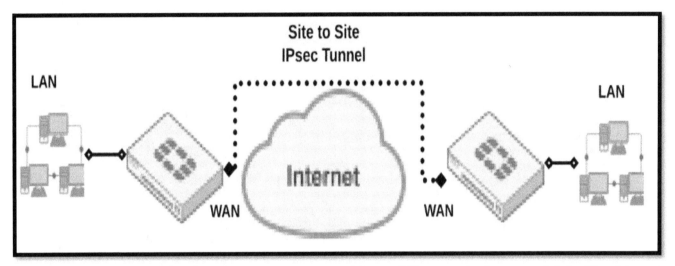

be used where one or both LANs are represented by a different single or multiple IP addresses when traversing an IPSec tunnel. Many organizations use a Site-to-Site tunnel to connect to cloud environments, remote offices, or external vendors. The possibilities are endless. The next topology to discuss is the Hub and Spoke.

Hub-and-Spoke IPsec Topology

A Hub-and-Spoke topology is a one-point (hub) to multiple points (spokes) topology. What is unique about this topology is all the spoke devices form their IPsec VPN connection with only the hub device. The advantage of this topology is that the FortiGate configuration is easy to manage. The spokes within this topology cannot directly communicate with each other but must transverse the Hub as a proxy essentially. Take a look at the diagram Image 8.13 on the next page.

Here we can see that there are three spokes, and most of the time, these would be lower end FortiGate models like 30E, 60E, or 100E models that act as a gateway device for a branch office LAN. The Spoke FortiGates would connect to the Hub FortiGate using a Dial-up VPN to access HQ resources and each other. Also, for each Spoke to communicate with each other's LAN, all traffic would be required to be proxied through the Hub device, which would increase latency and create a single point of failure. Most of the time, to eliminate this single point of failure, two independent Hubs would be used within the Hub-and-Spoke topology. Dual Hub Architecture is beyond the scope of this chapter. The Hub FortiGate would require more bandwidth and a

Image 8.13 – Hub and Spoke Topology

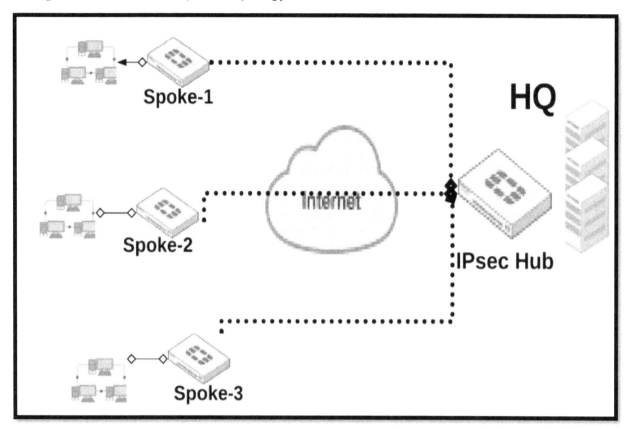

higher-end model platform, such as 1500D, 1800F, or 4200F. A Hub is also called a VPN concentrator or VPN aggregator. The Hub-and-Spoke Topology is the foundation for enterprise SDWAN deployments. We go through the Hub-and-Spoke configuration later in the chapter, so we are ready for our SDWAN chapter! The next VPN topology to discuss is Full Mesh.

Full and Partial Mesh IPsec Topology

The Full Mesh IPsec topology essentially is when every FortiGate has an IPsec Site-to-Site VPN built to every other FortiGate within an organization's WAN infrastructure. This might work ok for small businesses that only have 3-4 branch offices, but once the number of sites increases, then the number of IPsec tunnels becomes unmanageable. A ten-site business would require a total of 45 tunnels to obtain full mesh, and then routing would need to be implemented to obtain full connectivity, which creates a complex configuration. At the end of the day, Full Mesh IPsec VPN topologies are not scalable when there are many remote sites to account for. The Partial Mesh IPsec topology is the same concept expect not every FortiGate has direct access to every other FortiGate within the WAN infrastructure; maybe only half have access to all other FortiGate. This would be more like a hub-and-spoke VPN topology. Image 8.14 shows what the VPN tunnels would look like for a single FortiGate if full mesh were implemented.

Image 8.14 – Mesh IPsec Topology Example

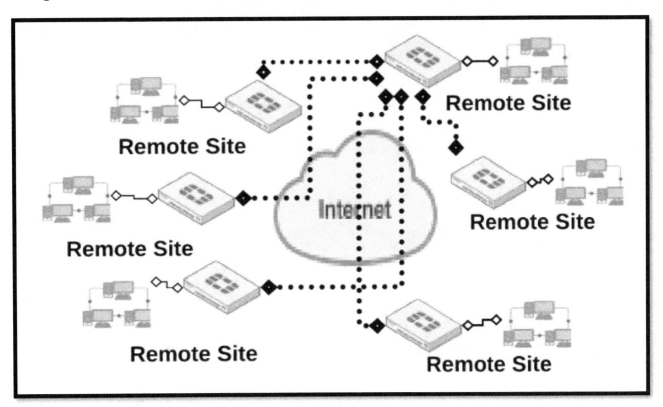

As you can see, I only connected one FortiGate to all other FortiGate's here. If the Full mesh diagram were true here, there would be so many lines, and it would no longer make sense. We would need a total of 15 tunnels to complete the full mesh IPsec topology here. The formula for the number of required VPNs in relation to the number of sites is:

X Site = X(X-1)/2 Tunnels

The last IPsec VPN topology to discuss in this section is ADVPN! No 'short-cuts' here! Maybe I should have waited until after the ADVPN section to try that joke... oh well.

Auto Discover IPsec Topology

Hub-and-Spoke architecture has gained a lot of popularity in the industry throughout the years. One of the major issues with this topology is that Spokes cannot directly communicate with each other. That is where the Auto Discover VPN (ADVPN) comes into play. With ADVPN, spokes are able to create '*shortcuts*' and bypass the Hub FortiGate. This makes for less latency in the communication between Spokes and saves resources on the FortiGate hub. Image 8.15 provides a nice high level visual of the IPsec ADVPN topology.

With ADVPN, you get to have your cake and eat it too. Meaning, the ADVPN provides all the benefits and features of a Full Mesh IPsec topology and does not come with the overhead complexity of managing it. FortiGate ADVPN dynamically negotiates tunnels between spokes with no prior configuration. In most ADVPN deployments, SDWAN is used on the spokes with dynamic routing like BGP to the hub so that all devices can learn Spokes LAN subnets and Hub networks. To enable ADVPN on FortiGate, under the Phase-1 configuration, we just need to add three settings:

Image 8.15- ADVPN Topology

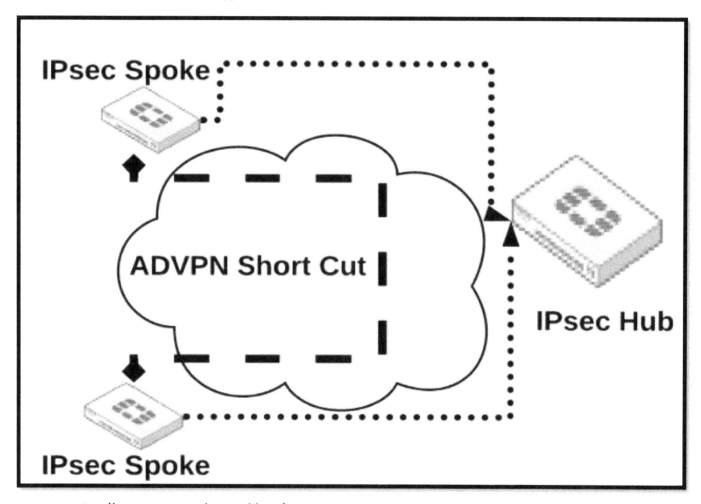

- auto-discovery-receiver //spoke
- auto-discovery-sender //hub
- auto-discovery-forward //hub

Look at the traffic flow for a SHORTCUT setup managed by ISAKMP between Spokes. Check out Image 8.16.

We are going to walk through the ADVPN Shortcut setup together:

Image 8.16 – ADVPN Shortcut setup

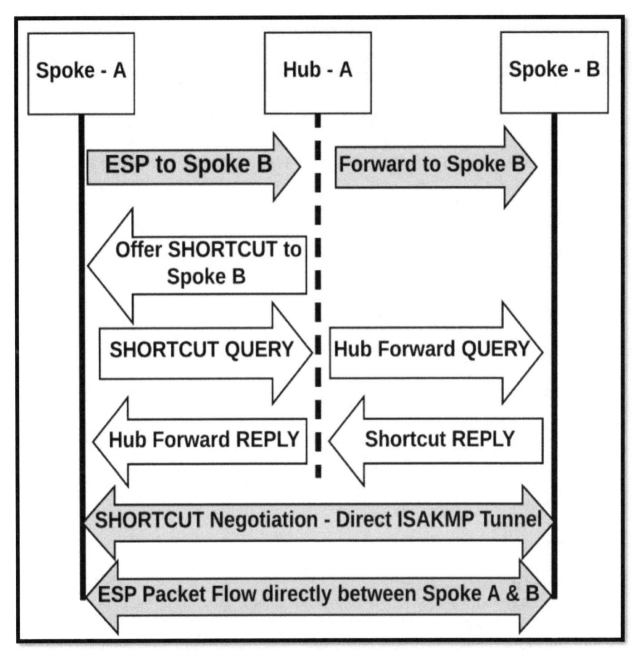

1) Spoke-A sends an ESP packet to the hub, but the encapsulated IP header has a destination IP address that is routable via Spoke-B.
    a. At this point, the Hub FortiGate does two things, forward the ESP packet to Spoke-B but then also send an OFFER Shortcut ISAKMP message to Spoke-A. Spoke-A
2) Spoke-A acknowledges the Shortcut OFFER by sending a Shortcut QUERY message to HUB-A in which HUB-A forwards to Spoke-B.

    a. An INFORMATIONAL SHORTCUT-QUERY message containing Spoke-A public IP address, local and destination subnet (quick mode selectors), and auto-generates a PSK to be used for the direct IPsec tunnel setup.

3) Spoke-B then creates an INFORMATIONAL reply message containing its external IP address and sends it back to HUB-A to be forwarded onward.

4) Since Spoke-A now knows the public IP of Spoke-B, Spoke-A will become the initiator for the Phase-1 and Phase-2 negotiations. Once the tunnel is established, communication between Spoke-A and Spoke-B can bypass the hub.

This section covers the *nuts and bolts* of ADVPN. However, ADVPN is a deep subject, and. Dynamic routing is required when using ADVPN as well. The NSE7 dives deeper into ADVPN. Before we shift gears into our configuration section, I want to provide a quick IPsec Topology overview.

IPsec Topologies Review

This section provides the high-level pros and cons for each VPN topology we have discussed so far.

1) Site-to-Site Topology
    a. Point to Pint, Easy to implement, allows transparent communication between private networks over the public Internet
2) Hub-and-Spoke Topology
    a. Easy to configure and manage.
    b. Requires higher-end FortiGate and bandwidth for Hub unit(s)
    c. Scalable solution
    d. No direct communication between spokes
    e. Requires multiple Hub for fault tolerance
3) Full Mesh Topology
    a. Complex configuration and management
    b. Many tunnels
    c. not scalable
    d. direct communication between sites
    e. Inherently fault-tolerant
    f. distributed processing load, medium-range FortiGate platforms.
4) Partial Mesh Topology
    a. Moderate complexity and management
    b. some fault tolerance
    c. distributed processing load, medium-range FortiGate platforms.
    d. more scalable than full
5) ADVPN
    a. Moderate complexity and management
    b. Direct communication between spokes
    c. Scalable solution

    d. Requires higher-end FortiGate and bandwidth for Hub unit(s)

Moving on, since we understand IPsec on a low level and a high level, our next steps are to configure it on FortiGate! There is a bunch of fun stuff to do in the next section!!

FortiGate IPsec Implementation

We will be implementing IPsec on FortiGate in this section. I will be focusing on FortiGate specific IPsec features and... what's a good word... *abilities*. Before we get started, I would like to provide a quick tour of the CLI and GUI IPsec configuration settings for you folks that are on

Image 8.17 – VPN GUI Menu

the 'newer' side working with FortiGate's. To find the IPsec configuration menus in the GUI, find the VPN dropdown.

In Image 8.17, I have highlighted *IPsec Tunnels,* which brings us to our IPsec configuration page. Once we select *Create New,* this actually brings us to a VPN Creation Wizard, which is a nice feature to have. Some folks don't like using Wizards, but if it makes my job easier, sign me up! Check out Image 8.18:

Image 8.18 - IPsec Wizard Menu

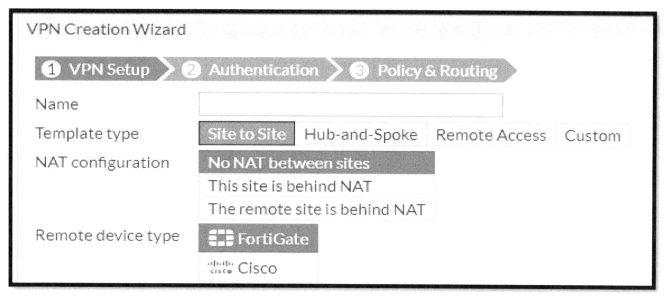

FortiGate makes it easy for novice firewall engineers to build complicated IPsec tunnels by having a slick walkthrough menu. We can even choose between building an IPsec tunnel to a FortiGate or to a Cisco device! Note, throughout this section, we use the Custom option so we can walk through all the Phase-1 and Phase-2 configuration. Also, notice in step three within Image 8.18, Policy & Routing, these are two things that are absolutely necessary when working with IPsec on FortiOS. When stepping through the IPsec wizard on the backend, FortiOS generates a CLI script, configure the required Policy Entries and Route Entry for you.

All these different possible topologies found in the wizard are mapped to IPsec Templates. If you wish to know what *under-the-hood* is, so to speak, then you can go to VPN -> IPsec Tunnel Template, and this page allows you to drill down into each template.

> *Also, remember the command #diag debug cli 7 – have this running before you submit your GUI configuration to view the CLI equivalent!*

Image 8.19 – IPsec Templates

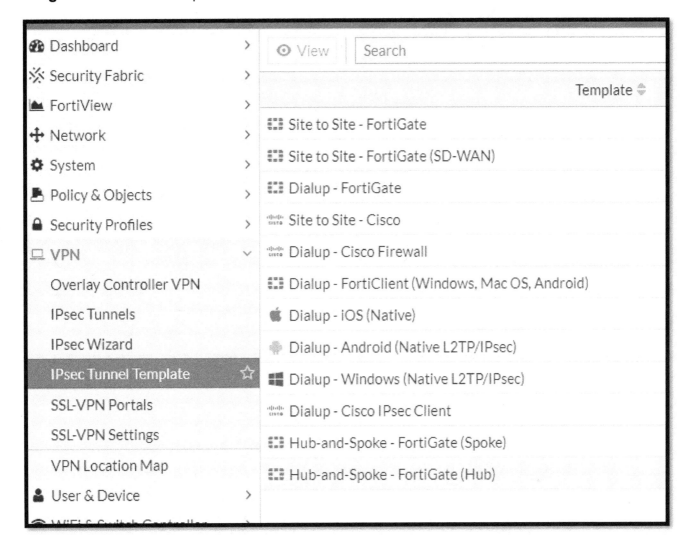

Image 8.19 provides a rundown of all the available VPN templates on FortiOS for 6.2.5 GA. We are moving on to our first FortiGate IPsec configuration example! I know I have been beating around the bush for long enough, and it's time to get to the meat and potatoes! We will be working with a basic Site-to-Site IPsec VPN between two FortiGate's running 6.2.5 GA. Let's check it out!

FortiGate Site to Site IPsec Tunnel

Here is a quick snapshot of the topology we are working with, see Image 8.20:

Image 8.20 – FortiGate IPsec Site to Site VPN

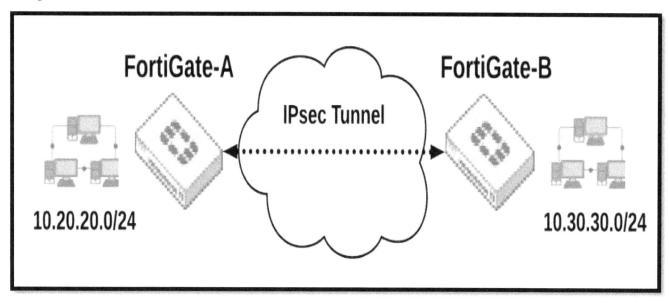

- FortiGate-A WAN IP = 172.16.10.1
    - LAN 10.20.20.0/24
- FortiGate-B WAN IP = 192.168.209.2
    - LAN 10.30.30./24

I have FortiGate-A and FortiGate-B in my lab, which are a 30E and 60F, respectfully. I will be representing the LAN subnets 10.20.20.0/24 and 10.30.30.0/24 with 10.20.20.1/32 loopback interface on FGT-A and 10.30.30.1/32 loopback interface on FGT-B. I will be focusing on IPsec content only in this section if you need to know how to create an interface reference Introduction to FortiGate Part-I.

I'm going to start our configuration on FGT-A. Our Phase-I and Phase-2 will have the following parameters:

1) Hash = SHA1
2) Authentication = PSK (*Password123*)
3) Group = DH Group 5
    a. Phase-2 = PFS DH 5
4) Encryption = AES256
5) Lifetime = 86400 Phase-1
    a. Phase-2 = 43200
        i. Phase-1 lifetime should be longer than phase-2

I am using the HAGEL method to configure our IPsec peers ISAKMP SA and Bi-directional Phase-2 SA's. Next, I display GUI options of Phase-1 and Phase-2 and then CLI output. Next, I configure a Policy Entry and a Static Route on each device.

Once all the configuration aspect is complete, I run the 'diag flow' commands as a Proof of Concept that the tunnels actually work. Lastly, I verify that IPsec ESP packets are indeed offloaded to the local ASIC. Let's get to it!

FortiGate-A Phase-1 GUI

The first device we are working on is FGT-A Phase-1 and Phase-2 GUI information; check out Image 8.21:

Image 8.21 – FortiGate-A Phase-1 GUI Configuration

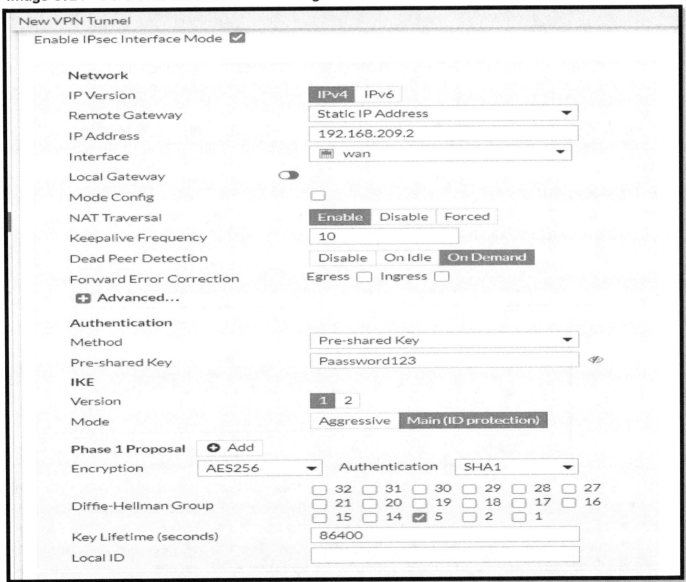

The first thing to note here is the 'Enable IPsec Interface Mode' box is selected. FortiGate has two IPsec implementation methods. Interface Mode, which is the most common, and Policy Mode, which is not used much anymore. The difference between these two methods is how transit traffic is directed to the IPsec tunnel and the additional configuration around the Firewall Policy Entry that governs traffic to the IPsec tunnel. FortiOS require Interface Mode IPsec to run routing protocol across IPsec. Also, Interfaced Based allows routing statements to be used to direct traffic to an IPsec tunnel. Policy-Based IPsec cannot directly use routing statements against the IPsec tunnel because there is no virtual interface to direct traffic to, but instead, Policy Mode IPsec uses the defined phase-2 Selector configuration to direct traffic to the tunnel. This chapter focuses on Interface Based IPsec VPN's.

To find current FQDN IP use the follow CLI command:

#diagnose test application dnsproxy 7

Take a moment to review FGT-A IPsec Phase-1 GUI configuration in Image 8.21. Try to see if you can find all the 'HAGEL' values. Now, let me go through some configuration items that you might have questions about. Starting at the top, IP Version – yes, the IPsec VPN peers can either be assigned an IPv4 or IPv6 address. Remember, this is only the cleartext IP header outside of the ESP payload. Within the ESP packet (the payload) can contain an IPv4 or IPv6 header as well.

Next, the Remote Gateway value in our case is a Static IP Address, meaning it does not change. For Main Mode Phase-1 to be used, a static IP is required. The other Remote Gateway options on FortiGate here are Dialup User and Dynamic DNS.

Image 8.22 - Remote Gateway Type

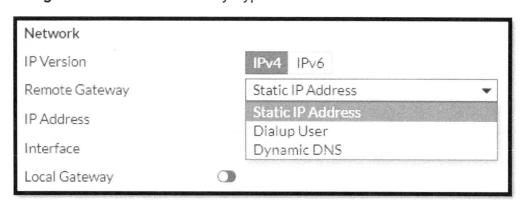

The Dialup User *Remote Gateway* would be used if this FortiGate was a Spoke in a Hub-and-Spoke IPsec topology and would use aggressive mode for Phase-I. The last Remote Gateway setting is Dynamic DNS. This allows FortiGate to use an IPsec peers FQDN IP address to form an IPsec tunnel with. Most of the time, this is used when the remote peer has a dynamically assigned IP or could be used to trigger a failover by updating a DNS record.

The next item is the <u>IP Address</u> setting; this is the IP for the remote IPsec peer and, in our case, is the FGT-B WAN interface. The next setting is <u>Interface</u>, which is the interface FortiGate expects to exchange ISAKMP messages and ESP packets. The next setting is <u>Local Gateway</u>; this setting can be used when there are multiple IP addresses assigned to the interface where the IPsec tunnel is built from. For example, if there was a secondary IP on WAN, we could tell IPsec to use 'this IP' to receive and send IPsec traffic for the remote IPsec peer.

Image 8.23 – IPsec Local Gateway Configuration

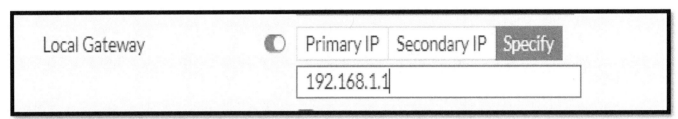

The next setting is Mode Config, a method to provide additional configuration settings to IPsec clients and provide clients with the required IP, DNS, WINS, and suffix to use while utilizing the IPsec tunnel. A Site-to-Site IPsec tunnel does not require this setting.

The next setting is the Keepalive Frequency. One of the issues with IPsec tunnels is timeouts because sessions age out if no traffic is passing. This can happen locally on FortiOS or a transit device. To keep an IPsec tunnel alive and active, it helps to periodically send data across the tunnel. This setting is meant to be used with NAT-T. The keepalive interval should be lower than the Lifetime Phase 1 & 2value(s) and is defined in seconds ranging from 0 – 900. The keepalive packet is 138 bytes sent via ISAKMP.

Next on the list is Dead Peer Detection (DPD); we spoke about this already some. FortiGate has three settings for DPD:

1) Disable
    a. FortiOS does not send DPD probes.
2) On-Idle
    a. FortiOS sends DPD probes if no <u>inbound</u> or <u>outbound</u> activity on the IPsec tunnel
3) On-Demand
    a. FortiOS only send DPD probes if no <u>inbound</u> ESP packets have been received.

Here is the CLI for the DPD Phase-1 interface.

```
config vpn ipsec phase1-interface
edit Phase-1_IPsec
NSE4-PASS (test_ph1) # set dpd ?
disable      Disable Dead Peer Detection.
on-idle      Trigger Dead Peer Detection when IPsec is idle.
on-demand    Trigger Dead Peer Detection when IPsec traffic is sent but no
reply is received from the peer.
..
set dpd-retryinveral 20
```

```
set dpd-retrycount 3
next
end
```

> *High volume of DPD exchange could impact the performance of IPsec. This is why the On-demand DPD option was created*

The next Phase-1 configuration item is Forward Error Correction (FEC). This is a new feature of 6.2 FortiOS.

FEC is defined in RFC 6363 https://tools.ietf.org/html/rfc6363, and its purpose is to protect against packet loss. This is accomplished by sending redundant data across IPsec.

Image 8.24 - IPsec Forward Error Correction Settings

This is used to control and correct errors that occur during transit but comes with a cost of more bandwidth. This subject is out of the scope of NSE4 certification and is covered in the NSE7.

The next item is Authentication. Here we are using the PSK method; FortiOS also allows authentication using certificates as well. IKEv1 is being used in this configuration. FortiGate also supports IKEv2. This IPsec tunnel is using Main Mode Phase-1 method because the two IPsec peers have known static IP addresses.

The Phase 1 Proposal is next; for the encryption, we specified AES256 value, the hash value of SHA1, Diffie-Hellman Group 5, and Key Lifetime 86400 (default).

Image 8.25 – Phase-1 Proposal

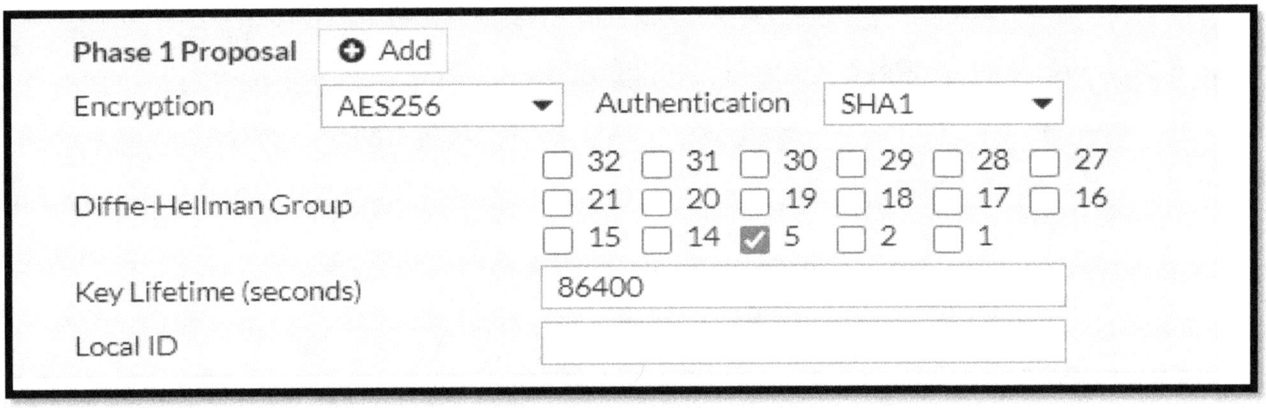

The last setting to touch on before we move onto the phase-2 settings is Local ID. This value is used to distinguish individual IPsec tunnels connected to the same Interface and Local Gateway. A common use cause is when multiple Dial-up VPNs are required to be built on a shared interface with only one IP available. By providing Local ID, this maps Dial-up IPsec users to the appropriate IPsec tunnel (Security Association). In the next configuration section, we cover the Phase-2 settings.

FortiGate-A Phase-2 GUI

Take your time and review Image 8.26 on the next page, which contains the Phase-2 configuration for FGT-A. We named FGT-A Phase-2 IPsec configuration FGT-A_IPsec_P2. The first thing to notice that is different from our Phase-1 configuration is that Phase-2 requires the configuration of Selectors. FGT-A has its Selectors source as 10.20.20.0/24 and destination 10.30.30.0/24. The encryption is AES256 and the hash SHA1. Next, the 'Enable Replay

---

Take note of IPsec tunnel MTU when using larger hashing algorithms like SHA512.

Detection' box is selected, meaning FortiGate keeps track of the ESP packet sequence and maintain a sliding window to prevent replay attacks. Next, Perfect Forward Secrecy (PSF) is used, meaning an additional DH exchange is performed to generate unique keys for the Phase-2 SA's, Group 5 is configured to be used. Next, note not only can we select traffic using source and destination IP addresses, but we can also select (or filter) traffic based on source and destination port numbers and IP protocol. Lastly, the Lifetime value is configured in seconds, which is the default. The other Lifetime option is Kilobytes or both. Once the 43200 seconds Lifetime expires, DH performs another exchange and provide fresh keys for the Phase-2 SA's.

Now that we have a handle on Phase 1 & 2 GUI configuration settings. Let's take a peek at the CLI equivalent.

<u>FortiGate-A Phase-A 1 & 2 CLI</u>

Image 8.26 – FortiGate-A IPsec Phase-2 Configuration

Here is the CLI output from the prior configuration on FGT-A:

IPsec-FGT-A (root) # show vpn ipsec phase1-interface

path=vpn.ipsec, objname=phase1-interface, tablename=(null), size=2640

```
config vpn ipsec phase1-interface
    edit "FGT-A_IPsec"
        set interface "wan"
        set peertype any
        set net-device disable
        set proposal aes256-sha1
        set dpd on-idle
        set dhgrp 5
        set nattraversal disable
        set remote-gw 192.168.209.2
        set psksecret ENC
e8CpltHvRrKW6kW2WnkHucUw8PLt+UUvCD4o4ACgZbeRx8azW+s8krkzECwvVzOWYDeXqcDewL+Sl
RcVSVsku47eH7KYVtQ+iAdgzT4Ld2ZExvRLYrnTLkaVMCKOR7MeAZ2WHdzu/PjCYVmmg0ZoUfkcOX
f/y2Zr6xCpT3Ay3MlAADumcQ5wOa6CSAfwfsCrYv39Uw==
    next
end
```

```
IPsec-FGT-A (root) # show vpn ipsec phase2-interface
path=vpn.ipsec, objname=phase2-interface, tablename=(null), size=676
config vpn ipsec phase2-interface
    edit "FGT-A_IPsec"
        set phase1name "FGT-A_IPsec"
        set proposal aes256-sha1
        set dhgrp 5
        set auto-negotiate enable
        set src-subnet 10.20.20.0 255.255.255.0
        set dst-subnet 10.30.30.0 255.255.255.0
    next
end
```

Most of the settings here are fairly intuitive in relation to the GUI settings. The one that might not be is the *peer type*; this is the Local ID setting. Since we did not specify a Local ID, this value is *any*. Also, you might have noticed the setting 'net-device disable'; this setting changes the behavior on a Dial-Up IPsec Hub device regarding IPsec virtual interfaces, which I will cover in our FortiGate Dial-up section.

<u>FortiGate-B Phase 1 & 2 CLI</u>

I won't pain you walking through the full GUI IPsec configuration on FortiGate-B here. So I will just provide you with the Phase-1 and Phase-2 settings we are working with.

```
IPsec-FGT-B (root) # 0: config vdom
0: edit root
```

```
0: config vpn ipsec phase1-interface
0: edit "FGT-B_IPsec"
0: set interface "wan1"
0: set peertype any
0: set net-device disable
0: set proposal aes256-sha1
0: set dpd on-idle
0: set dhgrp 5
0: set remote-gw 172.16.10.1
0: set psksecret ENC
GHaXjHD1ywdIkWW7quv2Y62ACq7gkPjeaxlN3O8Sd76gxOrq7ykHRiJ2bEYMxzz8/d7im3sJvsPJO
IB5J1dpLKPnXF1uc2GPv+BYtfqsjv8T5PYi5jsLYxbAKtwAkxN81l3g1B9fNvVRxWMlV6ZspzxM0h
iH1B7tYKIKOE0DUsxBgJRztAL1atEZfXi2vF0IvdqH2g==
0: end
0: end
0: config vdom
0: edit root
0: config vpn ipsec phase2-interface
0: edit "FGT-B_IPsec"
0: set phase1name "FGT-B_IPsec"
0: set proposal aes256-sha1
0: set dhgrp 5
0: set keepalive enable
0: set auto-negotiate enable
0: set src-subnet 10.30.30.0 255.255.255.0
0: set dst-subnet 10.20.20.0 255.255.255.0
0: end
```

The Phase-1 PSK hash is salted. Therefore they are unique on each FortiGate.

This covers our FGT-A and FGT-B Site-to-Site IPsec tunnel configuration, too easy, right? So the next question is, should our IPsec tunnel be up right now if we checked? Let's take a look via VPN -> IPsec Tunnels -> Custom:

Image 8.27 – IPsec Tunnel Status

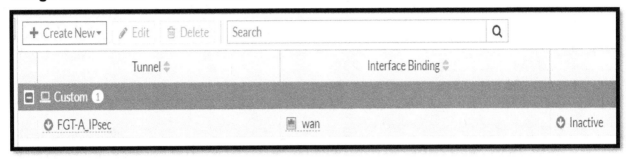

As you can see, the red down arrows are not a good indicator that our tunnel is up and operational. So what's the problem?

In this next section, I will try and bring up the tunnel we just built and go over the *other* required configuration to make traffic flow through this IPsec tunnel. Also, we will verify the tunnel's operational status and do some troubleshooting.

Policy and Routing

At this point, FGT-A and FGT-B have their respective IPsec configuration to form an IPsec Site-to-Site tunnel, so in theory, could we bring the tunnel up? And the answer is no. On FortiGate, we require at least one Firewall Policy Entry that references the IPsec tunnel of interest for Phase-1 ISAKMP to initiate. The policy we are going to build references a loopback interface. Once these policies are created, the IPsec tunnel should establish. Now, do you think our traffic can cross the tunnel?..

Nope, not yet! Because FortiGate does not know where to send our pings, so we need to add a host route that points to the IPsec tunnel interface. Now that we understand the additional configuration required for IPsec to function correctly, now it's time to configure it. First, on FGT-A, create the Firewall Policy Entry.

```
IPsec-FGT-A (root) #
0: config firewall policy
0: edit 0
0: set name "FGT-A_IPsec_FGT-B"
0: set srcintf "Lo_10.20.20.1"
0: set dstintf "FGT-A_IPsec"
0: set srcaddr "all"
0: set dstaddr "all"
0: set action accept
0: set schedule "always"
```

```
0: set service "ALL"
0: end
```

Note here the loopback interface has 10.20.20.1/32 assigned. The Policy Entry must contain the IPsec Phase-1 interface name within the destination field for egress traffic and source for ingress traffic, just like any other interface. The Next configuration is the routing statement:

```
0: config router static
0: edit 0
0: set dst 10.30.30.1 255.255.255.255
0: set device "FGT-A_IPsec"
0: end
0: end
```

Within the Static Route Entry, the device field must reference the Phase-1 interface for the IPsec tunnel. We are allowed to configure this because the IPsec tunnel is in Interface Mode. A Policy Mode tunnel would not allow us to point a static route to the virtual tunnel interface. Also, note here, the next-hope IP is not required for this to be functional. I replicated this configuration on the other FortiGate FGT-B in respect of local attributes and added bi-directional firewall policies between the IPsec tunnel interface and the loopback interface. Now let's double-check the status of our tunnel. I'm going to run the following debug set on FGT-A while I attempt to bring up the IPsec tunnel.

```
#diag vpn ike log-filter dst-addr4 192.168.209.2  // IPsec peer IP
#diag debug reset
#diag debug enable
#diag debug application ike -1
```



```
ike 0:FGT-A_IPsec:71:101: peer proposal is: peer:0:10.30.30.0-10.30.30.255:0,
me:0:10.20.20.0-10.20.20.255:0
ike 0:FGT-A_IPsec:71:FGT-A_IPsec:101: trying
ike 0:FGT-A_IPsec:71:FGT-A_IPsec:101: matched phase2
ike 0:FGT-A_IPsec:71:FGT-A_IPsec:101: autokey
ike 0:FGT-A_IPsec:71:FGT-A_IPsec:101: my proposal:
ike 0:FGT-A_IPsec:71:FGT-A_IPsec:101: proposal id = 1:
ike 0:FGT-A_IPsec:71:FGT-A_IPsec:101:    protocol id = IPSEC_ESP:
ike 0:FGT-A_IPsec:71:FGT-A_IPsec:101:    PFS DH group = 5
ike 0:FGT-A_IPsec:71:FGT-A_IPsec:101:      trans_id = ESP_AES_CBC (key_len =
256)
ike 0:FGT-A_IPsec:71:FGT-A_IPsec:101:      encapsulation =
ENCAPSULATION_MODE_TUNNEL
..
ike 0:FGT-A_IPsec:71:FGT-A_IPsec:101: replay protection enabled
ike 0:FGT-A_IPsec:71:FGT-A_IPsec:101: SA life soft seconds=42927.
ike 0:FGT-A_IPsec:71:FGT-A_IPsec:101: SA life hard seconds=43200.
..
```

```
ike 0:FGT-A_IPsec:71:FGT-A_IPsec:101: IPsec SA dec spi 03b94008 key
32:1A4FE8025722A21E62F1F7EFA3CB25C2B81EF048BB34597F644BE611617E8276 auth
20:1617342596E60C46E467DCF004E140AF88B0045B
ike 0:FGT-A_IPsec:71:FGT-A_IPsec:101: IPsec SA enc spi e65dff82 key
32:BF712F422F5362CF2B9F74957DC6E5D4D514471B2D9C627839293F5F020EC29F auth
20:F082C05DD51AA62B71FD3BAB334C0508929AC8D0
ike 0:FGT-A_IPsec:71:FGT-A_IPsec:101: added IPsec SA: SPIs=03b94008/e65dff82
ike 0:FGT-A_IPsec:71:FGT-A_IPsec:101: sending SNMP tunnel UP trap
ike 0:FGT-A_IPsec:71: enc ...
```

I bolded a few items of interest within the above debug output. We can see in this output part of the Phase-2 Negotiate taking place, and in the end, an SNMP tunnel up trap is sent. If you wish to confirm tunnel status, then go to the IPsec tunnel via the GUI, and make your way to *Monitor > IPsec Monitor > Refresh,* and we see green up arrows!

Next, let us test if our ICMP pings are successful across our brand-new IPsec tunnel. Essentially, I'm sourcing the loopback on FGT-A with my ping command and ping' ing FGT-B's loopback via IPsec tunnel. We will run the below debugs to verify connectivity.

Run-on FGT-A:

```
diag debug reset
diag debug enable
diag debug flow filter saddr 10.20.20.1    //FGT-A Loopback
diag debug flow filter daddr 10.30.30.1    //FGT-B Loopback
diag debug flow trace start 200
```

Run-on FGT-B

```
#diag sniffer packet any 'host 10.20.20.1 and host 10.30.30.1' 4
```

I want to come clean here, during my lab testing for this, I forgot to add a host route for the IPsec peer FGT-A (172.16.10.1) on FGT-B. So I only had one-way ISAKMP traffic and no return traffic. The moral of the story here, remember to have a route to your IPsec peer IP! Now we are ready for our ping test from FGT-A to FGT-B loopback addresses. See results below:

Results:

FGT-A

```
IPsec-FGT-A (root) # exe ping-options source 10.20.20.1
IPsec-FGT-A (root) # exe ping 10.30.30.1

PING 10.30.30.1 (10.30.30.1): 56 data bytes
id=20085 trace_id=201 func=print_pkt_detail line=5607 msg="vd-root:0 received
a packet(proto=1, 10.20.20.1:994->10.30.30.1:2048) from local. type=8,
code=0, id=994, seq=0."
id=20085 trace_id=201 func=init_ip_session_common line=5777 msg="allocate a
new session-0008db9d"
id=20085 trace_id=201 func=ipsecdev_hard_start_xmit line=788 msg="enter IPsec
interface-FGT-A_IPsec"
id=20085 trace_id=201 func=esp_output4 line=900 msg="IPsec encrypt/auth"
id=20085 trace_id=201 func=ipsec_output_finish line=617 msg="send to
172.16.10.2 via intf-wan"
64 bytes from 10.30.30.1: icmp_seq=0 ttl=255 time=1.4 ms
id=20085 trace_id=202 func=print_pkt_detail line=5607 msg="vd-root:0 received
a packet(proto=1, 10.20.20.1:994->10.30.30.1:2048) from local. type=8,
code=0, seq=1."
```

Within these debugs, we can confirm our IPsec tunnel is indeed up and allows traffic through!

FGT-B

```
IPsec-FGT-B (root) # diag sniffer packet any 'host 10.20.20.1 and host
10.30.30.1' 4
interfaces=[any]
filters=[host 10.20.20.1 and host 10.30.30.1]
20.237331 FGT-B_IPsec in 10.20.20.1 -> 10.30.30.1: icmp: echo request
20.237477 FGT-B_IPsec out 10.30.30.1 -> 10.20.20.1: icmp: echo reply
```

On the other side of the tunnel on FGT-B, we can see inbound packets coming through the tunnels, so we are good on this side as well! This completes our FortiGate Site-to-Site IPsec tunnel implementation. Note, this is the simplest IPsec implementation on FortiGate. You should definitely practice this lab for yourself because I guarantee if you work with FortiGate's, then at some point in time, you will be required to build a Site-to-Site IPsec tunnel with some stranger on the other side and work together to debug it! In the next section, we are going to walk through some IPsec debug commands, and I'm going to show you how to verify that IPsec traffic is indeed offloaded to the local NP ASIC.

Site to Site IPsec verification

The first command to know answers the simple question, is my IPsec tunnel up? Which is:

```
IPsec-FGT-B (global) # get ipsec tunnel list
```

Image 8.28 – IPsec Debug Confirm Tunnel Status

```
IPsec-FGT-B (global) # get ipsec tunnel list
NAME          REMOTE-GW        PROXY-ID-SOURCE         PROXY-ID-DESTINATION       STATUS TIMEOUT
FGT-B_IPsec  172.16.10.1:0   10.30.30.0/255.255.255.0 10.20.20.0/255.255.255.0 up     23070
```

This command runs the global level. Another simple IPsec debug command that must be run from the VDOM level is:

```
IPsec-FGT-B (root) # diagnose vpn ike status summary
connection: 1/40
IKE SA: created 1/41  established 1/1   times 9040/9040/9040 ms
IPsec SA: created 33/59  established 1/18   times 0/13/40 ms
```

The first line, 'IKA SA,' is our Phase-1 ISAKMP SA and shows us at a high level of how many SA's are established out of how many possible. We only have one Phase-1 on this FortiGate, and that one so happens to be established. The next line, 'IPsec SA' is for our Phase-2 establishment. The next command to know is:

```
IPsec-FGT-B (root) # diagnose vpn tunnel list
list all ipsec tunnel in vd 0
--------------------------------------------------------
name=FGT-B_IPsec ver=1 serial=1 192.168.209.2:0->172.16.10.1:0 dst_mtu=1500
bound_if=5 lgwy=static/1 tun=intf/0 mode=auto/1 encap=none/520
options[0208]=npu frag-rfc  run_state=0 accept_traffic=1 overlay_id=0

proxyid_num=1 child_num=0 refcnt=14 ilast=8 olast=8 ad=/0
stat: rxp=10 txp=26 rxb=1632 txb=1890
dpd: mode=on-idle on=1 idle=20000ms retry=3 count=0 seqno=3135
natt: mode=none draft=0 interval=0 remote_port=0
proxyid=FGT-B_IPsec proto=0 sa=1 ref=4 serial=1 auto-negotiate
  src: 0:10.30.30.0/255.255.255.0:0
  dst: 0:10.20.20.0/255.255.255.0:0
  SA:  ref=6 options=18227 type=00 soft=0 mtu=1438 expire=23126/0B
replaywin=2048
      seqno=9 esn=0 replaywin_lastseq=00000004 itn=0 qat=0 hash_search_len=1
  life: type=01 bytes=0/0 timeout=42932/43200
  dec: spi=e65dff84 esp=aes key=32
7c430115257a129ce89973a05fe0fea75dae0f241778261e0e9b3afa12e625a4
      ah=sha1 key=20 646d74207e567200b374502e2894a38b71a839f6
  enc: spi=03b94009 esp=aes key=32
9ae28c18bcb39b021460b0ba3c32fd83df6ac3fd57c2081b24761890ff6377d4
```

```
        ah=sha1 key=20 c92df0f23aca4592071dd9e83f3cc1aa08e8a16e
  dec:pkts/bytes=5/748, enc:pkts/bytes=14/1554
  npu_flag=03 npu_rgwy=172.16.10.1 npu_lgwy=192.168.209.2 npu_selid=0
dec_npuid=1 enc_npuid=1
run_tally=1
```

The 'diagnose vpn tunnel list' is useful for a few different things the big one is to check to see if traffic is offloaded to the local NP ASIC or not. The field/value that indicates if traffic is offloaded or not is 'npu_flag=03'. The '03' here means that traffic for both ingress and egress ESP packet are indeed offloaded to NP ASIC. Here are all the possible values for the npu_flag field:

1) npu_flag=00
    a. Indicates that ingress & egress ESP packets are not offloaded
2) npu_flag=01
    a. Indicates only egress ESP packets can be offloaded, ingress ESP packets are handled by the kernel
3) npu_flag=02
    a. Indicates only ingress ESP packets can be offloaded, egress ESP packets are handled by the kernel
4) npu_flag=03
    a. Indicates that both ingress & egress ESP packets are offloaded
5) npu_flag=20
    a. Indicates transform set is not supported by NP ASIC.

knowing if ESP packets are offloaded or not is very important for IPsec devices that are responsible for thousands of IPsec tunnels because the CPU alone might not be able to handle the processing load by itself. For a smaller environment where you are not pushing the limits of the hardware, then it does not matter as much other than generating latency. Note that only certain algorithms can be offloaded to certain NP ASIC chips. For details on these requirements, I would point you to the FortiGate hardware guide Fortinet offers:

https://fortinetweb.s3.amazonaws.com/docs.fortinet.com/v2/attachments/feb1d168-6d39-11ea-9384-00505692583a/fortios-hardware-acceleration-640.pdf

Sometimes it might be necessary to disable the NP ASIC for ISAKMP/ESP traffic, this can be performed within the Phase-1 configuration:

```
# config vpn ipsec phase1-interface
# edit Phase_1
# set npu-offload disable
# end
```

This might be necessary if you need to perform a packet capture because captures are only possible when traffic is not offloaded to ASIC. The kernel loses viability once the session is handed over the NP chip. Now back to the output at hand. The next line to review is:

```
..

dec:pkts/bytes=5/748, enc:pkts/bytes=14/1554

..
```

Did you know it is possible to decrypt ESP packet via Wireshark?
https://kb.fortinet.com/kb/documentLink.do?externalID=FD48280

For you Cisco folks out there, this should ring a bell. Your *Encrypts* and *Decrypts* which indicate if you see bi-directional traffic on an IPsec tunnel and how much. The last thing I want to point out in this output is 'mtu=1438'. It is important to know the MTU of your IPsec VPN because this could cause IP fragmentation, which could lead to latency. IPsec allocates different tunnel MTUs depending on the transform set used (3DES-SHA1 , AES256/SHA256..etc). From a theory standpoint, we could easily look at this output and see out Quick Mode Selectors or SPI's and secret keys. The last item I want to point out from the prior IPsec output is **replaywin_lastseq;** we can confirm that anti-replay is enabled, and the last sequence number received was 00000004.

Next, sometimes it might be necessary to bring up or take down an IPsec tunnel for testing in the CLI. The GUI has this option under Monitor -> IPsec, but the GUI may not always be available. In the CLI, the commands are:

```
IPsec-FGT-B (root) # diagnose vpn tunnel
down          Shut down tunnel.
up            Activate tunnel.
list          List all tunnel.
dialup-list   List dialup tunnel. [Take 0-8 arg(s)]
flush         Flush tunnel SAs. [Take 0-8 arg(s)]
delinbsa      Remove tunnel sa.
deloutbsa     Remove tunnel sa.
stat          Tunnel statistic info.
```

```
IPsec-FGT-B (root) # diagnose vpn tunnel down Your_Phase_2_Name
phase2    Name of phase2.
```

The last IPsec debug command I want to provide a rundown on is:

```
IPsec-FGT-B (root) # diagnose vpn ike gateway list
```

```
vd: root/0
name: FGT-B_IPsec
version: 1
interface: wan1 5
addr: 192.168.209.2:500 -> 172.16.10.1:500
```

```
created: 69367s ago
IKE SA: created 1/1  established 1/1  time 9040/9040/9040 ms
IPsec SA: created 1/19  established 1/18  time 0/13/40 ms

   id/spi: 40 4efe5d0442e33f4f/ba3585522c8bdc41
   direction: responder
   status: established 69367-69358s ago = 9040ms
   proposal: aes256-sha1
   key: 413fbe47a04e1152-c3cbd59fceb25aee-0558cd8c91869e25-ddb22ebe12c744ef
   lifetime/rekey: 86400/16771
   DPD sent/recv: 00000c7d/00000d4c
```

Here are the debug details around the ISAKMP SA for the Phase-1 and we can see the proposal selected is 'aes256-sha1' and details around the SPI and key being used. Sometimes it is necessary to know which IPsec peer is the Responder and which is the Initiator when troubleshooting IPsec. We can see here that FGT-B is indeed the responder. To make FortiGate the Responder turn off Phase-1 setting 'auto-negotiate' .

There are a lot of troubleshooting commands for IPsec, but these are the basic ones to know about. For advance trouble shooting most the time you will open a TAC case. Below are my personal IPsec debug commands I use when working odd IPsec types of issues that could be useful to you sometime in the future.

======Session One======

#diag vpn ike config list

#diag vpn ike gateway list

#diag vpn tunnel list

#get vpn ipsec tunnel details

#diag vpn ike status summary

#diag vpn ike status detailed

#get vpn ipsec tunnel summary

#get vpn ipsec stats tunnel

#diag vpn tunnel stat

#get vpn ipsec stats crypto

#diag vpn ipsec status

#diag vpn ike crypto stats

#get ipsec tunnel list

#diag netlink interface list

#diagnose vpn ike routes list

#diag vpn ike errors

#diagnose vpn ike counts

#diag vpn ike log terminal stats

=====IPSEC FILTER Session Two======

diag vpn ike log-filter dst-addr4 172.16.10.1

diag debug reset

diag debug enable

diag debug console timestamp enable

diag debug application ike -1

===================================

This wraps up IPsec tunnel verification and Site-to-Site topology. The next configuration we are going to review in this Chapter is IPsec Dial-Up.

FortiGate Hub and Spoke Implementation

If you are looking into FortiGate SDWAN or currently manage FortiGate SDWAN deployment(s), then this section is critical for you to know about. Almost all SDWAN deployments I have been involved in have been based on the IPsec Hub and Spoke topology. Fortinet split the NSE4 topics into infrastructure and security because of architectures like Hub-and-Spoke. These IPsec topologies are the roads and highways that all other network traffic use. If your Hub-and-Spoke IPsec architecture does not have a solid design, redundancy, and a great operational posture, nothing else is going to work right within your network.

I have spent many hours (if not days) configuring and troubleshooting Hub and spoke IPsec VPNs, and it is a topology that is not going away. The Hub-and-Spoke topology architecture is commonly used within the large enterprise and recently within Fortinet SDWAN design and deployments.

Image 8.29 – Hub and Spoke IPsec Diagram

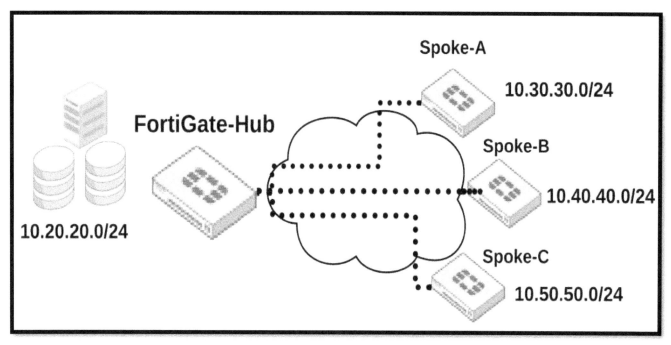

I'm going to start us off with a simple Hub-and-Spoke deployment implementation. In this example, we are going to be working with FortiGate to FortiGate Hub-and-Spoke IPsec and routing configuration. I'm going to follow the same format as the Site-to-Site configuration section. So firstly, we are going to review a high-level diagram before we get started with our configuration on the FortiGate's. Check out Image 8.29:

- FortiGate **Hub** WAN IP = 172.16.10.1
- FortiGate Spoke-**A** WAN IP = 192.168.209.2
- FortiGate Spoke-**B** WAN IP = 192.168.40.12
- FortiGate Spoke-**C** WAN IP = 192.168.50.13

We have three remote sites with FortiGate as their gateway, Spoke-A, Spoke-B, and Spoke-C, that connect to a FortiGate Hub device. Each Spoke has a dynamically assigned IP address and, therefore, must use Phase-1 aggressive mode. FortiGate-Hub is going to act as our IPsec concentrator. The first device to configure is the Hub; we will go ahead and take care of that piece of the puzzle. I'm going to go straight to the CLI for this configuration since GUI images are referenced in the prior configuration sections. See CLI Hub IPsec configuration:

```
IPsec-FGT-Hub (root) # 0: config vdom
0: edit root
0: config vpn ipsec phase1-interface
```

```
0: edit "Primary_Hub"
0: set type dynamic
0: set interface "wan"
0: set mode aggressive
0: set peertype any
0: set net-device enable
0: set proposal aes256-sha1
0: set dpd on-idle
0: set dhgrp 5
0: set nattraversal disable
0: set psksecret Password123
0: unset dpd-retryinterval
0: set dpd-retryinterval 60
0: end
0: end
..
0: config vpn ipsec phase2-interface
0: edit "Primary_Hub"
0: set phase1name "Primary_Hub"
0: set proposal aes256-sha1
0: set dhgrp 5
0: set keepalive enable
0: end
0: end
```

The main difference in the initial configuration so far is that the Phase-1 Type is dynamic, Phase-1 will use aggressive mode and we are using net-device enabled. Now let's take a look at the Spoke-C side configuration.

```
config vpn ipsec phase1-interface
    edit "Spoke-C_IPsec"
        set interface "Spoke-C_808"
        set mode aggressive
        set peertype any
        set net-device disable
        set proposal aes256-sha1
        set dpd on-idle
        set dhgrp 5
        set nattraversal disable
        set remote-gw 172.16.10.1
        set psksecret Password123
    next
end
config vpn ipsec phase2-interface
    edit "Spoke-C"
        set phase1name "Spoke-C_IPsec"
```

```
        set proposal aes256-sha1
        set dhgrp 5
        set auto-negotiate enable
        set src-subnet 10.50.50.0 255.255.255.0
        set dst-subnet 10.20.20.0 255.255.255.0
    next
end
```

Note, I've added a host route for IPsec peer IP and policies to allow IPsec traffic on all peers. We can check the tunnel status by running the ike debug provided earlier and output is as followed:

```
ike 4:Spoke-C_IPsec:625: initiator: aggressive mode get 1st response...
ike 4:Spoke-C_IPsec:625: VID DPD AFCAD71368A1F1C96B8696FC77570100
ike 4:Spoke-C_IPsec:625: DPD negotiated
ike 4:Spoke-C_IPsec:625: VID FORTIGATE 8299031757A36082C6A621DE00000000
ike 4:Spoke-C_IPsec:625: peer is FortiGate/FortiOS (v0 b0)
ike 4:Spoke-C_IPsec:625: VID FRAGMENTATION 4048B7D56EBCE88525E7DE7F00D6C2D3
ike 4:Spoke-C_IPsec:625: VID FRAGMENTATION
4048B7D56EBCE88525E7DE7F00D6C2D3C0000000
ike 4:Spoke-C_IPsec:625: peer identifier IPV4_ADDR 172.16.10.1
ike 4:Spoke-C_IPsec:625: negotiation result
ike 4:Spoke-C_IPsec:625: proposal id = 1:
ike 4:Spoke-C_IPsec:625:    protocol id = ISAKMP:
ike 4:Spoke-C_IPsec:625:       trans_id = KEY_IKE.
ike 4:Spoke-C_IPsec:625:       encapsulation = IKE/none
ike 4:Spoke-C_IPsec:625:          type=OAKLEY_ENCRYPT_ALG, val=AES_CBC, key-len=256
ike 4:Spoke-C_IPsec:625:          type=OAKLEY_HASH_ALG, val=SHA.
ike 4:Spoke-C_IPsec:625:          type=AUTH_METHOD, val=PRESHARED_KEY.
ike 4:Spoke-C_IPsec:625:          type=OAKLEY_GROUP, val=MODP1536.
ike 4:Spoke-C_IPsec:625: ISAKMP SA lifetime=86400
ike 4:Spoke-C_IPsec:625: NAT-T unavailable
ike 4:Spoke-C_IPsec:625: ISAKMP SA 37e1338fed54af1e/add2c17dda926a9a key
32:08CFF7B525585C69A534FC9BA1444F7B90355C160515FB5F5D1089A5485E21D6
ike 4:Spoke-C_IPsec:625: PSK authentication succeeded
ike 4:Spoke-C_IPsec:625: authentication OK
ike 4:Spoke-C_IPsec:625: add INITIAL-CONTACT
ike 4:Spoke-C_IPsec:625: enc
37E1338FED54AF1EADD2C17DDA926A9A081004010000000000000500B0000185D27592FB2CF5
9DEEAAED76AF8D8978EA468EE830000001C000000010110600237E1338FED54AF1EADD2C17DDA
926A9A
ike 4:Spoke-C_IPsec:625: out
37E1338FED54AF1EADD2C17DDA926A9A081004010000000000000005C63EADF6F0CEF918584FFC
6ED7375DEE4B5CC176BAAE795CE2612EB097FF5D66CB717CEF4153ABB6A4E089FE9620C7B126A
AB912190F473C5A8F65F5FD10D8876
```

```
ike 4:Spoke-C_IPsec:625: sent IKE msg (agg_i2send): 192.168.50.13:500-
>172.16.10.1:500, len=92, id=37e1338fed54af1e/add2c17dda926a9a
ike 4:Spoke-C_IPsec:625: established IKE SA 37e1338fed54af1e/add2c17dda926a9a
ike 4:Spoke-C_IPsec: set oper up
ike 4:Spoke-C_IPsec: schedule auto-negotiate
ike 4:Spoke-C_IPsec:625: no pending Quick-Mode negotiations
ike 4:Spoke-C_IPsec:Spoke-C: IPsec SA connect 37 192.168.50.13->172.16.10.1:0
ike 4:Spoke-C_IPsec:Spoke-C: using existing connection
ike 4:Spoke-C_IPsec:Spoke-C: config found
ike 4:Spoke-C_IPsec:Spoke-C: IPsec SA connect 37 192.168.50.13-
>172.16.10.1:500 negotiating
ike 4:Spoke-C_IPsec:625: cookie 37e1338fed54af1e/add2c17dda926a9a:13cab08f
ike 4:Spoke-C_IPsec:625:Spoke-C:9022: initiator selectors 0
0:10.50.50.0/255.255.255.0:0:0->0:10.20.20.0/255.255.255.0:0:0
ike 4:Spoke-C_IPsec:625: enc
```

Take a few moments to review the debug output and generate some questions. This is a great opportunity for folks that have not had to the *opportunity* to troubleshoot IPsec on FortiGate's.

If you start at the top of the debug output, you can see that Phase-1 is running in aggressive mode. We can conclude this from the explicit message:

```
..Spoke-C_IPsec:625: initiator: aggressive mode..
```

But also, if you remember, aggressive mode sends the Peer ID in clear text! So we can also extract out IPsec peer ID from the debugs:

```
..Spoke-C_IPsec:625: peer identifier IPV4_ADDR 172.16.10.1..
```

Next, I want to touch on the Phase-2 Quick Mode selectors. When I worked with Cisco devices, one of the checkboxes for an IPsec tunnel to come up was to be sure the Selectors matched; this is not the case for FortiGate's.

I want to tell you a quick story, back at my first Network Analyst Gig at a large MSSP, one of my first days, and I was training with one of my leads. And just for context, I had no prior FortiGate/Fortinet experience, only Cisco at this point in time.

So I was sitting behind him watching him work with one of the MSSP customers, and he was configuring an IPsec Site-to-Site VPN on their FortiGate cloud firewall. I overheard the conversation between him, and the customer told him their Encryption Domains (Selectors) they would be sent to us, but instead of configuring these values, he placed all zero's:

0.0.0.0/0.0.0.0

for the source and destination, Quick Mode Selectors and my immediate response was, "Hey man, and I think that might take down their network" because coming from a Cisco background, the quad zeros would match everything for an IPSec tunnel.

However, he looked back at me and grinned and said, 'Howard man, I got this!'. He later told me that he was glad I recognized that as a potential problem, and it showed I am familiar with

Cisco IPsec implementations. After this experience, I was thoroughly confused on how FortiGate Phase-2 Selectors worked. When I found that on FortiGate, we can just place quad zeros to match any Phase-2 Selector, I thought this was the absolute coolest feature ever. He later told me we could just point Static Route(s) to a virtual tunnel interface to define *Interesting Traffic*. So the moral of the story FortiGate running IPsec Interface Mode is not required to explicitly match the received Phase-2 Selector values.

Now let me clarify, I said FortiGate does require this; however, the other side of the IPsec tunnel might require FortiGate to send explicit Quick Mode Selectors values for Phase-2 to establish. I believe ASA's had this behavior at one point in time, which was very annoying when there were like 50+ Phase-2 Selector pairs to match. For static Site-to-Site IPsec VPN's FortiGate's has a feature to automatically match receive selector values. This can be enabled via:

```
IPsec-FGT-A (FGT-A_IPsec) # show ful | grep mesh
        set mesh-selector-type subnet
subnet     Enable addition of matching subnet selector.
```

This allows Address object groups to be configured and reference for dynamic Selectors to be created. Details on this can be found via:

https://kb.fortinet.com/kb/documentLink.do?externalID=FD36473

This is all I want to touch on right now regarding Phase-2 Selectors on FortiGate. The next item to complete for our Hub-and-Spoke IPsec VPN is verification. We are going to look at the established tunnels and some routing!

Hub and Spoke IPsec Verification

In this example, we have three spokes connected to one Hub FortiGate. On the Hub, we are going to confirm our three Spoke are indeed up.

```
IPsec-FGT-Hub (global) # get ipsec tunnel list
NAME          REMOTE-GW         PROXY-ID-SOURCE         PROXY-ID-DESTINATION     STATUS TIMEOUT
Primary_Hub  0.0.0.0:0
..
Primary_Hub_0 192.168.209.2:0  10.20.20.0/10.20.20.255  10.30.30.0/10.30.30.255  up
Primary_Hub_1 192.168.40.12:0  10.20.20.0/10.20.20.255  10.40.40.0/10.40.40.255  up
Primary_Hub_2 192.168.50.13:0  10.20.20.0/10.20.20.255  10.50.50.0/10.50.50.255  up
```

At first glance, we can see our three Spoke are up. I've bolded a few important items in the output.

```
Primary_Hub_0 192.168.209.2
Primary_Hub_1 192.168.40.12
Primary_Hub_2 192.168.50.13
```

Here list the Spoke IPsec peer IP addresses. In a production environment, these IP's would be public ones. When Dynamic IPsec is used, multiple peers can connect to a single Phase-1 and Phase-2 configuration on the IPsec concentrator FortiGate. When the *net-device* setting is enabled, these tunnels are indicated by the name of the Phase-1 name configuration with an appended '_x' value to notate an individual IPsec tunnel. Next, let's look at Spoke-C SA:

```
..
IPsec-FGT-Hub (root) # diagnose vpn tunnel list
..
------------------------------------------------------------
name=Primary_Hub_2 ver=1 serial=7 172.16.10.1:0->192.168.50.13:0 dst_mtu=1500
bound_if=4 lgwy=static/1 tun=intf/0 mode=dial_inst/3 encap=none/720
options[02d0]=create_dev no-sysctl rgwy-chg frag-rfc  accept_traffic=1
overlay_id=0

 parent=Primary_Hub index=2
proxyid_num=1 child_num=0 refcnt=11 ilast=14 olast=14 ad=/0
stat: rxp=0 txp=0 rxb=0 txb=0
dpd: mode=on-idle on=1 idle=60000ms retry=3 count=0 seqno=0
natt: mode=none draft=0 interval=0 remote_port=0
proxyid=Primary_Hub proto=0 sa=1 ref=2 serial=1 add-route
  src: 0:10.20.20.0-10.20.20.255:0
  dst: 0:10.50.50.0-10.50.50.255:0
  SA:  ref=3 options=283 type=00 soft=0 mtu=1438 expire=33729/0B
replaywin=1024
       seqno=1 esn=0 replaywin_lastseq=00000000 itn=0 qat=0 hash_search_len=1
  life: type=01 bytes=0/0 timeout=43191/43200
  dec: spi=03b94014 esp=aes key=32
50e67111a711cf17a6e5d58c1e59f39f63d7a3f6234fc49ede70345babc3510c
       ah=sha1 key=20 0b83e0abf5009338b147dffbe9fa3b2aaac2e628
  enc: spi=519b3fc3 esp=aes key=32
78f77310d88bf9af164ec10a6421d01c842e81cf46950a9b543a9972f4ef41ee
       ah=sha1 key=20 7a9a6e33ee05e4909fb8bdf0b2dded0ee2007e64
  dec:pkts/bytes=0/0, enc:pkts/bytes=0/0
```

Just like a Site-to-Site IPsec tunnel we can extract the SA's, key information and many other specific values for each tunnel. Another good command we can use to extract IPsec tunnel details is:

```
IPsec-FGT-Hub (root) # get vpn ipsec tunnel details
gateway
  name: 'Primary_Hub_2'
  type: route-based
  local-gateway: 172.16.10.1:0 (static)
  remote-gateway: 192.168.50.13:0 (dynamic)
  mode: ike-v1
  interface: 'wan' (4)
  rx  packets: 0  bytes: 0  errors: 0
  tx  packets: 0  bytes: 0  errors: 2
```

```
dpd: on-idle/negotiated   idle: 60000ms   retry: 3   count: 0
selectors
  name: 'Primary_Hub'
  auto-negotiate: disable
  mode: tunnel
  src: 0:10.20.20.0-10.20.20.255:0
  dst: 0:10.50.50.0-10.50.50.255:0
  SA
    lifetime/rekey: 43200/32978
    mtu: 1438
    tx-esp-seq: 1
    replay: enabled
    qat: 0
    inbound
      spi: 03b94014
      enc:  aes-cb
50e67111a711cf17a6e5d58c1e59f39f63d7a3f6234fc49ede70345babc3510c
      auth:   sha1  0b83e0abf5009338b147dffbe9fa3b2aaac2e628
    outbound
      spi: 519b3fc3
      enc:  aes-cb
78f77310d88bf9af164ec10a6421d01c842e81cf46950a9b543a9972f4ef41ee
      auth:   sha1  7a9a6e33ee05e4909fb8bdf0b2dded0ee2007e64
```

From this output we can see the remote IPsec peer is indeed dynamic. We can see how much information has been exchanged through this tunnel. We can see the current sequence number value and of course the SPI's. The next thing I want to look at with you are the Spoke routes within the routing table.

IPsec Reverse Route Injection Add-Route

Below is the routing table output from our Hub-and-Spoke example:

```
IPsec-FGT-Hub (root) # get router info routing-table  all

Routing table for VRF=0
Codes: K - kernel, C - connected, S - static, R - RIP, B - BGP
       O - OSPF, IA - OSPF inter area
       N1 - OSPF NSSA external type 1, N2 - OSPF NSSA external type 2
       E1 - OSPF external type 1, E2 - OSPF external type 2
       i - IS-IS, L1 - IS-IS level-1, L2 - IS-IS level-2, ia - IS-IS inter
area
       * - candidate default

S*      0.0.0.0/0 [10/0] via 172.16.10.2, wan
C       10.20.20.1/32 is directly connected, Lo_10.20.20.1
```

```
S       10.30.30.0/24 [15/0] via 192.168.209.2, Primary_Hub_0
S       10.40.40.0/24 [15/0] via 192.168.40.12, Primary_Hub_1
S       10.50.50.0/24 [15/0] via 192.168.50.13, Primary_Hub_2
C       172.16.10.0/24 is directly connected, wan
C       192.168.1.0/24 is directly connected, lan
```

I want to talk about the highlighted lines in this output. I did not add these route manuals under #config router static. So how did they appear? If you are familiar with RRI (Reverse Route Inject), which is Cisco lingo, then you can problem guess how this occurs. FortiGate just calls this 'Add-Route' under IPsec configuration, and how this occurs is Hub FortiGate parses the source Quick Mode Select received by IPsec Spoke peers and installs a route in the Routing Table for this subnet that points to the specific Spoke tunnel that leads to that peer.

It is common for any newly added Static route from IPsec Spoke to be redistributed into a routing protocol like BGP, so there can be bi-directional communication with spoke sites and internal resources.

The next item we need to discuss is FortiGate has two methods to handle Spoke IPsec tunnel interfaces and how traffic is steered to those tunnels. This behavior is controlled with the net-device setting under the Phase-1 configuration. The Route Table output above is from *net-device enable* setting

IPsec Net Device setting

The net-device setting is an important setting to understand. This controls how FortiOS handles the creation of IPsec virtual interfaces. When net-device is enabled, the kernel creates a virtual networking interface. We can find this virtual interface by looking in the debugs:

```
IPsec-FGT-Hub (root) # diagnose vpn tunnel list
..
--------------------------------------------------------
name=Primary_Hub_2
..
 parent=Primary_Hub index=2
..
```

Spoke-C was actually assigned index 2 off of the parent interface, which is the Phase-1 name. When using this method IPsec sends clear text packets to the virtual interface and uses the associated SA to create an ESP packet. We can see these interface in the kernel via:

```
IPsec-FGT-Hub (root) # diagnose netlink interface list | grep Hub
if=Primary_Hub family=00 type=768 index=25 mtu=1500 link=0 master=0
if=Primary_Hub_0 family=00 type=768 index=30 mtu=1438 link=25 master=0
if=Primary_Hub_1 family=00 type=768 index=31 mtu=1438 link=25 master=0
if=Primary_Hub_2 family=00 type=768 index=32 mtu=1438 link=25 master=0
```

Note, index=32 is a global index for all interfaces on FortiGate. The index=2, from IPsec debug is specifically related to the parent interface.

IPsec behavior changes when net-device is set to the disabled, hence when a Spoke connects to the Hub, a virtual interface is not created. All Spoke's share the same Phase-1 virtual interface. See below CLI output:

```
IPsec-FGT-Hub (Primary_Hub) # show ful
..
        set net-device disable
        set tunnel-search selectors
..
```

What this means is that IPsec needs to use a different method to map clear text traffic to the correct Spoke SA. You might be asking yourself why *net-device disable* was created. Essentially, for some very large Hub-and-Spoke deployments, the virtual interface can cause problems regarding the creation and removal process. So the option net-device disable was added to accommodate large deployments used with certain platforms.

To steer traffic to the correct SA when net-device is disabled, the setting 'tunnel-search selectors' is used by default. This tells IPsec to use the route injected into IKE from the destination Selector to steer traffic to the correct SA; IKE routes are found via:

```
IPsec-FGT-A (root) # diagnose vpn ike routes list
vd: root/0
vrf: 0
dst: 10.50.50.0/255.255.255.0
next-hop: 192.168.50.13  //Spoke-C
interface: Primary_Hub/25
distance: 15
priority: 0
overlap: use-new
virtual: false
ha-only: false
count: 1
```

The last option that can be used within the tunnel-search setting is 'next-hop', which is used when Spoke routes are learned via a routing protocol, see CLI:

```
IPsec-FGT-Hub (Primary_Hub) # set tunnel-search next-hop
```

That wraps up the FortiGate Hub-and-Spoke configuration section. In the next section, I'm going to walk through a FortiClient IPsec VPN configuration on FortiGate.

FortiClient IPsec Remote Access

Most organizations either use a remote access VPN based on SSL/TLS or IPsec. In general, FortiGate's IPsec VPNs are faster than its SSL/TLS since ESP packets are offloaded to the NP ASIC, which we know saves CPU cycles. Also, IPsec Dial-up inherently provides two-factor authentication because of the authentication requirement during the Phase-1 establishment, and users are required to provide their credentials (username/password) after the Phase-1 is complete during XAuth. This is another topic I would say to know by heart because I guarantee you if you continue to work with FortiGate's, you will be responsible one day to build and maintain an IPsec VPN for FortiClient.

This section aims to walk through building a remote access IPsec VPN or Dial-up (DU) for short. DU IPsec for remote users requires a couple of other parameters that fall under XAuth (extended authentication) and Mode Config. We are going to use the same FortiGate Hub device to perform this configuration. Check out Image 8.30.

- Remote Access Hub IP = 172.16.10.1
- FortiClient IP = 192.168.209.53

Image 8.30 - IPsec Remote Access VPN

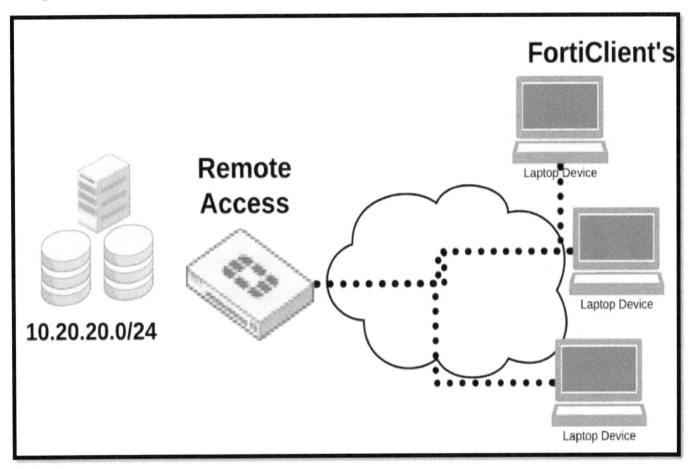

Most of the time, when folks use this type of VPN, they are at home or on public WiFi that could be anywhere. Once again, we do not know what the source IP will be, which is ok.

We begin with the configuration on the FortiGate Hub, and this time I am going to use the VPN

Image 8.31 – FortiClient Remote Access IPsec VPN - Wizard

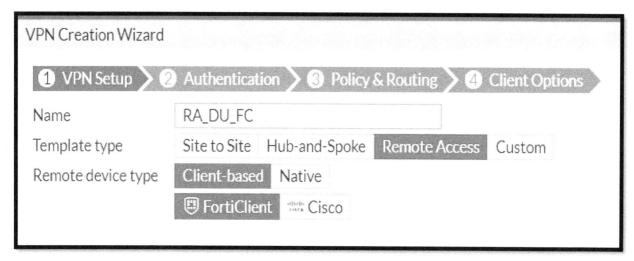

Wizard, do not hate on the Wizard folks (it is meant to make our lives easier!). I promise we will look over the CLI config as well! Go to VPN -> IPsec Tunnels -> Create New. We will call this tunnel RA_DU_FC for Remote Access Dial-up FortiClient.

In Image 8.31, we selected 'Remote Access' Template Type and Client-based for FortiClient. Next, we set up authentication parameters in Image 8.32.

Image 8.32 - FortiClient Remote Access IPsec VPN - Authentication

The local user group for XAuth authentication is *Guest-group*, which is a default built-in FortiOS object. A PSK is used for the Phase-1 authentication method using Password123. The VPN is bound to the WAN interface. Next, check out Image 8.33 on the next page.

Image 8. 33 - FortiClient Remote Access IPsec VPN – Policy & Routing

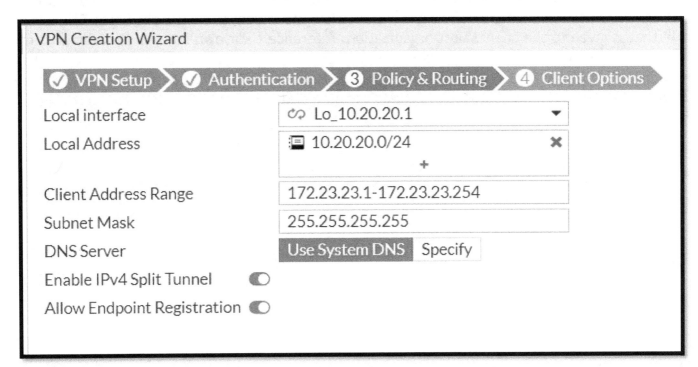

I'm using the local loopback interface as the local interface Lo_10.20.20.1 (10.20.20.1/32); most of the time, this is the LAN or internal port on FortiGate. The only reason the Local interface is required here is so a script on the backend can create an associated Firewall Policy Entry between the ingress Interface and RA_DU_FC tunnel interface. You may build other policies as needed. The Local Address value is significant for Remote Access VPNs because this is part of the split tunnel configuration. When split tunneling is enabled, this means only interesting traffic is routed through the client's IPsec VPN. Interesting traffic is defined within the Local Address object. It is common to use RFC 1918 address space here if you want all the clients' private communication to be routed through the IPsec tunnel but no public traffic. Also, if the split tunnel is disabled, then all traffic is routed through the IPsec tunnel to the FortiGate concentrator. The organization could do this for a few reasons, one of them being they wish to scrub the user's traffic with local UTM features before forwarding traffic to the Internet or restrict what users download and generate logs from their traffic to be referenced later.

Next, here is the Client Address Range setting, which is the address space the *Mode Config* function uses to allocate remote IPsec clients' IP addresses. You can think of this as your DHCP range. Clients are assigned a /32 host subnet mask by Mode Config. Next, specify the DNS server IP that is given to the client. Most organizations reference their own internal DNS server here, so internal server FQDN's can be resolved correctly. The last item to touch on here is Allow Endpoint Registration. FortiGate provides FortiClient registration access. This is where FortiGate stores metadata about the client machine that could be referenced for later use.

Image 8.34 - FortiClient Remote Access IPsec VPN – Client Options

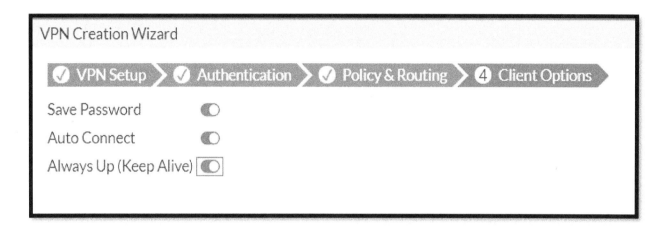

See Image 8.34; this stage defines client-side settings. Essentially, Save Password allows FortiClient to Save a VPN password locally. Auto Connect forces a VPN connection attempt automatically after FortiClient opens. Always Up is a keep-alive mechanism that causes the client to send data across a VPN when no traffic is on the tunnel to keep the session up. For more information around these settings, see:

https://kb.fortinet.com/kb/documentLink.do?externalID=FD41185

Once we click finish, FortiOS provide a synopsis of everything relating to the new IPsec DU VPN configuration. See Image 8.35:

Image 8. 35 - FortiClient Remote Access IPsec VPN – Complete

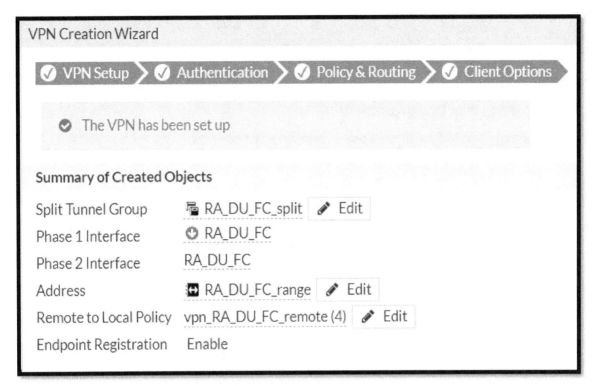

This last slide within the IPsec Remote Access Wizard provides details on a few Firewall Objects that were created. Split Tunnel Group, RA_DU_split is an address object that contains the network 10.20.20.0/24 that we defined earlier. The Phase-1 & Phase-2 newly created interfaces are shown. Next, The Address RA_DU_FC_range is used for IPsec Mode Config to assign IPsec clients IP addresses and DNS IP in our case. Remote to Local Policy vpn_RA_DU_FC_remote is an address object that holds the IP address of our loopback interface 10.20.20.1, which we will later use for testing. Lastly, it is notated we enabled Endpoint Registration.

Now that our brand-new Remote Access IPsec tunnel is built, its time to see what the configuration looks like in the CLI. First, take a look at the firewall policy that was built in the background for us.

```
IPsec-FGT-Hub (root) # show firewall policy
..
    edit 4
        set name "vpn_RA_DU_FC_remote"
        set uuid 85ce9f90-f6c0-51ea-8a9d-d919a1eeb052
        set srcintf "RA_DU_FC"
        set dstintf "Lo_10.20.20.1"
        set srcaddr "RA_DU_FC_range"
```

```
            set dstaddr "10.20.20.0/24"
            set action accept
            set schedule "always"
            set service "ALL"
            set comments "VPN: RA_DU_FC (Created by VPN wizard)"
            set nat enable
        next
end
```

Does anything look familiar?

Next, take a look at the Phase-1 configuration.

```
IPsec-FGT-Hub (root) # config vpn ipsec phase1-interface
IPsec-FGT- Hub (phase1-interface) # show
config vpn ipsec phase1-interface

..

    edit "RA_DU_FC"
        set type dynamic
        set interface "wan"
        set mode aggressive
        set peertype any
        set net-device disable
        set mode-cfg enable
        set proposal aes128-sha256 aes256-sha256 aes128-sha1 aes256-sha1
        set comments "VPN: RA_DU_FC (Created by VPN wizard)"
        set wizard-type dialup-forticlient
        set xauthtype auto
        set authusrgrp "Guest-group"
        set ipv4-start-ip 172.23.23.1
        set ipv4-end-ip 172.23.23.254
        set dns-mode auto
        set ipv4-split-include "RA_DU_FC_split"
        set save-password enable
        set client-auto-negotiate enable
        set client-keep-alive enable
        set psksecret ENC t+AbSXpr/UM3z4kb43Nhr851MZHx.........
    next
end
```

I bet your happy now we used the wizard! Memorizing CLI commands is not fun, and it is easy to forget parts of the configuration. However, we should still know what GUI settings relate to CLI settings because, as I said before, a GUI might not always be available. I am going to step through the new settings seen here for Remote Access IPsec. The first *mode-cfg enable* is set when we enable Mode Config. This provides additional configuration parameters that must be filled in, which are:

```
..
set xauthtype auto
set authusrgrp "Guest-group"
set ipv4-start-ip 172.23.23.1
set ipv4-end-ip 172.23.23.254
set dns-mode auto
..
```

These are the settings to assign to our FortiClients. The next group of settings are specific to FortiClient and are:

```
set save-password enable
set client-auto-negotiate enable
set client-keep-alive enable
```

Here we can find the CLI settings for 'Save Password', 'Auto-Connect', and 'Always Up(Keep Alive)' respectfully. Note, with these settings enabled; this modifies XML configuration on FortiClient locally. Next, take a peek at the Phase-2 CLI settings for Remote Access IPsec:

```
IPsec-FGT-Hub (root) # conf vpn ipsec phase2-interface
IPsec-FGT-Hub (phase2-interface) # show
config vpn ipsec phase2-interface
    ..
    edit "RA_DU_FC"
        set phase1name "RA_DU_FC"
        set proposal aes128-sha1 aes256-sha1 aes128-sha256 aes256-sha256
aes128gcm aes256gcm chacha20poly1305
        set comments "VPN: RA_DU_FC (Created by VPN wizard)"
    next
end
```

Nothing too surprising here; the Remote access Wizard basically attempts to match many different FortiClient Phase-2 transform-set proposals, which is fine in our case.

Next, I want to test this VPN from my local FortiClient, but I must configure a user for authentication before I can do this. I'm going to perform local authentication for this Proof of Concept; however, most organizations bind LDAP or Radius authentication to their Remote Access IPsec VPN on FortiGate, making things a lot easier because no one wants to manage hundreds of unique VPN credentials for users per device. Take a look at the following CLI output:

```
IPsec-FGT-Hub (root) # show user local
..
    edit "test123."
        set type password
        set passwd-time 2020-09-14 13:36:50
        set passwd Password123
    next
```

```
end
IPsec-FGT-Hub (root) # show user group Guest-group
config user group
    edit "Guest-group"
        set member "guest" "test123"
    next
```

Now that our test123 user is within the Guest-Group, which is referenced by RA_DU_FC XAuth, we can now authenticate. I'm going to run our IKE debug while this user attempts to authenticate.

Well, I almost forgot; this is not going to work because we have another aggressive mode Phase-1 IPsec VPN bound to this same WAN interface for the Hub-and-Spoke configuration. Therefore, to make this work, we need to provide the RA_DU_FC VPN, an additional setting, the Peer ID.

The Peer ID is a unique identifier delivered by ISAKMP and used by FortiOS IPsec to associate clients with dynamic IPs to certain Phase-1 SA. To configure this, run below CLI commands:

```
0: config vpn ipsec phase1-interface
0: edit "RA_DU_FC"
0: set peertype one
0: set peerid "101"
0: end
```

On the FortiClient side, the value of 101 must be entered in the Local ID field. Note, there is nothing special about *101* itself; it's just an arbitrary value. The only rule is, both sides of the tunnel must match.

Image 8.36 – FortiClient Local ID Configuration

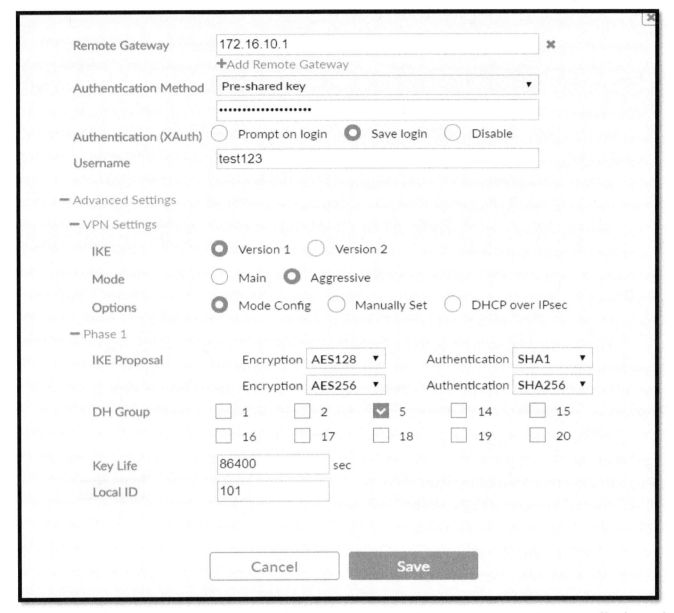

This was quite a bit of output, and I cleaned it up some for us. We are going to walk through this IKE debug, but on a high level, this is what happened:

1) Phase-1 Established
2) XAuth- Good
3) Mode Config – Good
4) Phase-2 Established

See CLI Debug output on the next page:

/// Initiator ISAKMP Phase-1 Aggressive Mode begins:

```
ike 0: comes 192.168.209.53:500->172.16.10.1:500,ifindex=4....
ike 0: IKEv1 exchange=Aggressive id=0bca52323a409f9f/0000000000000000 len=507
ike 0: in
```

..

/// peer ID found 101, map to correct SA, Initiator sends proposal

```
ike 0::718: received peer identifier FQDN '101'
ike 0: IKEv1 Aggressive, comes 192.168.209.53:500->172.16.10.1 4
ike 0:0bca52323a409f9f/0000000000000000:718: negotiation result
ike 0:0bca52323a409f9f/0000000000000000:718: proposal id = 1:
ike 0:0bca52323a409f9f/0000000000000000:718:    protocol id = ISAKMP:
ike 0:0bca52323a409f9f/0000000000000000:718:        trans_id = KEY_IKE.
ike 0:0bca52323a409f9f/0000000000000000:718:        encapsulation = IKE/none
ike 0:0bca52323a409f9f/0000000000000000:718:           type=OAKLEY_ENCRYPT_ALG,
val=AES_CBC, key-len=256
ike 0:0bca52323a409f9f/0000000000000000:718:           type=OAKLEY_HASH_ALG,
val=SHA2_256.
ike 0:0bca52323a409f9f/0000000000000000:718:           type=AUTH_METHOD,
val=PRESHARED_KEY.
ike 0:0bca52323a409f9f/0000000000000000:718:           type=OAKLEY_GROUP,
val=MODP1536.
ike 0:0bca52323a409f9f/0000000000000000:718: ISAKMP SA lifetime=86400
ike 0:0bca52323a409f9f/0000000000000000:718: SA proposal chosen, matched
gateway RA_DU_FC
ike 0:RA_DU_FC: created connection: 0x432bea8 4 172.16.10.1-
>192.168.209.53:500.
ike 0:RA_DU_FC:718: DPD negotiated
ike 0:RA_DU_FC:718: XAUTHv6 negotiated
```

..
```
ike 0:RA_DU_FC:718: PSK authentication succeeded
ike 0:RA_DU_FC:718: authentication OK
ike 0:RA_DU_FC: adding new dynamic tunnel for 192.168.209.53:500
```
..
// Phase-1 complete, send XAuth request to client
```
ike 0:RA_DU_FC_0:718: processed INITIAL-CONTACT
ike 0:RA_DU_FC_0:718: initiating XAUTH.
ike 0:RA_DU_FC_0:718: sending XAUTH request
ike 0:RA_DU_FC_0:718: enc
```
..

// XAuth Client credentials received

```
..ike 0:RA_DU_FC_0:718: received XAUTH_USER_NAME 'test123' length 7
ike 0:RA_DU_FC_0:718: received XAUTH_USER_PASSWORD length 7
```

```
ike 0:RA_DU_FC_0: XAUTH user "test123"
ike 0:RA_DU_FC: auth group Guest-group
ike 0:RA_DU_FC_0: XAUTH succeeded for user "test123" group "Guest-group"
ike 0:RA_DU_FC_0:718: enc
```
//Begin Mode Config

```
..
ike 0:RA_DU_FC_0:718: mode-cfg assigned (1) IPv4 address 172.23.23.1
ike 0:RA_DU_FC_0:718: mode-cfg assigned (2) IPv4 netmask 255.255.255.255
ike 0:RA_DU_FC_0:718: mode-cfg send (13) 0:10.20.20.0/255.255.255.0:0
ike 0:RA_DU_FC_0:718: mode-cfg send (3) IPv4 DNS(1) 208.91.112.53 // built in
```
FortiGate DNS servers
```
ike 0:RA_DU_FC_0:718: mode-cfg send (3) IPv4 DNS(2) 208.91.112.52

..
ike 0:RA_DU_FC_0:718: mode-cfg send APPLICATION_VERSION 'FortiGate-30E
v6.2.5,build1142,200819 (GA)'
ike 0:RA_DU_FC_0:718: mode-cfg send (28673) UNITY_SAVE_PASSWD
ike 0:RA_DU_FC_0:718: mode-cfg send (21514) FNT_AUTO_NEGOTIATE
ike 0:RA_DU_FC_0:718: mode-cfg send (21515) FNT_KEEP_ALIVE

..
ike 0:RA_DU_FC_0 HA send mode-cfg
```
//Receive client registration information

```
..
_0:718:3862: FCC request len = 287, data = 'VER=1
FCTVER=xxx
UID=xxx
IP=192.168.209.53
MAC=xxx
HOST=US-xxx
USER=test123
OSVER=Microsoft Windows 8.0 Professional Edition, 64-bit
REG_STATUS=0
```
///Begin Phase-2 negotiation

```
..
ike 0:RA_DU_FC_0:718:RA_DU_FC:3862: negotiation result
ike 0:RA_DU_FC_0:718:RA_DU_FC:3862: proposal id = 1:
ike 0:RA_DU_FC_0:718:RA_DU_FC:3862:    protocol id = IPSEC_ESP:
ike 0:RA_DU_FC_0:718:RA_DU_FC:3862:    PFS DH group = 5
ike 0:RA_DU_FC_0:718:RA_DU_FC:3862:       trans_id = ESP_AES_CBC (key_len =
128)
ike 0:RA_DU_FC_0:718:RA_DU_FC:3862:       encapsulation =
ENCAPSULATION_MODE_TUNNEL
ike 0:RA_DU_FC_0:718:RA_DU_FC:3862:          type = AUTH_ALG, val=SHA1
ike 0:RA_DU_FC_0:718:RA_DU_FC:3862: set pfs=MODP1536
```

```
ike 0:RA_DU_FC_0:718:RA_DU_FC:3862: using tunnel mode.
ike 0:RA_DU_FC_0:718:RA_DU_FC:3862: replay protection enabled
ike 0:RA_DU_FC_0:718:RA_DU_FC:3862: SA life soft seconds=43185.
ike 0:RA_DU_FC_0:718:RA_DU_FC:3862: SA life hard seconds=43200.
ike 0:RA_DU_FC_0:718:RA_DU_FC:3862: IPsec SA selectors #src=1 #dst=1
ike 0:RA_DU_FC_0:718:RA_DU_FC:3862: src 0 7 0:0.0.0.0-255.255.255.255:0
ike 0:RA_DU_FC_0:718:RA_DU_FC:3862: dst 0 7 0:172.23.23.1-172.23.23.1:0
ike 0:RA_DU_FC_0:718:RA_DU_FC:3862: add dynamic IPsec SA selectors
ike 0:RA_DU_FC:3862: add route 172.23.23.1/255.255.255.255 gw 192.168.209.53
oif RA_DU_FC(33) metric 15 priority 0
ike 0:RA_DU_FC_0:718:RA_DU_FC:3862: tunnel 4 of VDOM limit 0/0
ike 0:RA_DU_FC_0:718:RA_DU_FC:3862: add IPsec SA: SPIs=f62bb55a/58b47c38
..
ike 0:RA_DU_FC_0:718:RA_DU_FC:3862: added IPsec SA: SPIs=f62bb55a/58b47c38
ike 0:RA_DU_FC_0:718:RA_DU_FC:3862: sending SNMP tunnel UP trap
```

I know this was a lot of debug out for a book, but I feel like this is important information to know about. You need to know what debugs you are looking for, and if a client IPsec tunnel is failing to establish, you should be able to identify what step in the process it is failing at.

FortiClient IPsec verification time! In this next section, we walk through some FortiClient debugs commands.

FortiClient IPsec Verification

Now that our FortiClient is connected to the FortiGate Hub, we look at the CLI and confirm that everything looks ok.

```
IPsec-FGT-A (root) # get router info routing-table all
path=router, objname=info, tablename=(null), size=0
..
S*      0.0.0.0/0 [10/0] via 172.16.10.2, wan
C       10.20.20.1/32 is directly connected, Lo_10.20.20.1
S       10.30.30.0/24 [15/0] via 192.168.209.2, Primary_Hub
S       10.40.40.0/24 [15/0] via 192.168.40.12, Primary_Hub
S       10.50.50.0/24 [15/0] via 192.168.50.13, Primary_Hub
..
S       172.23.23.1/32 [15/0] via 192.168.209.53, RA_DU_FC
C       192.168.1.0/24 is directly connected, lan
```

We can see that a host route was added to the Routing Table. The next command to run here is our 'diag vpn ike gateway'; see CLI output below:

```
IPsec-FGT-A (root) # diagnose vpn ike gateway
...
vd: root/0
```

```
name: RA_DU_FC_0
version: 1
interface: wan 4
addr: 172.16.10.1:500 -> 192.168.209.53:500
virtual-interface-addr: 169.254.1.1 -> 169.254.1.1
created: 1424s ago
xauth-user: test123
peer-id: 101
peer-id-auth: yes
assigned IPv4 address: 172.23.23.1/255.255.255.255
IKE SA: created 1/1  established 1/1  time 110/110/110 ms // Phase-1
IPsec SA: created 1/1  established 1/1  time 10/10/10 ms // Phase-2

  id/spi: 718 0bca52323a409f9f/00191d670587a09c
  direction: responder
  status: established 1424-1424s ago = 110ms
  proposal: aes256-sha256
  key: ad98eb4d70de817a-ccbd2e51357b1e55-9190cf2c752d562b-33246dabf1a56ed8
  lifetime/rekey: 86400/84705
  DPD sent/recv: 00000000/00000498
  peer-id: 101
```

From the output of this command, we can find the IPsec client XAuth username information 'test123'. We can see the Peer ID is indeed 101, and lastly, we can find that Mode Config did assign an IP address within the range we specified earlier. The next items we can look at is the split tunnel route that was added to the Windows client routing table:

```
>route print
IPv4 Route Table
===========================================================================
Active Routes:
Network Destination        Netmask          Gateway        Interface  Metric
..
      10.20.20.0     255.255.255.0      172.23.23.2      172.23.23.1       1

..
```

This wraps up FortiClient verification and ends our IPsec Remote Access FortiClient section, and this actually wraps up all the IPsec topics within the NSE4, nice work! Moving on to the Chapter Summary!!

Chapter 8 Summary

What an amazing chapter to write! Don't get me wrong; some of the content was challenging at times and is most likely the most technical chapter I've written thus far in my career as an author. I think my eye's started watering about halfway through... jk. For you folks out there that had no clue what IPsec was until this chapter, a big congratulations to you. Not only did you work through the IPsec theory section but also how FortiGate uses the framework!

I always like to start my chapter off with background theory which I think is critical to becoming a great Fortinet engineer. Without theory, we could not visualize the network traffic and the internal processes taking place within Fortigate. I started Chapter 8, explaining how IPsec is not a protocol itself but a framework for protocols like ISAKMP and Oakley to operate within.

You can think of IPsec as the over the goal of securing IP network traffic, but IKE is the guy that will make it happen. Internet Key Exchange (IKE) uses the Internet Security Association Key Management Protocol (ISAKMP) to control the communication of IPsec parameters, key exchanges, Security Associations (SA) formatting, and negotiation functions between IPsec peers. Oakley group uses Diffie-Hellman to generate secret keys that are used by ISAKMP and IPsec SA's to seed encryption algorithms and generate HMACs.

An IPsec encrypted payload packets use Encapsulation Security Protocol (ESP) protocol 50, and authentication is performed with a Hash Message Authentication Code (HMAC), which is essentially an encrypted hash that only the IPsec peer can decrypt and so to compare with its own hash to verify data integrity and peer authentication.

Security Associations (SA's) are a set of parameters that are used together by IPsec to secure IP traffic. These parameters are Hash, Authentication, Group, Encryption, and Lifetime which can be remembered with HAGEL (no, I'm not trying to sell you a car!). SA's are negotiated using the ISAKMP framework. ISAKMP setups its own SA during the Phase-1 to secure IPsec management traffic (or control channel). Phase-1 can either be Aggressive Mode or Main Mode. Aggressive mode is quicker because there are only three packet exchanges but exposes the IPsec Peer ID, and the authentication Hash is sent in cleartext. Main Mode is a little bit slower because a six-packet exchange must occur to complete the negotiation; however, this method is more secure because the Peer IP and authentication information are encrypted before sent to IPsec peer. Phase-1 uses a single SA for ISAKMP management traffic.

Phase-2, two SA's are negotiated between IPsec peers for bi-directional transit traffic to use. Also, during Phase-2 Quick Mode, Selectors are negotiated, which define the source and destination IP addresses that can enter the tunnel. FortiGate can use quad zero's (0.0.0.0/0) to match all proposed Quick Mode Selectors, but sometimes FortiGate is required to explicitly send Selectors to IPsec Peer because of a requirement on their side. Within Interface Mode IPsec, Route Entries can be added to the config to steer traffic to IPsec tunnel interfaces and not the Phase-2 Selector values.

FortiGate has two methods of creating IPsec tunnels, Interface Mode and Policy Mode. This chapter covered Interface Mode because it is the most popular implementation, and there are very few use cases that require Policy Mode to be used anymore.

IPsec has an Anti-Replay mechanism to protect again packet duplication attacks (replay attacks). This is accomplished by issuing every ESP packet a sequence number, and both IPsec peers keep track of these sequence numbers within a sliding window. If the sequence number falls outside of the sliding window, then IPsec will drop ESP packets.

There are only a few major IPsec topologies. The most popular and basic is the Site-to-Site topology, where there are only two IPsec peers that know each other's public IP addresses, which are static in nature. Hub-and-Spoke topology is where the FortiGate acts as a Hub and has more processing power and bandwidth that acts as a concentrator. Most of the time, the Hub is located at corporate HQ. The Spoke FortiGate are smaller units in nature and are used to connect remote sites back to the Hub FortiGate. Spoke's have dynamic IP's most of the time and require Phase-1 to run in Aggressive Mode. Full and Partial Mesh IPsec topologies are less common and require each FortiGate to form a Site-to-Site IPsec tunnel to every other FortiGate at remote locations, which could easily become unfeasible to manage. The Partial Mesh does not form Site-to-Site tunnels to every other remote FortiGate, only a subset. The last topology we discussed was Auto-discovery VPN (ADVPN), which runs the same Hub-and-Spoke topology. However, the Hub acts as a proxy to relay SHORTCUT messages between Spoke's to allow Spokes to form directly connected IPsec tunnels and bypass the Hub, which saves resources.

We covered FortiGate IPsec implementation of Site-to-Site IPsec tunnels and worked through Phase-1 and Phase-2 configuration. We created Policies and Static Route Entries for reachability. We also covered FortiGate Hub-and-Spoke implementation, which involves the Add-Route features, which are known by other vendors as RRI (Reverse Route Injection). We also covered the net-device setting and how it affects IPsec virtual interface setups. Lastly, we covered Remote Access IPsec VPN with FortiClient using Peer ID values to differentiate the Hub IPsec VPN for the Spoke FortiGate's from the Remote Access VPN for FortiClient's.

What a ride! At this point, you should feel good working with IPsec and implementing it on FortiGate, and best of all, your one more step closer to obtain your NSE4 certificate! As always, within my chapters, it is time to challenge your knowledge by answer the end-of-chapter questions!

Chapter 8 End of Chapter Questions

1) What protocol number is assigned to ESP
   a. 1
   b. 6
   c. 50
   d. 51

2) What protocol is responsible for the exchange of the secret key information between IPsec peers?
   a. IPsec
   b. IKE
   c. ISAKMP
   d. Oakley Group

3) What function is responsible for generating the secret keying material to be used in the encryption function of ESP packets?
   a. IPsec
   b. IKE
   c. ISAKMP
   d. Oakley Group

4) What is a framework used to accomplish the overall goal of secure communication between two devices that have never communicated before over the public Internet?
   a. IPsec
   b. IKE
   c. ISAKMP
   d. Oakley Group

5) What does ESP stand for?
   a. Encrypted Security Protocol
   b. Encrypted Security Payload
   c. Encapsulated Security Protocol
   d. Encapsulated Security Payload

6) What is the purpose of an HMAC within the ESP trailer?
    a. To perform encryption on ESP packets
    b. To provide authentication for ESP packet
    c. To provide confidentiality
    d. To Provide authentication and integrity for ESP packets

7) What is the purpose of a SA?
    a. To provide interesting traffic values, also known as Quick Mode Selectors
    b. To generate the secret keying material used for encryption
    c. A common set of security protocols used between IPsec peers for secure communication
    d. Responsible for communicating the re-keying mechanism within IKE

8) What are the characteristics of Phase-1 Aggressive Mode?
    a. Three packets are exchanged, and the Peer ID is encrypted
    b. Six packets are exchanged, and the Peer ID and Authentication Hash are encrypted
    c. Three packets are exchanged, and the Authentication is encrypted
    d. Three packets are exchanged, and the Peer ID and Authentication Hash are unencrypted

9) What are the characteristics of Phase-1 Main Mode?
    a. Three packets are exchanged, and only Peer ID is encrypted
    b. Six packets are exchanged, and the Peer ID and Authentication Hash are encrypted
    c. Three packets are exchanged, and the Authentication Hash and Peer ID are encrypted
    d. Six packets are exchanged, and the Peer ID and Authentication Hash are unencrypted

10) ADVPN is where Shortcut messages are passed through Hub to IPsec Spokes
    a. True
    b. False

11) What is the sequence of events when XAuth and Mode Config is used within the IPsec framework?
    a. Phase-1 → Phase-2 → XAuth → Mode Config
    b. Phase-1 → Phase-2 → Mode Config → XAuth
    c. Phase-1 → Mode Config → XAuth → Phase-2

d. Phase-1 → XAuth → Mode Config → Phase-2

12) What command will show IPSec tunnel MTU and if Anti-Replay is being used?
   a. get vpn ipsec tunnel details
   b. diagnose vpn tunnel list
   c. get vpn ipsec status
   d. diagnose ike tunnel list

13) What debug command will show XAuth user information?
   a. diagnose ike vpn gateway
   b. get vpn ipsec tunnel
   c. diagnose gateway vpn ike
   d. diagnose vpn ike gateway

14) What sniffer command will allow you to see ISAKMP traffic with no NAT?
   a. diag sniffer packet any 'esp'
   b. diag sniffer packet any 'isakmp'
   c. diag sniffer packet any 'port 4500'
   d. diag sniffer packet any 'port 500'

15) What sniffer command will allow you to see ISAKMP traffic with NAT?
   a. diag sniffer packet any 'esp'
   b. diag sniffer packet any 'isakmp'
   c. diag sniffer packet any 'port 4500'
   d. diag sniffer packet any 'port 500'

16) What sniffer command will allow you to see ESP traffic?
   a. diag sniffer packet any 'esp'
   b. diag sniffer packet any 'isakmp'
   c. diag sniffer packet any 'port 4500'
   d. diag sniffer packet any 'port 500'

17) How does the Add-Route feature work on FortiOS?
   a. Detects if IPsec tunnel is up and adds policy routes depending on the condition
   b. ISAKMP sends informational Add-Route message to IPsec peer to Inject route for its source Quick Mode Selector

  c. Local IPsec peer performs a reverse route injection for source Quick Mode Selector value received into the local routing table

  d. Local IPsec peer

18) If the local IPsec peer is 10.10.10.10 and the remote IPsec peer is 192.168.1.1, what IPsec debug command must you run to see ISAKMP negotiations?

  a. diag vpn ike log-filter dst-addr4 10.10.10.10
    diag debug reset
    diag debug enable
    diag debug application ike -1

  b. diag vpn ike log-filter dst-addr4 192.168.1.1
    diag debug reset
    diag debug enable
    diag debug application ipsec -1

  c. diag vpn ike log-filter dst-addr4 192.168.1.1
    diag debug reset
    diag debug enable
    diag debug application isakmp -1

  d. diag vpn ike log-filter dst-addr4 192.168.1.1
    diag debug reset
    diag debug enable
    diag debug application ike -1

19) With the net-device setting enabled, then FortiOS will create virtual interfaces for each IPsec tunnel dynamic peer.

  a. True
  b. False

20) What IPsec function is responsible for assigning DNS IP information to the remote IPsec peer?

  a. ISAKMP
  b. IKE
  c. Phase-2
  d. Mode Config

Chapter 9 | SSL VPN

NSE4 Blueprint Topics Covered

- Understand SSL VPN concepts
- Describe the differences between SSL an IPsec
- Configure SSL VPN Modes
- Configure SSL VPN Realms
- Configure SSL VPN Portal
- Configure SSL VPN Settings
- SSL VPN Authentication
- Configure SSL VPN Bookmarks
- Configure SSL VPN Authentication
- Monitor SSL VPN users
- SSL VPN Client integrity checking
- Restrict by Mac Address

S SL/TLS Encryption mixed in with remote access, and we get an SSL-VPN! SSL-VPNs are extremely popular with large enterprises because of their simplicity for both the end-users and the administrator (us!). The SSL-VPN provides similar encryption services like IPsec behind the scenes but without the requirements of defining all the Phase-1 settings and Phase-2 settings. With SSL VPN, you can just tell your users what IP address to point their SSL VPN Client to and have them use their active directory credentials to authenticate to the VPN service. This, in turn, could provide them access to internal resources when working remotely. SSL/TLS VPN's is one of those technologies suites that are very complex 'under-the-hood' but extremely simple to manage. Like Chapter 8, I will be reviewing TLS theory before starting on the FortiGate configuration topics.

SSL-VPN configuration on FortiGate is heavily GUI driven. I don't think I've ever fully configured an SSL-VPN entirely from the CLI on FortiOS thus far in my career. In this chapter, I will still show you the CLI equivalent of the GUI configuration for reference. However, in general, you will not need to use it often unless you have specific requirements for certain cipher suites or have a particular corner case.

This chapter aims to show you how easy it is to set up an SSL-VPN for your organization. I'm going to review many of the major SSL-VPN features FortiOS offers and provide example configurations. Once we have our lab setup and SSL-VPN users connected, we will verify user connectivity and troubleshoot a few SSL-VPN issues together; and just like FortiGate can offload IPsec traffic to the NP ASIC, SSL/TLS traffic can be offload to the hardware Content Processor (CP) ASIC that is built to handle certain security-related processing on FortiGate like hash functions. We will explore the various debug commands to confirm that the local CP chipset is indeed processing user traffic. In the last part of Chapter 9, we compare the IPsec VPN to the SSL-VPN, touch on SSL-VPN logs, and operation verification methods.

Alright folks, the first topic we will tackle is TLS theory fundamentals because if you do not know how a TLS connection is established, it won't be very clear to understand how SSL-VPN works on FortiGate!

TLS Theory Fundamentals

I'll start by asking a simple question, what is an SSL-VPN (Secure Socket Layer VPN) ? and the answer is your very own Transport Layer Security (TLS) encrypted tunnel!! Wait a minute, I thought you said this was an 'SSL' VPN, yes.. yes I did.. but really, TLS is used to encrypt and secure our traffic (most likely!) I know, right, not confusing at all! The technology is labeled an 'SSL-VPN'; however, this is just the lingo now because before TLS was SSL! There are many versions of SSL and many versions of TLS, which is the newer standard of technology. I guess the name did not get updated because TLS-VPN doesn't roll off the tongue as well as SSL-VPN.

Netscape created the first SSL implementation in 1994 to secure web browser data. TLS was built on earlier SSL specifications published between 1994-1996. The TLS 1.0 standard was published in 1999 by the Internet Engineering Task Force (IETF) officially. The most current version of TLS is 1.3, which is defined in RFC 8446 in August 2018.

Over the years, there have been many iterations of SSL/TLS standards due to exploits being discovered in these standards. You may have heard of some of these exploits like Heartbleed, POODLE, Logjam, Luck13, FREAK, and BEAST. For some of these exploits to be successful, it requires TLS or SSL to use weak encryption standards like RC4, MD5, or SHA1, etc... Therefore, sometimes attackers trick the TLS client & server into negotiating weaker security suites.

The next question to ask is, how does TLS provide us our very own secure VPN tunnel? So to answer this question, we need to understand how a TLS connection is established first, and once we under this, we can understand the encrypted SSL-VPN tunnel used by FortiOS.

TLS 1.2 Connection Establishment

On a high-level, SSL/TLS uses public and private keys contained within certificates in line with key exchange protocols, symmetric/asymmetric encryption standards, and HMAC to accomplish Transport Layer Security. These parameters are agreed upon between the client & server via a Handshake Protocol. Once the transport layer is secured, then application data like HTTP can use the secure tunnel to transmit data, which makes it HTTPS (HTTP Secure). In our case regarding SSL-VPN, the application data is the IP header, transport header (TCP/UDP/etc.), and application payload packaged by the TLS Client, which will most likely be the FortiClient. This data is sent to the TLS Gateway, which is FortiGate, to be decrypted and routed onward to its final destination.

Before we discuss the initial TLS connection, I would like to review some TLS terminology and discuss some of the negotiated cryptographic parameters because I will be referencing these items within upcoming sections. Firstly, we need to understand the Cipher Suite used by TLS.

TLS Cipher Suites

A Cipher suite is a set of predefined cryptographic algorithms designed to work together to secure network connections. A TLS Cipher Suite usually contain the following items:

1) Key Exchange Algorithms
    a. For example, Diffie-Hellman, ECDHE, and RSA
2) Hash function
    a. For example, SHA1, SHA256, and MD5
3) Encryption Algorithm
    a. For example, AES128, RC4, and CAMELLIA
4) Cipher Type
    a. For Example, Galois/Counter Mode (GCM) or Cipher Blocker Chaining
5) Protocol Version
    a. TLS Version 1.0, 1.1, 1.2 or 1.3

These cryptographic functions are used to secure TLS tunnel maintenance and setup, but also the transit application data utilizing the tunnel. The next major component to discuss is the certificate, which contains the cryptographic key and identification attributes to be used by the TLS client & server.

Certificate Structure

Since TLS connections use certificates to secure network communication, it is important to understand what a certificate is and its structure. Certificates are sometimes referred to as digital certificates, public-key certificates, or identity certificates. The goal of a certificate is to validate the owner of a particular public encryption key to obtain confidence that the network connection is authentic. Many different framework standards were created to govern the certificate structure and define the certificate's attributes and how these attributes are formatted. In other words, public-key certificate owner attributes are bound to particular sets of encryption key pairings, which can be used in asymmetric encryption and authentication. Note, owners of a certificate can be many different things like systems, domains, or people.

This chapter uses the X.509v3 certificate format, a very general certificate structuring method with several defined encodings methods. We can view the built-in SSL-VPN certificate FortiGate uses by default via **Global > System > Certificates > Fortinet_SSL**; check out *Image 9.1* on the next page.

Image 9.1 – FortiOS Certificate Detail Information

Certificate Detail Information

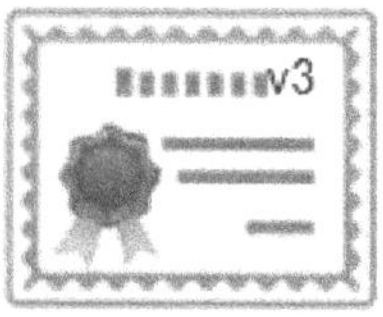

Fortinet_SSL
Serial Number: 5C

Subject Information

Common Name (CN)	FWF60D
Organization (O)	Fortinet
Organization Unit (OU)	FortiGate
Locality (L)	Sunnyvale
State (ST)	California
Country/Region (C)	US
Email Address	support@fortinet.com

Issuer

Common Name (CN)	FWF60D
Organization (O)	Fortinet
Organization Unit (OU)	FortiGate
Locality (L)	Sunnyvale
State (ST)	California
Country/Region (C)	US

Validity Period

Valid From	2019/04/22 09:03:32
Valid To	2029/04/22 09:03:32

Fingerprints

Take a few moments to look over the FortiGate certificate within Image 9.1 on the prior page, and reference back to it as needed as I explicitly go over a few of the displayed values next. It is time to review the X.509v3 certificate fields in detail; referencing RFC 5280, let's begin.

1) Certificate – Contains three required fields:
   a. tbsCertificate field
      i. Contains information associated with the subject (owner) of the certificate and the issuing CA
   b. signatureAlgorithm field
      i. contains the identifier for what hash algorithm was used by the issuing CA to sign this certificate.
   c. signatureValue field
      i. contains a hash (digital signature) output of the ASN.1 DER-encoded tbsCertificate. This hash string validates the information in the tbsCertificate field and certifies the relationship between the public key and the owner (subject) for this certificate.
2) TBSCertificate fields contain detailed information associated with the owner of the certificate and contain the following entries:
   a. Version Number
      i. X509 Version 1 structure provided in RFC 1422
      ii. X.509 Version 2 permits the reuse of issuers/subject name, not widely used
      iii. X.509 Version 3 provides additional extension fields
   b. Serial Number
      i. Every certificate issued by CA must have a unique Serial Number(SN). The issuer's name and SN should identify a unique certificate.
   c. Signature Algorithm ID
      i. A Hashing algorithm identifier is used by CA to sign the certificate.
   d. Issuer Name
      i. This field identifies the entity that issued and signed the certificate. Per RFC 5280, the following attributes must be present and defined as - country, organization, organizational unit, distinguished name qualifier, state or province name, common name (e.g., "Susan Housley"), and serial number. In addition, the following attributes SHOULD be present, subject names: locality, title, surname, given name, initials, pseudonym, and generation qualifier (e.g., "Jr.," "3rd", or "IV")."
   e. Validity period
      i. The certification validity fields state how long a CA will hold information about a certificate. This field is represented by two dates, which are:
         1. Valid Not Before *time*
         2. Valid Not After *time*
   f. Subject name
      i. The subject field identifies the entity associated with the public key stored in the subject public key field per RFC 5280

      g. Subject Public Key

          i. This field contains the actual public key and identifier of the key exchange algorithm in which the public key is used.

             1. Public Key Algorithm

             2. Subject Public Key

      h. Issuer Unique Identifier (optional)

      i. Subject Unique Identifier (optional)

   3) Extensions (optional)

Now that we know the X.509v3 certificate format structure, we are going to discuss how it is used within TLS 1.2.

TLS Public Key Certificate

A common type of public-key certificate is RSA, which stands for Rivest, Adi Shamir, and Leonard Adleman, which are the individuals who invented public-key cryptography back in 1977. RSA is called public-key cryptography because there are two keys used, one key is used to encrypt the data, and the other is required to decrypt data, which is also referred to as asymmetric encryption. We provide labels to these keys, one is labeled public key that is shared with the world, and the other key as private, that is kept safe locally. RSA public-key certificates can be used to encrypt keying material created from algorithms like DHE and ECDHE. The keying material can seed symmetric encryption standards like AES.

Certificates can be used within TLS to authenticate each point of the TLS connection. The TLS server must send a certificate whenever there is an agreed up key exchange method that uses certificates for authentication, which are most methods. The certificate sent by the server must be X.509v3 format unless another format is explicitly negotiated. TLS clients and servers negotiate a predefined security protocol set called a Cipher Suite. Line items one and two below is how A Cipher Suite code name would look.

TLS 1.2 – RFC 5246

   1) TLS_RSA_WITH_AES_256_CBC_SHA256 (rsa 2048)

TLS 1.3 – RFC 8446

   2) TLS_AES_128_GCM_SHA256

You may be able to decipher the coded names here. Each suite specifies a protocol, key exchange method, peer authentication method, encryption method, and packet authenticity/integrity method.

Many different types of certificates are used in TLS 1.2. Each certificate type has a specific function and is paired with a certain key exchange algorithm tactfully specified in a Cipher Suite, RFC 5246 states:

"- The end entity certificate's public key (and associated

restrictions) MUST be compatible with the selected key exchange algorithm."

This means, if ECDH key exchange is used, then a capable public key method must be used in parallel, and these two items would be bundled together within a single Cipher Suite. Here is an example of a Cipher Suite that can be used on FortiGate:

TLS_DHE_RSA_WITH_AES_256_CBC_SHA256 (dh 128)

This Cipher Suite states TLS 1.2 is used with DHE to generate secret keying material, and RSA will encrypt the secret keying material to be exchanged safely between TLS client & server to perform symmetric AES256 encryption using the generated DHE key(s) as seeding material using the encryption method of Block Cipher Encryption with a SHA256 hash as the source for the HMAC that provides authenticity and integrity for TLS control and data packets.

Wow! I felt like that was a mouth full! You need to read that last paragraph again to let those points sink in. We can take a look at the built-in Fortinet certificates on FortiGate. Next, since we understand Cipher Suites and Certificates, we can view built-in certificates on FortiOS. These certificates are provided for convenience, and Fortinet recommends customers to obtain their own certificate to be used on FortiGate. To find the built-in default certificates within the GUI, go to **Global > System > Certificates,** and you should see Image 9.2.

Public Key Infrastructure (PKI) and Digital Certificates are very large topics and I'll be dedicating a full chapter on these subjects in book three of the NSE4 study guide series when we discuss deep packet inspection (DPI)

Image 9.2 – FortiGate 6.2 Default Built in Certificates

Local CA Certificate ②	
🌐 Fortinet_CA_SSL	C = US, ST = California, L = Sunnyvale, O = Fortinet, OU = Certificate Aut...
🌐 Fortinet_CA_Untrusted	C = US, ST = California, L = Sunnyvale, O = Fortinet, OU = Certificate Aut...
Local Certificate ⑬	
🌐 Fortinet_Factory	C = US, ST = California, L = Sunnyvale, O = Fortinet, OU = FortiGate, CN =...
🌐 Fortinet_SSL	C = US, ST = California, L = Sunnyvale, O = Fortinet, OU = FortiGate, CN =...
🌐 Fortinet_SSL_DSA1024	C = US, ST = California, L = Sunnyvale, O = Fortinet, OU = FortiGate, CN =...
🌐 Fortinet_SSL_DSA2048	C = US, ST = California, L = Sunnyvale, O = Fortinet, OU = FortiGate, CN =...
🌐 Fortinet_SSL_ECDSA256	C = US, ST = California, L = Sunnyvale, O = Fortinet, OU = FortiGate, CN =...
🌐 Fortinet_SSL_ECDSA384	C = US, ST = California, L = Sunnyvale, O = Fortinet, OU = FortiGate, CN =...
🌐 Fortinet_SSL_ECDSA521	C = US, ST = California, L = Sunnyvale, O = Fortinet, OU = FortiGate, CN =...
🌐 Fortinet_SSL_ED448	C = US, ST = California, L = Sunnyvale, O = Fortinet, OU = FortiGate, CN =...
🌐 Fortinet_SSL_ED25519	C = US, ST = California, L = Sunnyvale, O = Fortinet, OU = FortiGate, CN =...
🌐 Fortinet_SSL_RSA1024	C = US, ST = California, L = Sunnyvale, O = Fortinet, OU = FortiGate, CN =...
🌐 Fortinet_SSL_RSA2048	C = US, ST = California, L = Sunnyvale, O = Fortinet, OU = FortiGate, CN =...
🌐 Fortinet_SSL_RSA4096	C = US, ST = California, L = Sunnyvale, O = Fortinet, OU = FortiGate, CN =...
🌐 Fortinet_Wifi	C = US, ST = California, L = Sunnyvale, O = "Fortinet, Inc.", OU = FortiWifi,...
Remote CA Certificate ④	
Fortinet_CA	C = US, ST = California, L = Sunnyvale, O = Fortinet, OU = Certificate Aut...
Fortinet_CA2	C = US, ST = California, L = Sunnyvale, O = Fortinet, OU = Certificate Aut...
Fortinet_Sub_CA	C = US, ST = California, L = Sunnyvale, O = Fortinet, OU = Certificate Aut...
Fortinet_Wifi_CA	C = US, O = DigiCert Inc, OU = www.digicert.com, CN = DigiCert SHA2 Hi...

As you can see, there are many different types of certificates, and each one is a little different and provides different services. I encourage you to do some independent research before moving forward to the next page by picking one of these certificate names out of this list and see what you can find out about it and what makes it unique. Since this chapter aims to learn FortiGate SSL-VPN, we are moving on to the next topic!

Since we understand the X.509v3 certificate structure, the purpose of a Cipher Suite, and the basic purpose of the public key certificate, we can move on to talk more about the TLS 1.2 protocol itself and how it uses these items to create our very own TLS encrypted tunnel!

<u>TLS Record Protocol</u>

The first two TLS protocols to discuss are the TLS Record Protocol and the TLS Handshake Protocol. The TLS Record Protocol is built right on top of TCP or UDP in most cases. The high-level purpose of the TLS Record Protocol is to provide a framework to carry management messages between TLS client & server. The TLS Record Protocol is used for encapsulating higher level TLS protocols like the TLS Handshake Protocol. Here are a few of the higher-level TLS protocols encapsulated by the TLS Record Protocol.

- Handshake Protocol
  - o Provides the server and client a method to authenticate each other, negotiate security algorithms, and exchange cryptographic keys.
- Alert Protocol
  - o Used to communicate alert type messages which contain the severity and a description of the alert, for example, connection closure, errors, and handshake issues. Note that Alert Protocol messages with a level of fatal result in the termination of the TLS connection. Lastly, note that Alert messages are indeed encrypted and compressed by the negotiated connection parameters.
- Application Protocol
  - o The upper layer protocol that would normally use transport layer protocols like TCP or UDP directly instead uses the TLS tunnel. Network applications would include, for example, HTTP, TELNET, FTP, and SMTP.

Now that we understand the base TLS structure, we can start to build on that concept. Next, I would like to discuss more details around the TLS Handshake Protocol itself.

<u>TLS Handshake Protocol</u>

A secure TLS connection between a client and server requires each endpoint to negotiate several different underlying cryptographic security protocols with related keying material in a confidential & secure manner. The TLS Handshake Protocol is the mechanism used to perform this initial exchange between client & server, RFC 5246 states:

"The cryptographic parameters of the session state are produced by the

TLS Handshake Protocol, which operates on top of the TLS record

layer. When a TLS client and server first start communicating, they

agree on a protocol version, select cryptographic algorithms,

optionally authenticate each other, and use public-key encryption

techniques to generate shared secrets."

The very first message is sent by the TLS client and is the Handshake Protocol 'Client Hello' message, which contains the client's supported Cipher Suites and capabilities. The server should respond with a Server Hello message back to the client. The goals of the Client Hello and Server Hello messages are to establish the following attributes for the TLS 1.2 connection.

1) Protocol Version,
2) Session ID
3) Cipher Suite
4) Compression Method.
5) Two random values

Image 9.3 – TLS 1.2 Handshake Client Hello Message

```
> Transmission Control Protocol, Src Port: 50846, Dst Port: 8443, Seq: 1,
˅ Secure Sockets Layer
  ˅ TLSv1.2 Record Layer: Handshake Protocol: Client Hello
      Content Type: Handshake (22)
      Version: TLS 1.2 (0x0303)
      Length: 147
    ˅ Handshake Protocol: Client Hello
        Handshake Type: Client Hello (1)
        Length: 143
        Version: TLS 1.2 (0x0303)
      ˅ Random: 5f7dd55d572485e33296b67cae3390f050668e288a169462...
          GMT Unix Time: Oct  7, 2020 07:49:01.000000000 Pacific Daylight Ti
          Random Bytes: 572485e33296b67cae3390f050668e288a169462d9d75927...
        Session ID Length: 0
        Cipher Suites Length: 38
      ˅ Cipher Suites (19 suites)
          Cipher Suite: TLS_ECDHE_ECDSA_WITH_AES_256_GCM_SHA384 (0xc02c)
          Cipher Suite: TLS_ECDHE_ECDSA_WITH_AES_128_GCM_SHA256 (0xc02b)
          Cipher Suite: TLS_ECDHE_RSA_WITH_AES_256_GCM_SHA384 (0xc030)
          Cipher Suite: TLS_ECDHE_RSA_WITH_AES_128_GCM_SHA256 (0xc02f)
          Cipher Suite: TLS_ECDHE_ECDSA_WITH_AES_256_CBC_SHA384 (0xc024)
          Cipher Suite: TLS_ECDHE_ECDSA_WITH_AES_128_CBC_SHA256 (0xc023)
          Cipher Suite: TLS_ECDHE_RSA_WITH_AES_256_CBC_SHA384 (0xc028)
          Cipher Suite: TLS_ECDHE_RSA_WITH_AES_128_CBC_SHA256 (0xc027)
```

Next, the TLS server responds with a Handshake Server Hello message back to the client, which most likely contains a single Cipher Suite the server chosen from the client's proposed list. This message also contains the TLS version, Compression method, and server random string value. See Image 9.4 for details.

Image 9.4 – TLS 1.2 Handshake Server Hello Message

```
Secure Sockets Layer
  TLSv1.2 Record Layer: Handshake Protocol: Server Hello
    Content Type: Handshake (22)
    Version: TLS 1.2 (0x0303)
    Length: 65
    Handshake Protocol: Server Hello
      Handshake Type: Server Hello (2)
      Length: 61
      Version: TLS 1.2 (0x0303)
      Random: 003d08abfb49dcadc3a08edf5cc9bda1627bb3cbf526feb0...
        GMT Unix Time: Feb 15, 1970 23:05:15.000000000 Pacific Standard Time
        Random Bytes: fb49dcadc3a08edf5cc9bda1627bb3cbf526feb0444f574e...
      Session ID Length: 0
      Cipher Suite: TLS_ECDHE_RSA_WITH_AES_256_GCM_SHA384 (0xc030)
      Compression Method: null (0)
      Extensions Length: 21
      Extension: renegotiation_info (len=1)
      Extension: ec_point_formats (len=4)
      Extension: SessionTicket TLS (len=0)
      Extension: extended_master_secret (len=0)
```

In this example, the Cipher Suite selected by the server was:

TLS_ECDHE_RSA_WITH_AES_256_GCM_SHA384

which should be the strongest Cipher Suite available on the server and compatible with the client as well. From Image 9.4, we can find that TLS version 1.2 was selected with Session ID zero and no compression method (null) used. The next set of TLS messages to be exchanged are for the actual key exchanges. TLS uses up to four messages for key exchange.

First, the TLS server sends the client the following Handshake Messages - Certificate, Server Key Exchange, and Server Hello Done. The Certificate Message contains the server Public Key used for asymmetric encryption to accomplish confidentiality, authenticity, and integrity for the management and data communication channels. In other words, the TLS client & server relationship and the transit data using the tunnel. Check out *Image 9.5* on the next page to see what these messages would look like on the wire.

Image 9.5 – TLS 1.2 Server Handshake Key Exchange Messages

```
Transmission Control Protocol, Src Port: 8443, Dst Port: 50846,
[5 Reassembled TCP Segments (5914 bytes): #12(1390), #13(1460),
Secure Sockets Layer
  TLSv1.2 Record Layer: Handshake Protocol: Certificate
    Content Type: Handshake (22)
    Version: TLS 1.2 (0x0303)
    Length: 5909
    Handshake Protocol: Certificate
Secure Sockets Layer
  TLSv1.2 Record Layer: Handshake Protocol: Server Key Exchange
    Content Type: Handshake (22)
    Version: TLS 1.2 (0x0303)
    Length: 365
    Handshake Protocol: Server Key Exchange
  TLSv1.2 Record Layer: Handshake Protocol: Server Hello Done
    Content Type: Handshake (22)
    Version: TLS 1.2 (0x0303)
    Length: 4
    Handshake Protocol: Server Hello Done
      Handshake Type: Server Hello Done (14)
      Length: 0
```

Now that the TLS client has received the servers' certificate and ECDHE *pubkey* value, it checks the servers' certificate to check if it is expired or not and could also query the issuing CA to request a Certificate Revocation List (CRL) to be sure the certificate has not been revoked for whatever reason. The client verifies the digital signature by decrypting the hash with the public key and then performs a local hash function on the TLS message to see if the hash values match. If they match, then the TLS client transmits its own key to the server. Take a look at Image 9.6 for TLS client Key Exchange response messages.

Image 9.6 – TLS 1.2 Client Response Key Exchange Messages

```
Secure Sockets Layer
ˇTLSv1.2 Record Layer: Handshake Protocol: Client Key Exchange
  Content Type: Handshake (22)
  Version: TLS 1.2 (0x0303)
  Length: 102
 ˇHandshake Protocol: Client Key Exchange
   Handshake Type: Client Key Exchange (16)
   Length: 98
  ˇEC Diffie-Hellman Client Params
    Pubkey Length: 97
    Pubkey: 044ea763ec1f12cc2540f98b98796746030ef82f24dc630e...
ˇTLSv1.2 Record Layer: Change Cipher Spec Protocol: Change Cipher Spec
  Content Type: Change Cipher Spec (20)
  Version: TLS 1.2 (0x0303)
  Length: 1
  Change Cipher Spec Message
ˇTLSv1.2 Record Layer: Handshake Protocol: Encrypted Handshake Message
  Content Type: Handshake (22)
  Version: TLS 1.2 (0x0303)
```

Notice here the client now sends its ECDHE *pubkey* value to the server along with the Change Cipher Spec message, which indicates the proposed Cipher Suite is agreed to be used by the Client. Lastly, to end the Handshake Protocol, the server responds with the Handshake Messages - New Session Ticket, Change Cipher Spec, and Encrypted Handshake Message. Note here that the New Session Ticket message is only available as a TLS extension. In this case, Fortigate uses this to keep track of various TLS 'SSL-VPN' clients. The Change Cipher Spec message again means the server agrees with the client to put in use the proposed Cipher Suite, and all further communication will be encrypted. The Encrypted Handshake Message is the last message to ensure the client and server can understand each other regarding their implemented Cipher Suite. Check out Image 9.8 for details on final server messages on the next page. At this point, the TLS client and server can start sending application data traffic to each other.

Since you understand the certificate structure, the basics of how the TLS protocol works regarding associated Cipher Suite, we almost ready to move on and shift gears from TLS theory to FortiGate SSL-VPN implementation! On the next page, you will also find a diagram that outlines this entire process from a high level within Image 9.7.

Image 9.7 – TLS Server Handshake Protocol Final Messages

```
Secure Sockets Layer
˅ TLSv1.2 Record Layer: Handshake Protocol: New Session Ticket
    Content Type: Handshake (22)
    Version: TLS 1.2 (0x0303)
    Length: 170
  › Handshake Protocol: New Session Ticket
˅ TLSv1.2 Record Layer: Change Cipher Spec Protocol: Change Cipher Spec
    Content Type: Change Cipher Spec (20)
    Version: TLS 1.2 (0x0303)
    Length: 1
    Change Cipher Spec Message
˅ TLSv1.2 Record Layer: Handshake Protocol: Encrypted Handshake Message
    Content Type: Handshake (22)
    Version: TLS 1.2 (0x0303)
    Length: 40
    Handshake Protocol: Encrypted Handshake Message
```

Take a moment to walk through the Handshake Message flow in the below Image. Time to shift gears and look at how FortiGate uses certificates in SSL-VPNs.

Image 9.8 – TLS Handshake Protocol Diagram

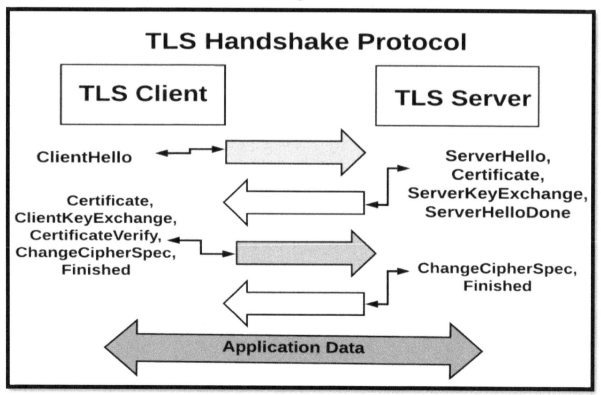

FortiGate SSL-VPN Introduction

Are you ready to learn about SSL-VPN on FortiGate? I hope so! You're going to start noticing a pattern when working with FortiOS that everything is object-oriented. Meaning, we first built a configuration object (a module) and then applied it to be referenced in an active configuration. For example, remember how we first needed to build an Address Object and then reference it in a Firewall Policy Entry? Well, the SSL-VPN configuration is no different. The SSL-VPN's object workbench is found in the GUI via VPN -> SSL-VPN Portal; see Image 9.9 for reference.

Image 9.9 – VPN Menu Portals

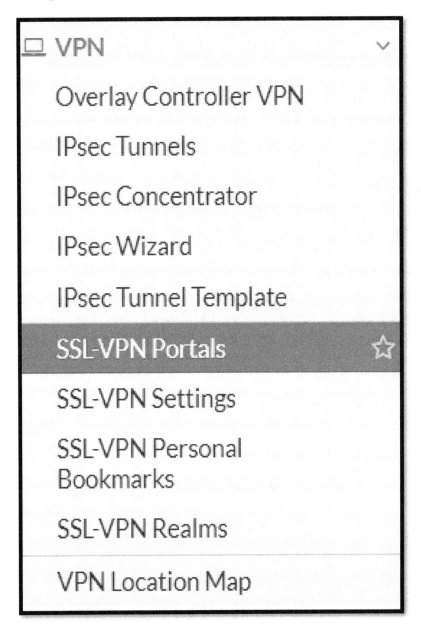

When I first started working with FortiGates, I found the SSL-VPN Portal configuration confusing because I didn't understand why the SSL-VPN Settings Menu was needed as well. So to clear this up, you first build your SSL-VPN requirements using the SSL-VPN Portals configuration GUI and then you reference this within the SSL-VPN settings to make those configurations active on FortiGate. There are three major SSL-VPN Portal configurations available which are:

1) Tunnel Mode
2) Web Mode
3) Tunnel & Web Mode

You can think of Tunnel mode SSL-VPN similar to a Dial-up IPsec VPN. Users are connected to FortiGate using an encrypted tunnel and can browse to internal resources that are not available publicly. To connect to an SSL-VPN using Tunnel Mode, an SSL client software is required. Fortinet provides FortiClient for this function. FortiGate assigns SSL-VPN users a unique IP address to be used while traversing the SSL-VPN to FortiGate. This IP uniquely identifies the SSL-VPN users while browsing enterprise resources. Essentially, Tunnel Mode SSL-VPN simulates your device as if it were sitting within your corporate HQ LAN on a high level. Just like ESP packets, this is accomplished by encrypting the transport protocol header (UDP/TCP), IP header, and data payload within the packet and re-creating the IP header using the SSL-VPN gateway IP address as the new destination IP over the public internet. This public IP address will most likely be assigned to the FortiGate WAN interface.

Web Mode SSL-VPN is clientless. Meaning, the service only requires a user to have access to a regular web browser. This is where FortiGate host an encrypted web page that has various functions that provide access to backend resource that could be manually defined by the administrator or the user. These functions are called *Bookmarks*. These Bookmarks can be configured with many different protocols that will touch on later in this chapter.

The SSL-VPN settings are used to tie all the configuration together into one usable purpose, and that is to service SSL-VPN client's remote access to internal resources. In later sections, we will step through all the various SSL-VPN settings and configuration requirements to obtain an operational SSL-VPN on FortiGate. The first topic I want to dive into is the SSL-VPN Portal options since this is our fundamental building blocks.

SSL-VPN Portals

Navigate within the GUI to VPN -> SSL-VPN Portals. On FortiOS 6.4, there are three default Portal profiles. See Image 9.10.

1) full-access
2) tunnel-access
3) web-access

Image 9.10 – SSL-VPN Default Portal Profiles

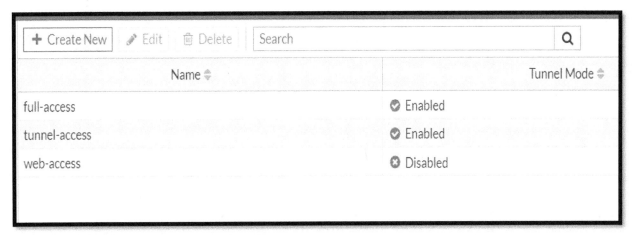

Next, we create a customer Portal profile so we can check out all the available settings. Select Create New, and you should see the configuration options displayed in image 9.11. I went ahead and disabled all the available settings to fit better all the settings onto the Image to see all the available options. I'm going to toggle on each setting one at a time and explain its purpose.

The first option is "Limit Users to One SSL-VPN Connection at a Time" setting; wow, that was a mouth full! This setting is located within Image 9.11 on the next page. So intuitively, you should be able to tell what the purpose of this setting is. Essentially, if left disabled, I could create one local user called 'Test-SSL-User', and if I did not have this option enabled, then anyone that wanted to use the SSL-VPN could share this single-user which makes it easier to manage. However, we lose accountability because our log messages and monitor debug are now generic, and if someone did something malicious, it would be much harder to track down. Most environments I've worked in have this setting enabled, so users are forced to use their own credentials to log onto the SSL-VPN. The next toggle to discuss is *Tunnel Mode*. These settings hold specific parameters for the remote SSL-VPN clients to use while utilizing the SSL-VPN..

Image 9.12 – New SSL-VPN Portal Profile Settings

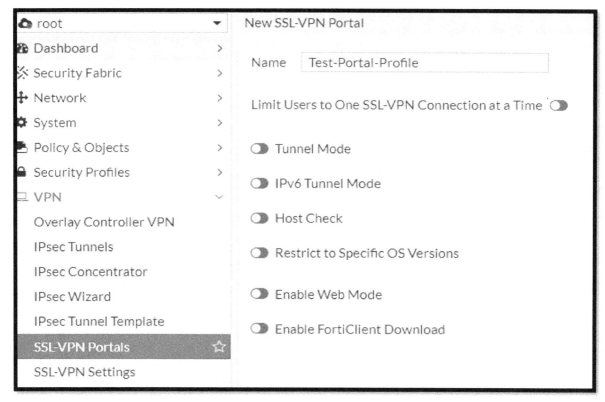

Within the Tunnel Mode settings, there are three options *Enable Split Tunneling*, Routing Address, and Source IP Pools. Split Tunneling we discussed in our IPsec chapter. This value defines interesting traffic that transverses the SSL-VPN, and If a split tunnel value is not set, then all traffic is forced through the SSL-VPN tunnel. The *Routing Address* is what defines the split tunnel addresses, and in this case, internal is being referenced. Internal holds the subnet range of the FortiGate internal LAN in this case. Next, Source IP Pool is the IPv4 address range

Image 9.11 – Tunnel Mode Portal Options

that FortiGate is offering SSL-VPN clients. The SSLVPN_TUNNEL_ADDR1 object is a default Address Object on FortiGate that contains the address range of 10.212.134.200-10.212.134.210. This address range would need to be advertised from FortiGate, or static routes would need to be configured within the enterprise network that points to FortiGate so bi-directional communication can occur.

The next toggle is IPv6 Tunnel Mode. This is used if you wish to assign the SSL-VPN clients an IPv6 address instead of an IPv4 address. The same concepts apply regarding Split Tunnel and Source IP Pool configuration settings that we covered in IPv4 Tunnel Mode. The next toggle to discuss is 'Tunnel Mode Client Options'. Check out Image 9.13.

The first three toggles here might be familiar to you if you read the IPsec chapter. The first

Image 9.13 – SSL-VPN Tunnel Mode Client Options

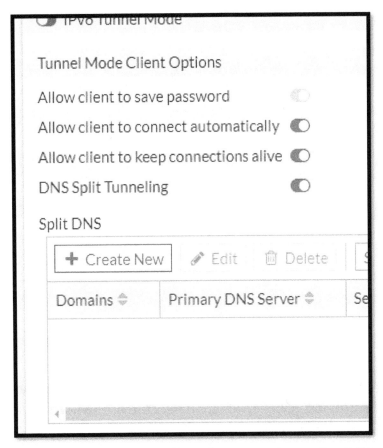

toggle, 'Allow client to save password' pushes a setting to FortiClient, which gives the user the option to save their password locally, so not having to enter it every time they need to use the SSL-VPN, which is a convenience feature. The next toggle, 'Allow client to connect automatically', is another setting that is pushed to FortiClient to enable the option to use the 'Auto Connect' FortiClient feature that triggers a VPN connection once FortiClient is launched automatically. The last setting here is 'Allow client to keep connections alive', another setting that is pushed to FortiClient that enables the 'Always up' features, which is essentially a keep-alive where FortiClient sends keep-alive packets to FortiGate. If a connection terminates for some reason, FortiClient continues to send probes to FortiGate and detect when the SSL-VPN service on FortiGate is available again and, if true, then reconnect to the SSL-VPN.

The last toggle here is for 'DNS Split Tunnel', which is a relatively new feature. When an SSL-VPN client connects to FortiGate, it receives a DNS IP address while accessing the VPN resources. The Split DNS Tunnel provides the ability to specify what DNS IP address to use for certain FQDN's. I'll click the Create New icon and configure a few options; check out Image 9.14 below.

Image 9.14 – SSL-VPN DNS Split Tunneling

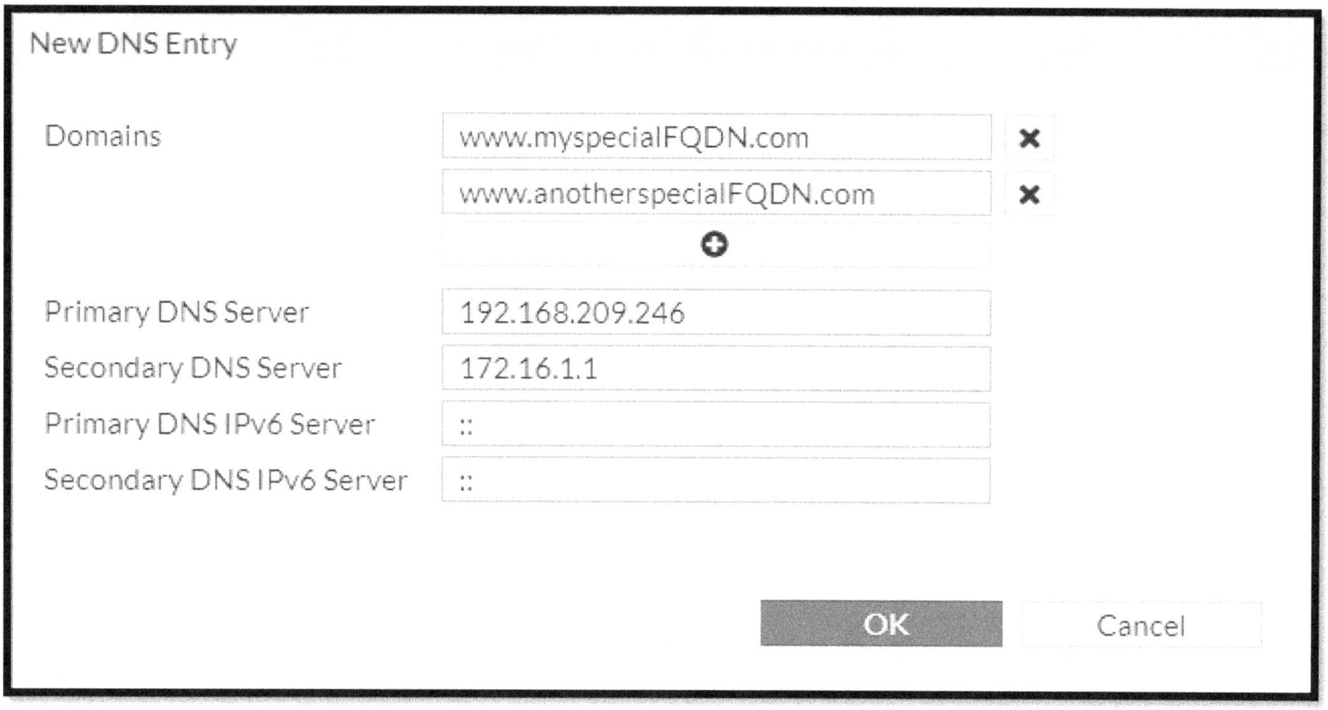

New DNS Entry

Domains	www.myspecialFQDN.com ✕
	www.anotherspecialFQDN.com ✕
	➕
Primary DNS Server	192.168.209.246
Secondary DNS Server	172.16.1.1
Primary DNS IPv6 Server	::
Secondary DNS IPv6 Server	::

OK   Cancel

With this DNS split tunnel configuration, the SSL-VPN client uses the Primary DNS Server value to perform DNS lookups for the provide FQDN's, which in my case are: www.myspecialFQDN.com & www.anotherspecialFQDN.com . Only these two FQDN use the DNS IP at 192.168.209.246 for IP lookup; the default DNS server handles all other requests.

The next toggle is 'Host Check', which provides the ability to validate endpoints security posture before allowing endpoint access to the FortiGate SSL-VPN. See Image 9.15.

Image 9.15 – SSL-VPN Host Checking

At the beginning of this chapter, I said most things could be done from the GUI regarding SSL-VPN on FortiGate; the Host Check feature is not one of them. If you wish to customize host checking for your SSL-VPN users, then this is all CLI driven. The GUI Host Check toggle provides a generic check for popular AV software and local firewall settings, but beyond this would be all CLI configuration. Let's check out some popular AV software pre-configured on FortiOS that we can check for:

```
IPsec-FGT-B (host-check-software) # show
config vpn ssl web host-check-software
    edit "FortiClient-AV"
        set guid "1A0271D5-3D4F-46DB-0C2C-AB37BA90D9F7"
    next
    edit "FortiClient-FW"
        set type fw
        set guid "528CB157-D384-4593-AAAA-E42DFF111CED"
    next
    edit "FortiClient-AV-Vista"
        set guid "385618A6-2256-708E-3FB9-7E98B93F91F9"
    next
..
```

This is a fairly lengthy list, but this gives you an idea of what FortiGate is looking for. The AV GUID can be found on Windows PowerShell CLI using the following command:

```
PS C:\Users\user> gwmi -Namespace root\securitycenter2 -Class
AntivirusProduct
```

```
\\DESKTOP-ROOT\securitycenter2:AntiVirusProduct.instanceGuid="{1A0271D5-3D4F-
46DB-0C
```

```
                                2C-AB37BA90D9F7}"
displayName            : FortiClient AntiVirus
instanceGuid           : {1A0271D5-3D4F-46DB-0C2C-AB37BA90D9F7}
..
```

Next, I provide a quick example of how you could customize your host checking requirements on FortiGate SSL-VPN. In this example, we are going to look for a certain domain setting within the Windows registry

```
FGT-B (root) # config vpn ssl web host-check-software
FGT-B (host-check-software) # edit Domain
new entry 'Domain' added
FGT-B (Domain) # set
os-type     OS type.
type        Type.
version     Version.
guid        Globally unique ID.
..
config vpn ssl web host-check-software
    edit "Domain"
        set type fw
        config check-item-list
            edit 1
                set type registry
                set target
"HKEY_LOCAL_MACHINE\\SYSTEM\\CurrentControlSet\\services\\Tcpip\\Parameters:D
omain==local.local"
            next
        end
    next
end
..
show vpn ssl web portal full-access
config vpn ssl web portal
    edit "full-access"
..
        set host-check-policy "Domain"
    next
end
```

Note, the NSE4 certification does not require you to have in-depth knowledge regarding SSL-VPN host checking. However, I do want you to understand what is happening behind the scenes when you make GUI changes.

The next toggle is 'Restrict to Specific OS Versions'; this is part of the host checking feature as well. This allows the ability to specify what Windows or MAC versions can connect to FortiGate SSL-VPN. Check out Image 9.16 for a complete list. Note, FortiOS provides the ability to enforce by OS patch level as well by just right-clicking one of these OS types, but this is beyond the scope of this book and the NSE4 exam currently.

Image 9.16 – Restrict OS SSL-VPN Access

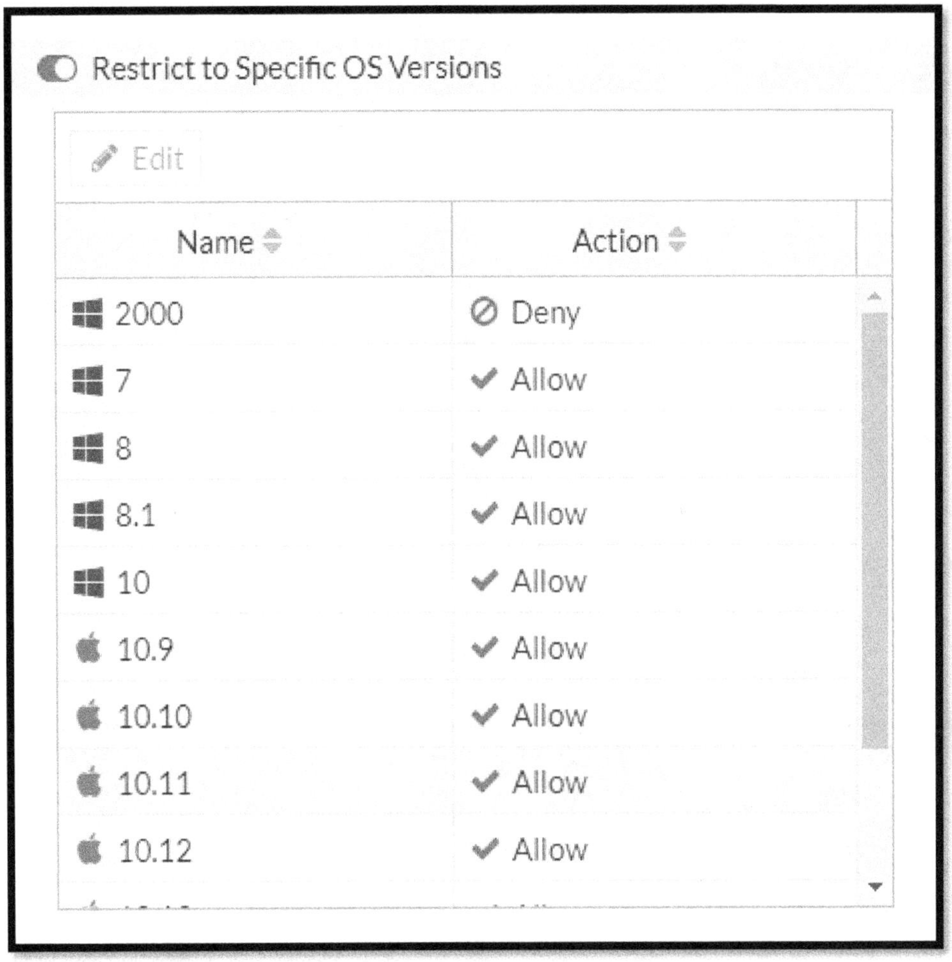

The next toggle is 'Enable Web Mode' and this is one of the two major features of the FortiGate SSL-VPN. With this setting enabled, this provides the ability for remote users to access a secure web portal on FortiGate without the need for client SSL-VPN software. The web portal then acts as a proxy to access specific resources located on FortiGate's private side. To see the configuration options available for Web Mode, see Image 9.17.

Image 9.17 – SSL-VPN Web Mode Configuration Settings

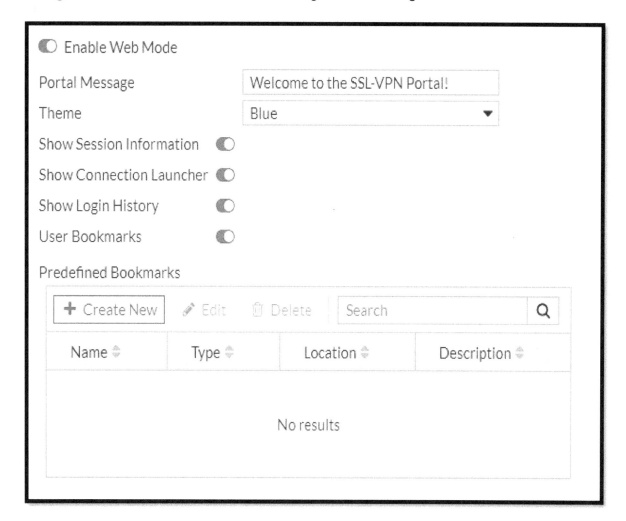

The first thing I want to mention is all these settings will make more sense once you see the front of the Web Mode portal that the client interacts with. The first couple of settings, Portal Message and Theme, are just to customize the user experience. The Portal Message could be used as a warning banner that states only authorized users may utilize this Portal for company X. Also, Fortinet provides a few different options regarding the color scheme, which is a nice feature. Next, toggle settings will be a little arbitrary to you right now until we look at the front end of the Portal, and at that point, I will double back to these settings so we can see what is actually presented to the user when these settings are enabled. Lastly, the most important item to touch on here is Predefined Bookmarks! This is where the magic happens within Web Mode and where we can provide our users with GUI widgets to access certain resources. Once you click '+ Create New' you will see the Bookmark configuration screen; check out Image 9.18.

Image 9.18 – SSL-VPN Web Mode Bookmark Configuration Example

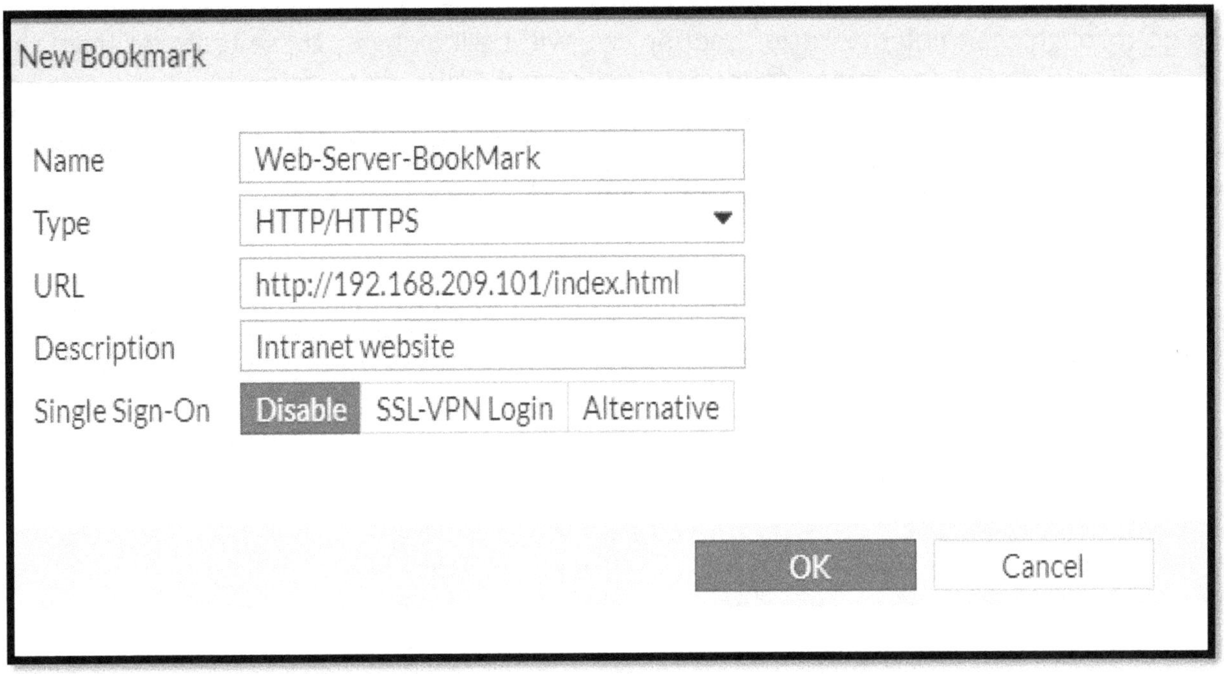

In this example, the Bookmark allows the SSL-VPN user to access an HTTP server located at the private IP of 192.168.209.101. Once again, this makes more sense once we start looking at the user Portal GUI which is the other half of the puzzle here;

The last toggle within the SSL-VPN Portal configuration GUI is 'Enable FortiClient Download'. This setting provides SSL-VPN Web Mode users the ability to obtain a FortiClient installer directly from the FortiGate and this could be used as a method to enable users to user Tunnel Mode via FortiClient.

Image 9.19 – FortiClient Download SSL-VPN Portal

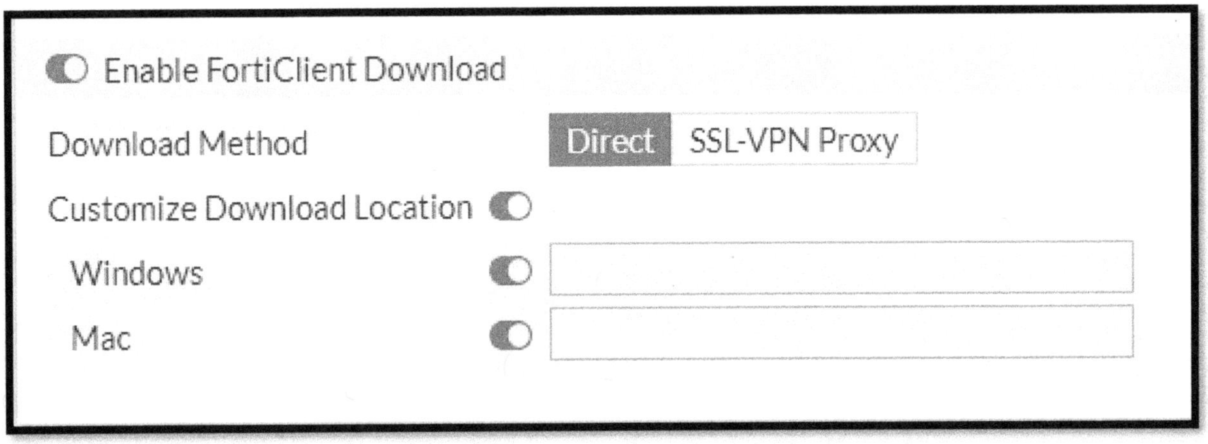

Once we go through the implementation section, we will be looking at these features from the user perspective. The CLI equivalent of the SSL-VPN Portal GUI configuration is:

```
config vpn ssl web portal
    edit "NSE-4-VPN-Portal"
        set tunnel-mode enable
        set web-mode enable
        set ip-pools "SSLVPN_TUNNEL_ADDR1"
        set split-tunneling-routing-address "internal"
        config bookmark-group
            edit "gui-bookmarks"
                config bookmarks
                    edit "Web-Server-BookMark"
                        set description "Intranet website"
                        set url "http://192.168.209.101/index.html"
                    next
                end
            next
        end
        set heading "Welcome to the NSE4 SSL-VPN Por"
        set customize-forticlient-download-url enable
        set windows-forticlient-download-url "windows-fc"
        set macos-forticlient-download-url "mac-fc"
    next
end
```

Now that we have covered the SSL-VPN Portal configuration section, next we move into the SSL-VPN Settings configuration where we reference the *NSE-4-VPN-Portal* object we just created.

SSL-VPN Settings

The SSL-VPN Settings Menu is where the VPN becomes active, and we tie together all our configuration objects into one goal which is TLS access for remote users. I will walk through the SSL-VPN Settings configuration page, just like I did with the SSL-VPN Portal. In the GUI, go to VPN -> SSL-VPN Settings and check out Image 9.20.

Image 9.20 – SSL-VPN Settings GUI Configuration Page

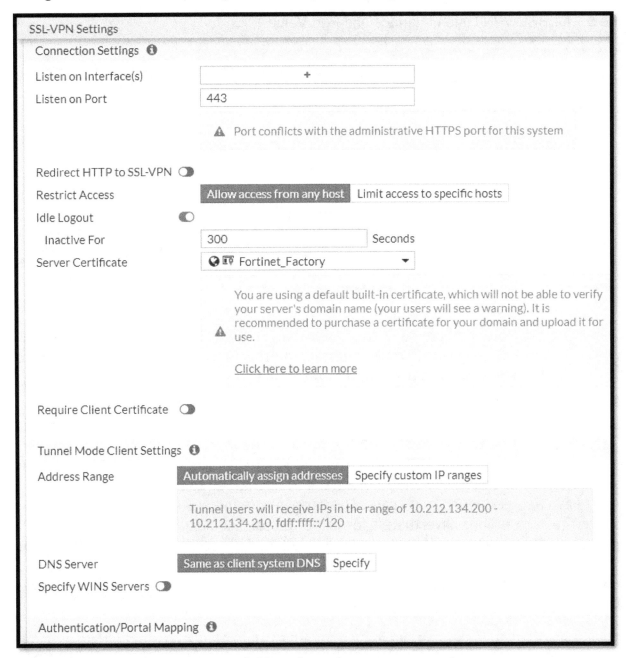

Take a moment to review Image 9.20 and generate some questions.

The first configuration setting is 'Listen on Interface(s)'; once you select this option, a list of interfaces display, and this is where we can select which interface(s) the SSL-VPN server listens on. Note that multiple interfaces can be selected for redundancy. The next setting is 'Listen on Port'. A port must be specified for the SSL-VPN server to listen on. If HTTPS administrator access is allowed on the same interface as the SSL-VPN server, then the SSL-VPN server must use something other than port 443 because this port conflicts with the local HTTPS administrative access function. In our example, I use port 8443 for the SSL-VPN server to accept inbound connections. See Image 9.21.

Image 9.21 – SSL-VPN Listen Interface and Port Value

Notice here that the socket is provided to access the SSL-VPN,192.168.209.2:8443 . The IP address 192.168.209.2 is assigned to WAN1 interface on this FortiGate. To access the secure Portal, a user would simply need to use a web browser and go to https://192.168.209.2:8443, and if tunnel mode is used then, 192.168.209.2 would be the SSL-VPN gateway address.

Next, see Image 9.22 on the next page. This image shows a few more settings that we could use for the SSL-VPN. The first toggle, Redirect HTTP to SSL-VPN, which means, if a user attempts to access a secure Portal page via HTTP, then the user will be redirected to the HTTPS. Next is 'Restrict Access'; this is essentially an IP whitelist of users allowed to access the SSL-VPN. This is a setting I have not used much in my career because most remote access users have dynamic IP's. Still, the feature is here nevertheless for corner cases. The next setting is 'Idle Logout', which is default 300 seconds; this setting sets the threshold for how long SSL-VPN users can be idle while connected to the VPN. A common setting for this value is 28800, which is 8 hours and is also the common workday for most folks.

Image 9.22 – SSL-VPN GUI Settings

The next item to note in Image 9.22 is the 'Server Certificate'. The Server Certificate field provides a dropdown to select which certificate you wish the SSL-VPN to utilize to secure communication for VPN users. Fortinet provides a recommendation to purchase and upload your own domain certificate. The next toggle option is "Require Client Certificate", this setting is required when clients authenticate using certificates. Certificates authentication is beyond the scope of this chapter.

Next is the 'Tunnel Mode Client Settings' settings; check out Image 9.23 on the next page. You might be thinking we already configured the SSL-VPN Address Range settings within the SSL-VPN Portal settings GUI page, which we did.

At this part of the configuration is where some folks get confused when working with FortiGate SSL-VPN, and it's not really going to make sense to you until we cover the 'Authentication/Portal Mapping' section and configure the *Identity* Firewall Policy Entry. Essentially, FortiGate provides the granularity to map users to different SSL-VPN Portals depending on which group they authenticate to. Since most organizations use LDAP and Active Directory group infrastructure to provide particular sets of permissions to user groups, this also provides the function to restrict SSL-VPN user access based on the user group.

For now, think of the VPN-SSL Tunnel Mode Client Settings -> Address Range values as the default settings and that SSL-VPN Portal profiles can be used to override the default settings by binding them to certain user groups. Next, just like we configured in the IPsec Dial-up VPN, we can also specify SSL-VPN users a DNS and WINs server IP to use; this is important for Enterprises that communicate to internal resources using FQDN.

Image 9.23 –Tunnel Mode Settings

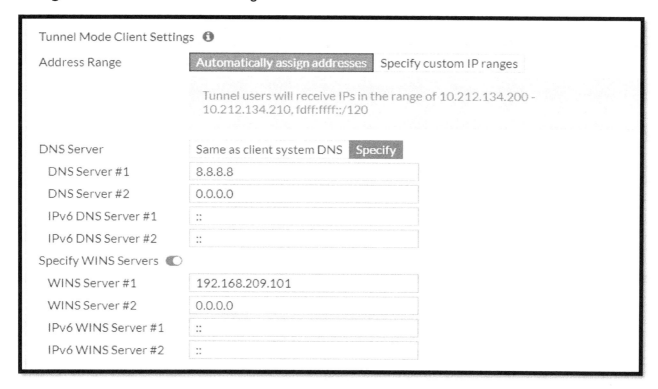

SSL-VPN Authentication & Portal Mapping Settings

The last part of the SSL-VPN Settings to cover and one of the more important features is the 'Authentication/Portal Mapping'. See Image 9.24 below:

Image 9.24 – SSL-VPN Authentication/Portal Mapping

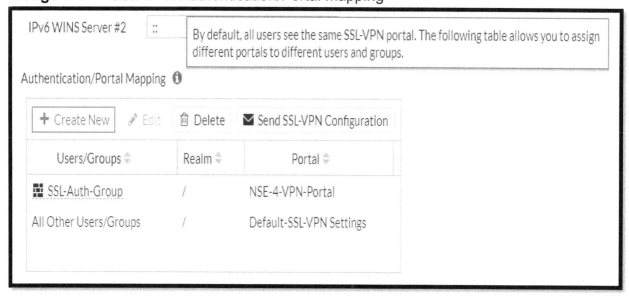

This is the configuration section where we tell FortiGate what user groups are authorized to use the SSL-VPN. We can also provide the granularity to provide users unique settings dependent on which user-group they authenticate to. I configured an additional SSL-VPN Portal and named it 'Default-SSL-VPN-Settings' and mapped it to the *Users/Groups* setting field 'All Other Users/Groups'. So the authentication part of the chapter makes more sense.

At this point, the SSL-VPN settings are almost complete. The SSL-VPN differentiates from the IPsec Dial-up VPN because authentication is performed within the Firewall Policy Entry.

<u>SSL-VPN Authentication</u>

The last piece of the puzzle to have an operational SSL-VPN is to create a Firewall Policy Entry that references a user group, which makes this entry an *identity* policy. For our first example, I reference the Portal object 'NSE-4-VPN-Portal' and use the Group object 'SSL-Auth-Group' for

Image 9.25 – SSL VPN Authentication Identity Policy

a Proof of Concept (PoC). Check out policy configuration in Image 9.25.

Something new here we have not touched on, is the SSL network interface, which is a single virtual interface per VDOM. Since we are working out of the root VDOM, the SSL-VPN virtual interface name is 'ssl.root'. We treat this interface just like every other virtual interface on FortiOS, except we must provide a user group value within the Source field when referencing it. There can only be one SSL-VPN virtual interface per VDOM. Group Object(s) within the identity policy contains the users allowed to access the SSL-VPN. Within the 'SSL-Auth-Group' object is a user named 'NSE4'. We will attempt to authenticate to the SSL-VPN with this user and access the encrypted tunnel so to ping the loopback interface on FortiGate. During the test, we will run the SSL-VPN debug, which is:

```
FGT-B (root) # diagnose debug application sslvpn 255
Debug messages will be on for 30 minutes.
FGT-B (root) # diagnose debug enable
```

Next, I will navigate to the SSL-VPN client and configured the necessary FortiClient parameters to access Tunnel Mode.

Image 9.26 – FortiClient SSL-VPN Settings

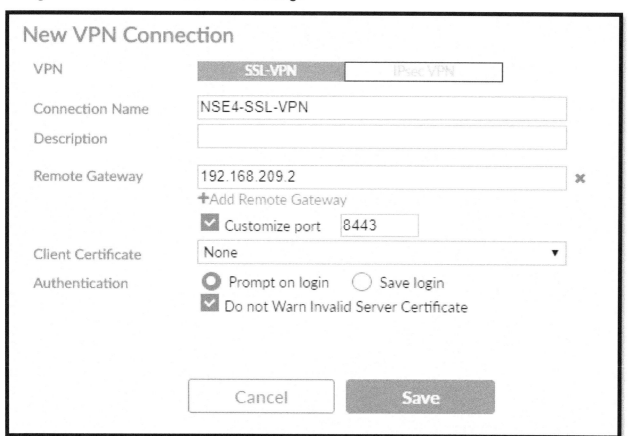

Note here a custom SSL-VPN port is being used, which is 8443. It is a common mistake to forget to modify the default value here to match what is configured locally on FortiGate. Next, we will run our debugs while we connected and check the parameters.

Before we review the debugs, review the SSL-VPN topology at hand; check out Image 9.27.

Image 9.27 - SSL-VPN Tunnel Mode Diagram

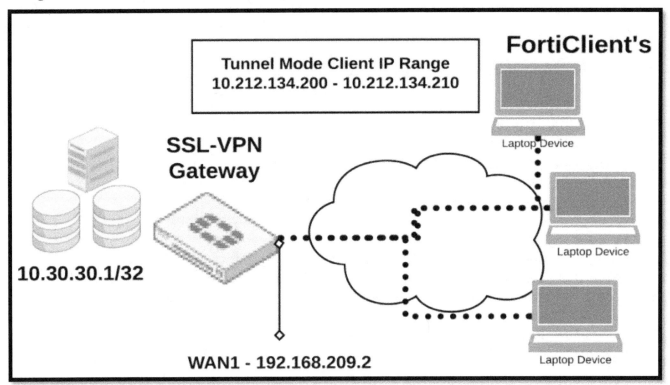

The SSL-VPN Gateway is WAN1, and the IP is 192.168.209.2. Clients will receive an SSL-VPN IP address between 10.212.134.200 - 10.212.134.200 to identify the SSL-VPN client while traversing the VPN. The server resource is represented by the 10.30.30.1/32 loopback IP on FortiGate SSL-VPN Gateway. Now that we understand the topology let's go ahead and connect to the VPN! Review the following SSL-VPN Tunnel Mode debugs:

```
FGT-B (root) # diagnose debug application sslvpn 255
Debug messages will be on for 30 minutes.
FGT-B (root) # diagnose debug enable

[30415:root:7]client cert requirement: no
[..
[30409:root:8]SSL established: TLSv1.2 ECDHE-RSA-AES256-GCM-SHA384
[30409:root:8]rmt_web_auth_info_parser_common:461 no session id in auth info
[30409:root:8]rmt_web_get_access_cache:793 invalid cache, ret=4103

..
[30410:root:8]SSL established: TLSv1.2 ECDHE-RSA-AES256-GCM-SHA384
[30410:root:8]rmt_web_auth_info_parser_common:461 no session id in auth info

..
```

[30410:root:8]rmt_logincheck_cb_handler:1181 user 'NSE4' has a matched local entry.
[30410:root:8]two factor check for NSE4: off
[30410:root:8][fam_auth_send_req_internal:597] **The user NSE4 is authenticated.**
[30410:root:8]SSL VPN login **matched rule (1).**

..

[30410:root:8]deconstruct_session_id:426 decode session id ok, user=[NSE4],group=[SSL-Auth-Group],authserver=[],portal=[**NSE-4-VPN-Portal**],**host=[192.168.209.7]**,realm=[],idx=0,auth=1,sid=714941cf,login=1601391 193,access=1601391193,saml_logout_url=no

..

[30410:root:8]Destroy sconn 0x7f95be2800, connSize=0. (root)
[30412:root:8]allocSSLConn:298 sconn 0x7f95be2800 (0:root)
[30412:root:8]client cert requirement: no
[30412:root:8]SSL established: TLSv1.2 ECDHE-RSA-AES256-GCM-SHA384
[30412:root:8]deconstruct_session_id:426 decode session id ok, user=[NSE4],group=[SSL-Auth-Group],authserver=[],portal=[NSE-4-VPN-Portal],host=[192.168.209.7],realm=[],idx=0,auth=1,sid=714941cf,login=1601391 193,access=1601391193,saml_logout_url=no

..

[30415:root:8]allocSSLConn:298 sconn 0x7f96986c00 (0:root)
[30415:root:8]DTLS established: **DTLSv1 ECDHE-RSA-AES256-SHA from 192.168.209.7**
[30415:root:8]sslvpn_dtls_handle_client_data:632 got type clthello
[30415:root:8]sslvpn_dtls_handle_client_data:642 got cookie:
Ff1n4l199TCaq7ay44bdekAbgX8HxTQu7IVC8AXbMvKD0I02NA6l1GGjxv2w2knmcAxinf4Phbl1N
8zWsiUvznItAyyaczMs77YjBeKnV0hqbIeSNShiMyF0Zpx2bxQX714BjkLJB+KKtE/28AsHyDsZMH
zFB2ZhvKeGfa+XZLXE1HhM36RjJNe1RP37x2ADWAb+ehplcL/VjQdJbYbPWw==

..

[30415:root:8]sslvpn_dtls_handle_client_data:650 got **dns0 8.8.8.8**
[30415:root:8]sslvpn_dtls_handle_client_data:657 got **dns1 4.2.2.2**
[30415:root:8]sconn 0x7f96986c00 (0:root) vfid=0 **local=[192.168.209.2]** remote=[192.168.209.7] dynamicip=[10.212.134.200]
[30415:root:8]Prepare to launch ppp service ...
[30415:root:8]tun: ppp 0x7f95cd0000 dev (ssl.root) opened fd 31
[30415:root:8]Will add auth policy for **policy 5 for user NSE4:SSL-Auth-Group**
[30415:root:8]Add auth logon for user **NSE4:SSL-Auth-Group, matched group** number 1
[30415:root:8]sslvpn_send_ctrl_msg:914 0x7f96986c00 message: svrhello ok 192.168.209.7

..

RCV: LCP Configure_Request id(1) len(14) [Maximum_Received_Unit 1354] [Magic_Number 1A448360]

..

```
SND: LCP Configure_Request id(1) len(10) [Magic_Number 170F3879]
[30415:root:0]lcp_reqci: returning CONFACK.
[30415:root:0]SND: LCP Configure_Ack id(1) len(14) [Maximum_Received_Unit
1354] [Magic_Number 1A448360]
[30415:root:0]RCV: LCP Configure_Ack id(1) len(10) [Magic_Number 170F3879]
[30415:root:0]lcp_up: with mtu 1354
[30415:root:0]SND: IPCP Configure_Request id(1) [IP_Address 192.168.209.2]
[30415:root:0]RCV: IPCP Configure_Request id(0) [IP_Address 0.0.0.0]
[Primary_DNS_IP_Address 0.0.0.0] [Secondary_DNS_IP_Address 0.0.0.0]
[30415:root:0]ipcp: returning Configure-NAK
[30415:root:0]SND: IPCP Configure_Nak id(0) [IP_Address 10.212.134.200]
[Primary_DNS_IP_Address 8.8.8.8] [Secondary_DNS_IP_Address 8.8.8.8]
[30415:root:0]RCV: IPCP Configure_Ack id(1) [IP_Address 192.168.209.2]
[30415:root:0]RCV: IPCP Configure_Request id(1) [IP_Address 10.212.134.200]
[Primary_DNS_IP_Address 8.8.8.8] [Secondary_DNS_IP_Address 8.8.8.8]
[30415:root:0]ipcp: returning Configure-ACK
[30415:root:0]SND: IPCP Configure_Ack id(1) [IP_Address 10.212.134.200]
[Primary_DNS_IP_Address 8.8.8.8] [Secondary_DNS_IP_Address 8.8.8.8]
[30415:root:0]ipcp: up ppp:0x7f95cd0000 caller:0x7f96986c00 tun:31
[30415:root:0]Cannot determine ethernet address for proxy ARP
[30415:root:0]local  IP address 192.168.209.2
[30415:root:0]remote IP address 10.212.134.200
[30415:root:8]sslvpn_ppp_associate_fd_to_ipaddr:281 associate 10.212.134.200
to tun (ssl.root:31)
```

Take a few moments and step through this output. I've highlighted a few important lines and cleaned up the debug somewhat. If you walk through the output, you can see user 'NSE4' is successfully authenticated by group *SSL-Auth-Group* which is mapped to portal *NSE-4-VPN-Portal*, which contains the default SSL-VPN IP range 10.212.134.200 - 10.212.134.210. We can check the Windows machine NIC adapter configuration to confirm this.

```
C:\Users\user>ipconfig
..
Ethernet adapter Ethernet 3:

    Connection-specific DNS Suffix  . :
    Link-local IPv6 Address . . . . . : fe80::acb0:f3ef:1234:53ad%10
    IPv4 Address. . . . . . . . . . . : 10.212.134.200
    Subnet Mask . . . . . . . . . . . : 255.255.255.255
    Default Gateway . . . . . . . . . :

..
```

Jumping back to the debugs, I want to point out after authentication is successful, FortiOS utilizes PPP to assigned SSL-VPN clients IP parameters.

```
[30415:root:8]Prepare to launch ppp service ...
```

We can also see in the debugs the explicit IP and DNS information assigned:

```
IPCP Configure_Nak id(0) [IP_Address 10.212.134.200] [Primary_DNS_IP_Address 8.8.8.8]
```

Before we move onto SSL-VPN verification, I want to share one more debug we can run for authentication troubleshooting, which is:

```
IPsec-FGT-B (root) # diagnose debug application fnbamd 255
Debug messages will be on for 30 minutes.
```

In this example, I disabled the *sslvpn* debug and only have *fnbamd* enabled.

---

fnbamd stands for Fortinet Non-Blocking Authentication Module Daemon.

The fnbamd daemon handles all authentication processes for other daemons on FortiOS and, in this case, SSL-VPN authentication. I'm going to disconnect '*NSE4*' SSL-VPN users and connecting again while fnbamd debug is running.

```
IPsec-FGT-B (root) # diagnose debug application  fnbamd 255
Debug messages will be on for 30 minutes.

IPsec-FGT-B (root) # diagnose debug enable
IPsec-FGT-B (root) # local auth is done with user 'NSE4', ret=0
```

Here is an example of a successful authentication attempt; this can sometimes show useful information when debugging more complex authentication methods. Now that the SSL-VPN is configured and we can authenticate with a local user, the next step is verification. Meaning, what user(s) are currently authenticated and the metadata around that session. We also review SSL-VPN traffic offload onto CP ASIC.

SSL-VPN Tunnel Mode Verification

Once users are connected to FortiGate SSL-VPN services, we have a few tools to gather details around the user sessions. First, check out what CLI options are available:

```
FGT-B (root) # diagnose vpn ssl ?
list                    List current connections.
mux                     Show mux information.
```

```
mux-stat                   Show mux statistics.
statistics                 SSL VPN statistics
hw-acceleration-status     SSL hardware acceleration status.
tunnel-test                Enable/disable SSL VPN old tunnel mode IP
allocation method.
web-mode-test              Enable/disable random session ID in proxy URL for
testing.
info                       SSL VPN information
debug-filter               SSL-VPN debug message filter.
..
FGT-B (root) # get vpn ssl ?
monitor       SSL VPN session.
settings      Configure SSL VPN.
web           web
FGT-B (root) # get vpn status ssl ?
..
hw-acceleration-status     SSL hardware acceleration status.
list                       List current connections.
```

We don't cover all of these but I want you see the CLI notes for each command.

Monitor SSL VPN users

The first command we are going to use if the '#diagnose vpn ssl list' :

```
FGT-B (root) # diagnose vpn ssl list
[30415:root]sconn=0x7f96986c00 from(192.168.209.7) dtls state: loop
```

From this output, we can pull the users public IP, which in our case is my lab IP, and that the user is connecting using DTLS ; note that DTLS is TLS using UDP as a transport protocol instead of TCP, this is configurable on FortiGate SSL-VPN, and I'll touch on this more later in the Advanced Features section of this chapter. The next command provides a few more details about the users currently using the SSL-VPN:

```
FGT-B (root) # get vpn ssl monitor
SSL VPN Login Users:
 Index  User   Group      Auth Type    Timeout        From       HTTP in/out
HTTPS in/out
 0      NSE4   SSL-Auth-Group 1(1)         297     192.168.209.7  0/0
0/0
```

The #get vpn ssl monitor , command displays what users are currently logged on and what group they are authenticated with. Next is a more detailed command that provides information around the number of users, tunnels, and memory:

```
FGT-B (root) # diagnose vpn ssl statistics
SSLVPN statistics (root):
-----------------
```

```
Memory unit:              1
System total memory:      2012004352
System free memory:       881889280
SSLVPN memory margin:     201200435
SSLVPN state:             normal

Max number of users:      1
Max number of tunnels:    1
Max number of connections: 4

Current number of users:       1
Current number of tunnels:     1
Current number of connections: 1
```

This command could be useful if FortiGate is running low on resources and SSL-VPN users report issues. In general, this command can provide a quick snapshot of your connected SSL-VPN users. When I worked for a major MSSP, we always knew when a FortiGate hit something called 'conserve mode', which is a state FortiGate enters when memory usage is very high for the entire system. Conserve mode would then prevent SSL-VPN users from connecting to FortiGate. I go over Conserve Mode in detail in our troubleshooting chapter within this book. The next command provides the most detailed information around SSL-VPN authenticated users:

```
FGT-B (root) # diagnose firewall auth list

10.212.134.200, NSE4
        type: fw, id: 0, duration: 319, idled: 319
        expire: 28480, allow-idle: 28799
        flag(80): sslvpn
        packets: in 0 out 0, bytes: in 0 out 0
        group_id: 2
        group_name: SSL-Auth-Group

----- 1 listed, 0 filtered ------
```

Within the output of this command, we can determine how long the user has been logged-on to the SSL-VPN and when they expire, and this command also provides how much data the user has sent to FortiGate to be processed, which could be useful for troubleshooting.

The last verification command to discuss is one to ensure SSL-VPN traffic is indeed offloaded to CP ASIC. The command that provides this information is:

```
IPsec-FGT-B (root) # diagnose vpn ssl hw-acceleration-status
Acceleration hardware detected: kxp=on cipher=on
```

The command to determine the FortiGate Content Processor chip is, #get hardware status. Here is what output would look like for a 60F.

```
FGT-B (global) # get hardware status
```

```
Model name: FortiGate-60F
ASIC version: SOC4
CPU: ARMv8
Number of CPUs: 8
RAM: 1918 MB
EMMC: 3662 MB(MLC) /dev/mmcblk0
Hard disk: not available
USB Flash: not available
Network Card chipset: FortiASIC NP6XLITE Adapter (rev.)
```

Note the SoC4 chip contains the NP and the CP processing logic. Sometimes it might be necessary to disable the CP for troubleshooting. This can be performed on a Firewall Policy Entry.

```
config firewall policy
edit 0
set auto-asic-offload disable
```

This covers SSL-VPN verification. The next topic to discuss is SSL-VPN routing.

SSL-VPN Routing

When a user connects to the SSL-VPN successfully, FortiGate injects a route into the kernel routing table. The Local SSL-VPN IP on Windows client is 10.212.134.200. This can be cross-referenced on FortiOS.

```
Ethernet adapter Ethernet 3:

    Connection-specific DNS Suffix  . :
    Link-local IPv6 Address . . . . . : fe80::acb0:1234:1234:53ad%10
    IPv4 Address. . . . . . . . . . . : 10.212.134.200
    Subnet Mask . . . . . . . . . . . : 255.255.255.255
    Default Gateway . . . . . . . . . :
```

On FortiGate:

```
FGT-B (root) # get router info kernel | grep 10.212.134.200
tab=254 vf=0 scope=0 type=1 proto=17 prio=10 0.0.0.0/0.0.0.0/0-
>10.212.134.200/29 pref=0.0.0.0 gwy=0.0.0.0 dev=19(ssl.root)
```

From the output we can see that FortiGate holds the route 10.212.134.200/29 that will route traffic back to the SSL-VPN tunnel interface. Next we will attempt to ping the loopback interface on FortiGate with the Windows client through the SSL-VPN. The IP address of the loopback interface is 10.30.30.1/32. The first item to check is that split tunneling includes this IP address and that FortiClient installed it correctly on the Windows machine. Since user 'NSE4' is indeed connected to the SSL-VPN currently then we will run #route print – on Windows machine to check for a route:

```
C:\Users\user>route print
```

```
..
IPv4 Route Table
===========================================================================
Active Routes:
Network Destination        Netmask          Gateway         Interface  Metric
..
       10.30.30.1   255.255.255.255   10.212.134.201   10.212.134.200       1
..
       172.16.10.0      255.255.255.0   10.212.134.201   10.212.134.200       1
```

I've bolded the split tunnel routes received by FortiClient. Since the route for 10.30.30.1/32 is present, then we should be able to communicate with the loopback interface once a policy is configured. I'm going to show the Firewall Policy Entry on the CLI:

```
FGT-B (5) # show
config firewall policy
    edit 5
        set name "SSL-VPN-Policy"
        set uuid 994f00f2-003c-51eb-517a-1469b7053edb
        set srcintf "ssl.root"
        set dstintf "Lo_10.30.30.1"
        set srcaddr "all"
        set dstaddr "10.30.30.1/32"
        set action accept
        set schedule "always"
        set service "ALL"
        set logtraffic disable
        set groups "SSL-Auth-Group"
    next
end
```

I've bolded the important items within the Firewall Policy Entry to take notice of. Firstly, the source interface must be the ssl.root interface. Next, the allowed destination address (10.30.30.1/32) must be within the provided split-tunnel address range(s) within the Portal configuration. Lastly, the *groups* value (**SSL-Auth-Group**) must contain the SSL-VPN users to be authenticated. Next, we will run a flow debug before initiating the ICMP Echo Request on the Windows machine.

```
diag debug reset
diag debug enable
diag debug flow show console enable // This line is required in 5.6 code and
prior
diag debug flow filter addr 10.30.30.1
diag debug flow trace start 200
..
```

```
FGT-B (root) # id=20085 trace_id=9 func=print_pkt_detail line=5639 msg="vd-
root:0 received a packet(proto=1, 10.212.134.200:1->10.30.30.1:2048) from
ssl.root. type=8, code=0, id=1, seq=1489."
id=20085 trace_id=9 func=init_ip_session_common line=5810 msg="allocate a new
session-0017ffd3"
id=20085 trace_id=9 func=vf_ip_route_input_common line=2598 msg="find a
route: flag=84000000 gw-10.30.30.1 via root"
id=20085 trace_id=10 func=print_pkt_detail line=5639 msg="vd-root:0 received
a packet(proto=1, 10.30.30.1:1->10.212.134.200:0) from local. type=0, code=0,
id=1, seq=1489."
id=20085 trace_id=10 func=resolve_ip_tuple_fast line=5720 msg="Find an
existing session, id-0017ffd3, reply direction"
id=20085 trace_id=10 func=ipd_post_route_handler line=439 msg="out ssl.root
vwl_zone_id 0, state2 0x0, quality 0."
```

Again, I've bolded a few important items in the debug, but our ping traffic was essentially successful. FortiGate should now have a Route Cache entry for SSL-VPN host IP address for end-user.

```
FGT-B (root) # diagnose ip rtcache list | grep 10.212.134.200 -A 1 -B 1
..
--
family=02 tab=254 vrf=0 vf=0 type=03 tos=0 flag=90000200
10.212.134.200@19(ssl.root)->255.255.255.255@18(root) gwy=0.0.0.0
prefsrc=26.179.117.27
ci: ref=0 lastused=29 expire=0 err=00000000 used=335 br=0 pmtu=16436

..
```

The last item I want to touch on regarding SSL-VPN routing is the Static Route Entry. FortiGate allows us to provide static route(s) that point to the virtual SSL-VPN interface. The reason for this is because most of the time, the SSL-VPN IP range needs to be advertised to other routers in the network to obtain reachability. This can be done in many ways, but a common method is to redistribute a Static Route into a routing protocol to be shared throughout the network. Here is the CLI for a static route example:

```
FGT-B (root) # 0: config vdom
0: edit root
0: config router static
0: edit 0
0: set dst 10.212.134.0 255.255.255.0
0: set device "ssl.root"
0: end
0: end
```

And check out Image 9.28 for the GUI equivalent for reference.

Image 9.28 – SSL-VPN Static Route

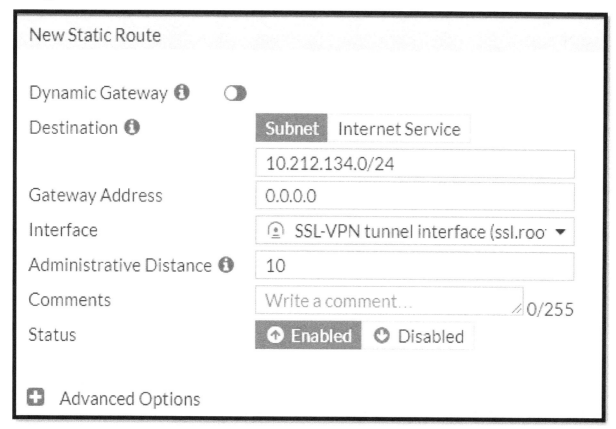

This brings us to the end of the routing section for the SSL-VPN users using Tunnel Mode. The next topic to cover is SSL-VPN Web Mode!

SSL-VPN Web Mode

So we have discussed some aspects of Web Mode SSL-VPN already, and in this section, we are going to run through a few examples. Web Mode is clientless secure access to a hosted web portal on FortiGate. Within this Portal, items called Bookmarks can be configured to that act as

Image 9.29 - SSL-VPN Portal Gateway Socket

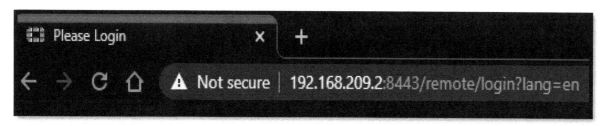

a proxy to private LAN resources. To access the SSL-VPN Portal, we must navigate to the gateway IP with the specified port number, which in our case is 8443.

Image 9.30 – SSL-VPN Web Mode Portal Login

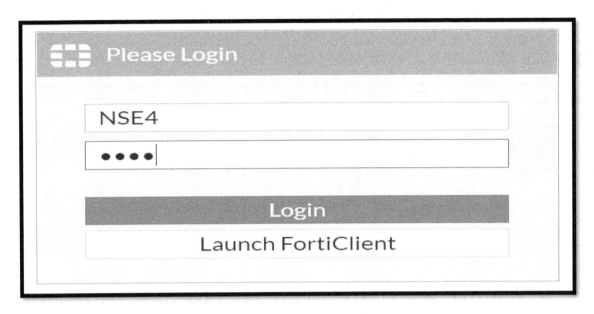

Next, a login screen is presented, and we must enter the credentials of our SSL-VPN users, 'NSE4'. If login is successful, then the default Web Mode GUI portal displays. Post login, you are

Image 9.31 – Edit Bookmark Portal Page

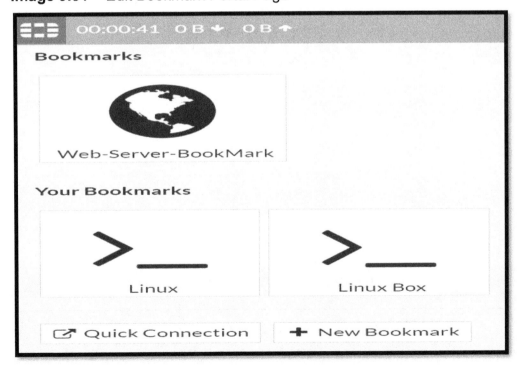

going to see the Bookmarks section. The first sections houses the predefined Bookmarks configured on the backend. The next section allows the SSL-VPN users to define their own Bookmarks via the '+New Bookmark' icon. Check out the next page, Image 9.31. The next item to touch on regarding Web Portal Bookmarks is the list of protocols that are configurable by the SSL-VPN users. See Image 9.32 for all the options.

Image 9.32 – SSL-VPN User Portal Web Mode

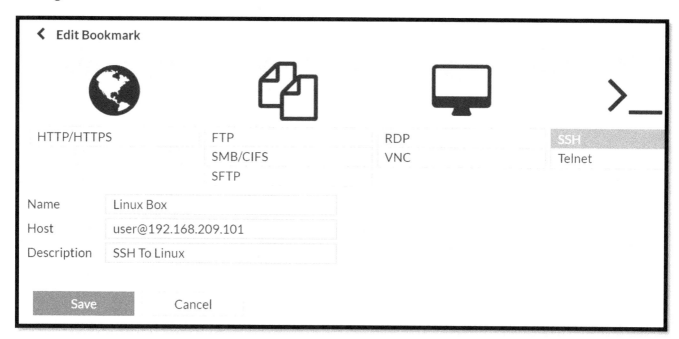

The last topic to discuss for Web Mode SSL-VPN is realms.

SSL-VPN Realm Settings

The purpose of Realms is to differentiate Web Mode Portals by assigning users to different authentication groups. To configure this on FortiGate, first in the GUI, go to VPN-> SSL-VPN Realms and select '+Create New'. We are going to create a Realm named 'realm2'; check out Image 9.33 below.

Image 9.33 – Create New Realm GUI

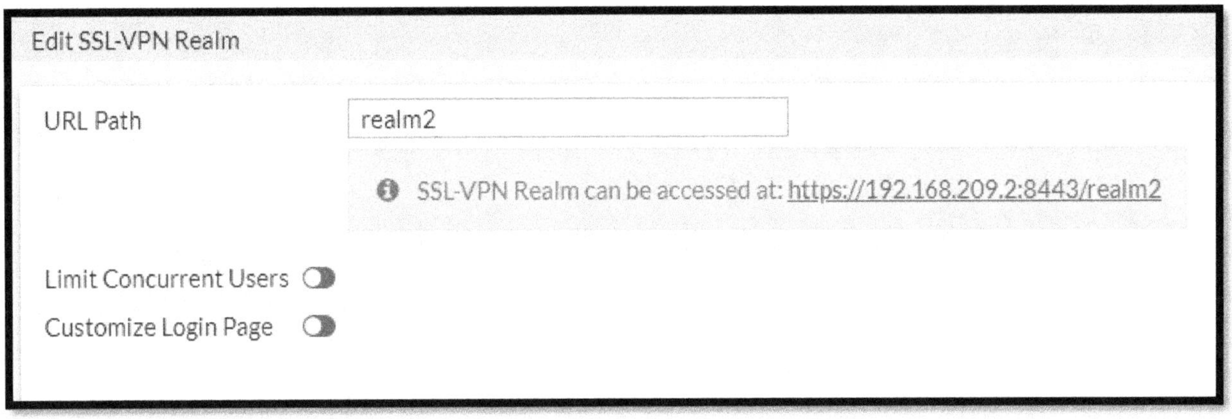

Now that the 'realm2' object is created to access the realm2 GUI portal, the user would browse to 'https://192.168.209.2:8443/realm2'. Next, to make this configuration live on FortiGate, A user group and SSL-VPN Portal must be mapped to realm2. I have already performed this configuration change under the SSL-VPN Settings GUI page. Check out Image 9.34 for details:

Image 9.34 – SSL-VPN Realm to Portal Mapping

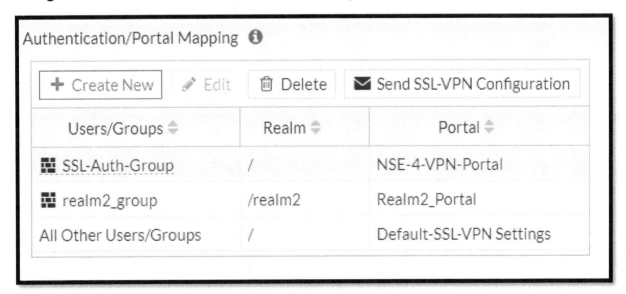

Notice the 2nd entry from the top with the 'realm2_group' user group. This line is what associates the user group authentication to the Realm and to the SSL-VPN Portal configuration. This configuration provides the ability to explicitly control the SSL-VPN Portal that users receive. Note, realms can also be accessed with FQDN via host headers. To configure this, see below CLI output:

```
FGT-B (Realm) # show
config vpn ssl web realm
..
    edit "realm2"
..

FGT-B (realm) # edit realm2 ?

FGT-B (realm2) # set
max-concurrent-user    Maximum concurrent users (0 - 65535, 0 means
unlimited).
login-page             Replacement HTML for SSL-VPN login page.
virtual-host           Virtual host name for realm.
virtual-host-only      Enable/disable enforcement of virtual host method for
SSL-VPN client access.
radius-server          RADIUS server associated with realm.
FGT-B (realm2) # set virtual-host hr.company.com
```

Lastly, remember for newly configured *realm2_group* to be active on FortiGate, a Firewall Policy Entry must be configured, referencing the SSL-VPN virtual interface as a source with the *realm2_group* user group referenced in the source field of the policy. This brings us to the end of Tunnel Mode and Web Mode overview on FortiGate. In the next section, we dive a little deeper into some more advanced features SSL-VPN has to offer and some of the details around the underlying technology.

SSL-VPN Advance Features

So far, in this chapter, we have discussed many things around FortiGate SSL-VPN and TLS theory. At this point, you should feel confident in how TLS works and how FortiGate uses these technologies to provide remote users their very own encrypted VPN tunnel. For networks with no odd requirements, then what you know about SSL-VPNs on FortiGate will be enough to perform your job well. However, sometimes specific conditions require more knowledge of the underlying technologies and advanced configuration methods. The first item I want to touch on is DTLS.

SSL-VPN DTLS

DTLS stands for Datagram Transport Layer Security. Meaning, TLS uses UDP instead of TCP. As for 5.4 FortiOS, SSL-VPN uses DTLS. The reason for this is because UDP is faster than TCP and does not have some of the issues that come along with TCP. With TCP, you can hit issues with TCP Window sizing, delay in TCP ACK messages and can cause other issues when inside tunnel TCP communication is being carried by TLS-TCP. To remove all of this, DTLS is used. Here are the CLI DTLS parameters:

```
FGT-B (settings) # show ful | grep dtls
    set dtls-hello-timeout 10
    set dtls-tunnel enable
    set dtls-max-proto-ver dtls1-2
    set dtls-min-proto-ver dtls1-0
```

The first setting to cover is the DTLS hello timeout time value; by default, this is 10 seconds. This timer is the mechanism that detects if TLS endpoints are still reachable. When FortiClient connects to the FortiGate SSL-VPN server, by default, a TLS TCP connection first establishes, and if successful, then the two points negotiate a DTLS connection if the configuration and code versions allow it. Next, to only use TCP based TLS, then DTLS must disable in the CLI via:

```
#set dtls-tunnel disable
```

I'm sure you noticed the max and min version settings as well. As of FortiOS 6.4, DTLS can run TLS versions 1.2 or 1.0. These settings can be adjusted to fit your organization's needs. This section covers DTLS in a nutshell. The next topics to discuss are stability of the SSL-VPN and the tools we have to account for TLS packet loss because of end-user unstable networks.

SSL-VPN stability

If you work with SSL-VPNs on FortiGate's long enough, eventually, you will run into issues where your users report they are getting 'kicked off' or disconnected from the VPN. So what do you do?

Well, there are a couple of options. The problem could be with the end host, the transit network, or the FortiGate. If the problem is with the transit network, then there are specific SSL-VPN settings we can adjust. The first set of values to review are the ones controlling the SSL-VPN timeout; see below CLI:

```
FGT-B (settings) # show ful | grep timeout
    set idle-timeout 300
    set auth-timeout 28800
    set login-timeout 30
    set dtls-hello-timeout 10
```

The first setting to touch on is `idle-timeout 300`, (5 minutes) this is how long the FortiGate can receive no traffic before it disconnects the user's TLS tunnel. It is common to set this value much higher. I've seen many organizations set this to be 8 hours, which is 28800 seconds, which is usually the individual's work shift. I just want to note here; this might be the fix to the problem for the end-user but does increase the security risk because what if a user walks away from their computer at the wrong location and someone else is using their VPN?

The next setting is `auth-timeout 28800`, which states the user <u>must</u> reauthenticate to the SSL-VPN after this timer expires (8 hours by default). The maximum value for this setting is 259200 seconds, which is three days or 72 hours, and this value might need to adjust in production. This feature was created because there are some users that work longer than 8 hours straight. To disable this feature, set the `auth-timeout 0`, which tells FortiOS never to disconnect remote SSL-VPN users. This may help stabilize the VPN user experience, but once again, this introduces increase security risks.

The next setting is `login-timeout 30;` this setting comes into effect during the actual SSL-VPN log on process. Sometimes this value may need to be increased if remote authentication occurs, meaning LDAP or RADIUS etc., because remote authentication methods require more time for SSL-VPN users to be verified. Also, if two-factor authentication is used, then this value may need to be increased to provide more time for the end-user to enter their 2-factor OTP.

The next setting to discuss controls FortiOS behavior when an SSL-VPN client is changing source IP often, which causes SSL-VPN to disconnect. Having a dynamic IP address is common for a user that works off roaming Wi-Fi or LTE, where their IP address may change depending on their physical location. In cases like this, Fortinet has provided a few tools; see below CLI settings.

```
FGT-B (settings) # show
..
    set auth-session-check-source-ip disable    //default enabled
    set tunnel-connect-without-reauth enable     // default disable
..
```

These settings should correct any disconnect issue regarding IP address change of the client. Note, this benefits stability and the user experience; however, convenience is again a trade-off for increased security risk, so be sure to evaluate your network's security posture before implementing these settings.

This section covers the SSL-VPN stability settings on FortiGate. For the next topic within this chapter, we discuss features around SSL-VPN Hardening on FortiGate.

SSL-VPN Hardening

The reason there are many different versions of SSL and TLS is because of security enhancements and vulnerability fixes. Over the years, there have been many security concerns addressed in each SSL/TLS standard. In this chapter, the goal is to show you how to harden the SSL-VPN on FortiGate and make it more secure. The first item to discuss is weak Cipher Suites.

Weak Cipher Suites

Some attacks leverage weak security Cipher Suites. Some protocols are inherently vulnerable, for example MD5 or RC4 encryption. The goal is not to allow weak cryptographic protocols negotiated between TLS clients & servers. FortiGate has a global setting that prevent certain Cipher Suites from being used within TLS connections and enforce strong Cipher Suites. The command is enabled by default on 6.0+; see below CLI output:

```
FGT-B (global) # conf sys glo
FGT-B (global) # show ful | grep strong
    set strong-crypto enable
```

Fortinet KB on Strong Crypto command:

https://kb.fortinet.com/kb/viewContent.do?externalId=FD36915

When the strong-crypto command is set to enabled, then FortiOS only allows the following TLS 1.2 and 1.3 Cipher Suites

```
TLSv1.2:
    ciphers:
        TLS_DHE_RSA_WITH_AES_128_CBC_SHA (dh 128)
        TLS_DHE_RSA_WITH_AES_128_CBC_SHA256 (dh 128)
        TLS_DHE_RSA_WITH_AES_128_GCM_SHA256 (dh 128)
        TLS_DHE_RSA_WITH_AES_256_CBC_SHA (dh 128)
        TLS_DHE_RSA_WITH_AES_256_CBC_SHA256 (dh 128)
        TLS_ECDHE_RSA_WITH_AES_128_CBC_SHA (dh 256)
        TLS_ECDHE_RSA_WITH_AES_128_CBC_SHA256 (dh 256)
        TLS_ECDHE_RSA_WITH_AES_128_GCM_SHA256 (dh 256)
        TLS_ECDHE_RSA_WITH_AES_256_CBC_SHA (dh 256)
        TLS_ECDHE_RSA_WITH_AES_256_CBC_SHA384 (dh 256)
        TLS_ECDHE_RSA_WITH_AES_256_GCM_SHA384 (dh 256)
        TLS_RSA_WITH_AES_128_CBC_SHA (rsa 1024)
        TLS_RSA_WITH_AES_128_CBC_SHA256 (rsa 1024)
        TLS_RSA_WITH_AES_256_CBC_SHA (rsa 1024)
        TLS_RSA_WITH_AES_256_CBC_SHA256 (rsa 1024)
        TLS_RSA_WITH_AES_128_CBC_SHA (rsa 2048)
        TLS_RSA_WITH_AES_128_CBC_SHA256 (rsa 2048)
        TLS_RSA_WITH_AES_256_CBC_SHA (rsa 2048)
        TLS_RSA_WITH_AES_256_CBC_SHA256 (rsa 2048)
TLSv1.3
    ciphers
        TLS_AES_256_GCM_SHA384
        TLS_CHACHA20_POLY1305_SHA256
```

```
    TLS_AES_128_GCM_SHA256
```

Sometimes it might be necessary to obtain more granular control of what TLS Cipher Suites are negotiated. FortiOS provides further tools for this. Check out the CLI options under config vpn ssl settings; see below output:

```
FGT-B (settings) # show ful | grep tls
    set ssl-max-proto-ver tls1-3
    set ssl-min-proto-ver tls1-2
```

In this output, we can see the minimum and maximum TLS versions for FortiOS 6.4. Since most folks have not completely adopted TLS 1.3, the defaults are a minimum of TLS 1.2 for backward compatibility. These values can, of course, be adjusted to fit your environment as needed. The next topic I want to discuss is the Banned Cipher Suites feature. The reason this feature was created is that vulnerability scanners would detect that FortiGate offers certain Cipher Suites that certain security vendors would deem to be an issue. So the ban cipher tool was created to give customers the power to explicitly limit what the FortiGate would offer, hence the Banned Cipher Suites feature. This feature is configurable in the CLI; see below output:

```
IPsec-FGT-B (root) # config vpn ssl settings
FGT-B (settings) # set banned-cipher ?
RSA         Ban the use of cipher suites using RSA key.
DHE         Ban the use of cipher suites using authenticated ephemeral DH key
agreement.
ECDHE       Ban the use of cipher suites using authenticated ephemeral ECDH
key agreement.
DSS         Ban the use of cipher suites using DSS authentication.
ECDSA       Ban the use of cipher suites using ECDSA authentication.
AES         Ban the use of cipher suites using either 128 or 256 bit AES.
AESGCM      Ban the use of cipher suites AES in Galois Counter Mode (GCM).
CAMELLIA    Ban the use of cipher suites using either 128 or 256 bit
CAMELLIA.
3DES        Ban the use of cipher suites using triple DES
SHA1        Ban the use of cipher suites using HMAC-SHA1.
SHA256      Ban the use of cipher suites using HMAC-SHA256.
SHA384      Ban the use of cipher suites using HMAC-SHA384.
STATIC      Ban the use of cipher suites using static keys.
```

We cannot only force FortiOS to use strong Cipher Suites and define which TLS versions are acceptable, but now we can explicitly tell FortiOS which ones not to use. This feature can help you pass your security audit. The last tool to specify Cipher Suites on SSL-VPN is the Low, Medium, and High settings under SSL-VPN.

```
FGT-B (root) # config vpn ssl settings
FGT-B (settings) #
FGT-B (settings) # set algorithm
high        High algorithms.
```

```
medium      High and medium algorithms.
low         All algorithms.
```

The *high* setting value means is that FortiOS only uses the strongest cryptographic algorithms available. You might be asking yourself why medium or low algorithms are offered, and the answer is functionality. Older SSL/TLS client software might require certain Cipher Suites to be used. So be careful when removing or banning Cipher Suites because this could break TLS for some applications.

Fortinet KB on controlling TLS versions and Cipher Suites:

https://kb.fortinet.com/kb/documentLink.do?externalID=FD43679

This wraps up SSL-VPN Cipher Suite security hardening section. The next topic to discuss is the authentication lockout on SSL-VPN.

SSL-VPN Lockout

SSL-VPN lockout can occur if a user enters the wrong password too often and is ban for a certain amount of time. These values can be adjusted on SSL-VPN within the CLI. Look at the default values for this feature via CLI output below:

```
FGT-B (settings) # show ful | grep login
    set login-attempt-limit 2
    set login-block-time 60
```

This output states that by default, on 6.4 FortiOS SSL-VPN, users are allowed two authentication attempts, and if both fail, then the user is locked out for 60 seconds. These values can be adjusted. For login-attempt-limit settings, we can configure up to 10 failed attempts before the user is locked out. Also, if 0 (zero) is specified here, then there is no limit to how many failed login attempts users can have, which is most likely a bad idea for production environments. The no-limit setting would most likely just be used in testing. Next, the login-block-time setting max value is 86400 seconds, which is one day or 24 hours. The last security SSL-VPN method I want to cover with you is MAC address restriction.

Restrict by Mac Address

For very secure environments, FortiGate administrators may need to explicitly state which machines can connect to the SSL-VPN, which can be accomplished through the MAC Address restriction feature on FortiOS. This feature is available in the CLI via:

```
FGT-B (root) # conf vpn ssl web portal
FGT-B (Portal) # edit NSE-4-VPN-Portal
FGT-B (NSE-4-VPN-Portal) # set mac-addr-check enable
IPsec-FGT-B (NSE-4-VPN-Portal) # set mac-addr-action ?
```

```
allow    Allow connection when client MAC address is matched.
deny     Deny connection when client MAC address is matched.
..
        config mac-addr-check-rule
            edit "Mac-Rule-1"
                set mac-addr-list 11:22:33:44:55:66
            next
        end
..
```

We must first enable the feature via 'mac-addr-check enable' settings and explicitly tell FortiOS what to do with the MAC address if matched, which is allow or deny, meaning a whitelist or blacklist type of configuration. Lastly, we must specify a MAC address rule that lists out all the MAC addresses of interest. This covers SSL-VPN hardening topics; the next topic we jump into is the difference between SSL-VPN and IPsec.

SSL VPN vs. IPsec

Describe the differences between SSL-VPN and IPsec VPN. One of the biggest reasons to understand the differences between these two protocols is to successfully configure a policy to allow or deny the various network traffic. For example, if I told you to configure a policy that only blocks IPsec traffic, what configuration items would you require?

For IPsec, from Chapter 8, we learned that ISAKMP is used to set up VPN parameters for ESP packets. ISAKMP uses UDP on port 500 by default, and if there is a NAT device between IPsec peers, then ISAKMP switches to 4500 and encapsulate ESP in 4500 as well. ESP packets themselves use their own layer-3 protocol 50, which can be referenced in a Firewall Policy Entry.

It would be much harder to block an SSL-VPN because TLS traffic could be configured to use any port. We would need to look at our application control tools to help control this type of traffic or perform a Man-in-the-Middle attach to intercept the server public key and proxy FortiGate's own Public key to the TLS client. In summary, IPsec traffic can use the following ports and protocol:

1) Protocol 50
2) UDP Port 500
3) UDP Port 4500

and TLS can use any port as long as the client and server agree on that port with UDP or TCP as a transport protocol.

SSL-VPN Logs and Events

In the last section, we discuss log events around SSL-VPN users. The Log to review is Event Type. I've configured my lab FortiGate to log local, so we are not required to log into FortiAnalyzer to see these log messages. In general, it is best practice to configure remote logging, but for this lab to find SSL-VPN Event logs on FortiGate in the GUI, go to **VDOM -> Log & Report -> Events**, check out the below image:

In Image 9.35, we can see various events for the NSE4 test users. We can see auth-logon, auth-

Image 9.35 – SSL-VPN Event Logs

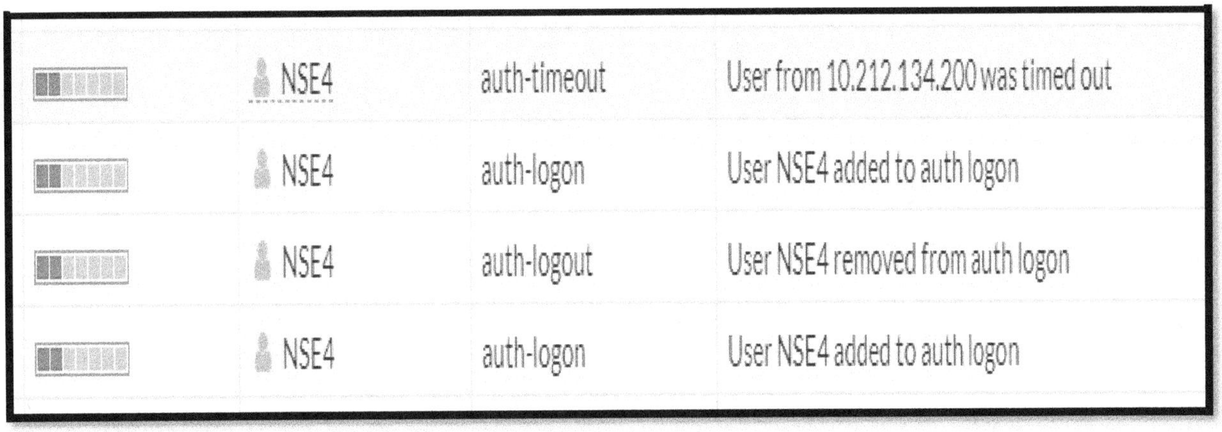

	NSE4	auth-timeout	User from 10.212.134.200 was timed out
	NSE4	auth-logon	User NSE4 added to auth logon
	NSE4	auth-logout	User NSE4 removed from auth logon
	NSE4	auth-logon	User NSE4 added to auth logon

logout and auth-timeout. These logs would be useful for SSL-VPN auditing or troubleshooting. I've downloaded the raw events logs from the lab FortiGate and this is what a raw SSL-VPN timeout event log would look like:

```
date=2020-10-01 time=23:53:19 logid="0102043011" type="event" subtype="user"
level="notice" vd="root" eventtime=1601621599612047251 tz="-0700"
logdesc="Authentication timed out" srcip=10.212.134.200 user="NSE4"
authserver="N/A" action="auth-timeout" status="timed_out" msg="User from
10.212.134.200 was timed out"
```

Next, FortiGate can also pull active Firewall authentication sessions that show what users have been authenticated and to what user group. In 6.4, we must add a Firewall User Monitor Dashboard to see this information via VDOM -> Dashboard -> '+' and select Firewall User Monitor. Check out Image 9.36 below:

Image 9.36 – Firewall User Monitor Dashboard

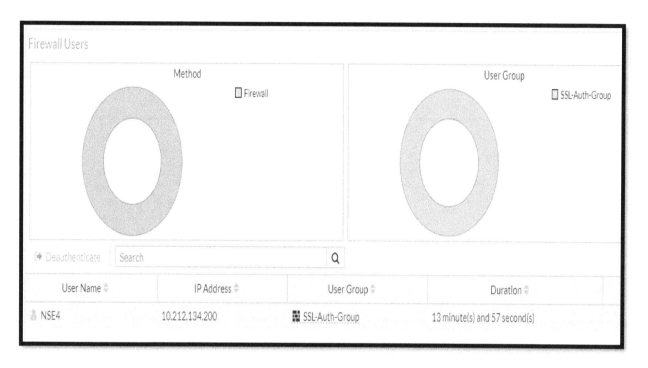

We can see our test SSL-VPN user NSE4 with a source IP of 10.212.134.200 that is authenticated to SSL-Auth-Group for 13 minutes and 57 seconds. This feature would be a great tool to determine what users are actively connected to SSL-VPN on FortiGate. FortiGate administrators also can terminate active sessions from the GUI via VDOM - > Dashboard -> SSL-VPN Monitor; see Image 9.37 on the next page. Terminating SSL-VPN sessions is also possible from the CLI via:

```
IPsec-FGT-B (root) # execute vpn sslvpn list
SSL VPN Login Users:
 Index   User    Group     Auth Type      Timeout        From      HTTP in/out    HTTPS in/out
 0       NSE4    SSL-Auth-Group 1(1)            283      192.168.209.7  0/0        0/0

SSL VPN sessions:
 Index   User    Group     Source IP      Duration       I/O Bytes      Tunnel/Dest IP
 0       NSE4    SSL-Auth-Group            192.168.209.7  1375      79864/5572     10.212.134.200

FGT-B (root) # execute vpn sslvpn del-tunnel 0
```

Image 9.37 – End SSL-VPN Session GUI

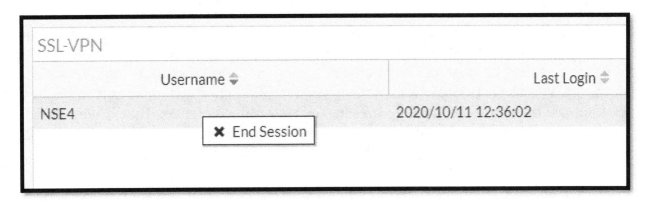

Within this CLI example, the SSL-VPN user index value is 0 (zero), so the del-tunnel command's argument is 0. There is also an option to disconnect all SSL-VPN users if needed.

```
FGT-B (root) # execute vpn sslvpn ?
del-all          Delete all connections under current VDOM.
del-tunnel       Delete tunnel connection.
del-web          Delete web connection.
list             List tunnel connections.
```

This brings us to the end of the SSL-VPN logs and events sections and Chapter 9! Move on to the Chapter summary on the next page and test your knowledge with the end of chapter questions!!

Chapter 9 Summary

What an exciting chapter to write! I love working with SSL-VPNs in general, especially on FortiGate. TLS is a fascinating technology that packages very complex security functions in a digestible and transparent manner to the end-user and the FortiGate administrator. Implementing SSL-VPN on FortiGate is very simple; however, I feel like it is important to respect and understand the underlying technology that makes everything possible. That is why at the beginning of Chapter 9, I took the time to break down TLS and discussed some background theory so you can appreciate the intuitive interface the FortiGate provides us for these various technologies.

TLS has many module components that can be moved in and out of the framework. A few important components to know about is the certificate that contains the server public key, which is used for encryption and authentication functions between TLS client & servers. Next, it is important to understand that the client and server negotiate a Cipher Suite that contains the TLS protocol version, authentication method, encryption method, and hashing method. These TLS components are negotiated using the TLS Handshake protocol, which is housed by the TLS Record Protocol. TLS can use either TCP or UDP as a transport protocol. When UDP is used, the communication is referred to as DTLS.

After completing our TLS theory review, we stepped into the GUI tour for SSL-VPN and the various features available. FortiGate offers two SSL-VPN modes, which are the Tunnel Mode and Web Mode. Tunnel Mode requires a TLS client, which is FortiClient most of the time, to establish a direct TLS tunnel to FortiGate. FortiGate uses PPP to assign FortiClient IP attributes to be used while connected to the SSL-VPN. FortiGate can also provide split-tunnel IP subnets to FortiClient using Tunnel Mode, which defines what traffic sends through the SSL-VPN to FortiGate, which is RFC 1918 subnets most of the time. If no split tunnel is defined, then all traffic generated from FortiClient is sent through SSL-VPN. On FortiGate, the host IP of the SSL-VPN client is injected in the kernel by default, but an explicit static route could be configured if route advertisement is a requirement. It is required for SSL-VPN Firewall Policy Entries to contain a user group for authentication.

Different user groups in SSL-VPN authentication could be mapped to separate Portals, which contains unique settings for Tunnel Mode and Web Mode VPN methods. Portal configuration can also be mapped to unique Realms to differentiate the SSL-VPN user experience further.

Web Mode SSL-VPN provides clientless TLS access to a secure web page hosted on FortiGate that provides Bookmarks proxies that provide access to resources through widget configuration. Realms are different instances that could be configured per authentication group to provide a unique GUI interface per user group.

It is important to know and understand a few advanced configuration settings for SSL-VPN, like the various timers available. The Idle timeout timer controls how long a user can be inactive while connected to the SSL-VPN before being disconnected; by default, this value is 300 seconds. The Authentication timeout controls how long a user can stay connected to the SSL-VPN before FortiOS forces an authentication by default; this is 28000 seconds, which is 8 hours. The login timer controls how long the authentication process can occur and can be increased when using remote or two-factor authentication methods because this increases the amount of time for SSL-VPN users to be verified.

FortiOS provides a few options to harden the SSL-VPN service. One of the easiest configurations to know about is the strong crypto setting, which limits what Cipher Suites FortiOS can offer TLS clients. To obtain further granularity regarding Cipher Suites, the Banned Cipher Suite feature could be used to explicitly ban certain cryptographic protocols for passing security audits. Lastly, under SSL-VPN settings, there are configuration settings to control the maximum and minimum TLS/SSL versions that could be used between client and servers. Older SSL/TLS client might require the use of older insecure Cipher Suites, so be mindful when adjusting these values because it could cause older SSL/TLS applications not to function.

FortiOS also provides lockout settings by default FortiOS allows two failed authentication attempts before the user is locked out for 60 seconds. Both these values could be adjusted as needed. Lastly, for very secure environments, the Restrict By Mac address feature could be used to either whitelist or blacklist certain Mac addresses regarding SSL-VPN access.

IPsec VPN differs from TLS VPNs (SSL-VPN) in the fact that IPsec uses explicitly define ports, IP protocols, and transport protocol. IPsec ISAKMP uses port 500 UDP to negotiate Phase-1 and Phase-2 SA's and uses ESP packets with protocol 50 for transit traffic data. Also, when NAT is used between IPsec peers, then port 4500 UDP is used between peers. TLS can use either TCP or UDP as a transport protocol and can be configured to use any port as long as both sides agree. TLS uses mainly public key certificates with PKI methods to obtain cryptographic function while IPsec could use certificates, but common IPsec implementations use the Pre-Shared Key (PSK) method to seed cryptographic functions.

Lastly, SSL-VPN generates various logs throughout FortiOS. There are Event Type logs, User logs, and Endpoint logs. SSL-VPN GUI Monitor feature allows for FortiGate administrators to view connected SSL-VPN users and terminate sessions as required. It is also possible to terminate SSL-VPN sessions from the CLI.

That is it, folks! This covers the SSL-VPN topics for the NSE4 exam, nice work, but you're not finished just yet! Go ahead and knock out those end of chapter questions to be sure you understand the material!

Chapter 9 End of Chapter Questions

1) What protocol is used for the initial TLS client to server communication to set up a secure encrypted channel?
   a. Record protocol
   b. Alert Protocol
   c. Handshake Protocol
   d. Cipher Suite Protocol

2) What TLS protocol message means the client & server agree to put in use the proposed Cipher Suite, and all further communication will be encrypted?
   a. Handshake Message
   b. Record Message
   c. Key Exchange Message
   d. Change Cipher Spec Message

3) What is DTLS?
   a. Only available in 1.3 TLS
   b. Only Available in 1.2 TLS
   c. encryption services for transit data
   d. TLS using UDP as a transport protocol

4) A set of cryptographic protocols used by TLS client & server for authentication, encryption, and authentication?
   a. DTLS
   b. Cipher Suite
   c. HMAC
   d. x.509v3

5) What types SSL-VPN Modes could be defined within Portal settings?
   a. Web Mode
   b. Tunnel Mode
   c. Web and Tunnel Mode
   d. Portal Mode

6) What configuration controls when SSL-VPN authentication becomes active?
   a. Authentication mappings under SSL-VPN Settings
   b. Authentication Mappings under Portal Settings
   c. Authentication Group being referenced in SSL-VPN Firewall Policy Entry
   d. Authentication under Realm settings

7) It is required to explicitly add a route to the SSL-VPN interface for SSL-VPN user IP subnet address(s).
   a. True
   b. False

8) What is the purpose of Realms?
   a. To differentiate Web Mode Portals by assigning users to different authentication groups.
   b. To hold user authentication information.
   c. To assigned SSL-VPN users unique transit Firewall Policies
   d. So SSL-VPN users can use RADIUS authentication

9) What SSL-VPN setting controls how long a connected user can be inactive before being disconnected?
   a. idle-timeout
   b. auth-timeout
   c. login-timeout
   d. inactive-timeout

10) What SSL-VPN setting controls how long the initial authentication process can take?
   a. idle-timeout
   b. auth-timeout
   c. login-timeout
   d. inactive-timeout

11) What SSL-VPN setting controls when a connected user is forced to reauthenticate?
   a. idle-timeout
   b. auth-timeout
   c. login-timeout
   d. inactive-timeout

12) What two settings could help in the SSL-VPN stability regarding user IP frequently changing?
    a. auth-session-check-source-ip & tunnel-connect-without-reauth
    b. dynamic-ip-auth & no-auth-reconnect
    c. auth-connected-allow & auth-session-dynamic-ip
    d. source-ip-checking & source-reauth-checking

13) What Global FortiOS setting is used to enforce the use of strong Cipher Suites?
    a. crypto- strong
    b. strong-crypto
    c. cipher-strong-crypto
    d. strong-cipher-suite-only

14) What SSL-VPN setting is used to explicitly restrict certain cryptographic algorithms from be negotiated?
    a. crypto-strong
    b. banned-cipher
    c. cipher-restrict-list
    d. cipher-suite-ban

15) On FortiOS, SSL-VPN can only use known default HTTPS standard port.
    a. True
    b. False

16) For SSL-VPN to restrict what machines can connect, what setting must be enabled?
    a. machine-check
    b. host-addr-check
    c. mac-addr-check
    d. source-mac-check

17) What CLI command will delete a SSL-VPN active session index value 5
    a. diagnose vpn sslvpn rm-tunnel 5
    b. get vpn sslvpn del-tunnel 5
    c. execute vpn sslvpn del-tunnel 5
    d. execute vpn sslvpn rm-session 5

18) What debug command is used for SSL-VPN?

    a. diagnose debug application ssl 255
    b. diagnose debug application vpn 255
    c. diagnose debug application ssl-vpn 255
    d. diagnose debug application sslvpn 255

19) It is recommended to use the default built-in SSL-VPN Fortinet certificate for production use.
    a. True
    b. False

20) When building a Firewall Policy Entry for an SSL-VPN interface, what unique specific attribute is require?
    a. user or group in the source field
    b. user or group in the destination field
    c. SSL-VPN Portal in the source field
    d. SSl-VPN Realm in the source field

21) When building an SSL-VPN Firewall Policy Entry, why would the error 'Destination Address of split tunnel policy is invalid' occur?
    a. A split tunnel is required for SSL-VPN
    b. Split Tunnel 'all' object is not allowed on SSL-VPN
    c. The policy destination subnet does not match the specified related Portal split-tunnel subnet.
    d. The destination subnet is not referenced in the Realm configuration

Chapter 10 | SD-WAN

NSE4 Blueprint Topics Covered

- Understand SD-WAN concepts
- Understand SD-WAN design
- Understand SD-WAN requirements
- Configure SD-WAN virtual link and load balance
- Configure SD-WAN routing and policies
- Configure SD-WAN health check
- understand SLA link quality measurements
- Understand SD-WAN rules
- configure dynamic link selection
- Monitor SD-WAN
- Verify SD-WAN traffic
- Understand Basic QoS
- Understand Basic Traffic Shaping
- Understand SD-WAN traffic flow

I Spent a solid year working with a major MSSP certifying FortiOS SD-WAN features for production use and another year certifying FortiManager for SD-WAN orchestration based on 6.0 GA. It was an *enlightening* experience. Everything that could go wrong did go wrong. During some periods of the certification process, I was worried that we were going to fail to get the product where it needed to be and meet the needs of the MSSP. However, the various teams I was working with at the time, internal and external, all doubled down and pushed forward by adding software fixes, new features, and integrating ASIC technology to support the complete FortiOS SD-WAN offering. I am happy to say as of today; this large MSSP is indeed re-selling the Fortinet SD-WAN solution to their end-customers, which is a win for everyone. The end customer receives awesome SD-WAN and security services for a low cost via the MSSP. The MSSP can generate revenue for their organization and Fortinet benefits by selling the hardware and software to the MSSP.

I must say I had my doubts when Fortinet announced it would compete in the SD-WAN market. Most network security vendors just paired their solutions with a well-known SD-WAN vendor like Viptela (Cisco Now) or Velocloud (VMware). Because these well-known SD-WAN vendors did not perform network-based security functions very well and each side made up for their shortcomings of the other, and so, these *pure-play* SD-WAN vendors added value to their solutions through these partnerships with reputable cybersecurity companies. This would seem like a perfect fit at first. However, the multi-entity WAN edge solution became quite complicated to manage because having multiple virtual or physical machines per deployment increases the total cost of ownership of the solution, decreasing profits. Also, this caused the network orchestration piece of the puzzle to become much more complex because of the requirement of having multiple vendor central management structures, one for the SD-WAN solution and one for the security solution(s). Carriers and large enterprises did not like this very much because it was unfeasible to scale, manage, and expensive! This is how Fortinet found its niche in the SD-WAN market.

When I started working at Fortinet, SD-WAN did not exist in the production environment. Various vendors were just starting to develop these types of solutions. So, in general, these technologies and methods are new to everyone. But just like everyone else at the time, I started hearing about Software-Defined WAN here and there back in 2016. When I first read about It, I kinda laughed to myself because I thought it was just a fancy marketing scheme that large networking vendors were using to coin certain phrases so to be used by their sales folks just so they can step into their sales pitch meetings and say, "we are the only vendor that offers *true* SD-WAN,."

and I'll be honest with you, SD-WAN means different things to different organizations. A few RFCs published attempting to clarify what Software Defined Network (SDN) is, but vendors have branched into what they feel SD-WAN should be, and this started the SD-WAN competition for market share. Over time, more and more *features* were added to the mix by various vendors. In this light, it is hard to provide an honest technical evaluation of SD-WAN. Here is one statement I pulled out of RFC 7149 to try and clarify what SD-WAN is:

" Dynamically adaptive decision-making processes, which can

properly operate according to a set of input data and metrics,

such as current resource usage and demand, traffic forecasts

and matrices, etc., all for the sake of highly responsive

dynamic resource allocation and policy enforcement schemes."

Statements like these leave a lot of wiggle room for interpretation. Vendors started adding terms like Zero-Touch deployment, Dynamic application routing, or presenting SD-WAN as a true replacement to MPLS networks, which it is not.

I'm going to take like ten steps back and attempt to clarify SD-WAN. The first thing I want to say is that it's not magical. I've heard too many podcasts, marketing overviews, and explanations attempting to describe what SD-WAN is and how it works that seem to come off to me as fluff. These folks have implied that SD-WAN will replace Network Engineers around the world. It seems that not too many folks really know what it is. Well, I'll start by saying SD-WAN will not be replacing network engineers anytime soon. If anything, we will need more engineers that require more advanced skill sets and API knowledge because at the end of the day, computer networks use IPv4 or IPv6, and these protocols operate under a set of rules and methods. With SD-WAN, it is required to know how to route traffic via IP header, but we must also know how to route traffic by first matching the layer-7 application, which adds to the complexity and increases the probability of software defects or anomalies.

I am a nuts and bolts type of guy. I don't like fluff or to have technologies presented to me like there magical with no logic in how they work. I find it confusing and frustrating. As you should know, I always like to start off my chapter by going over the theory behind the technology we are working with on FortiGate, but I don't think that is possible for SD-WAN because there are a lot less specific technical theory and a whole lot more of computer networking philosophy. I feel like folks are taking SD-WAN as a way of life or something instead of studying it in a functional manner.

I cannot go over SD-WAN theory specifically because SD-WAN is a compilation of technologies with each having sub-technologies. It would be comparable to going over how the Internet works in which we use the OSI model. SD-WAN uses a broad technology suite that all works together to accomplish application layer dynamic best quality path selection.

Alright, it's time to share a dirty little secret.. step a little closer... 95% of all technologies that make up SD-WAN functionality existed before they were labeled as SD-WAN. Maybe 90% at this point, that number is up for debate. But Essentially, FortiGate already had the majority of the components to accomplish SD-WAN in 5.4 & 5.6 FortiOS before officially labeling the features as SD-WAN. Features and enhancements were built around these base subsets of components to make the rollout and operations of SD-WAN more streamlined and effective to compete for market share.

Here is the grant list of base components of FortiOS SD-WAN, which are IPsec, Virtual WAN interface, QoS/Traffic Shaping, IP routing, FortiOS Application Control, and Link Monitor (SLA). *(mic drop)*

To start us off in this chapter by going over the major building blocks that make up the complete Fortinet SD-WAN solution and *unmask* those underlying core technologies. I list and break down all the SD-WAN components and then specify which ones we are covered in this chapter and why.

Introduction to FortiOS SD-WAN

What are the goals for SD-WAN? I break down the goals into three categories: Technical FortiOS goals, Orchestration goals, and Business goals.

Technical FortiOS goals.

1) Media independent high availability network paths
2) Application visibility
3) A per application, dynamic selection of most optimum network path
4) Security
5) Ease of local SD-WAN configuration and management
6) Traffic Management (Quality of Service (QoS))
7) High-performance throughput (ASIC technologies)

Orchestration Goals

1) SD-WAN central management, provisioning, and visibility
2) Overlay Management

Business Goal

1) Cost-efficient SD-WAN solution
2) Zero Touch Provisioning
   a. reduction of operational cost
3) Reduced Complexity
   a. reduction in engineering and operational cost
4) SD-WAN SLA and traffic visibility for reporting & traffic steering

This is a good start to classify SD-WAN goals. The confusing part is that all these topics are bundled into SD-WAN deliverables or *true* SD-WAN services. That is a nightmare for technical folks trying to engineer the solution. I understand we all report to some sort of boss, which might be a high-level director or vice president who are required to make strategic budgeting decisions and business cases; just know where you fit into the conversation because if your job is to engineer FortiOS to accomplish SD-WAN for your organization, then you might not need to concern yourself with all these items. Maybe your organization does not require an Overlay Controller or Zero Touch Provisioning, but you still want secure dynamic application routing, that's fine, and this is still SD-WAN. Next, I want to review Fortinet SD-WAN components' in further detail. Here are the items covered in this chapter and why.

SD-WAN components

The underlined items below are addressed in this chapter. Take a moment to review. Every other item could be used in SD-WAN but are not covered in this chapter.

1) Dynamic Gateway
    a. DHCP
2) Zero Touch Deployment
    a. FortiCloud
    b. FortiManager
        i. FortiManager Orchestration
    c. FortiDeploy
3) FortiManager Integration
    a. SD-WAN Manager
    b. VPN Manager
4) SD-WAN topologies
5) Routing and route selection
    a. Layer-3 IP Routing
        i. Static Routing
        ii. Advanced Dynamic Routing
            1. iBGP
            2. BGP tags with SD-WAN rules
    b. Application Routing (steering)
        i. Application Control Database
    c. Internet Service Database (ISDB) Routing
6) SD-WAN Session Table considerations
    a. SNAT Route Change
    b. Preserve Session route change no SNAT
7) Performance Service Level (SLA) Agreement or health checks
    a. Latency measurement
    b. Jitter measurement
    c. Packet Loss measurement
8) Traffic steering Methods
    a. Manually Assigned

b. <u>Best SLA Quality</u>
c. <u>Maximized Bandwidth ECMP</u>
    i. <u>Load Balancing Methods</u>
d. <u>Lowest Cost SLA</u>
9) <u>SD-WAN Rule Matching Methods</u>
a. <u>Source IP, Destination port, and/or IP</u>
b. <u>ISDB</u>
c. <u>Applications</u>
d. <u>User Groups</u>
e. <u>Type of Service</u>
10) Deep Packet Inspection
a. Block QUIC
b. Application visibility
11) <u>Traffic Shaping and QoS</u>
12) Advanced IPsec
a. ADVPN
b. Hub-and-spoke topology
c. Overlapping routes
d. FEC
e. Multiple IPsec tunnels
f. OCVPN
13) <u>FortiOS SDWAN configuration</u>
14) Fortinet Overlay Controller VPN
15) <u>FortiOS SDWAN Diagnostics</u>
16) SD-WAN UTM Security
a. AV
b. IPS
c. Web-Filtering
d. Application Control
17) Alternative media types
a. LTE
b. WiFi
18) SD-WAN API Integration & Automation

Even though we will not be covering all SD-WAN topics in this chapter, I feel that it is important for you to know what other technologies a production SD-WAN deploy could use. You might have noticed, but I tactfully selected all the FortiOS specific items. However, I did not select <u>all</u> FortiOS specific SD-WAN related technologies because we've not discussed BGP, UTM, ADVPN, or advanced topologies using a combination of these protocols and features. We must walk before we can run, meaning we must learn the basic SD-WAN functions on FortiOS before we start designing and implementing large scale FortiOS SD-WAN deployments. For that reason, I am not going over technologies supporting SD-WAN deployment methods or anything around central SD-WAN management. Once we understand the FortiOS requirements, then we can move into more design and orchestration related conversations. Finally, here is the short and sweet list of SD-WAN topics are covered in this chapter:

1) SD-WAN Topology
2) Basic FortiOS SD-WAN Configuration
3) Application Identification
4) QoS and Traffic Shaping
5) SD-WAN Path Control
6) SD-WAN Traffic Flow
7) SD-WAN Uses Cases

SD-WAN Topology

Now that you're starting to piece together what makes up SD-WAN services, we can go over a basic topology use case. Most SD-WAN topologies are the same as IPsec topologies. One difference is the concern with what applications are taking what path and why. One of the goals for SD-WAN is Application identification; therefore, it is important to know where critical applications are hosted so probes can be sent to the correct location. Since many organizations are moving their services to hosted cloud environments like AWS or Azure, then probes would be forwarded using redundant IPsec tunnels to cloud applications, but obviously, IPsec tunnels are not limited to cloud environments. FortiGate could easily use IPsec tunnels to obtain connectivity to application services anywhere in your environment.

Image 10.1 – SDWAN Topology

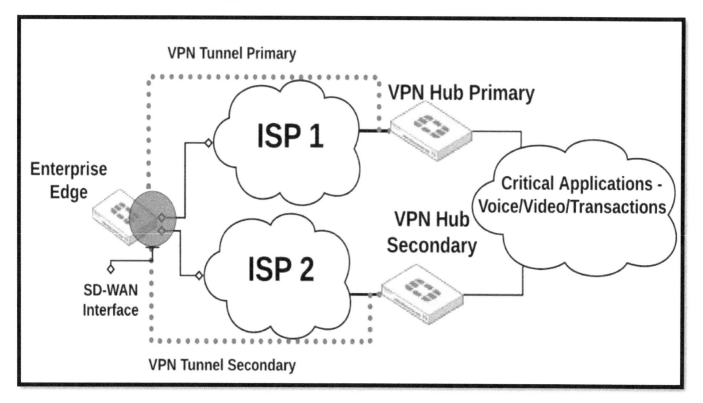

One other item to touch on is some specific SD-WAN terminology. The term Overlay refers to a virtual path, like a VPN tunnel and an Underlay refers to the physical median like Ethernet circuit, Fiber, LTE, etc...

Image 10.1 provides a typical SDWAN edge deployment. Two ISP circuits for redundancy with each having IPsec VPN's build on them. Most of the time, each physical interface has two IPsec VPN built, one that connects back to the primary VPN concentrator and one to the secondary, but for simplicity sakes, the diagram only shows one per interface. This topology would have two Overlay WAN network interfaces and two underlay network interfaces. All four interfaces would be bundled together into one virtual interface and labeled SD-WAN. Once interfaces are referenced into an SD-WAN interface, then they become members. Each member has an SLA probe configured to measure the quality of its network path. All probe SLA Link monitors are indexed, so rules can be configured to always send certain applications down the path with the best quality. So if the primary IPsec VPN has the best quality per SLA Link Monitor, then, for example, voice traffic could be configured to take the best path, which is the primary VPN. If network degradation occurs and the secondary VPN SLA Link Monitor becomes the best quality, then FortiOS dynamically re-route voice traffic to the secondary IPsec VPN.

SD-WAN seems fairly simple at this level, but once you start increasing the SD-WAN members to say, for example, 10 SD-WAN members performing SLA Link monitoring for hundreds of applications, then things become a little more interesting but remember the foundation does not change. The first FortiOS SD-WAN topic we dive into is the basic configuration used to setup SD-WAN for an enterprise edge.

Basic SD-WAN Configuration

For me, new technology always makes more sense once I configure it and make it useful. If I can't understand its purpose, then most likely, I'm not going to give it much attention. My goals for us in this section are to set up a very basic SD-WAN lab with FortiGate. We are going to create a virtual SD-WAN zone interface, basic SD-WAN rule, and SD-WAN route. The first item on the docket is the SD-WAN interface. So before we start configuring, take a look at our topology we are working with via Image 10.2.

<u>SD-WAN Interface</u>

In 5.4 MR, FortiOS labeled this interface as a Virtual WAN interface; in 6.4 MR, this is labeled as an SD-WAN interface. You might be asking yourself, what is an SD-WAN virtual interface? It is a lot like a Zone interface. A Zone interface can reference multiple interfaces and represent them to FortiOS as one logical interface regarding things like policy creations. The SD-WAN virtual interface takes this concept a step further and can relate a single routing statement that points to an SD-WAN interface and distributes this route to all member interfaces so traffic can be load-balanced across them or so certain path selection policies can be created.

Image 10.2 – Basic SD-WAN Topology Example

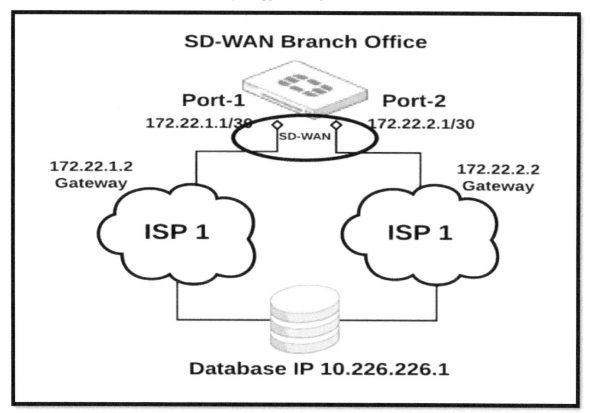

I've already configured the basic IP information on port1 and port2. Next, we must create SD-WAN member objects which are referenced by the SD-WAN Zone object

Image 10.3 – SD-WAN Zone and Member GUI

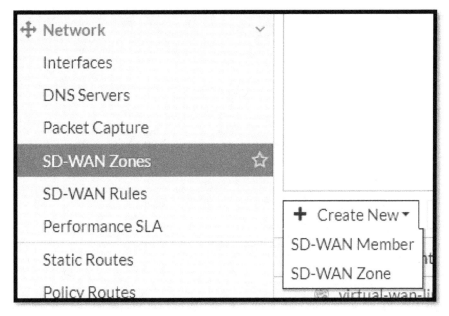

In the GUI, go to VDOM -> Network -> SD-WAN Zones -> Create New -> SD-WAN Member. See Image 10.3 for details. Next, we configure interface Internal1 to be an SD-WAN member.

Image 10.4 – SD-WAN Member GUI Configuration

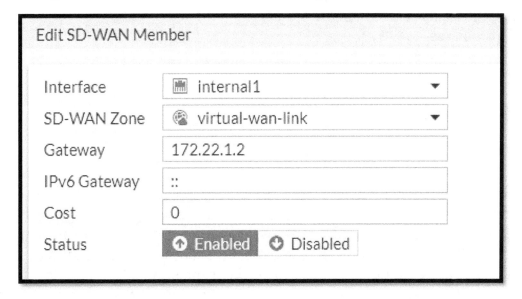

The CLI equivalent of the initial SD-WAN configuration is:

```
config system sdwan
    set status enable
    config zone
        edit "virtual-wan-link"
        next
        edit "SD-WAN_ZONE_2"
        next
    end
    config members
        edit 1
            set interface "internal1"
            set gateway 172.22.1.2
        next
        edit 2
            set interface "internal2"
            set gateway 172.22.2.2
        next
    end
```

Note here the default zone is <u>virtual-wan-link</u> for SD-WAN member interface, and if I run a show full-on interface members, then the following configuration would be seen in the CLI:

```
FGT-B (members) # show ful
path=, objname=members, tablename=(null), size=128
config members
    edit 1
        set interface "internal1"
        set zone "virtual-wan-link"
        set gateway 172.22.1.2
        set source 0.0.0.0
        set gateway6 ::
        set source6 ::
        set cost 0
        set priority 0
        set status enable
        set comment ''
    next
```

To build an SD-WAN Zone, we are required to reference SD-WAN Member interfaces as dependencies. Each member interface can be assigned a gateway IP if using static interface configuration. If DHCP client is used on SD-WAN members, then the gateway would be all zeros in this example. The gateway IP is resolved to a MAC address to be used in the destination MAC address field within the ethernet header per member underlay interface. Also, the gateway IP is used to create the kernel route so as to reach the Performance SLA remote IP addresses and used as the next-hop address for <u>sdwan</u> static routes.

SD-WAN Zone

The next configuration aspect is the SD-WAN zone, and the default is <u>virtual-wan-link</u>. Within FortiOS 6.4+, it is possible to create multiple SD-WAN Zones to make policy creation more granular. I went ahead and configured an additional SD-WAN Zone interface as a PoC, *SD-WAN_ZONE_2*.

```
config system sdwan
    set status enable
    config zone
        edit "virtual-wan-link"
        next
        edit "SD-WAN_ZONE_2"
        next
```

Once created, this object can be referenced via the SD-WAN Member configuration page. If you look back at Image 10.4 on the prior page, you see that the SD-WAN Zone virtual-wan-link is referenced. We could easily assign Internal1 to SD-WAN_ZONE_2 with a few mouse clicks. Once our SD-WAN Zone and Members are created and assigned, next is the routing configuration.

SD-WAN Static Route

When configuring Static Route Entries for SD-WAN Zones, a special parameter is required for 6.4 MR; the setting is **"set sdwan enable"** under the static route configuration section. In 6.2 GA, the command is **"set virtual-wan-link enable"** Here is the configuration.

```
0: edit root
0: config router static
0: edit 0
0: set sdwan enable
0: end
0: end
```

```
IPsec-FGT-B (root) # get router info routing-table all
path=router, objname=info, tablename=(null), size=0
Codes: K - kernel, C - connected, S - static, R - RIP, B - BGP
       O - OSPF, IA - OSPF inter area
       N1 - OSPF NSSA external type 1, N2 - OSPF NSSA external type 2
       E1 - OSPF external type 1, E2 - OSPF external type 2
       i - IS-IS, L1 - IS-IS level-1, L2 - IS-IS level-2, ia - IS-IS inter
area
       * - candidate default

Routing table for VRF=0
S*      0.0.0.0/0 [1/0] via 172.22.1.2, internal1
                  [1/0] via 172.22.2.2, internal2
```

I've also grabbed the routing table on this device so you can see that a default has been added for each member interface, and if we added an additional member interface, it would also receive a default route entry. The SD-WAN configuration so far load-balances traffic across internal1 and internal2 once a Firewall Policy Entry is created. Another good CLI command to display the SD-WAN member interface details is:

```
FGT-B (root) # diagnose sys sdwan member
Member(1): interface: internal1, gateway: 172.22.1.2, priority: 0, weight: 0
Member(2): interface: internal2, gateway: 172.22.2.2, priority: 0, weight: 0
```

The priority and weight fields here relate to path selection, which we dive into later. Next, we cover the default load-balancing algorithm for an SD-WAN Zone, also referred to as the 'Implicit Rule'.

SD-WAN Implicit Rule

The next part of SD-WAN is how basic traffic load-balancing is accomplished and what the default settings are. The *Implicit Rule* controls SD-WAN traffic steering behavior when no other rules are configured and is automatically generated when SD-WAN is enabled on FortiOS. This rule ECMP load-balances traffic to all available SD-WAN member interfaces. The default load-balancing algorithm is based on the source IP address. Here is a CLI configuration snippet:

```
FGT-B (sdwan) #  show ful
config system sdwan
    set status enable
    set load-balance-mode source-ip-based
```

This can be adjusted of course. The following options are available.

```
FGT-B (sdwan) #   set load-balance-mode ?
source-ip-based        Source IP load balancing. All traffic from a source
IP is sent to the same interface.
weight-based           Weight-based load balancing. Interfaces with higher
weights have higher priority and get more traffic.
usage-based            Usage-based load balancing. All traffic is sent to
the first interface on the list. When the bandwidth on that interface exceeds
the spill-over limit new traffic is sent to the next interface.
source-dest-ip-based   Source and destination IP load balancing. All
traffic from a source IP to a destination IP is sent to the same interface.
measured-volume-based  Volume-based load balancing. Traffic is load
balanced based on traffic volume (in bytes). More traffic is sent to
interfaces with higher volume ratios.
```

I've bolded the available options. The source IP load balance method hashes the source IP and selects the egress SD-WAN member interface based on hashed value. All sessions from the same source IP transverses the SD-WAN member interface.

Next, the weight-based load-balancing method is related to the amount of session each interface member is carrying. FortiOS, by default, uses a 1:1 radio for each member interface. For example, in this configuration with only two members, the session load is split between them 50/50. For further clarification, If there were a total of four interface members within the SD-WAN zone, then each member would be assigned 25% of the total sessions. This could be useful for environments with a high session setup rate but low throughput. The GUI configuration can be found via Network -> SD-WAN Rules -> Edit Rule > Load Balancing Algorithm > Sessions.

For details, check out Image 10.5. In this example, Internal1 is configured with a value of 2 and Internal2 with a value of 8. This is so that we can easily see that 80% of the new sessions are indeed created on the Internal2 member interface and 20% on Internal2. The defaults, in this

Image 10.5 – Session (weight-based) Load Balance Method

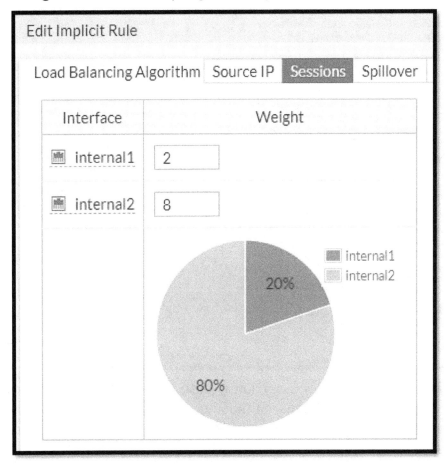

example, would display a pie chart showing 50/50. The next *Implicit Rule* load balancing option is usage-based or *Spillover*.

The Spillover load balancing method requires to set thresholds on every member interface. This threshold defines the amount of throughput the given interface member can send, and if the throughput hits the threshold limit, then FortiOS then use the next member interface to transmit data. In this example, the Internal1 threshold is 100Mbps and Internal2 to be 900Mbps. Since Internal1 is the first interface listed, it is utilized first. Once the throughput becomes greater than 100Mbps, then Internal2 will be used to forward SD-WAN traffic. Image 10.6 contains the GUI equivalent of these parameters.

Image 10.6 – Spillover (usage) Load Balance Method

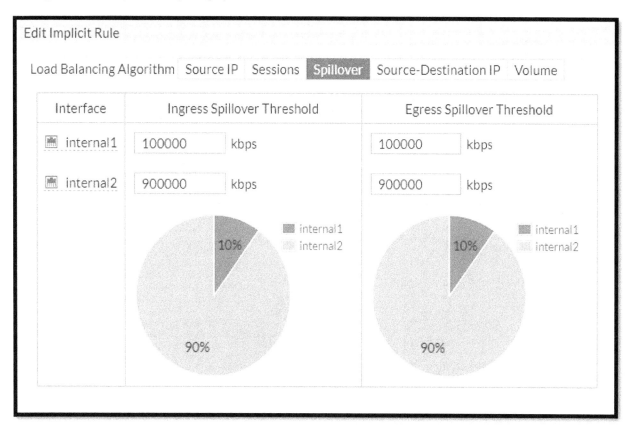

The next *Implicit Rule* load balancing setting is based on source and destination IP (**source-dest-ip-based**). This method creates more randomness for traffic distribution between member interface and keeps all traffic from a single source IP to a single destination IP on the same member interface.

The last *Implicit Rule* load balancing method is throughput Volume-based load balancing. Once again, it is required to configure a ratio value, so FortiOS knows how you wish to load balance traffic across member interfaces. Traffic is measured in bytes, and interface members with the highest ratio value receives more traffic. This is accomplished on the backend by assigning a 'volume room' value to interface members based on the ratio configured. For example, if Internal1 has a ratio value of 33 and Internal2 has a ratio value of 66, then FortiOS would allocate *volume room* for data transmission:

Internal1 volume room 33MB:

Internal2 volume room 66MB

and when one-member interface fills up their *volume* room space, the SD-WAN member interfaces are more likely to be utilized for new sessions. Once the volume room is full, the interface is marked with *overload volume* from debug output of:

```
diagnose sys virtual-wan-link member
```

To configure this load balancing method in the GUI go to Network -> SD-WAN Rules -> Edit Rule > Load Balancing Algorithm > Volume – See Image 10. below:

Image 10.7 - Volume (measured-volume-based) Load Balance Method

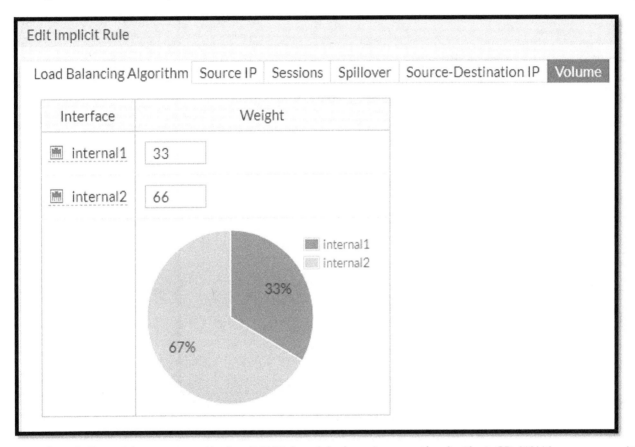

Alright, folks, this covers all the ECMP load balancing methods that SD-WAN can use. At this point, this is technically an SD-WAN configuration, but just one with no application-level routing or SLA configuration. It is important to understand that the routing table is always used, no matter how complex the SD-WAN rules get. Also, note that ECMP requires routes to be learned from the same source that has the same metric/distance/priority. For example, FortiOS cannot ECMP load balance using a BGP default route and a static default route. Each routing protocol has its own ECMP caveats, so keep that in mind when configuring or design ECMP solutions as a whole.

SD-WAN becomes interesting when we start talking about path precedence when ECMP is in play with SD-WAN Rules, which is the next topic to review.

Basic SD-WAN Rule

So we have touched on the *Implicit Rule,* which is essentially ECMP routing. In this section, we start moving up the TCP/IP protocol stack regarding what items within the packet FortiOS are matching to make a forwarding decision. To configure SD-WAN Rules in the GUI, go to Network

Image 10.8 – SD-WAN Rule Example

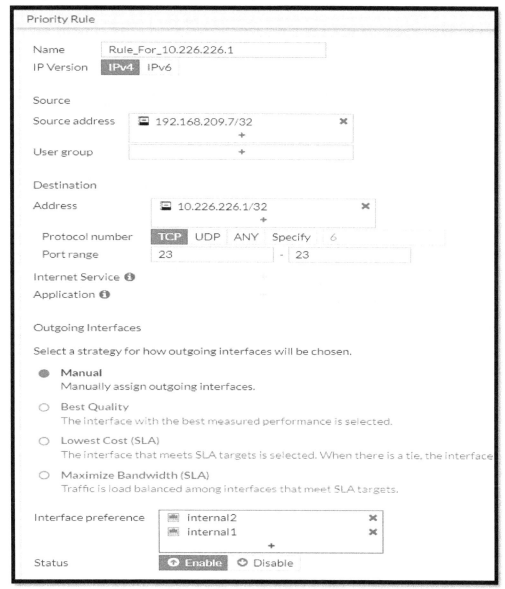

-> SD-WAN Rules -> Create New, and you should see Image 10.8.

Here is the CLI equivalent:

```
0: config system sdwan
0: config service
0: edit 0
0: set name "Rule_For_10.226.226.1"
0: unset input-device
0: set protocol 6
0: set start-port 23
0: set end-port 23
0: set dst "10.226.226.1/32"
0: set src "192.168.209.7/32"
0: unset users
0: unset groups
0: set priority-members "2" "1"
0: end
0: end
0: end
```

There is a lot of information here but don't fret; we will break it down to a more digestible manner. Firstly, know that SD-WAN Rules are essentially Policy Routes and are evaluated <u>before</u> the regular routing table (most of the time). Next, I kept this example simple; the below settings are essentially the matching requirements for traffic to use this rule:

```
set protocol 6
set start-port 23
set end-port 23
set dst "10.226.226.1/32"
set src "192.168.209.7/32"
```

This rule states traffic must be coming from 192.168.209.7 and going to 10.226.226.1/32 using transport protocol TCP with destination port being 23, which you might know is the default port for Telnet. If a match occurs, then FortiOS routes traffic to SD-WAN member 2, which is the Internal2 interface. The next configuration line to review is:

```
set priority-members "2" "1"
```

The numbers 2 and 1 here respectively are index value found under the sdwan configuration via:

```
config system sdwan
..
    config members
        edit 1
            set interface "internal1"
            set gateway 172.22.1.2
        next
        edit 2
            set interface "internal2"
```

```
          set gateway 172.22.2.2
      next
  end
```

The sequence order of the SD-WAN interface member indexed value referenced by the *priority-members* setting determines the interface preference when steering traffic within SD-WAN Rules. In this example, index value 2 is preferred before index value 1 because it is the first referenced interface. To make index value 1 be preferred for this SD-WAN rule, we would re-arrange these to be like so

```
set priority-members "1" "2"
```

This rule is like configuring a hot standby interface; if one fails, then traffic is re-routed, very basic. To see this rule in the Firewall Policy Table, we can issue the below command:

```
FGT-B (root) # diagnose firewall proute list
list route policy info(vf=root):

id=0x7f090001 vwl_service=1(Rule_For_10.226.226.1) vwl_mbr_seq=2 1
dscp_tag=0xff 0xff flags=0x0 tos=0x00 tos_mask=0x00 protocol=6 sport=0:65535
iif=0 dport=23 oif=9(internal2) oif=8(internal1)
source(1): 192.168.209.7-192.168.209.7
destination(1): 10.226.226.1-10.226.226.1
hit_count=0 last_used=2020-10-21 16:34:49
```

This output shows the rule's details like the outgoing interface, source/destination IP, and port numbers to match. Lastly, you can see the hit counts of the rule and the last time it was used.

The last configuration required to make SD-WAN operational is the Firewall Policy Entry. This is built just like any other policy referencing the SD-WAN zone.

```
FGT-B (8) # show
path=firewall, objname=policy, tablename=8, size=2816
config firewall policy
    edit 8
        set name "SD-WAN-Policy"
        set srcintf "wan1"
        set dstintf "virtual-wan-link"
        set srcaddr "all"
        set dstaddr "all"
        set action accept
        set schedule "always"
        set service "ALL"
    next
end
```

One thing that might be odd within this policy is that SD-WAN members would be the 'wan' interfaces most of the time. The reason I have wan1 as the source interface within this policy is because it interfaces with my lab environment, and the test traffic ingresses wan1 and then load-balanced across the SD-WAN members. For a PoC, we can run the diagnose flow debug command set to see the behavior of this rule. I'm going make it, so Internal2 is preferred within the rule; check out the debugs below:

```
id=20085 trace_id=29 func=print_pkt_detail line=5639 msg="vd-root:0 received
a packet(proto=6, 192.168.209.7:57774->10.226.226.1:23) from wan1. flag [S],
seq 2452217991, ack 0, win 64240"
id=20085 trace_id=29 func=init_ip_session_common line=5810 msg="allocate a
new session-0032f8cc"
id=20085 trace_id=29 func=vf_ip_route_input_common line=2580 msg="Match
policy routing id=2131296257: to 10.226.226.1 via ifindex-9"
id=20085 trace_id=29 func=vf_ip_route_input_common line=2598 msg="find a
route: flag=04000000 gw-172.22.2.2 via internal2"
id=20085 trace_id=29 func=fw_forward_handler line=796 msg="Allowed by Policy-
8: SNAT"
id=20085 trace_id=29 func=__ip_session_run_tuple line=3427 msg="SNAT
192.168.209.7->172.22.2.1:57774"
id=20085 trace_id=29 func=ipd_post_route_handler line=439 msg="out internal2
vwl_zone_id 1, state2 0x0, quality 1.
```

At this point, we could easily steer traffic to Internal1 by updating the Rule interface preference, so Internal1 has priority. Note, *ifindex 9* is the global index value for Internal1, not the SD-WAN index value. This wraps up FortiGate basic SD-WAN configuration, not much to it. There are many layers of configuration we are missing to make SD-WAN intelligent enough to perform application steering based on the best path.

Also note, SD-WAN rules are evaluated from top to bottom, just like firewall policies. Combinations of the following attributes can be used to match network traffic within an SD-WAN rule:

1) Source IP
2) Destination IP
3) Destination Port
4) ISDB Object(s)
5) Application Control signatures
6) User and user groups
7) Type of Service (ToS) value

In the next section, we focus on how FortiOS determines the best path for SD-WAN traffic.

SD-WAN Path Control

SD-WAN path control requires Link-Monitor tools, which are also referred to as Performance Service Level Agreement (SLA) tools. These tools tell FortiOS, which links have the lowest packet loss, packet jitter, and packet latency. With this information, FortiOS can dynamically steer traffic across the best SD-WAN interface members. On 6.4 MR FortiOS, there are default SLA objects that can be used within the configuration. These can be seen within Image 10.9. The method these default Performance SLA objects use is HTTP message exchanges to gauge link SLA metrics. The default SLA objects are for AWS, FortiGuard, Gmail, Google Search, and Office 365, which are some of the most commonly used well-known applications being routed across SD-WAN environments. Performance SLA is referred to as Health Checks within the CLI.

Image 10.9 – Default Performance SLA Objects

Performance SLA Object

Next, review the parameters that make up an SLA object. To do this, create a new custom SLA object. Check out Image 10.10 on the next page. I named this object *SLA_Tester_Object*. The first parameter is an IPv4/IPv6 toggle, which specifies the layer-3 protocol the probe uses; here, we are using IPv4. Next is the Protocol field, which is the type of message that is going to be transmitted through the network used for measurement. In the GUI, we have three choices, ICMP (PING), HTTP, or DNS. These protocols should be self-explanatory, but one thing to note here, the probe you decide to use, be sure the machine you are sending the probe to is *listening* and responds to the expected protocols. Meaning, be sure you can ping your target or don't use a DNS probe to an HTTP server because FortiOS is expecting certain information back. Also, be sure to set up multiple probes of different types because what if your DNS probe target is having a systems-level issue? Now all your links are marked as degraded when in reality, they are good.

I've seen 500+ SD-WAN sites go down because a PING SLA probe-target became unreachable. Nothing was wrong with the links or the FortiGate. However, someone did remove a certain loopback IP address, which caused a massive event. Redundancy is your friend. In this example, I am using the DNS probe and pointing to FortiGuard DNS. The *Participants* parameter, seen in Image 10.10, marks what SD-WAN members SLA probe packets are sent down; this parameter allows granularity of controlling what SLA probes go where.

Image 10.10 – Custom SLA Performance Object Example

The next parameter is the *Enable Probe packets* toggle, which, if turned off, disables the function of this SLA object. Next is *SLA Target* toggle, which is turned on and reveals three more options: Latency Threshold, Jitter Threshold, and Packet Loss Threshold. These metrics for FortiOS to determine which SD-WAN member has the best path. To elaborate on these items:

1) Latency
   a. Latency is the time it takes for packets to travel the round trip between two network devices. Also referred to as Round-Trip Delay. Latency SLA threshold is used to measure how fast data can be transmitted from a client to the server and back, in other words.
2) Jitter
   a. It is not measuring the total round-trip time of a packet but is measuring the time variance between multiple packets. For example, if packets A & B are sent at 1:00PM and packet A is received back at 1:01PM, and packet B is received back at 1:05PM then the jitter is 4 minutes. This causes an issue with real-time applications like audio/video.

Image 10.11 – SD-WAN Rule with SLA Probe

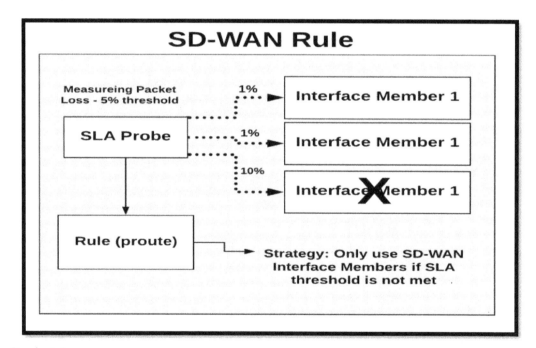

3) Packet Loss
   a. FortiOS can also keep up with packet loss to an SLA target. For example, if 100 ICMP echo-request are sent and only 90 return, then the SD-WAN member will report a 10% packet loss.

FortiOS SD-WAN can set thresholds for each of these values and steer traffic accordingly if said thresholds are exceeded, which is referred to as SD-WAN *strategy*. The strategy determines which egress interface is chosen. The next parameter to review under within the Performance SLA configuration is the *Link Status* section.

Image 10.12 – SD-WAN Rule Link Status Section

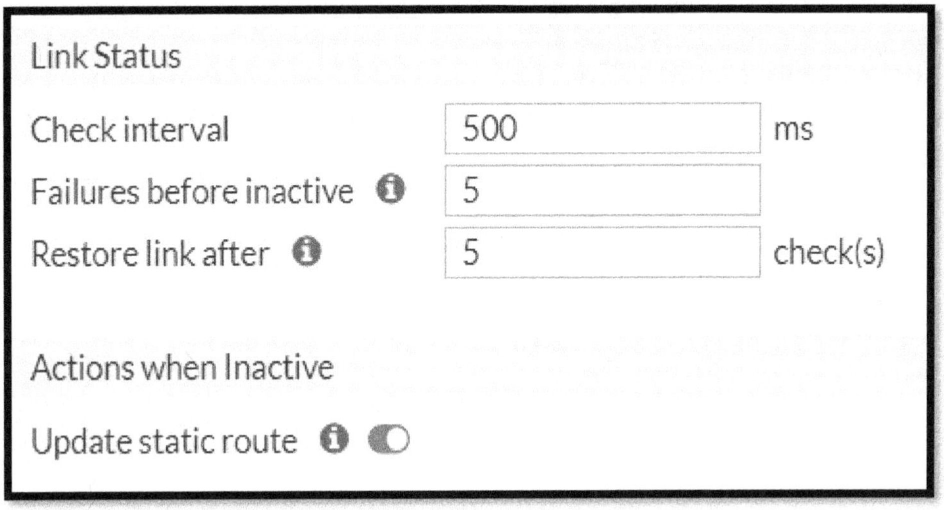

The Check interval parameters tell the SLA performance object how often to send a probe to the target destination. This measurement is in Milliseconds, in which the default is 500. The *Failure before inactive* parameter notates how many probe messages can be lost before marking an SD-WAN member interface as DOWN. The *Restore Link after* parameters is how many successful probes must be received to mark an SD-WAN member interface UP again. The Update static route toggle by default is on and removes any static route entries bound to DOWN interfaces. Next, we are going to review the SLA Performance object via CLI under *config system sdwan*:

```
FGT-B (SLA_Tester_Object) # show ful
config health-check
    edit "SLA_Tester_Object"
        set probe-packets enable
        set addr-mode ipv4
        set system-dns enable
        set ha-priority 1
        set dns-request-domain "www.example.com"
        set dns-match-ip 0.0.0.0
        set interval 500
        set probe-timeout 500
        set failtime 5
        set recoverytime 5
        set probe-count 30
        set diffservcode 000000
        set update-cascade-interface enable
```

```
        set update-static-route enable
        set sla-fail-log-period 0
        set sla-pass-log-period 0
        set threshold-warning-packetloss 0
        set threshold-alert-packetloss 0
        set threshold-warning-latency 0
        set threshold-alert-latency 0
        set threshold-warning-jitter 0
        set threshold-alert-jitter 0
        set members 0
        config sla
            edit 1
                set link-cost-factor latency jitter packet-loss
                set latency-threshold 150
                set jitter-threshold 150
                set packetloss-threshold 5
            next
        end
    next
end
```

I've bolded some of the items we covered in the Performance SLA GUI settings. I won't be going over all these settings in this chapter, but I think it is important to see the full picture of what CLI settings are available. This covers the SLA Performance object. In the next section, we are going to dive into the SD-WAN strategies available with the SD-WAN Rule settings.

SD-WAN Rule Strategies

For FortiOS 6.4 MR, the following strategies are available:
1) Manual
    a. This is where the administrator specifies the egress interface preference; no SLA probe is required. This method uses *priority-members* under *Config Service* in CLI and within SD-WAN Rule *Interface Preference* in GUI. This is the method we used in our first example.
2) Best Quality
    a. The SD-WAN member interface with the best measured SLA performance is chosen for traffic matched within Rule.
3) Lowest Cost
    a. This strategy states if the SLA threshold is not met, then the SD-WAN interface member is ok to be used. If all or multiple members are within SLA, then the Cost value is the tiebreaker. I show you where the Cost value in one moment.
4) Maximize Bandwidth
    a. This strategy load-balances traffic across all SD-WAN member interfaces if they are under the SLA Probe threshold.

The *cost* value is located in CLI under SD-WAN members via:

```
config sys sdwan
config members
    edit 1
        set interface "internal1"
        set zone "virtual-wan-link"
        set gateway 172.22.1.2
..
        set cost 0
..
    next
    edit 2
        set interface "internal2"
        set zone "virtual-wan-link"
        set gateway 172.22.2.2
..
        set cost 0
..
```

Image 10.13 – SD-WAN Rule Steering Strategies

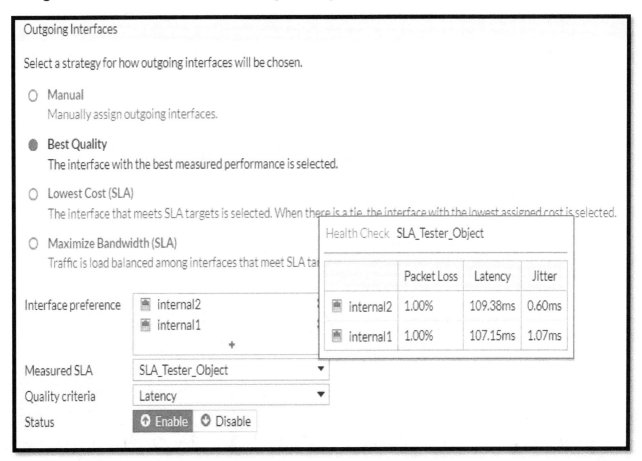

Image 10.13 displays the available Rule steering strategies in the GUI. Within this Image, the Best Quality strategy is selected, which requires the Rule to reference a Performance SLA object. In this example, we are going to use the object we just configured *SLA_Tester_Object*. Within this example, the quality criteria is marked as Latency. This means, if there is a variance of more than 10% between SD-WAN member interfaces, then traffic is steered to the member with the best quality. If the variance is under 10%, then traffic will be steered using the Interface Preference list. This same logic goes with any Quality Criteria selected, which can be found. If you click the chevron within the Quality criteria field, you receive a drop-down menu that lists all the available options.

Image 10.14 – Quality Criteria Drop Down

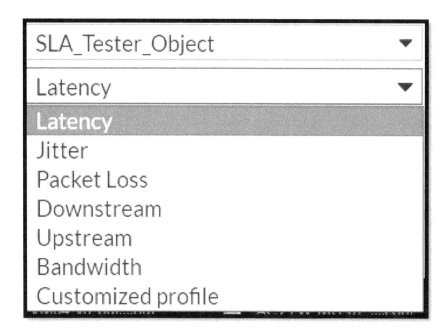

The items we have not covered here are Upstream Bandwidth, Downstream Bandwidth, bi-directional and Customized Profile. Here is the CLI equivalent of bi-directional quality :

```
config service
    edit 1
        set name "Rule_For_10.226.226.1"
..
        set health-check "SLA_Tester_Object"
        set link-cost-factor bibandwidth
..
    next

end
```

As an example, I have selected 'Bandwidth' in the GUI, which is **bibandwidth** in the CLI, which means the best quality member is based on bi-directional bandwidth. With this Quality criteria,

FortiOS references estimated upstream and downstream bandwidth values configured on the interfaces. See below CLI output:

```
FGT-B (internal1) # show ful | grep bandwidth
..
        set estimated-upstream-bandwidth 0 // kbps
        set estimated-downstream-bandwidth 0   // kbps
..
```

The last item to cover here is the Customized profile options, which could be used for specific requirements. The formula for the custom profile is:

Link Quality = (a * packet loss) + (b * latency) + (c * jitter) + (d / bandwidth)

Once the custom profile option is selected, then a drop-down is displayed containing the following field names:

1) packet loss weight (a)
2) latency weight (b)
3) Jitter weight (c)
4) bandwidth weight (d)

The next strategy to discuss is *Lowest Cost (SLA)*. This strategy states that if the Performance SLA threshold is not met, then interface members are available to receive traffic. Next, if all SD-WAN interface members' SLA are under the target threshold, then the next value to be evaluated is the Cost value that is assigned to an SD-WAN member interface directly. If all the Cost values are the same, then Interface Preference is the tiebreaker. So, in short, the evaluation process goes:

1) Under Performance SLA threshold
2) Lowest Cost value
3) Interface Preference list
       a. first in sequence index value for member interface is most preferred

Lastly, the Lowest Cost (SLA) strategy also requires a Performance SLA object. The CLI configuration is:

```
config service
    edit 1
        set name "Rule_For_10.226.226.1"
        set mode sla
..
    next
end
```

The last strategy available is the Maximize Bandwidth (SLA) and essentially load balances traffic across all SD-WAN interface members if Performance SLA metrics are under the configured threshold. The CLI configuration is:

```
config service
    edit 1
        set name "Rule_For_10.226.226.1"
        set mode load-balance
..
end
```

To recap, we know how to build the SD-WAN zone and add members to it. We know how to configure static routing to the SD-WAN zone. We reviewed details for SD-WAN *Implicit Rule*. We discuss SD-WAN Rule creation and how they are used to steer traffic across SD-WAN member interfaces. Lastly, we discussed path control and how FortiOS uses Performance SLA probes so FortiOS can pick the best interface to steer traffic to using metrics like latency, jitter, or packet loss.

In the next section, we start discussing application routing and focus on methods to identify applications within FortiOS because we first need to match applications so we can then tell FortiOS what to do with them.

Identify SD-WAN Application

There are two major methods to identify applications on FortiOS. The first one we already discussed in Part-I book of the series, which is the Internet Service Database (ISDB). The second method is the Application Control feature. The ISDB uses IP/Port/Protocol values mapped to well- known applications. Application Control we have not covered yet, and this is a fairly large topic, but I felt like it is important to include it in the SD-WAN chapter since application routing is a keystone in SD-WAN. So this will be a crash course in Application Control for you knew folks.

Application Control Traffic Identification

Application Control on FortiOS as of 2020 has over 4,300+ application signatures updated via FortiGuard. Application signatures are built with the same syntax used to create IPS signatures. FortiOS IPS engine is used for Application Control as well. This section will not dive deep into how App Control works on the backend, but we will indeed match and steer applications with SD-WAN Rules. We navigate back to the SD-WAN Rules via Network -> SD-WAN Rules -> Create New - and create an Application Control rule that steers traffic for AWS over Internal1.

Here is the CLI equivalent:

```
0: config system sdwan
0: config service
0: edit 0
0: set name "SDWAN_AWS_RULE"
..
0: set internet-service enable
```

```
..
0: set internet-service-app-ctrl "27210" "37172" "36740" "35944" "47432"
"47433"
..
0: set priority-members "1"
0: end
```

Image 10.15 – SD-WAN Application Steering Rule

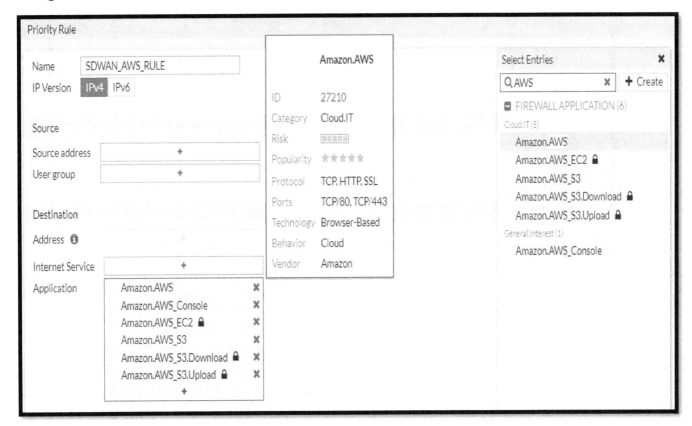

When using Application Control for steering traffic be sure that an Application Control profile and Deep Packet Inspection is configured in the Firewall Policy Entry

Next is to configure the Firewall Policy Entry with Application Control and Deep Packet inspection. See the next page, Image 10.16. The Application Control profile is required because traffic matched to this policy is identified by the App. Control signature database. Deep Packet Inspection (DIP) is required because most application these days uses TLS encryption. So for FortiOS to see what applications are running through a Firewall Policy Entry, then it must decrypt it first.

Image 10.16 – Application Control and SSL Inspection

The time for FortiOS to identify an application using App. Control is called the learning phase. This means the first session that establishes for any given application might not take the expected SD-WAN Rule. After the initial learning phase for said application, FortiOS dynamically caches application layer-3 and layer-4 information and store the values within the ISDB to avoid performing the learning phase again for applications that have already been evaluated. This being said, FortiOS is a stateful device and requires a little time to learn the applications on the network. The more dynamic cached ISDB entries App. Control creates allows SD-WAN Rules using this traffic steering method to work as expected. Dynamic cached ISDB entries contain the destination IP(s), protocol, and destination port(s) mapped back to any given application matched. Any other traffic using the same protocol, destination IP, and port are routed using the correct SD-WAN Rule.

To recap on this concept, have you ever heard of machine learning (ML)? Essentially, when using App. Control this activates ML to identify what applications are on the network and dynamically build cached ISDB entries that are run in parallel with the static ISDB entries that are updated via FortiGuard. Both are used to steer traffic to the correct SD-WAN member interface. Note that the dynamic ISDB entries that are created by App. Control has a limit of 512 entries, and once this fills up, the oldest entry is removed. That being said, be very specific about what applications you want FortiOS to perform machine learning for, do not just apply ALL known applications for this feature; this will most likely break things. Remember a smooth FortiGate deployment requires effective certification testing before rollout.

Next, we will go over an example of App. Control SD-WAN traffic steering. Below is the SD-WAN Rule we are testing:

```
config system sdwan
```

```
..
config service
..
    edit 2
        set name "SDWAN_AWS_RULE"
        set mode sla
        set internet-service enable
        set internet-service-app-ctrl 27210
        config sla
            edit "SLA_Tester_Object"
                set id 1
            next
        end
        set priority-members 1 2
    next
end
```

This rule states that the Application ID 27210 (Amazon.AWS) is steered towards SD-WAN interface members using the Lowest Cost (SLA) method. Next, I will generate some traffic on our test PC for Amazon AWS. Below is the debug output of the traffic:

```
FGT-B (root) # diagnose sys sdwan internet-service-app-ctrl-list

Amazon.AWS(27210 4294836311): 13.225.139.73 6 80 Thu Oct 29 14:00:51 2020
Amazon.AWS(27210 4294836311): 13.225.139.73 6 443 Thu Oct 29 14:00:51 2020
Amazon.AWS(27210 4294836311): 13.225.142.150 6 443 Thu Oct 29 14:00:51 2020
Amazon.AWS(27210 4294836311): 99.84.197.194 6 443 Thu Oct 29 14:00:52 2020
```

You can see now that FortiOS identified Amazon AWS traffic, and four dynamic cached ISDB entries were created. These entries contain the Application name, ID, Destination IP, Protocol, Port, and time stamp when created.

Remember, this first AWS session took the implicit SD-WAN rule, and once FortiOS used ML to ID the AWS, for any subsequent packets to the same IP/Protocol/Port AWS, traffic will be steered using Rule 2 in the configuration here. This wrap of App. Control traffic steering. Next, we will discuss ISDB traffic steering and the differences.

Internet Service Database Traffic Identification

I went over ISDB in Part-I of this series, but essentially, the ISDB contains well-known applications and maps them to their respective IP subnet ranges, ports, and protocols, which is referred to as a three tuple. The ISDB can be explored in the GUI via *Policy & Objects -> Internet Service Database*. Review Image 10.18 on the next page. The next SD-WAN Rule example will be created with an ISDB.

The ISDB entry must be referenced within the SD-WAN rule. To do this, navigate to the GUI via Network -> SD-WAN Rules -> Create New, see image 10.17:

The CLI equivalent for the AWS ISDB SD-WAN Rule is:

Image 10.17 – Internet Service Database GUI

```
FGT-B (root) # config system sdwan
FGT-B (sdwan) # config service
FGT-B (service) #edit 3
FGT-B (3) # show
```

Image 10.18 – SD-WAN Rule ISDB Example

```
config service
    edit 3
        set name "AWS_ISDB_Rule"
        set mode sla
        set internet-service enable
        set internet-service-name "Amazon-AWS" "Amazon-
AWS.WorkSpaces.Gateway"
        config sla
            edit "SLA_Tester_Object"
                set id 1
            next
        end
        set priority-members 2
    next
end
```

Next, to find details for Amazon-AWS ISDB via CLi, then go to Global context and issue the following commands:

```
FGT-B (global) # diagnose internet-service id-summary | grep AWS
id: 393320 name: "Amazon-AWS"
id: 393403 name: "Amazon-AWS.WorkSpaces.Gateway"
FGT-B (global) # diagnose internet-service id 393320
..
223.71.71.96-223.71.71.255 country(156) region(195) city(2018) blacklist(0x0)
reputation(4), domain(5) popularity(665) botnet(0) proto(6) port(1-65535)
223.71.71.96-223.71.71.255 country(156) region(195) city(2018) blacklist(0x0)
reputation(4), domain(5) popularity(665) botnet(0) proto(17) port(1-65535)
FGT-B (global) # config firewall internet-service 393320

IPsec-FGT-B (393320) # get
id                    : 393320
name                  : Amazon-AWS
icon-id               : 504
direction             : both
database              : isdb
ip-range-number       : 11797
extra-ip-range-number: 11797
ip-number             : 54706987
singularity           : 7
obsolete              : 0
```

Next is to confirm that the SD-WAN Service 3 (CLI Output) created a Policy Route entry within FortiOS, run the following command to see Policy Routes:

```
FGT-B (root) # diagnose firewall proute list
list route policy info(vf=root):
```

```
id=0x7f000003 vwl_service=3(AWS_ISDB_Rule) vwl_mbr_seq=2 1 dscp_tag=0xff 0xff
flags=0x0 tos=0x00 tos_mask=0x00 protocol=0 sport=0:65535 iif=0 dport=1-65535
oif=9(internal2)
source wildcard(1): 0.0.0.0/0.0.0.0
destination wildcard(1): 0.0.0.0/0.0.0.0
internet service(2): Amazon-AWS(393320,0,0,0) Amazon-
AWS.WorkSpaces.Gateway(393403,0,0,0)
hit_count=0 last_used=2020-11-01 13:56:45
```

I've bolded a few important items in the output here, field/value of vwl_service=3 specifies the SD-WAN Rule index number. In the CLI, the SD-WAN rule is referred to as a 'service' found under *config service*. The next portion of the output to review is vwl_mbr_seq=2 1, which indicates this Rule has an interface preference of index 2, which is mapped to *internal2*. The next portion *of the output to review is:*

"dscp_tag=0xff 0xff flags=0x0 tos=0x00 tos_mask=0x00 protocol=0 sport=0:65535 iif=0 dport=1-65535 oif=9(internal2)
source wildcard(1): 0.0.0.0/0.0.0.0
destination wildcard(1): 0.0.0.0/0.0.0.0
"

The above snippet of the output is what traffic this Rule will match. For example, we could filter this rule so only certain source IPs can utilize this Rule for AWS. FortiOS also provides options to match the ToS field within the packet header. This can be configured in the CLI via

```
FGT-B (sdwan) # config service
FGT-B (3) # show ful | grep tos
        set tos 0x00
        set tos-mask 0x00
```

The last portion of this output indicates the ISDB entry(s) being used and how much network traffic has matched this Rule from hit count and the last time used timestamp.

```
internet service(2): Amazon-AWS(393320,0,0,0) Amazon-
AWS.WorkSpaces.Gateway(393403,0,0,0)
hit_count=0 last_used=2020-11-01 13:56:45
```

> *To contact Fortinet regarding ISDB go to https://www.fortiguard.com/faq/isdb-contact*

FortiOS contains many ISDB entries for various applications, but there are sometimes cases where the destination IP/Port/Protocol bindings you are looking for might not be available. In cases like these, FortiOS provide options to modify an ISDB entry. In this example, the Amazon-AWS entry 393320 is used. We are going to add UDP protocol 17 with a destination port of 8888 and still use the same destination IP ranges. This method is referred to as an ISDB addition or extension.

```
FGT-B (global) # config firewall internet-service-addition

IPsec-FGT-B (internet-service~ion) # edit 393320
new entry '393320' added
FGT-B (393320) # show
config firewall internet-service-addition
    edit 393320
        set comment ''
        config entry
            edit 1
                set protocol 17
                config port-range
                    edit 1
                        set start-port 8888
                        set end-port 8888
                    next
                end
            next
        end
    next
end
FGT-B (393320) # end
Warning: Configuration will only be applied after rebooting or using the
'execute internet-service refresh' command.

IPsec-FGT-B (global) # execute internet-service refresh
```

> Note: ISDB entries can be used for SD-WAN Rules, Static Routing and Firewall Policy Entries

As a PoC that this actually works, we can issue the following command:

```
FGT-B (global) # diagnose internet-service info root 17 8888 3.1.1.1
Internet Service: 393320(Amazon-AWS) country(702 Singapore) region(1740
(null)) city(22292 Singapore)
```

This section wraps up Application identification with ISDB. The last identification method available for SD-WAN rules is the FQDN method

Fully Qualified Domain Name (FQDN) SD-WAN Rule

The last method SD-WAN Rules can use to identify applications is the FQDN method. In this method, the administrator is required to create an Address object with type FQDN. This procedure was discussed in the Part-I book of this NSE4 study guide series. Once the object is created, then referencing it in the SD-WAN Rule is straightforward. See Image 10.19.

Image 10.19 – SD-WAN Rule FQDN

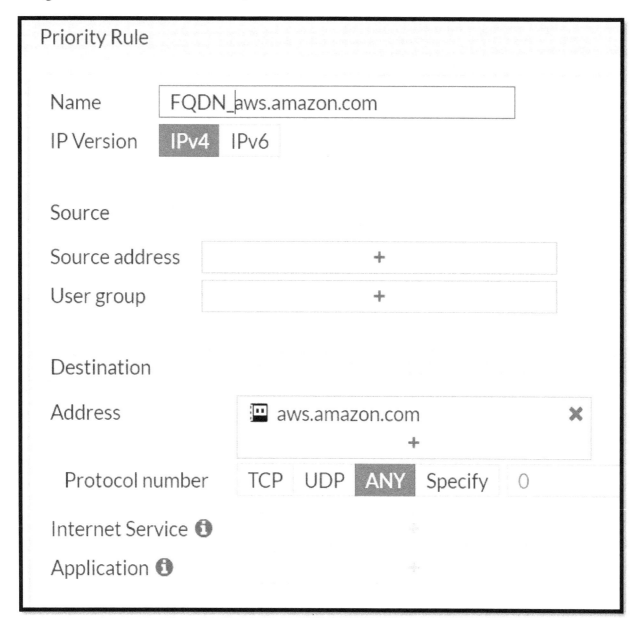

Once this is configured, FortiOS will attempt to resolve aws.amazon.com and insert the IP address within the Policy Routing Table. This can be check via CLI:

```
FGT-B (root) # diagnose firewall proute list
list route policy info(vf=root):

id=0x7f050004 vwl_service=4(FQDN_aws.amazon.com) vwl_mbr_seq=1 dscp_tag=0xff
0xff flags=0x0 tos=0x00 tos_mask=0x00 protocol=0 sport=0:65535 iif=0 dport=1-
65535 oif=8(internal1)
destination fqdn(1):
        aws.amazon.com ID(108) ADDR(13.226.224.72) ADDR(13.35.91.74)
source wildcard(1): 0.0.0.0/0.0.0.0
hit_count=0 last_used=2020-11-01 15:58:27
```

This brings us to the end of the Application identification section. At this point, you should know how FortiOS identifies applications used within SD-WAN Rules. The next FortiOS SD-WAN component to discuss is QoS & Traffic Shaping!

QoS & Traffic Shaping

So you might be thinking, what is the difference between QoS and Traffic Shaping? You might also be thinking, why are we even talking about these items within the SD-WAN chapter? Like I said at the beginning of the chapter SD-WAN is a compilation of technologies to accomplish dynamic best path application steering. QoS and Traffic Shaping create quality paths for network traffic.

The difference between QoS and Traffic Shaping in this context is, Traffic Shaping is a FortiGate-specific technology that allows administrators to explicitly define policies to match traffic so as to prioritize, deprioritize, limit bandwidth, or guarantee bandwidth for certain traffic flows. QoS conforms to traffic classification industries standards defined in RFC's 2474 & 2475 and has its own set of terminology and methodology to obtain End-To-End Quality of Service. The first topic to discuss is QoS

Quality of Service (QoS)

I hope you're ready for a crash course in QoS! The goal of QoS is the ability to handle different classes of traffic uniquely. Meaning, the ability to separate traffic flows and then perform an action. To separate traffic flows, an 8-bit field in the IPv4/IPv6 header was decided to be used and was labeled Type of Service (ToS), which was initially defined in RFC 791. The 8-bit ToS field was broken up into three parts, and the first three high order bits are labeled as Precedence; the next three high order bits were labeled Type of Service, and the last two bits were unused. See Image 10.20 for details.

Image 10.20 – RFC 971 Type of Service Field Definition

7	6	5	4	3	2	1	0
Precedence			Type of Service			Unused (0)	

The precedence field is a 3-bit value to indicate what packets have a higher priority than others. The ToS field was used to specify how IP packets are handled during processing. This ToS model was deprecated by RFC 2474 and was renamed the Differentiated Services (DS) field or could be referred to as DiffServe for short. The DS field held Differentiated Services Code Point (DSCP) values, which define a Class Selector (CS).

DSCP uses a 6-bit value (Code Point), which are the high order bits within the DS field within the IPv4/IPv6 header, and this value is used to affect the Per-Hop-Behavior (PHB) of devices process packets with DSCP markings. Meaning, a certain priority is set per packet, and each router in the full transit path can take action on this value. This could be to prioritize or deprioritize the packet processing. DSCP values are mapped to names and Service Classes that define the treatment of the packet. Per RFC 4594, here is the table mapping Classification to DSCP names and values. Some common DiffServ Classifications are:

1) Default Forwarding (DF)
    a. which is typically best-effort traffic
    b. Value 000000
2) Expedited Forwarding (EF)
    a. dedicated to low-loss, low-latency traffic
    b. Value 101110
3) Assured Forwarding (AF)
    a. gives assurance of delivery under prescribed conditions
    b. Many values
4) Class Selector (CS)
    a. Used to maintain backward compatibility with the ToS IP precedence field.

In short, an application that requires low latency and jitter like voice should use DiffServ class EF. Meaning, the DS field should be marked with 10111000 to let all devices know in the transit path that this packet is high priority and cannot tolerate latency. One of the benefits of having an MPLS network is the ability to perform end-to-end QoS markings and prioritization for enterprise voice traffic. SD-WAN cannot do this because IPsec is simulating a private network, and any DSCP values might not be honored by the ISP unless there is a prior agreement.

Regarding SDWAN, most of the time, BGP operates over IPsec, and transit routers need to know which IPsec packets contain BGP control packets so they can be prioritized over the others. This is accomplished by marking these packets with a DSCP value of <u>CS6</u>, which is the Class Name for Internet Control traffic. The full listing of CS names are:

Legacy ToS IP Precedence Values (CS names)

1) Routine or Best Effort
   a. 000 (CS0)
2) Low Priority
   a. 001 (CS1)
3) Immediate
   a. 010 (CS2)
4) Flash (mainly used for voice signaling or for video)
   a. 011 (CS3)
5) Flash Override
   a. 100 (CS4)
6) Critical (RTP)
   a. 101 (CS5)
7) **Network Control**
   a. 110 (CS6)

These values can also be found in RFC 4594 via:

https://tools.ietf.org/html/rfc4594#section-1.5.4

"

```
  ------------------------------------------------------------------
  |    Service      |  DSCP   |    DSCP     |      Application       |
  |  Class Name     |  Name   |    Value    |      Examples          |
  |=================+=========+=============+=======================|
  |Network Control|   CS6   |    110000   | Network routing        |
  |---------------+---------+-------------+------------------------|
  |  Telephony      |   EF    |    101110   | IP Telephony bearer    |
  |---------------+---------+-------------+------------------------|

  ...
  ...

  |   Standard      | DF (CS0)|    000000   | Undifferentiated       |
  |                 |         |             | applications           |
  |---------------+---------+-------------+------------------------|
  | Low-Priority    |   CS1   |    001000   | Any flow that has no BW|
  |    Data         |         |             | assurance              |
  ------------------------------------------------------------------
```

"

For reference, as of 6.4 MR FortiOS supports the following DiffServ RFCs

1) RFC 3260: New Terminology and Clarifications for Diffserv
2) RFC 2597: Assured Forwarding PHB Group
3) RFC 2475: An Architecture for Differentiated Services
4) RFC 2474: Definition of the Differentiated Services Field (DS Field) in the IPv4 and IPv6 Headers

I'm not going to lie, QoS is a large subject, and there are a lot of table mappings between the various classes and values. The goal of this section is to provide a high-level overview of QoS. You should remember that BGP data encapsulated within IPsec ESP packets should be marked with DSCP CS6 to be prioritized correctly. FortiGate can apply DSCP markings to packets via Firewall Policy as well, which can be configured in the CLI. For example, FortiOS can mark packets that cross the SD-WAN policy with Expedited Forwarding (EF), which is DSCP value 101110. See configuration below:

```
config firewall policy
    edit 8
        set name "SD-WAN-Policy"
        set uuid aee009c8-1709-51eb-395d-80491b26b567
        set srcintf "wan1"
        set dstintf "virtual-wan-link"
        set srcaddr "all"
        set dstaddr "all"
        set action accept
        set schedule "always"
        set service "ALL"
        set utm-status enable
        set ssl-ssh-profile "deep-inspection"
        set application-list "g-default"
        set diffserv-forward enable
        set diffserv-reverse enable
        set diffservcode-forward 101110
        set diffservcode-rev 101110
        set nat enable
    next
end
```

Any packet excepted by Firewall Policy 8, in this example, the IP DS field value is marked with 101110. This configuration overrides any prior DSCP markings the IP packet may have. What this configuration doesn't do is prioritize packets already marked with 101110. FortiOS separates this function from the Firewall Policy Table. To understand DS/ToS prioritization, you first need to understand FortiOS packet queues.

FortiOS Interface Queues

FortiOS has a total of <u>six egress</u> <u>queues</u> <u>per physical interface</u> used for traffic prioritization. Virtual interfaces use the parent's physical interface queues and do not have their own.

FortiOS assigns a Global Priority that partly specifies how traffic is prioritized within these six queues. The other method of traffic prioritization is with the Traffic Shaper feature used to govern transit traffic that flows through FortiGate. Queue 0 has the highest priority and is

Image 10.21 – FortiOS Interface Egress Queues

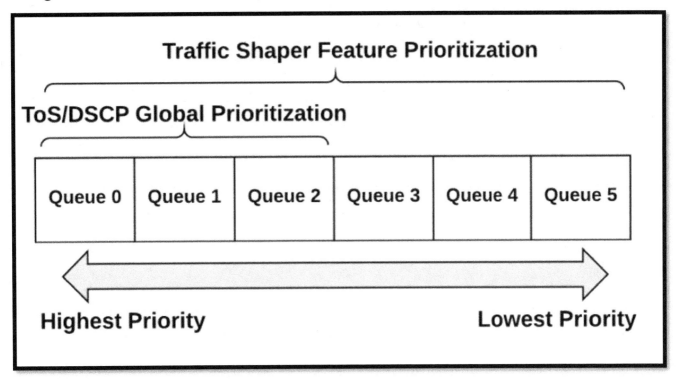

reserved for administrative access.

FortiOS separates traffic streams into the following groups:

1) Local-out // Generated locally from FortiOS // Including AV Proxying
2) Local-In or ingress traffic
3) Transit Traffic // Traffic processed by Firewall Policy

Network traffic that matches a security policy with no Traffic Shaper applied can use the following queues 0, 1, or 2, and by default, the Medium (1) queue is used. Traffic matching Firewall Policy Entry with Traffic Shaping applied traffic can be configured to use any queue. FortiOS runs a first-in-first-out FIFO packet processing strategy per egress queue with 0 being the first processed and then queue 1 and so on. FortiOS processes all packets within higher priority queues before moving down to lower priority queues. By default, Firewall Policy Entries with no Traffic Shaper applied places packets within priority queue one by default.

Remember, there are two methods to assign a priority value to a packet, the Global ToS method, which occurs by default, and the Policy method, which requires a Traffic Shaper.

FortiOS Global Priority

Global priority options govern ingress, Local-out, and transit traffic. These options are found in the CLI via:

```
FGT-B (global) # conf sys glo
FGT-B (global) # show ful | grep priority
    set traffic-priority tos
    set traffic-priority-level medium
```

For 6.4 MR FortiOS, the default method to prioritize traffic uses the 4-bit ToS value within the IP header outlined in RFC 1349. The default priority level is Medium for all possible ToS values. FortiOS maps Global ToS/DS priority levels (High, Medium, and Low) to the following queues:

1) High   = queue 0
2) Medium   = queue 1
3) Low   = queue 2

To see all the current ToS values to priority level mappings, run the following CLI command:

```
FGT-B (global) # diagnose sys traffic-priority list
Traffic priority type is set to TOS.
00:medium 01:medium 02:medium 03:medium 04:medium 05:medium 06:medium
07:medium
08:medium 09:medium 10:medium 11:medium 12:medium 13:medium 14:medium
15:medium
```

The first value in the '00:medium' pair is the ToS marking on the packet, and the second value, ':medium' is the priority level, which is mapped to an egress queue. To adjust these mappings, the below configuration can be used:

```
(global) # config system tos-based-priority
end
IPsec-FGT-B (tos-based-priority) # edit 0
new entry '0' added
IPsec-FGT-B (0) # show ful
config system tos-based-priority
    edit 1
        set tos 0
        set priority high
    next
end
..
IPsec-FGT-B (global) # diagnose sys traffic-priority list
Traffic priority type is set to TOS.
00:high    01:medium 02:medium 03:medium 04:medium 05:medium 06:medium
07:medium
```

```
08:medium 09:medium 10:medium 11:medium 12:medium 13:medium 14:medium
15:medium
```

Global Priority mapping can be changed from ToS based to DSCP based by global CLI configuration, see below:

```
FGT-B (global) # conf sys glo
IPsec-FGT-B (global) # set traffic-priority dscp
FGT-B (global) # end
FGT-B (global) # config sys dscp-based-priority
IPsec-FGT-B (dscp-based-priority) # edit 0
new entry '0' added
IPsec-FGT-B (0) # set ds 00
IPsec-FGT-B (0) # set priority high
IPsec-FGT-B (0) # show
config system dscp-based-priority
    edit 1
    next
end
FGT-B (global) # diagnose sys traffic-priority list
Traffic priority type is set to DSCP (DiffServ).
00:high   01:medium 02:medium 03:medium 04:medium 05:medium 06:medium
07:medium
08:medium 09:medium 10:medium 11:medium 12:medium 13:medium 14:medium
15:medium
16:medium 17:medium 18:medium 19:medium 20:medium 21:medium 22:medium
23:medium
24:medium 25:medium 26:medium 27:medium 28:medium 29:medium 30:medium
31:medium
32:medium 33:medium 34:medium 35:medium 36:medium 37:medium 38:medium
39:medium
40:medium 41:medium 42:medium 43:medium 44:medium 45:medium 46:medium
47:medium
48:medium 49:medium 50:medium 51:medium 52:medium 53:medium 54:medium
55:medium
56:medium 57:medium 58:medium 59:medium 60:medium 61:medium 62:medium
63:medium
```

This configuration will use the 6-bit DSCP value within the DS field within the IP header to associate packet to a priority queue of Low, Medium or High. In this example, DSCP 000000 was configured to be mapped to the High priority queue which maps to queue 0. Using Global ToS/DS Priority prioritization method does not implicitly limit or guarantee bandwidth, this is accomplished by Traffic Shaper.

Remember, Global ToS/DS Priority queues High, Medium, and Low map to priority values of 0, 1, and 2, respectively.

Traffic Shaper Policy

Traffic Shaper maps priority levels High, Medium, and Low to the following queues:

1) High   = queue 1
2) Medium   = queue 2
3) Low   = queue 3

FortiOS Traffic Shaper feature is used to control transit traffic through FortiGate. The goal is to match traffic flows and then guarantee or limit bandwidth values or session count values. Traffic Shaper can be used in conjunction with Global Priority for transit traffic. This is calculated by taking the Global Priority queue value High, Medium and Low (0, 1, or 2) a packet is associated with and the Traffic Shaper queue High, Medium and Low (1, 2, or 3) and adding them together to get the total priority value. It might be a bit confusing that Traffic Shaper priority labels (High, Medium, or Low) map to different values (1, 2, or 3) than the Global ToS/DS Priority label to value mappings (0, 1, or 2), but this is just something we must notate moving forward.

For example, if Global ToS/DS Priority associates packet to queue 1 (Medium - Global) and the packet is also matched by a Traffic Shaper within a policy that associates the packet to queue 2 (Medium - Policy), then the total priority value for this packet would be queue 3.

This is a bit misleading; let me explain why. Traffic Shaper can provide a guaranteed bandwidth value for specific traffic flows, and if the packet is matched by a Traffic Shaper and is marked as under the guaranteed bandwidth, then this packet is placed in queue 0 regardless. Only when a packet breaks the guaranteed bandwidth threshold and is under the maximum bandwidth threshold will the packet be placed in the Medium queue (queue 3) in this example. If the packet is deemed to be above the maximum bandwidth, then the packet is discarded.

Another point to note is that the maximum and guaranteed bandwidth threshold only comes into play on traffic sharing an egress port. For example, if one device is transmitting and goes out WAN1 and WAN2, then Traffic Shaper measures bandwidth utilized on WAN1 and WAN2 independently, which could cause unexpected behavior. To control this traffic flow, the Global Priority method would need to be utilized.

Since we have covered some of the basics for Traffic Shaper, I'm sure the big question on your mind is how do we configure and apply the Traffic Shaper? To accomplish this in the GUI, go to Policy & Objects -> Traffic Shapers; see Image 10.22.

Image 10.22 – Traffic Shaping Menu's

For older FortiOS releases, the Traffic Shaper was required to be configured within the Firewall Policy Entry; this is no longer true. Fortinet changed their Traffic Shaping strategy to allow independent VDOM Traffic Shaper Policy to be configured that is separate from the Firewall Policy Table. FortiOS still allows for Traffic Shaper to be applied directly to Firewall Policy Entry via CLI only. This section will focus on the new method. Go to Policy & Objects -> Traffic Shapers > +Create New

Image 10.23 – Traffic Shaping Policy

In Image 10.23, the Traffic Shaper Policy is named *Match_Streaming_Media*. The matching criteria are any source IP, any destination IP, HTTP or HTTPS, URL Category Streaming Media, and Download. URL Categories are something we have not covered yet, but essentially a category represents many related domains into one object. This is performed by FortiGuard. For example, I would expect sites like youtube.com or pandora.com to be a part of the Streaming Media and Download URL Category. This is a convenience feature, so administrators do not need to explicitly specify individual domains, which is very time-consuming. Once traffic is matched, then the Action is to apply a *Shaper* to this traffic that egresses all SD-WAN interface members apart of *virtual-wan-link* SD-WAN zone. The type of Shaper applied to this policy is *low-priority*, which is a pre-defined Traffic Shaper object. This object is using the Shared shaper method, which means any traffic match shares one pool of resources.

Let me explain; when I say one pool of resources, I mean the guaranteed and maximum bandwidth that is allocated by this object. This is defined within the *low-priority* Shaper object that can be found in the GUI via Policy & Objects -> Traffic Shapers - > low-priority -> Edit.

Image 10.24 – Default low-priority Shaper Object

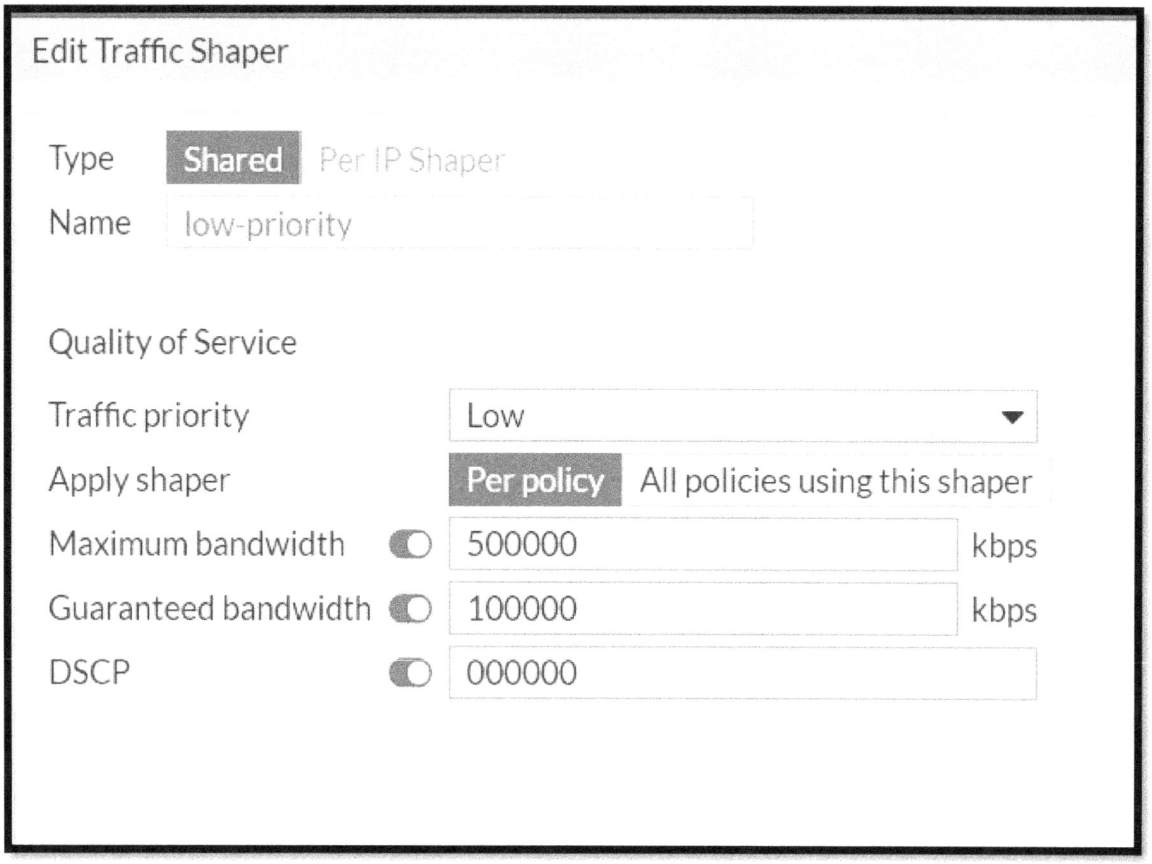

The *low-priority* Shaper currently is configured to map traffic to the Low queue (queue 3) and allows a maximum bandwidth of 500Mbps and a Guaranteed bandwidth of 100Mbps, and packets accepted by this policy is marked with DSCP 000000. Also, note the Shaper is applied *Per policy* and not *'All policies using this shaper'* method. The difference is how the maximum and guaranteed bandwidth resources are allocated. If *Per policy method* is used then, each Firewall Policy Entry is allocated the full Guaranteed and Maximum bandwidth for Shaper. If *'All policies*

Image 10.25 – Traffic Shaper Thresholds

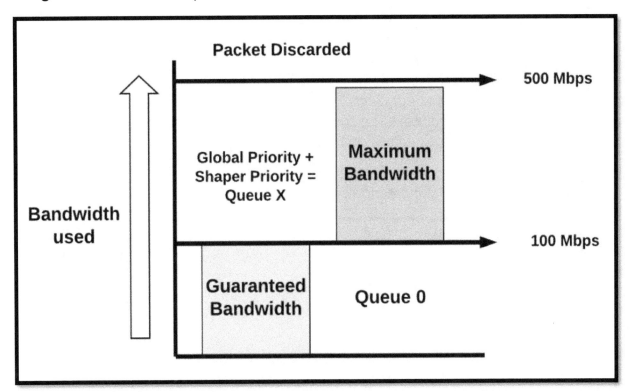

using this shaper' method is used, then all firewall policies that utilize Shaper is divided equally. So if there are four Firewall Policy Entries that are using the Shaper in this example, then each policy would be allocated 25Mbps for Guaranteed bandwidth and 125Mbps for Maximum bandwidth for matched traffic.

Next, each Shaper has a direction; it regulates traffic flow (upload/download). The Shared shaper in *Match_Streaming_Media* is only useful in policing bandwidth for uploading. To police download bandwidth, then the *Reverse shaper* would need to be referenced. These Shapers require an ingress-to-egress interface binding to be effective. Sessions with different ingress-to-egress bindings are treated independently from each other regarding Traffic Shaping.

The last option is to apply Shaper to a Traffic Shaper Policy as *a Per-IP shaper*. As the name indicates, the resources allocated within the Shaper object is based on source IP. Meaning, if Match_Streaming_Media policy were configured with a Per-IP shaper in this example, then every connection would be allocated a maximum bandwidth of 500Mbps and a Guaranteed bandwidth of 100Mbps, which really makes no sense because independent clients will never reach these thresholds (most likely!). One unique feature of the Per-IP shaper is that it can limit concurrent sessions per source IP. This configuration can safeguard your network; in fact, FortiOS can cap outbound sessions from a single source IP if a client on your network decides to join a botnet! The configuration below limits a single client to 100 outbound sessions and 10Mpbs.

```
FGT-B (per-ip-shaper) # show
config firewall shaper per-ip-shaper
    edit "Per-IP-Shaper_Limit_Sessions"
        set max-bandwidth 10000
        set max-concurrent-session 100
    next
end
```

These shapers can be found in the Traffic shaping profile; see Image 10.26 for reference. Shared & Per-IP Shaper can be mixed and matched. The Shared shaper could be configured to police bandwidth, and the Per-IP shaper could be configured to limit sessions. If using both Shared & Reverse shaper profiles, then both upload and download are policed.

Image 10.26 – Traffic Shaper Policy Options

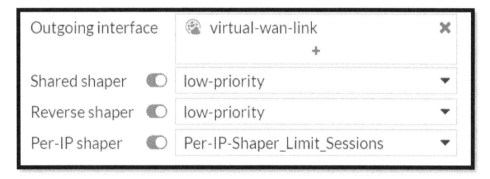

Application Traffic Shaping

If using Application Control within a Traffic Shaping Policy, then the Application bandwidth calculation is separated from the source IP and has its own autonomous counters of the total bandwidth used. For example, if Youtube was being matched with App. Control and if the Youtube application reaches its maximum allocated bandwidth via Shaper; then, Youtube packets will be discarded; however, the source user would still have bandwidth resources available for other activities on the network, just not Youtube. Note, just like SD-WAN Application steering, it is required to apply an App. Control profile to the Firewall Policy Entry, the same goes here. For Application Traffic Shaping to work correctly, then an App. Profile with deep SSL inspection should be used in the transit policy.

Image 10.27 – YouTube Application Traffic Shaper Policy

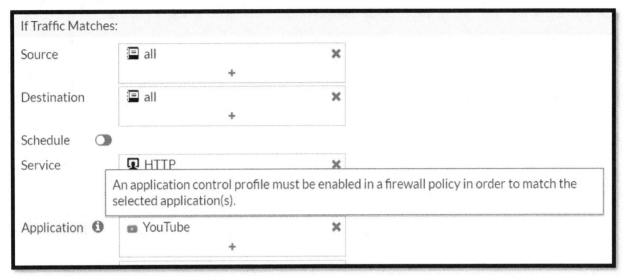

The next Traffic Shaper topic to discuss is Shaping Classes.

Traffic Shaping Profile

The Traffic Shaping Profile uses the Traffic Shaper Class ID feature and is a way to organize different tiers of services delivered by the FortiGate within the single windowpane of *Traffic Shaping Profile*. Essentially, instead of creating ad-hoc Traffic Shaper Policies to control traffic streams with Class ID's each ID can be assigned certain levels of guaranteed and maximum bandwidth attributes and indexed within a single Traffic Shaper Profile. Each index value is called a class. This can be configured in the GUI via Policy & Objects -> Traffic Shaping Profile -> Create New. Check out Image 10.28 on the next page. In this example, the Traffic Shaping Profile has three classes defined.

1) Class_ID_2 (Default)
2) Class_ID_3
3) Low-Priority-Class-4

Each class has three attributes, which are Maximum bandwidth, Guaranteed bandwidth, and Priority. Class_ID_2 is the default class that is required for each Shaping Profile. The default class ID within the profile is implicitly referenced in two conditions:

1) Any traffic that does not match any Shaping Policy for egress interface
2) Any traffic matched by an external Traffic Shaper not defined in a Shaping Profile.

Image 10.28 – Traffic Shaping Profile with Class ID's

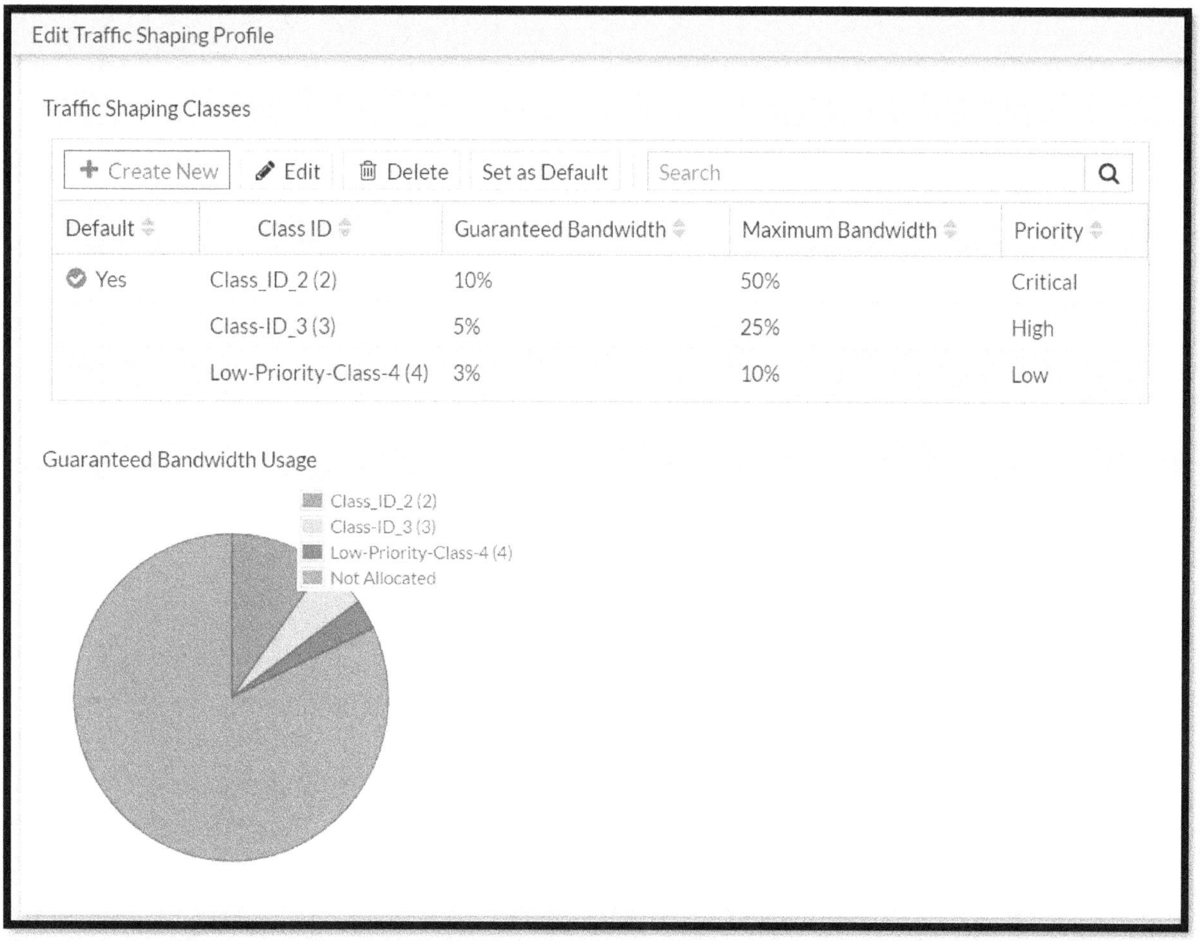

Edit Traffic Shaping Profile

Traffic Shaping Classes

| + Create New | ✏ Edit | 🗑 Delete | Set as Default | Search | Q |

Default ⇕	Class ID ⇕	Guaranteed Bandwidth ⇕	Maximum Bandwidth ⇕	Priority ⇕
✓ Yes	Class_ID_2 (2)	10%	50%	Critical
	Class-ID_3 (3)	5%	25%	High
	Low-Priority-Class-4 (4)	3%	10%	Low

Guaranteed Bandwidth Usage

- Class_ID_2 (2)
- Class-ID_3 (3)
- Low-Priority-Class-4 (4)
- Not Allocated

Once various classes are created within a single Traffic Shaping Profile, a snapshot pie-chart displays all the guaranteed bandwidth across all Class ID's. This is a *convenience* feature to help you keep track of all the allocated guaranteed bandwidth per Shaping Profile. Once all the Classes are defined, these can easily be referenced within Traffic Shaping Policy, making the configuration live. Image 10.29 on the next page contains an example configuration of a Traffic Shaping Policy that references the Low-Priority-Class-4 Class that matches any source or destination using the URL Category *Streaming Media and downloads*. The Low-Priority-Class-4 Class object restricts all traffic flow egressing WAN1 for this URL category outlined in the specified parameters. Note that a Web Filter profile and DPI are required on the transit for this Shaper configuration to work correctly.

Image 10.29 – Traffic Shaping Policy with Traffic Class

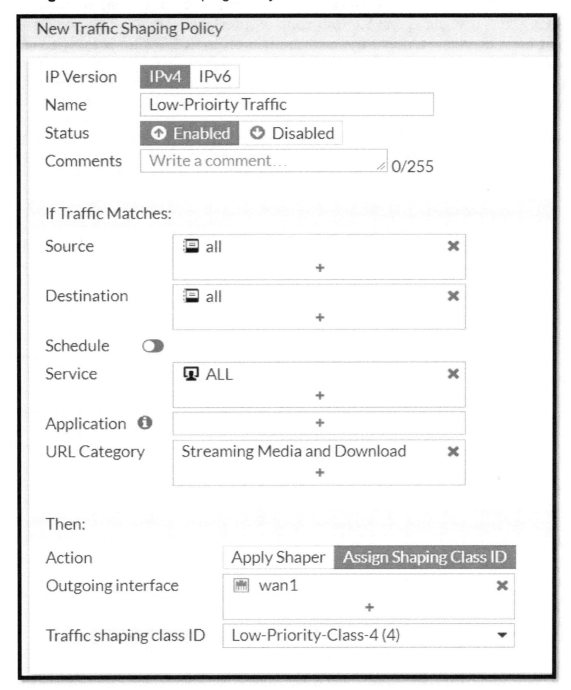

To check that the specific traffic is put into the correct shaping group or class ID:

 # diagnose firewall iprope list 100015

It is best to keep things as simple as possible for manageability when using Traffic Shaping Profiles and Traffic Shaping Policies. It would be best practice to not overlap multiple Traffic Shaping Profiles across a single egress SD-WAN zone or interface member. This completes the Traffic Shaping Class overview section; the next method of FortiOS Traffic Shaping to cover is Interface based.

Interface Based Traffic Shaping

FortiOS allows you to directly configure ingress & egress bandwidth limiting on a per-interface basis. Also, FortiOS provides the option to apply a Traffic Shaping Profile directly to the interface. The interface GUI menu looks like Image 10.30 below:

Image 10.30 – Interface Based Traffic Shaping Profile

The CLI configuration would show the following configurations:

```
config system interface
    edit "wan1"
        set vdom "root"
        set ip 192.168.209.2 255.255.255.0
        set allowaccess ping https ssh snmp http telnet
        set type physical
        set outbandwidth 500000
        set set egress-shaping-profile "Wan-1-Shaping-Profile"
        set snmp-index 1
    next
```

Next, the two items to review within the wan1 interface configuration output is the *egress shaping profile* and *outbandwidth*. The easier one to explain is outbandwidth; this limits the available interface bandwidth and, in this example, is set to 500Mbps. The *outbandwidth* value is also used within the Traffic Shaping Profile to allocate bandwidth between Class ID Guaranteed Bandwidth value. In the next example, the Traffic Shaping Profile references three Class ID's 6, 7, and 8. See configuration details in the below output:

```
FGT-B (root) # show fire shaping-profile
config firewall shaping-profile
...
    edit "Wan-1-Shaping-Profile"
        set default-class-id 7
        config shaping-entries
            edit 2
                set class-id 7
                set priority low
                set guaranteed-bandwidth-percentage 10
                set maximum-bandwidth-percentage 25
            next
            edit 1
                set class-id 6
                set guaranteed-bandwidth-percentage 50
                set maximum-bandwidth-percentage 75
            next
            edit 3
                set class-id 8
                set priority medium
                set guaranteed-bandwidth-percentage 20
                set maximum-bandwidth-percentage 40
            next
        end
    next
end
```

These Class ID's each have a priority value, Guaranteed Bandwidth value, and Maximum Bandwidth Value, with Class ID 7 being the default. These Class ID's are referenced in the Traffic Shaping Policy, which is used to match interesting traffic; check out the below CLI output:

```
FGT-B (root) # show fire shaping-policy
config firewall shaping-policy
    ..
    edit 5
        set name "Wan1-Int-Medium"
        set service "ALL"
        set url-category 49 // business
        set dstintf "wan1"
        set class-id 8
        set srcaddr "all"
        set dstaddr "all"
```

```
    next
    edit 4
        set name "Wan1-Class-7-Low-Prioirty"
        set service "ALL"
        set dstintf "wan1"
        set class-id 7
        set srcaddr "all"
        set dstaddr "all"
    next
    edit 3
        set name "Wan1-Int-Class-6"
        set service "HTTP" "HTTPS"
        set dstintf "wan1"
        set class-id 6
        set srcaddr "all"
        set dstaddr "all"
    next
end
```

This configuration matches traffic within the Traffic Shaping Policy, which is HTTP/HTTPS with any source, any destination that egresses wan1 which is mapped to service class id 6, which is prioritized High with guaranteed bandwidth of 50% of total allocated bandwidth and a maximum bandwidth of 75% of total allocated bandwidth which would be 250Mbps and 375Mbps respectively because the **outbandwidth** wan1 is configured for 500000 Kbps (500Mbps). The logic holds true for the other Class IDs referenced in this configuration. The last item I want to mention in this section is this configuration only governs egress traffic. To govern ingress traffic via interface then the below CLI commands would be referenced:

```
FGT-B (wan1) # show ful
..
set inbandwidth 0
set ingress-shaping-profile ''
```

Traffic Shaper Debug

FortiOS provides a few good commands that provide insight into what is happening behind the scenes with Traffic Shaper. The first one to review is:

```
FGT-B (root) # diagnose netlink interface list wan1

if=wan1 family=00 type=1 index=5 mtu=1500 link=0 master=0
ref=31 state=start present fw_flags=8000 flags=up broadcast run multicast
Qdisc=mq hw_addr=04:d5:90:xxxxxxx broadcast_addr=ff:ff:ff:ff:ff:ff
egress traffic control:
        bandwidth=500000(kbps) lock_hit=0 default_class=7 n_active_class=3
```

```
        class-id=7    allocated-bandwidth=5000(kbps)  guaranteed-
bandwidth=5000(kbps)
                      max-bandwidth=5000(kbps)           current-
bandwidth=8(kbps)

                      priority=low    forwarded_bytes=8916K
                      dropped_packets=0       dropped_bytes=0
        class-id=8    allocated-bandwidth=5000(kbps)  guaranteed-
bandwidth=5000(kbps)
                      max-bandwidth=5000(kbps)           current-
bandwidth=0(kbps)

                      priority=medium          forwarded_bytes=0
                      dropped_packets=0       dropped_bytes=0
        class-id=6    allocated-bandwidth=5000(kbps)  guaranteed-
bandwidth=5000(kbps)
                      max-bandwidth=5000(kbps)           current-
bandwidth=0(kbps)

                      priority=high    forwarded_bytes=0
                      dropped_packets=0       dropped_bytes=0
stat: rxp=3170632 txp=1806967 rxb=778062257 txb=490194324 rxe=0 txe=0 rxd=0
txd=0 mc=0 collision=0
re: rxl=0 rxo=0 rxc=0 rxf=0 rxfi=0 rxm=0
te: txa=0 txc=0 txfi=0 txh=0 txw=0
misc rxc=0 txc=0
input_type=0 state=3 arp_entry=0 refcnt=31
```

The output of this command provides a synopsis of the Traffic Shaper for the interface and if any dropped packets have occurred. Next, when troubleshooting a transit traffic issue with the diagnose flow debug commands, if Traffic Shaper is dropping packets then the follow debug messages will be presented:

```
d=10455 trace_id=15 msg="Find an existing session, id-0000aabc, original
direction"
id=10455 trace_id=15 msg="exceeded shaper limit, drop"
```

This will be the message for a Shared Traffic Shaper configuration threshold being hit. The Per-IP Shaper debug message is a little different if packets are discarded. This message is:

```
d=10455 trace_id=15 msg="Find an existing session, id-0000aabc, original
direction"
id=10455 trace_id=15 msg="block by quota check, drop"
```

The output for session table entry related to Traffic shaper are:

```
origin-shaper=High_priority
reply-shaper= High_priority
per_ip_shaper=Per-IP-Shaper
```

The last two commands to provide here are:

```
FGT-B (root) # diagnose firewall shaper per-ip-shaper list

name Per-IP-Shaper_Limit_Sessions
maximum-bandwidth 1250 KB/sec
maximum-concurrent-session 100
tos ff/ff
packets dropped 0
bytes dropped 0
FGT-B (root) # diagnose firewall shaper traffic-shaper list

name guarantee-100kbps
maximum-bandwidth 131072 KB/sec
guaranteed-bandwidth 12 KB/sec
current-bandwidth 0 B/sec
priority 2
overhead 0
tos ff
packets dropped 0
bytes dropped 0
```

Next, we step into how the Network Process ASIC comes into play when utilizing traffic shapers.

Interface Based Network Processor Acceleration Traffic Shaping

One of the limitations I ran into when certifying 6.0.x GA FortiOS on certain lower-end platforms was the NP ASIC. As Fortinet progresses into their development of more SD-WAN features, to keep a competitive edge, the ASIC is a big item because you might be aware that Fortinet takes a lot of pride that the FortiGate is the fastest firewall on the market, and this must hold true for SD-WAN technologies as well to maintain the precedence that has been placed.

One of the major driving factors for the creation of the SoC4 ASIC chip for lower-end FortiGate models was not only to increase speed but also to integrate new features. Fortinet created the ability to off-load interface-based traffic shaping and interface bandwidth, limiting to the NP ASIC. This feature can be enabled via CLI:

```
config system npu
    set intf-shaping-offload enable
end
```

As I've said many times, during your planning stages for deployment, be sure to test features like these against the code and platforms you have chosen for your environment and make sure everything works as you expected. The last Traffic Shaping Section will summarize everything we have covered thus far.

Traffic Shaping Summary

The SD-WAN Traffic Shaping and bandwidth limiting section covers many different topics and concepts. I thought It would be useful to allocate a section just to recap on everything we have learned so far before more into the SD-WAN traffic flow section.

1) QoS is an industry-standard that defines various levels of service classifications for packets and how to handle classified packets.
2) Traffic Shapers are proprietary FortiOS features used to control what traffic streams are allocated what bandwidth resources and can enforce limits on bandwidth and session utilization.
   a. Traffic Shaping features can be combined with industry-standard QoS for packet handling.
3) FortiOS Packeting Queuing Review
   a. Packets are prioritized by an internal Priority Value, which maps to respective packet processing queues on each physical egress interface. The Queues are numbered between 0 to 5, with 0 being the highest priority and processed first.
   b. FortiOS uses a First-In-First-Out packet processing method per Queue; queue 0 is processed first and then queue 1 and so on.
   c. Any packet Matching a Firewall Policy Entry with no Traffic shaper defined still receives a Global Priority value via ToS or DSCP between 0 to 2 and a Firewall Policy Priority value of High (1).
   d. Queue 0 is used for administrative access.
   e. Traffic matched by Traffic Shaper that is operating below the guaranteed bandwidth threshold utilizes Queue 0.
   f. Traffic matched by Traffic Shaper that is operating above guaranteed bandwidth threshold but below maximum bandwidth, the packet is assigned to a Queue by using the following formula, Total Priority = Global Priority value (ToS/DSCP 0,1,2) + Traffic Shaper Priority (1,2,3)
4) Global Priority can be based on either IP ToS or DSCP, which are mapped to various local priority values which are High, Medium, or low, which are mapped to priority values 0, 1, and 2, respectively
5) Traffic Shaper High, Medium, and Low settings are mapped to priority values 1, 2, and 3, respectively
6) Application Signatures used in Traffic Shapers are evaluated independently from other traffic from the source IP and can be dropped without dropping all traffic from a single IP source.
7) A Traffic Shaping Policy is used to match traffic so to policy bandwidth.
   a. Traffic Shaping Policy can either use local Guarantee Bandwidth, Maximum Bandwidth, and Priority Values or can reference these values within a Class ID.
   b. Traffic Shaper Object can be referenced within the Traffic Shaping Policy
8) A Traffic Shaping Class ID is used to setup tiered service levels. Each Class ID is configured with a Guarantee Bandwidth value, Maximum Bandwidth value, and Priority Values.

   a. The Traffic Shaping Policy References Class IDs instead of configuring Shaper Objects locally
9) Class IDs are indexed within a Traffic Shaping Profile
10) Traffic Shaping Profiles present a single pane of glass for all Class ID's and how much Guaranteed Bandwidth has been allocated between them
   a. A default class is assigned to packets that do not fall within a Traffic Shaping Policy or are matched by a different shaper policy.
11) Interface bandwidth limiting caps available bandwidth on a logical level and drops packets that exceed this user define threshold.
12) SoC4 chips can offload interface-based Traffic Shaper feature.

This covers SD-WAN traffic shaping topics. As I stated at the beginning of the chapter SD-WAN is a compilation of technologies that work together to accomplish high-quality application delivery. Traffic Shaping and QoS are a *must* to prevent Application degradation on busy networks. If this section was your first exposure to FortiOS Traffic Shaping and QoS, then the information here is a solid foundation of knowledge for sure, but I promise you the rabbit hole goes way deeper. I encourage you to do some independent research and explore these topics more on your own for completion because, for the sake of chapter scope, we must move onward into more SD-WAN topics so to obtain that solid foundation of understanding!

In the next section, we will be reviewing SD-WAN traffic flows and details around how and when route lookup occurs.

SD-WAN Traffic Flow

It is important to understand how packets are evaluated by FortiOS when SD-WAN is in play. The first section to cover is the route lookup process.

<u>Route Table Look Up</u>

All routing decisions are made by the Forwarding Information Base (FIB). The FIB is essentially the kernel routing table. The goal of this section is to walk through the routing lookup process. Take a moment to review Image 10.31.

Image 10.31 – Route Lookup Process Part-I

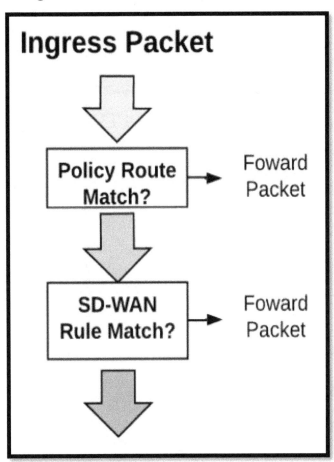

Once FortiOS accepts the packet into the memory buffer, the header information is evaluated against all VDOM Policy Routes first. If no Policy Routes match, then the packet is evaluated against the SD-WAN Rules. It is important to note, technically, the Policy Routes and the SD-WAN are both provisioned within the Policy Route table. During this process, if the packet is matched <u>and</u> Policy Route Action is Forward Traffic, then FortiOS forwards the packet onward. The following CLI command to display the Policy Route Entries on FortiOS.

FGT-B (root) # diagnose firewall proute list

```
id=0x7f0a0001 vwl_service=1(Rule_For_10.226.226.1) vwl_mbr_seq=2 1
dscp_tag=0xff 0xff flags=0x10 load-balancehash-mode=round-robin  tos=0x00
tos_mask=0x00 protocol=6 sport=0:65535 iif=0 dport=23 oif=9(internal2)
num_pass=1 oif=8(internal1) num_pass=1
source(1): 192.168.209.7-192.168.209.7
destination(1): 10.226.226.1-10.226.226.1
hit_count=0 last_used=2020-11-01 13:56:45
```

A Policy Route Entry contains the option to *Stop Policy Routing* and if a match occurs with this option enabled then the packet evaluation process will skip the rest of the PBR entries. if no match is found for within the Policy Route Table and SD-WAN Rules, then the Route Cache is evaluated next. The Route Cache entries are provisioned post successful route look using the FIB. This table is used to save CPU cycles so FortiOS does not need to perform multiple FIB lookups.

Image 10.32 - Route Lookup Process Part-II

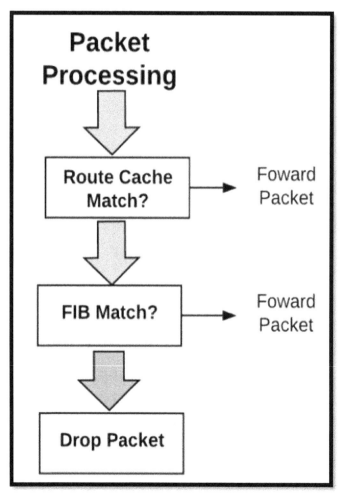

To view the Route Cache entries on FortiOS, run the following CLI command:

```
FGT-B (root) #    diagnose ip rtcache list
family=02 tab=254 vrf=0 vf=0 type=01 tos=0 flag=00000200
172.22.2.1@0->13.226.224.72@9(internal2) gwy=172.22.2.2 prefsrc=0.0.0.0
ci: ref=0 lastused=1 expire=0 err=00000000 used=29 br=0 pmtu=1500
```

Next, if no Route Cache entry is matched, then the final table to look at is the Forward Information Base (FIB). The FIB is populated by all learned routes and directly connected routes.

Introduction to FortiGate Part-I goes over Policy Based Routing in more detail

---

Essentially the FIB is constructed by the Routing Table. For this example, a static route is configured for 172.16.10.1/32 next-hop being 192.168.209.2. To find this entry in the FIB, run the following CLI command:

```
FGT-B (root) # get router info kernel | grep 172.16.10.1
..
tab=254 vf=0 scope=0 type=1 proto=11 prio=0 0.0.0.0/0.0.0.0/0->172.16.10.1/32
pref=0.0.0.0 gwy=192.168.209.1 dev=5(wan1)
```

The regular Routing Table will display the following related entry:

```
FGT-B (root) # get router info routing-table all
Codes: K - kernel, C - connected, S - static, R - RIP, B - BGP
       O - OSPF, IA - OSPF inter area
       N1 - OSPF NSSA external type 1, N2 - OSPF NSSA external type 2
       E1 - OSPF external type 1, E2 - OSPF external type 2
       i - IS-IS, L1 - IS-IS level-1, L2 - IS-IS level-2, ia - IS-IS inter
area
       * - candidate default

Routing table for VRF=0
..
S       172.16.10.1/32 [10/0] via 192.168.209.1, wan1
..
```

From a high level, this covers the FortiOS route lookup process. In the next section, we take a more detailed view of what occurs once an SD-WAN Rule is matched and what action FortiOS takes when there are conflicting default routes within and outside of the SD-WAN Zone.

SD-WAN Rule Selection Flow

Two major settings within the SD-WAN Rule controls the routing behavior of FortiOS when evaluating Rules and egress SD-WAN member interfaces. These two commands are:

```
config sys sdwan
config service
edit test
set default disable
set gateway disable
```

The two settings in bold here are what controls how SD-WAN rules are processed. The default behavior for both are *disable*. This is important because this forces the destination IP address to be evaluated by the FIB, and if the egress interface is matched within the FIB, this interface must be an SD-WAN member interface for the SD-WAN Rule to be utilized. This creates scenarios where the Routing Table can indeed take precedence over SD-WAN Rules.

Now, if these two settings are enabled:

```
config sys sdwan
config service
edit test
set default enable
set gateway enable
```

This allows SD-WAN Rules to have autonomy from the FIB. Meaning even if the FIB and SD-WAN disagree on the egress interface, the SD-WAN Rule takes precedence. These options have come into play to accommodate unique situations. For example, when there is an LTE connect that receive a default route but is not a part of the SD-WAN zone. We go over an SD-WAN use case at the end of this chapter so we can see the change in behavior regarding these two settings.

Self-Originating Traffic

Another challenge for FortiGate SD-WAN is self-originating traffic. During my FortiOS 6.0 GA very in-depth SD-WAN certification process, we found that BGP peering traffic was following SD-WAN rules causing FortiOS to drop routes and BGP to become generally unstable. Up to this point, FortiOS Policy Routes always took precedent over all FIB entries, even directly connected one! Yes, you heard me correct. This became a major obstacle when attempting many BGP peering relationships over many different IPsec overlay tunnels. As of 2020, Fortinet's final solution to the problem, starting with 6.2.3+ & 6.4.0+, was to have Local-Out (self-Originating) traffic not to follow SD-WAN Rules.

Also, FortiOS 6.4.0+ & 6.2.3+, SD-WAN policy routes are skipped when the destination IP for a packet belongs to a directly connected subnet.

This brings us to the end of the SD-WAN traffic flow section. In the next section, we start putting together everything we have learned so far into SD-WAN use cases.

SD-WAN Use Case

In this use case, we have a basic SD-WAN setup. Here is a rundown of the topology:

1) Two WAN interfaces
    a. wan1/wan2
2) One Internal LAN Interface
3) Two VLAN's build onto each WAN interface
    a. VLAN 220 & 221 for wan1
    b. VLAN 222 & 223 for wan2
4) IPsec Tunnel build off of each VLAN interface
    a. vlan221wan1-p1
    b. vlan222wan2-p1
    c. vlan223wan2-p1
5) Only the IPsec tunnels are part of the SD-WAN Zone
6) Default Route pointed to all SD-WAN members
7) Source NAT on each IPsec interface

Check out diagram 10.33 for details:

Image 10.33 – SD-WAN Use Case Lab Diagram

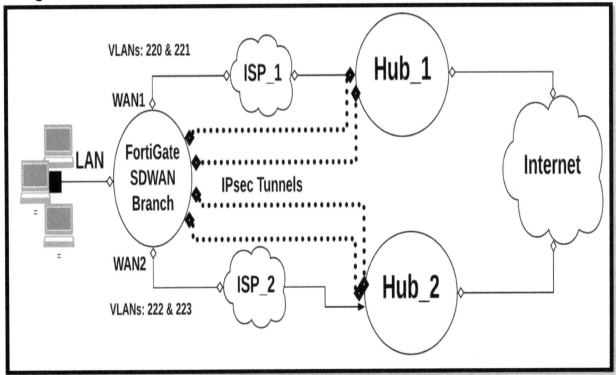

The first thing I want to show you is the routing table of our FGT device so you can get a feel for the environment; take a moment to review the following output:

```
FGT-B-232 # get router info routing-table all
```

```
Codes: K - kernel, C - connected, S - static, R - RIP, B - BGP
       O - OSPF, IA - OSPF inter area
       N1 - OSPF NSSA external type 1, N2 - OSPF NSSA external type 2
       E1 - OSPF external type 1, E2 - OSPF external type 2
       i - IS-IS, L1 - IS-IS level-1, L2 - IS-IS level-2, ia - IS-IS inter
area
       * - candidate default

Routing table for VRF=0
S*       0.0.0.0/0 [1/0] via 172.21.220.2, vlan220wan1-p1//IPsec tunnel
                   [1/0] via 172.21.221.2, vlan221wan1-p1//IPsec tunnel
                   [1/0] via 172.22.222.2, vlan222wan2-p1//IPsec tunnel
                   [1/0] via 172.22.223.2, vlan223wan2-p1//IPsec tunnel
C        172.21.220.1/32 is directly connected, vlan220wan1-p1
C        172.21.220.2/32 is directly connected, vlan220wan1-p1
C        172.21.221.1/32 is directly connected, vlan221wan1-p1
C        172.21.221.2/32 is directly connected, vlan221wan1-p1
C        172.22.222.1/32 is directly connected, vlan222wan2-p1
C        172.22.222.2/32 is directly connected, vlan222wan2-p1
C        172.22.223.1/32 is directly connected, vlan223wan2-p1
C        172.22.223.2/32 is directly connected, vlan223wan2-p1
C        192.168.208.0/24 is directly connected, wan2
C        192.168.209.0/24 is directly connected, wan1
C        192.168.220.0/24 is directly connected, vlan-220
C        192.168.221.0/24 is directly connected, vlan-221
C        192.168.222.0/24 is directly connected, vlan-222
C        192.168.223.0/24 is directly connected, vlan-223
```

I tried to stick to an intuitive naming scheme for this lab but for clarification the IPsec interfaces are:

```
vlan220wan1-p1
vlan221wan1-p1
vlan222wan2-p1
vlan223wan2-p1
```

I've bolded the number in the middle for each IPsec tunnel name to indicate which VLAN the VPN is bound to. For example, vlan220wan1-p1 = vlan 220 = vlan interface 'vlan-220', and the same logic goes for the other three tunnels. Next, I went ahead and configured an IP address for each IPsec interface; see below output:

```
C        172.21.220.1/32 is directly connected, vlan220wan1-p1
C        172.21.220.2/32 is directly connected, vlan220wan1-p1
C        172.21.221.1/32 is directly connected, vlan221wan1-p1
C        172.21.221.2/32 is directly connected, vlan221wan1-p1
C        172.22.222.1/32 is directly connected, vlan222wan2-p1
C        172.22.222.2/32 is directly connected, vlan222wan2-p1
```

```
C        172.22.223.1/32 is directly connected, vlan223wan2-p1
C        172.22.223.2/32 is directly connected, vlan223wan2-p1
```

Each of these directly connected addresses here are assigned to their respective IPsec tunnel interfaces. FGT-B has the first IP, and the remote side of the IPsec tunnel has the 2nd IP. For example, the following output means 172.21.220.1 is assigned to FGT-B, and 172.21.220.2 is assigned to the head-end FortiGate IPsec tunnel interface.

```
C        172.21.220.1/32 is directly connected, vlan220wan1-p1
C        172.21.220.2/32 is directly connected, vlan220wan1-p1
```

Here is a local configuration snippet for FGT-B (branch).

```
FGT-B-232 # 60F-B-232 # show sys int | grep  -f
config system interface
    edit "vlan220wan1-p1"
        set vdom "root"
        set ip 172.21.220.1 255.255.255.255 <---
        set allowaccess ping https
        set type tunnel
        set remote-ip 172.21.220.2 255.255.255.255
        set snmp-index 14
        set interface "vlan-220"
    next
```

Now that we have a feel for the SD-WAN lab environment next, we walk through a couple of different scenarios. The first one being the gateway enable/disable setting within the SD-WAN rule and review the different behavior.

SD-WAN Use Case: Rule Vs. Regular Route

The first thing to do here is to configure an SD-WAN Rule and a regular routing statement that conflicts with each other. We are going to use destination IP 10.226.226.1 during the testing. See the following CLI configuration:

```
config router static
    edit 1
        set distance 1
        set sdwan enable
    next
    edit 2
        set dst 10.226.226.1 255.255.255.255
        set gateway 192.168.209.62
        set device "wan1"
    next
end
FGT-B-232 # config sys sdwan
FGT-B-232 (service) # show
```

```
config service
    edit 1
        set name "Rule_dst_10.226.226.1"
        set mode priority
        set dst "10.226.226.1/32"
        set health-check "Default_DNS"
        set priority-members 1 4 3 2
..
        set gateway disable      // note default values for
        set default disable      // these two lines
    next
end
```

Currently FortiOS has conflicting information where to send **10.226.226.1/32**. The static route states to send this traffic out wan1 next hop being 192.168.209.62 and the SD-WAN Rule states to send 10.226.226.1/32 over all the SD-WAN member interface which are the VPN tunnels using best quality steering method. So what is going to happen? Time to test. The client machine is behind the Internal interface at source IP 192.168.1.110. A ping is performed from client machine to 10.226.226.1 and here is the daig flow debug output:

```
FGT-B-232 # diag debug flow filter addr 10.226.226.1
FGT-B-232 # diag debug flow trace start 200
FGT-B-232 # id=20085 trace_id=47 func=print_pkt_detail line=5665 msg="vd-
root:0 received a packet(proto=1, 192.168.1.110:1->10.226.226.1:2048) from
internal. type=8, code=0, id=1, seq=13."
id=20085 trace_id=47 func=init_ip_session_common line=5836 msg="allocate a
new session-000395e9"
id=20085 trace_id=47 func=vf_ip_route_input_common line=2584 msg="find a
route: flag=04000000 gw-192.168.209.62 via wan1"
id=20085 trace_id=47 func=fw_forward_handler line=796 msg="Allowed by Policy-
5: SNAT"
id=20085 trace_id=47 func=__ip_session_run_tuple line=3453 msg="SNAT
192.168.1.110->192.168.209.232:60417"
id=20085 trace_id=47 func=ipd_post_route_handler line=490 msg="out wan1
vwl_zone_id 0, state2 0x0, quality 0.
```

From the debug output you can see that the ICMP echo request packet was routed out wan1 interface and did not follow the SD-WAN Rule configured. This is because of the follow Service (SD-WAN) Rule Settings:

```
set gateway disable
set default disable
```

With these settings disabled, a FIB lookup is performed on 10.226.226.1 and FortiOS found that the best route egress interface was wan1. FortiOS then checks to see if wan1 is indeed a SD-WAN member interface and since it is not, the FIB takes precedence over this SD-WAN Rule. Note, if multiple SD-WAN Rules are configured, then they will be evaluated from top to bottom.

Furthermore, if I created an additional Rule to steer destination IP 10.226.226.1 with *gateway* and *default* <u>Service</u> (Rule) settings set to *enable*, then traffic would follow the second Rule. Because the logic goes, when gateway/default are disabled (default settings) if FIB egress interface is not a SD-WAN member interface then go to next Rule in the list. In this case, I only have one Rule configured, so there is no 'next rule' therefore, the FIB is used to route traffic to 10.226.226.1.

This next example, I will create an additional rule with gateway/default Service settings enabled, see below configuration.

FGT-B-232 (service) # show

```
config service
    edit 1
        set name "Rule_dst_10.226.226.1"
        set mode priority
        set dst "10.226.226.1/32"
        set health-check "Default_DNS"
        set priority-members 1 4 3 2
    next
    edit 2
        set name "Rule_dst_10.226.226.1-enabled"
        set mode priority
        set dst "10.226.226.1/32"
        set health-check "Default_DNS"
        set priority-members 1 4 3 2
        set gateway enable
        set default enable
    next
end
```

Entry 2 had been added with gateway/default enabled. Next is to clear session for 10.226.226.1 and re-test ping from 192.168.1.110 to 10.226.226.1. See below debug output.

```
FGT-B-232 # diag debug flow filter addr 10.226.226.1
FGT-B-232 # diag debug flow trace start 200
FGT-B-232 # id=20085 trace_id=55 func=print_pkt_detail line=5665 msg="vd-
root:0 received a packet(proto=1, 192.168.1.110:1->10.226.226.1:2048) from
internal. type=8, code=0, id=1, seq=21."
id=20085 trace_id=55 func=init_ip_session_common line=5836 msg="allocate a
new session-0003a9b4"
id=20085 trace_id=55 func=vf_ip_route_input_common line=2566 msg="Match
policy routing id=2098724866: to 172.21.220.2 via ifindex-26"
id=20085 trace_id=55 func=vf_ip_route_input_common line=2584 msg="find a
route: flag=04000000 gw-172.21.220.2 via vlan220wan1-p1"
id=20085 trace_id=55 func=fw_forward_handler line=796 msg="Allowed by Policy-
4: SNAT"
```

```
id=20085 trace_id=55 func=__ip_session_run_tuple line=3453 msg="SNAT
192.168.1.110->172.21.220.1:60417"
id=20085 trace_id=55 func=ipd_post_route_handler line=490 msg="out
vlan220wan1-p1 vwl_zone_id 1, state2 0x0, quality 1.
"
id=20085 trace_id=55 func=ipsecdev_hard_start_xmit line=789 msg="enter IPsec
interface-vlan220wan1-p1"
id=20085 trace_id=55 func=_ipsecdev_hard_start_xmit line=666 msg="IPsec
tunnel-vlan220wan1-p1"
id=20085 trace_id=55 func=esp_output4 line=901 msg="IPsec encrypt/auth"
```

The important items in the debug output has been bolded. You can see that packet ingress Internal interface and the SD-WAN Rule was matched (Policy Route) and forwarded traffic out IPsec tunnel *vlan220wan1-p1*. With gateway/default enabled, FortiOS does not performed any FIB lookup on the destination IP and FortiOS looks at the possible SD-WAN Rule egress interfaces within the Outbound Interface (oif) list and choses the egress interface based off selection criteria configured within SD-WAN Rule. The oif list can be found within the Policy Route entry via CLI:

```
FGT-B-232 # diagnose firewall proute list
list route policy info(vf=root):

id=2132279297(0x7f180001) vwl_service=1(Rule_dst_10.226.226.1) vwl_mbr_seq=1
4 3 2 dscp_tag=0xff 0xff flags=0x0 tos=0x00 tos_mask=0x00 protocol=0 sport=0-
65535 iif=0 dport=1-65535 oif=26(vlan220wan1-p1) oif=29(vlan223wan2-p1)
oif=28(vlan222wan2-p1) oif=27(vlan221wan1-p1)
destination(1): 10.226.226.1-10.226.226.1
source wildcard(1): 0.0.0.0/0.0.0.0
hit_count=0 last_used=2020-11-12 10:24:40

id=2098724866(0x7d180002) vwl_service=2(Rule_dst_10.226.226.1-enabled)
vwl_mbr_seq=1 4 3 2 dscp_tag=0xff 0xff flags=0x0 tos=0x00 tos_mask=0x00
protocol=0 sport=0-65535 iif=0 dport=1-65535 oif=26(vlan220wan1-p1)
gwy=172.21.220.2 oif=29(vlan223wan2-p1) gwy=172.22.223.2 oif=28(vlan222wan2-
p1) gwy=172.22.222.2 oif=27(vlan221wan1-p1) gwy=172.21.221.2 default
destination(1): 10.226.226.1-10.226.226.1
source wildcard(1): 0.0.0.0/0.0.0.0
hit_count=1 last_used=2020-11-12 10:26:37
```

This wraps up the first use case of SD-WAN Rules Vs. Regular Routes conflicting. The next use case we will review Local-out traffic with SD-WAN.

Use Case: FortiOS Local Out with SD-WAN

The default behavior for Local out (self-organization) traffic changed in 6.2.3 GA and 6.4.0 GA FortiOS. Before these versions were released, FortiOS would place Policy Routes (SD-WAN Rules) before any FIB lookup, even locally connected routes. This caused many issues when trying to control FortiGuard traffic and BGP peering traffic on overlay links. Clever workarounds were created to overcome these limitations, like matching all BGP peer IP addresses within a Policy Route to stop policy routing. Fortinet decided the better long-term method to handle local-out traffic was to bypass all Policy Routes (SD-WAN Rules) and only use the FIB (Regular Routing Table).

In this use case we will use the same lab as before but in this case we will use FortiGate itself to generate ICMP traffic to 10.226.226.1, see below flow debug output:

```
FGT-B-232 # exe ping 10.226.226.1
PING 10.226.226.1 (10.226.226.1): 56 data bytes
id=20085 trace_id=59 func=print_pkt_detail line=5665 msg="vd-root:0 received
a packet(proto=1, 192.168.209.232:3840->10.226.226.1:2048) from local.
type=8, code=0, id=3840, seq=0."
id=20085 trace_id=59 func=init_ip_session_common line=5836 msg="allocate a
new session-0003b70f"
id=20085 trace_id=59 func=ipd_post_route_handler line=490 msg="out wan1
vwl_zone_id 0, state2 0x0, quality 0.
"
id=20085 trace_id=60 func=print_pkt_detail line=5665 msg="vd-root:0 received
a packet(proto=1, 10.226.226.1:3840->192.168.209.232:0) from wan1. type=0,
code=0, id=3840, seq=0."
id=20085 trace_id=60 func=resolve_ip_tuple_fast line=5746 msg="Find an
existing session, id-0003b70f, reply direction"
id=20085 trace_id=60 func=vf_ip_route_input_common line=2584 msg="find a
route: flag=80000000 gw-192.168.209.232 via root"
id=20085 trace_id=61 func=ipd_post_route_handler line=490 msg="out wan1
vwl_zone_id 0, state2 0x0, quality 0.
```

The above debug output confirms that traffic did not follow the SD-WAN Rules configured and instead referenced the Static Route Entry that's points to 192.168.209.62 via wan1.

This logic holds true for all local-out traffic like Syslog/FortiAnalzyer logging, FortiGuard traffic, remote authentication (RADIUS, LDAP, etc.), DNS queries FortiManager traffic, FortiSandbox, FSSO, NTP. There are some exceptions; for example, explicit/implicit proxy and VXLAN traffic uses SD-WAN Rules. In FortiOS 6.4, there are options to specify for various protocols to use SD-WAN Rules or FIB. For example, to modify how FortiGuard traffic is handed locally, the below CLI settings are available:

6.4.2 FortiOS Self Originating per protocol configuration:

https://docs.fortinet.com/document/fortigate/6.4.2/administration-guide/848980/self-originating-traffic

```
FGT-B-232 #  config sys fortiguard
FGT-B-232 (fortiguard) # set interface-select-method
auto        Set outgoing interface automatically.
sdwan       Set outgoing interface by SD-WAN or policy routing rules.
specify     Set outgoing interface manually.
```

Use Case: SD-WAN Failover

The high-level purpose of SD-WAN is best dynamic path selection for applications, meaning FortiOS will change traffic flows based on SLA criteria. This causes no issue for stateless devices, but FortiGate being a stateful firewall we need to understand how session entries are handed when traffic flows change. The first example will be a basic interface failover using SLA Best Quality method. The same lab environment will be used. The client machine will issue a constant ping request for 10.226.226.1. We will note which IPsec SD-WAN interface is chosen and then I will degrade the SLA monitor probe upstream using traffic shaper for this overlay which will mark the overlay as down because does not meet SLA and traffic for 10.226.226.1 will be re-route traffic. The following debugs shows the current state of traffic from 192.168.1.110 to 10.226.226.1:

```
FGT-B-232 # id=20085 trace_id=69 func=print_pkt_detail line=5665 msg="vd-
root:0 received a packet(proto=1, 192.168.1.110:1->10.226.226.1:2048) from
internal. type=8, code=0, id=1, seq=25."
id=20085 trace_id=69 func=init_ip_session_common line=5836 msg="allocate a
new session-0003d4cf"
id=20085 trace_id=69 func=vf_ip_route_input_common line=2566 msg="Match
policy routing id=2098724866: to 172.21.220.2 via ifindex-26"
id=20085 trace_id=69 func=vf_ip_route_input_common line=2584 msg="find a
route: flag=04000000 gw-172.21.220.2 via vlan220wan1-p1"
id=20085 trace_id=69 func=fw_forward_handler line=796 msg="Allowed by Policy-
4: SNAT"
id=20085 trace_id=69 func=__ip_session_run_tuple line=3453 msg="SNAT
192.168.1.110->172.21.220.1:60417"
id=20085 trace_id=69 func=ipd_post_route_handler line=490 msg="out
vlan220wan1-p1 vwl_zone_id 1, state2 0x0, quality 1.
```

```
FGT-B-232 # diagnose sys session list
```

```
session info: proto=1 proto_state=00 duration=25 expire=59 timeout=0
flags=00000000 socktype=0 sockport=0 av_idx=0 use=3
origin-shaper=
reply-shaper=
per_ip_shaper=
class_id=0 ha_id=0 policy_dir=0 tunnel=vlan220wan1-p1/ vlan_cos=0/255
state=may_dirty
statistic(bytes/packets/allow_err): org=1500/25/1 reply=1500/25/1 tuples=2
```

```
tx speed(Bps/kbps): 58/0 rx speed(Bps/kbps): 58/0
orgin->sink: org pre->post, reply pre->post dev=25->26/26->25
gwy=172.21.220.2/192.168.1.110
hook=post dir=org act=snat 192.168.1.110:1-
>10.226.226.1:8(172.21.220.1:60417)
hook=pre dir=reply act=dnat 10.226.226.1:60417-
>172.21.220.1:0(192.168.1.110:1)
misc=0 policy_id=4 auth_info=0 chk_client_info=0 vd=0
serial=0003d4cf tos=ff/ff app_list=0 app=0 url_cat=0
sdwan_mbr_seq=1 sdwan_service_id=2
rpdb_link_id=fd000002 rpdb_svc_id=0 ngfwid=n/a
npu_state=0x1000001 no_offload
no_ofld_reason:  disabled-by-policy
total session 1
```

From the debug output here we can conclude that FortiOS used SD-WAN member *vlan220wan1-p1* to forward traffic. Next is to check the SLA monitor for each SD-WAN interface member in this lab. The following debug command can be used:

```
FGT-B-232 # diagnose sys sdwan health-check
Health Check(Default_DNS):
Seq(1 vlan220wan1-p1): state(alive), packet-loss(0.000%) latency(109.974),
jitter(1.467) sla_map=0x1
Seq(2 vlan221wan1-p1): state(alive), packet-loss(1.000%) latency(104.896),
jitter(0.579) sla_map=0x1
Seq(3 vlan222wan2-p1): state(alive), packet-loss(0.000%) latency(107.292),
jitter(1.054) sla_map=0x1
Seq(4 vlan223wan2-p1): state(alive), packet-loss(1.000%) latency(108.994),
jitter(0.212) sla_map=0x1
```

Now that we know what SD-WAN interface member the traffic is using and the current SLA measurement values, now we can degrade the SLA probe upstream for **vlan220wan1-p1**. Below are the SLA values while **vlan220wan1-p1** is within a degraded state.

```
FGT-B-232 # diagnose sys sdwan health-check
Health Check(Default_DNS):
Seq(1 vlan220wan1-p1): state(dead), packet-loss(100.000%) sla_map=0x0
Seq(2 vlan221wan1-p1): state(alive), packet-loss(2.000%) latency(107.029),
jitter(0.289) sla_map=0x1
Seq(3 vlan222wan2-p1): state(alive), packet-loss(0.000%) latency(104.400),
jitter(0.448) sla_map=0x1
Seq(4 vlan223wan2-p1): state(alive), packet-loss(0.000%) latency(106.737),
jitter(0.464) sla_map=0x1
```

Now that the SLA for *vlan220wan1-p1* has been degraded, we can check the traffic flow to see which SD-WAN member the ICMP traffic is being forwarded on.

```
FGT-B-232 # id=20085 trace_id=259 func=print_pkt_detail line=5665 msg="vd-
root:0 received a packet(proto=1, 192.168.1.110:1->10.226.226.1:2048) from
internal. type=8, code=0, id=1, seq=4828."
id=20085 trace_id=259 func=resolve_ip_tuple_fast line=5746 msg="Find an
existing session, id-00046755, original direction"
id=20085 trace_id=259 func=ipv4_fast_cb line=53 msg="enter fast path"
id=20085 trace_id=259 func=ip_session_run_all_tuple line=6936 msg="SNAT
192.168.1.110->172.22.223.1:60417"
id=20085 trace_id=259 func=ipsecdev_hard_start_xmit line=789 msg="enter IPsec
interface-vlan223wan2-p1"
id=20085 trace_id=259 func=_ipsecdev_hard_start_xmit line=666 msg="IPsec
tunnel-vlan223wan2-p1"
```

From this debug output we can conclude the Session Entry was updated to steer traffic to IPsec tunnel *vlan223wan2-p1*. When SLA probe comes back online for vlan220wan1 then new sessions could use this path. The next section we discuss how SD-WAN behaves during routing table changes.

Route Change and Preserve Session Route

Most SD-WAN deployments run BGP across IPsec overlay connections. Since the NSE4 does not cover BGP in this use case to simulate the route change event, I will just add and remove static routes that current sessions are using. The logic stays the same when BGP routes are updated and how it affects active sessions. The first command to discuss is *preserve session route*, which is found in the CLI via:

```
FGT-B-232 # config system interface

FGT-B-232 (interface) # edit vlan220wan1-p1

FGT-B-232 (vlan220wan1-p1) # show ful | grep preserve
        set preserve-session-route disable
```

The preserve session route setting is found under the interface configuration. By default, this command is set to disable, meaning all sessions that egress a certain interface if route change occurs, then traffic could be re-routed out a different interface. This could become an issue when working with dynamic routing protocols that are unstable and cause many routing updates. If this setting is set to *enable,* then if route change occurs, then active sessions remain flowing out the same interface, and no new route lookup is performed. Only new sessions are affected by routing table changes. Also note, this setting only affects traffic sessions with no SNAT. When SNAT is applied to sessions, then we must use a different command to modify traffic flow behavior.

SNAT Route Change Setting

After a route change occurs, sessions with not SNAT routing and cache information are flushed by default. The next packet accepted by an active session entry is evaluated by new route entries. RPF is performed again for the original direction, and Session Entry are marked with the *dirty* flag. For SNAT sessions, when route change occurs, the setting that controls FortiOS behavior is found via CLI:

```
FGT-B-232 # conf sys glo
FGT-B-232 (global) # show ful | grep snat
    set snat-route-change disable
```

A few years back, my customer hit an issue where if there IPsec tunnel bounced (lost routes), then RFC1918 private traffic that was originally routed through the IPsec tunnel would then be routed out the public WAN interface via default route, and SNAT was being applied to the newly created Session Entries. The tunnel would be only down for a couple of seconds, and after routes re-established for the IPsec tunnel, traffic was no longer flowing between the two VPN sites; instead, traffic kept flowing out the WAN interface. The workaround is to clear the session manually, but this is not a feasible long-term solution every time an IPsec tunnel bounces. Hence, the snat-route-change command was created. This setting is disabled by default, and SNAT sessions are not flushed when route change occurs. When *snat-route-change* is set to *enable*, then when a route table update occurs, the next packet is evaluated by the new route table entries.

Within the lab I've updated the Static Routes for 10.226.226.1/24 to prefer vlan220wan1-p1. Note, that SNAT if configured for all egress traffic across IPsec tunnel overlays. Here is the static route configuration:

```
config router static
    edit 1
        set distance 1
        set sdwan enable
    next
    edit 2
        set dst 10.226.226.1 255.255.255.255
        set gateway 192.168.209.62
        set device "wan1"
    next
    edit 3
        set dst 10.226.226.1 255.255.255.255
        set priority 1
        set device "vlan220wan1-p1"
    next
    edit 4
        set dst 10.226.226.1 255.255.255.255
        set priority 4
```

```
        set device "vlan222wan2-p1"
    next
end
```

Next, we will start a continuous ping from Internal host 192.168.1.110 to 10.226.226.1/32.

id=20085 trace_id=659 func=__ip_session_run_tuple line=3453 msg="**SNAT 192.168.1.110->172.21.220.1:60417**"
id=20085 trace_id=659 func=ipd_post_route_handler line=490 msg="out **vlan220wan1-p1 vwl_zone_id 1**, state2 0x1, quality 1.

Next, we tigger a route table update by removing the static route to *vlan220wan1-p1*.

```
FGT-B-232 # config router static
FGT-B-232 (static) # delete 3
FGT-B-232 (static) # end
FGT-B-232 # get router info routing-table  all
Codes: K - kernel, C - connected, S - static, R - RIP, B - BGP
       O - OSPF, IA - OSPF inter area
       N1 - OSPF NSSA external type 1, N2 - OSPF NSSA external type 2
       E1 - OSPF external type 1, E2 - OSPF external type 2
       i - IS-IS, L1 - IS-IS level-1, L2 - IS-IS level-2, ia - IS-IS inter
area
       * - candidate default


Routing table for VRF=0
..
S        10.226.226.1/32 [10/0] via 192.168.209.62, wan1
                         [10/0] via 172.22.222.2, vlan222wan2-p1, [4/0]
..
```

See that vlan222wan2-p1 IPsec tunnel interface is now preferred. Next, is to check to see where FortiOS is forwarding this traffic now:

```
FGT-B-232 # diagnose sys session filter dst 10.226.226.1
FGT-B-232 # diagnose sys session list

session info: proto=1 proto_state=00 duration=33 expire=27 timeout=0
flags=00000000 socktype=0 sockport=0 av_idx=0 use=3
origin-shaper=
reply-shaper=
per_ip_shaper=
class_id=0 ha_id=0 policy_dir=0 tunnel=vlan220wan1-p1/ vlan_cos=0/255
state=log dirty may_dirty f00
statistic(bytes/packets/allow_err): org=120/2/1 reply=120/2/1 tuples=2
tx speed(Bps/kbps): 3/0 rx speed(Bps/kbps): 3/0
orgin->sink: org pre->post, reply pre->post dev=0->26/26->0
gwy=0.0.0.0/0.0.0.0
```

```
hook=post dir=org act=snat 192.168.1.110:1-
>10.226.226.1:8(172.21.220.1:60417)
hook=pre dir=reply act=dnat 10.226.226.1:60417-
>172.21.220.1:0(192.168.1.110:1)
misc=0 policy_id=4 auth_info=0 chk_client_info=0 vd=0
serial=00062242 tos=ff/ff app_list=0 app=0 url_cat=0
sdwan_mbr_seq=1 sdwan_service_id=2
rpdb_link_id=fd000002 rpdb_svc_id=0 ngfwid=n/a
npu_state=0x1000001 no_offload
no_ofld_reason:  disabled-by-policy
total session 1
```

As you can see, no update occurred on egress interface. The next test is to use the snat-change-route settings to modify this behavior.

```
FGT-B-232 # config system global
FGT-B-232 (global) # set snat-route-change enable
FGT-B-232 (global) # end
FGT-B-232 # config router static
    edit 3
        set dst 10.226.226.1 255.255.255.255
        set priority 1
        set device "vlan220wan1-p1"
..
```

The static route has been added back to the configuration and next I will clear the session table for 10.226.226.1. Next, check the egress interface for traffic flow.

```
msg="SNAT 192.168.1.110->172.21.220.1:60417"
id=20085 trace_id=721 func=ipd_post_route_handler line=490 msg="out
vlan220wan1-p1 vwl_zone_id 1, state2 0x1, quality 1.
..
FGT-B-232 # diagnose sys session list

session info: proto=1 proto_state=00 duration=43 expire=59 timeout=0
flags=00000000 socktype=0 sockport=0 av_idx=0 use=3
origin-shaper=
reply-shaper=
per_ip_shaper=
class_id=0 ha_id=0 policy_dir=0 tunnel=vlan220wan1-p1/ vlan_cos=0/255
state=log may_dirty f00
statistic(bytes/packets/allow_err): org=2400/40/1 reply=2400/40/1 tuples=2
tx speed(Bps/kbps): 59/0 rx speed(Bps/kbps): 59/0
orgin->sink: org pre->post, reply pre->post dev=25->26/26->25
gwy=172.21.220.2/192.168.1.110
hook=post dir=org act=snat 192.168.1.110:1-
>10.226.226.1:8(172.21.220.1:60417)
```

```
hook=pre dir=reply act=dnat 10.226.226.1:60417-
>172.21.220.1:0(192.168.1.110:1)
misc=0 policy_id=4 auth_info=0 chk_client_info=0 vd=0
serial=000624a0 tos=ff/ff app_list=0 app=0 url_cat=0
sdwan_mbr_seq=1 sdwan_service_id=2
rpdb_link_id=fd000002 rpdb_svc_id=0 ngfwid=n/a
npu_state=0x1000001 no_offload
no_ofld_reason:  disabled-by-policy
total session 1
```

Now we are going to run the same test by deleting the static route to create a routing table update and check the session for 10.226.226.1.

```
FGT-B-232 # config router static
FGT-B-232 (static) # delete 3
FGT-B-232 (static) # end
FGT-B-232 # diagnose sys session list

session info: proto=1 proto_state=00 duration=5 expire=59 timeout=0
flags=00000000 socktype=0 sockport=0 av_idx=0 use=3
origin-shaper=
reply-shaper=
per_ip_shaper=
class_id=0 ha_id=0 policy_dir=0 tunnel=vlan222wan2-p1/ vlan_cos=0/255
state=log may_dirty f00
statistic(bytes/packets/allow_err): org=360/6/1 reply=360/6/1 tuples=2
tx speed(Bps/kbps): 63/0 rx speed(Bps/kbps): 63/0
orgin->sink: org pre->post, reply pre->post dev=25->28/28->25
gwy=172.22.222.2/192.168.1.110
hook=post dir=org act=snat 192.168.1.110:1-
>10.226.226.1:8(172.22.222.1:60417)
hook=pre dir=reply act=dnat 10.226.226.1:60417-
>172.22.222.1:0(192.168.1.110:1)
misc=0 policy_id=4 auth_info=0 chk_client_info=0 vd=0
serial=0006272e tos=ff/ff app_list=0 app=0 url_cat=0
sdwan_mbr_seq=3 sdwan_service_id=0
rpdb_link_id=80000000 rpdb_svc_id=0 ngfwid=n/a
npu_state=0x1000001 no_offload
no_ofld_reason:  disabled-by-policy
total session 1
```

As you can see now, FortiOS changed the egress interface for the session because the best route points out vlan222wan2-p1. This same logic holds true when working with dynamic routing protocols.

This completes our SD-WAN use case section. It is important to understand how FortiOS behaves when SLA probes mark SD-WAN member interfaces as down and when routing changes occur in

SD-WAN environments and how this affects session handling. The last part of the chapter goes over SD-WAN logging and monitoring.

SD-WAN Logging and Monitoring

FortiOS 6.4 contains fantastic features in the GUI to monitor SD-WAN. FortiOS changed how Monitor widgets work in 6.4. Now you must explicitly add the widgets you want via Dashboard -> '+'. You must select the plus icon, and FortiOS presents a new screen that lists all the available Monitor widgets, and search SD-WAN.

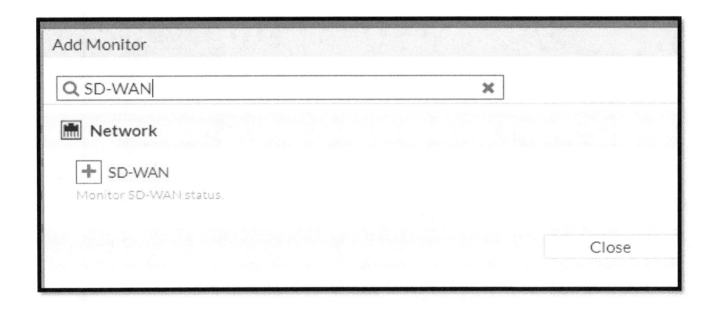

You are presented with a GUI page that displays all the available SD-WAN member interfaces with their respective SLA monitor attributes.

Within Image 10.34, we can see all the SD-WAN zones; in this case, only one is configured. This screen displays how many sessions are being handled for each SD-WAN member interface. Lastly, this page provides the upload and download bandwidth currently being utilized. This method is ok for smaller SD-WAN deployments but for large enterprise networks or carrier networks that may have thousands of devices, it is not feasible to log into every device and see what's going on, which is why logs and API calls are used instead.

Image 10.34 – SD-WAN GUI Monitor Page

SD-WAN Traffic Logs

FortiOS generates many different SD-WAN events. We are only going to cover a subset of these in this section. SD-WAN logs can be found locally in GUI via Log & Report -> Events -> SD-WAN Events.

FortiOS generates Syslog messages around SD-WAN events. These events can be captured at remote logging solutions. Once Syslog data is captured, then SD-WAN analytics or triggered events can occur. For example, some MSSP's build front end portal for their end customers that presents link quality data for a customers' entire SD-WAN deployment. In theory, they can obtain a visual to see which underlays or overlays are performing the best and worse. This data can lead to investigations to optimize traffic flows. Most of the time, to build web portals like this, the FortiOS API is used along with Syslog data. Here are a few examples of the SD-WAN Syslog.

Image 10.35 – SD-WAN GUI Logs

Level	Message	Log Description
	SD-WAN health-check member initial state.	Virtual WAN Link SLA inform ▲
	SD-WAN health-check member initial state.	Virtual WAN Link SLA inform
	Service prioritized by performance metric will be redirected in sequence order.	Virtual WAN Link status
	Member link is available. Start forwarding traffic.	Virtual WAN Link status
	Service prioritized by performance metric will be redirected in sequence order.	Virtual WAN Link status
	Member link is available. Start forwarding traffic.	Virtual WAN Link status
	Number of pass member changed.	Virtual WAN Link status
	Member status changed. Member in sla.	Virtual WAN Link status
	Service prioritized by performance metric will be redirected in sequence order.	Virtual WAN Link status
	Member link is unreachable or miss threshold. Stop forwarding traffic.	Virtual WAN Link status
	Service prioritized by performance metric will be redirected in sequence order.	Virtual WAN Link status
	Member link is unreachable or miss threshold. Stop forwarding traffic.	Virtual WAN Link status

```
date=2020-11-13 time=10:48:04 eventtime=1605293284419290781 tz="-0800"
logid="0113022923" type="event" subtype="sdwan" level="notice" vd="root"
logdesc="Virtual WAN Link status" eventtype="Service" interface="vlan221wan1-
p1" member="2" serviceid=2 service="Rule_dst_10.226.226.1-enabled"
gateway=172.21.221.2 msg="Member link is available. Start forwarding traffic.
"
```

This Syslog states that the vlan221wan1-p1 overlay is good to forward traffic for the 10.226.226.1 Rule (Service). This Rule could easily become Office_365_Traffic, so it would be possible to match application data to the transit path. We could also build a program that queries SD-WAN events and states if I see "msg=Member link is available. Start forwarding traffic." for device X, interface Y, then mark Y as green (UP) and application XY (Service) is currently egressing device X interface Y. API programming is a lot of fun but is far outside the scope for the NSE4 requirements.

SD-WAN SLA Logging

FortiOS also logs on SLA probe metrics. For example, the following syslog event report data around a health check probe:

```
date=2020-11-13 time=13:02:19 eventtime=1605301339759114040 tz="-0800"
logid="0113022923" type="event" subtype="sdwan" level="notice" vd="root"
logdesc="Virtual WAN Link status" eventtype="Health Check"
healthcheck="Default_DNS" slatargetid=1 member="3" msg="Member status
changed. Member out-of-sla."
```

This Syslog states that the health-check SLA Default_DNS marked SD-WAN member 3 as not meeting the SLA threshold. The next log is an example of when an SD-WAN member interface stops forwarding traffic because of the SLA probe threshold.

```
date=2020-11-13 time=5:51:33 eventtime=1605293493019176181 tz="-0800"
logid="0113022923" type="event" subtype="sdwan" level="notice" vd="root"
logdesc="Virtual WAN Link status" eventtype="Service" interface="vlan222wan2-
p1" member="3" serviceid=1 service="Rule_dst_10.226.226.1"
gateway=172.22.222.2 msg="Member link is unreachable or miss threshold. Stop
forwarding traffic. "
```

The last log to review in this section is when the SD-WAN Rule dynamic steers traffic to a different SD-WAN interface member.

```
date=2020-11-13 time=5:50:58 eventtime=1605293458619410821 tz="-0800"
logid="0113022923" type="event" subtype="sdwan" level="notice" vd="root"
logdesc="Virtual WAN Link status" eventtype="Service" serviceid=2
service="Rule_dst_10.226.226.1-enabled" metric="latency" seq="1,4,3,2"
msg="Service prioritized by performance metric will be redirected in sequence
order."
```

In this log, you can see that the priority sequence number was updated to seq="1,4,3,2" with SD-WAN interface index value 1 being most preferred next being 4.

Alright, folks! This completes our SD-WAN Chapter! So much great information, and it is now time to recap everything we learned in this chapter. Move onto the next page to review the chapter summary, and lastly, complete those end of chapter questions!

Chapter 10 Summary

Congratulations! You have just made a massive step into your FortiOS SD-WAN journey. For any new technology, learning the foundation is the most important and sometimes the toughest.

SD-WAN is a large topic with many different components; chapter 10 focuses on SD-WAN technologies that pertain directly to FortiGate itself. SD-WAN topologies can be very similar to IPsec topologies like hub-and-spoke, and redundancy is the name of the game. Common SD-WAN topologies could include two WAN interfaces, each with two IPsec tunnels that go to redundant VPN concentrators.

The FortiGate full SD-WAN solution can be broken up into a hand full of categories. The first is local FortiGate SD-WAN configuration and management, which is the focus of chapter 10. Next, SD-WAN orchestration with external tools like Fortinet Overlay Controller to help maintain IPsec tunnel topologies. Next, SD-WAN management and analytical Integration focuses on managing FortiGate using SD-WAN features from a central point like FortiManager and FortiAnalyzer, which can ingest SD-WAN logs to be used in reports. Next, Zero Touch Provisioning (ZTP) focuses on low cost and operational efforts for new site turn-ups and makes new FortiGates essentially a plug-and-play device. ZTP requires the use of FortiCloud, FortiManager, and possibly API's and Bulk Keys. Next, dynamic best path selection, which FortiGate uses SD-WAN Rules steering strategies based on health checks and BGP dynamic routing. Next, IPsec and ADVPN technologies to create virtual network environments. Next, high-quality application service delivery, which requires QoS, Traffic Shapers, IPsec FEC, and Health Check monitors. The last category for SD-WAN deployment is security, which includes UTM modules like AV, IPS, or Web-Filtering with deep packet inspection (DPI).

SD-WAN topologies can quickly become very complex. We begin with the basics in chapter 10. We started this chapter off by reviewing the basic SD-WAN FortiOS configuration, which is essentially declaring an SD-WAN Zone interface and then creating an interface member within the zone. Once interface members are apart of an SD-WAN zone, FortiOS provides functions to dynamically steer traffic over the best quality path by sending SLA probes called health checks.

Health checks measure latency, jitter, and packet loss across each SD-WAN member interface by sending ICMP, DNS, or HTTP probes to remote servers. SD-WAN Rules are used to match traffic either by layer-3 or layer-4 header attributes or application layer signatures. Once traffic is matched, SD-WAN Rules can use a few different traffic steering strategies. These strategies are Manual, Best Quality, Lowest Cost, and Maximized Bandwidth. The Manual strategy, the administrator must explicitly define which SD-WAN member interface forwards' traffic. The Best Quality strategy selects the egress interface with the highest performing SLA stats. The Maximized Bandwidth Strategy will essentially load-balances sessions across all SD-WAN member interfaces that meet SLA thresholds.

Application steering requires the use of the ISDB and/or Application Signatures. ISDB is a predefined database maintained by FortiGuard that holds well-known Applications protocol, destination IP ranges, and port ranges mappings. When using Application Signature to steer SD-WAN traffic, a learning phase must occur to identify the application protocol, destination IP, and ports, which is be placed in an ISDB cache. The first session might not match the expected SD-WAN Rules, but all other sessions created using the same application will. The dynamic ISDB cache can hold up to 512 entries as of 6.4 GA FortiOS. Once full, the oldest entry is removed. Lastly, for Application Signature steering to work as expected, full TLS/SSL inspection and Application Control must be configured within the transit policy.

QoS is a well-known industry standard outlined in various RFCs that allocate certain IP ToS/DS field markings and how each marking should be prioritized on each router hop. Traffic Shaping is a Fortinet proprietary method to guarantee certain bandwidth availability for matched traffic and police sessions that exceed the thresholds. FortiGate using Traffic Shaper Policy and application Traffic Shaper objects to match network traffic. FortiOS can also use Shaper Profiles to define various traffic classes which each having their own guaranteed bandwidth, maximum bandwidth, and priority value.

FortiOS has a total of 6 egress traffic queues per interface, which are 0 to 5. Queue zero takes precedence above all others. Administrative access uses Queue 0. FortiOS uses a First-In-First-Out packet processing method on a per queue basis. All packets awaiting in higher precedence queues must be processed first before any packets being held in lower precedence queues are processed. FortiOS can assign packets to egress queues by assigning them a priority value that corresponds to the queue value. There are two methods to assigned priority to a packet, Global Priority, and Policy Priority. The Global Priority uses predefined values for ToS and/or DSCP. The Policy Priority is assigned using a Firewall Policy or a Traffic Shaper. All Firewall Policy Entries, by default, assign the priority value of 1 (high). A Traffic Shaper can modify the default priority assignment by assigning packets 1, 2, or 3 priority values that map to High, Medium, and Low, respectively

SD-WAN Rules have two important settings which are, *gateway* & *default* disable or enable, which are disabled by default, which forces a FIB lookup for destination IP and egress interface must be an SD-WAN member for the Rule to be used. When gateway/default settings under service rules are enabled, then no FIB lookup is performed to correlate the egress interface to SD-WAN member. As of GA 6.2.3+ & 6.4.0+, FortiGate local out traffic does not follow SD-WAN Rules or Policy Routes, only FIB. The preserve session route setting under the interface configuration when enabled if a Route Table update occurs any active Session Table Entries using this egress interface are kept on the same interface until sessions close with no new routing lookup. By default, if the route table update occurs, then Session Entries are marked as dirty, and the next packet is evaluated by the update routing table. If SNAT occurs, then by default, these SNAT sessions are not reevaluated if route change occurs. The global command *snat-route-change enable* changes this behavior and re-evaluate any SNAT sessions if route changes occur.

SD-WAN traffic event Syslog messages are generated by various events that occur on FortiOS. These events can be used in analytical reporting or logic triggers. FortiOS also offers SD-WAN API integration.

This completes our SD-WAN Chapter 10 summary! This was a challenging chapter to write because, on the one hand, the information here does not even come close to a comprehensive approach to the topic. So, for folks that are looking to engineer a complete Fortinet SD-WAN solution, this chapter is not enough information to accomplish that, which could be frustrating. On the other hand, folk completely new to FortiGate technologies require stepping-stone into more advanced SD-WAN use cases. The NSE4 caters to folks new to Fortinet and FortiGate technologies. I really hope there comes a time in my life where I have time to write a complete SD-WAN solution guide. This would be extremely rewarding and would be its own entire book! My goal for this chapter is for you to gain that fundamental knowledge around SD-WAN and how to use it on FortiGate so that your confidence level can grow. If you want to learn more about SD-WAN, I recommend first learn BGP and setup a BGP network over IPsec hub and spoke environment with Spokes being FortiGate SD-WAN branch setup.

As always! The only thing left to do is those pesky end of chapter questions. It's time to test your knowledge!

Chapter 10 End of Chapter Questions

1) FortiGate 6.2.5 GA SD-WAN local out traffic follow Policy Routes and SD-WAN Rules.
   a. True
   b. False

2) What SD-WAN Rule Strategy load-balancs across all SD-WAN members that meet SLA Health-Check threshold?
   a. Manual Strategy
   b. Best Quality Strategy
   c. Maximum Strategy
   d. Lowest Cost

3) What SD-WAN Rule Strategy steers traffic to SD-WAN member interfaces that meet SLA targets and has the lowest cost value?
   a. Manual Strategy
   b. Best Quality Strategy
   c. Maximum Strategy
   d. Lowest Cost

4) What SD-WAN Rule Strategy steers traffic to SD-WAN interface members based on the most desirable health check statistics?
   a. Manual Strategy
   b. Best Quality Strategy
   c. Maximum Strategy
   d. Lowest Cost

5) What SD-WAN Rule Strategy is managed directly by the administrator?
   a. Manual Strategy
   b. Best Quality Strategy
   c. Maximum Strategy
   d. Lowest Cost

6) SD-WAN Health Check probes measure what metrics?
   a. Only Packet Loss
   b. Only Packet Loss, Available Bandwidth, and Latency
   c. Only Latency, Jitter, and Packet Loss

    d. Health Checks only monitor directly connected interface health

7) How many priority queues are on each egress interface?
    a. FortiOS only uses QoS, which are static pre-defined values
    b. one through ten
    c. zero through five
    d. ingress queues and egress queues total to ten

8) If priority queues are used, which queue is processed first?
    a. FortiOS only uses FiFo packet processing only
    b. Queue Zero
    c. Queue Ten
    d. Traffic matching Traffic Shaper is processed first

9) What is the 6.4 FortiOS GA default method is used to assigned Global Priority Value?
    a. ToS
    b. DSCP
    c. Traffic Shaper
    d. Firewall Policy Entry

10) Once Global Priority is assigned, what is the next function to assign additional priority values?
    a. Firewall Policy Entry or Traffic Shaper
    b. Only Firewall Policy Entry
    c. Only Traffic Shaper
    d. Interface QoS Mapper

11) What Priority are packets that match a Traffic Shaper and has a transmission rate below the guaranteed threshold?
    a. Ten
    b. One
    c. Zero
    d. Five

12) How is the packet priority value determined if the packet matched a Traffic Shaper and is above the Guaranteed threshold but below the maximum threshold?
    a. This packet will be placed in queue zero

b. The Global Priority value is added to the Policy Priority value, and the result will be the egress interface queue.

c. The Global Priority value is subtracted from the Policy Priority value, and the result will be the egress interface queue.

d. The Firewall Policy Entry, by default, will place the packet into the High queue.

13) Source NAT sessions will not be flushed from the routing table by default if route change occurs.

    a. True

    b. False

14) Service Rule with gateway & default settings enabled, how will FortiGate process traffic against Rule entries?

    a. FortiOS will look up the destination IP to see if it matches an egress SD-WAN member interface as a condition to be processed.

    b. FortiOS will skip FIB lookup

    c. FortiOS only route traffic based on SLA health monitor checks

    d. A FIB lookup will occur, and FortiOS will only process packet if the egress interface is outside of SD-WAN member interfaces

15) By default, if a Route Table update occurs, all sessions without SNAT are marked as dirty.

    a. True

    b. False

16) What command will prevent sessions from being marked as dirty that do not have SNAT?

    a. snat-route-change enable

    b. preserve-session-route enable

    c. session-route-change enable

    d. snat-preserve-session enable

17) What are the requirements to use Application Signatures within SD-WAN Rules?

    a. Only Application Control profile within transit Firewall Policy Entry

    b. Only Application Control profile and Deep Packet Inspection Profile within transit Firewall Policy Entry

    c. Only Application Control profile, Deep Packet Inspection Profile within transit Firewall Policy Entry and active FortiGuard license

    d. Application Control Profile must be placed on ingress and egress interfaces per SD-WAN member

18) Why is a learning phase required when using Application Signatures within SD-WAN Rules?
   a. Because FortiOS needs time to use Machine Learning to identify application and associate protocol, destination IP, and destination Port to detected application.
   b. Because FortiOS needs time to lookup applications within the ISDB stored locally.
   c. Because FortiOS needs time to use Machine Learning to identify the application and associate application to the ingress interface
   d. FortiOS does not require a learning phase because all application are stored within ISDB, which is updated by FortiGuard

19) If an Application is learned and used in SD-WAN Rule, then its header attributes will be temporarily cached in the ISDB.
   a. True
   b. False

20) Application matched within Traffic Shaper is accounted for separately from other traffic being generated from the same source IP.
   a. True
   b. False

21) BGP encapsulated in IPsec ESP packets are marked with what DSCP value?
   a. CS1
   b. 1011101
   c. CS2
   d. CS6

Chapter 11 | Troubleshooting

NSE4 Blueprint Topics Covered

- System Level Troubleshooting
- Advanced System Troubleshooting
- Network Level Troubleshooting
- FortiGuard Troubleshooting
- VPN Troubleshooting
- Session Helpers
- High Availablity Troubleshooting
- Troubleshoot Logging
- Troubleshoot SDWAN

Troubleshooting is more of an art than a science. I believe figuring out why something is broken is all about getting into the right mindset and asking the right questions. One thing I've always been good at is breaking down problems and really hearing the customer. In my first computer networking role, I worked for a large MSSP and managed various firewalls within the environment. My title was Network Analyst. This role provided plenty of *opportunities* to increase my troubleshooting talents, and just like everything else, if you want to get better at something, you must do it!

Many folks think if you know a bunch of super-secret commands will increase your ability to troubleshoot networks or systems; this just isn't true. Instead of memorizing various specialized commands, I recommend memorizing a troubleshooting methodology. It only takes a couple of seconds to look up the syntax for CLI commands, in which everyone must do, so don't fret if you don't remember commands off the top of your head; this is normal. It might be months or years when we must run certain specialized commands.

I'll admit walking into unknown troubleshooting situations with limited context with people you don't know is a scary thing. I honestly thought I was going to get fired from my first role because I didn't have solutions to problems right away. The first time I built an SSL-VPN on FortiGate, I was on the phone with one of our MSSP customers requesting it. And let me tell you right now, it did not happen quickly. I think it took me an hour or two to figure it out because I was reading the documentation on FortiGate SSL-VPNs while I had him on the phone. You might be wondering why didn't you just tell him it would be ready by the end of business on that day; good question! I had to keep him on the phone because I was operating in a high volume call queue, and if I hung up, I would receive another call, and I could not be in pause status as a tier-one analyst. But let me tell you, I asked about this guy's entire life and IT career. As he chatted away, I was figuring out how to build this SSL-VPN on an FMG pointing to geo-redundant firewalls! My point here, it is not what you know that matters (mostly), but the knowledge you can obtain is paramount. Fear is a gift in the Information Technology field. Fear is a pointer to your personal growth. Put yourself in a position to give yourself these uncomfortable experiences, and you will build internal and external confidence to conquer that fear. The best Network Engineers I've met have a certain edge about them or a little grittiness. So the next time your boss asks everyone for volunteers to help a customer with a high-profile problem that you don't know much about, do it! Figure it out and put yourself out there.

I say troubleshooting is more of a mindset and methodology than just knowing CLI commands. It is also about staying calm under pressure and maintaining your ability to act. I'll share a story with you, I accepted my Fortinet TAM Role at the beginning of 2016, and this was a very big jump in my career going to work for the vendor. The level of intensity of the issues I worked on increases drastically. During my first year working as a Carrier TAM, one of my most memorable troubleshooting calls was not even for my assigned accounts. My boss called me up, and he wanted me to join a troubleshooting call, as a ringer, for a large carrier account because they were in the middle of an outage. The primary TAM was out on PTO, but he was called in any way as well because the issue was so large. When I joined the call, the Primary TAM, Backup TAM, my boss, and I were on the call representing Fortinet. The first thing the customer Senior Engineer said to us was, "We currently have 80,000 customers down, fix it". About 3-5 seconds went by; these seconds were the longest seconds of my entire life when no one was talking; it was just silent on the call, so this was my first exposure working with my peers and boss on a live troubleshooting call (in addition to a very large customer); panic was in the air, and this is about the point I referred back to my basic troubleshooting methodology.

1) Is the system ok?
2) When did the issue begin? Any changes?
3) Are interfaces taking errors?
4) Can we see ARP entries? or ND for IPv6?
5) Can we ping our next-hop IP?
6) What does the Routing Table look like?
7) Do we see transit traffic?
8) What type of traffic is it?
9) Do we have security modules affecting this traffic flow?

After a few minutes of troubleshooting, I'm happy to say I was able to obtain a workaround for the issue at hand; I believe this earned me some cool points with the team. Don't be the guy running around like a chicken with its head cut off; stay calm, stay relaxed, and stay focused and stick to the basics.

Another tip of advice before we jump into the chapter, I've solved many complex issues while taking walks, having lunch, or driving, then I've solved by just sitting in front of my computer. You can only break down a problem so much and try so many different things before hitting a wall and needing to take a break. I've worked on issues where hospitals' MPLS firewall traffic was taking 50% packet loss for 8 hours straight. Things to try and possible solutions came to me while I was doing other things. Take time to yourself and give yourself a fresh mind to evaluate things. For many cases like this, I come in the next morning and solve the problem in five minutes.

Next, in this chapter, I step through this troubleshooting methodology with FortiGate. I felt like this would be a good chapter to notate various troubleshooting commands. The first topic will be system-level troubleshooting to confirm that basic resource allocations are as expected. Next will be network interface troubleshooting and then network traffic. After we complete the network traffic review, we will move into FortiGuard troubleshooting and then move into IPsec & SSL VPNs. We step back into Session Helpers in this chapter with an FTP use case. This chapter finishes with logging, HA, and SD-WAN troubleshooting.

I want to be clear, some of the troubleshooting commands I provide in this chapter are for reference only, so you know they exist, and I do not provide context around them.

System Level Troubleshooting

Before engaging on most networking issues, it is best to check system-level resources before moving onto more specific troubleshooting. I can't tell you how many times I've troubleshot symptoms of underlying system issues. Think about it, if someone said "the router is dropping packets" or "has low throughput", a logical next step is to obtain a PCAP. But I warn you; you might not be able to take a true PCAP if system CPU, memory, or disk resources are maxed out. Operating System kernels drop packets during a packet capture if the resources are available to store them. So before engaging on issues like 'the router is dropping packets', take a quick look at system-level resources. On FortiGate, there are few good commands to validate system integrity.

```
30E-B-231 # get sys performance status
CPU states: 0% user 0% system 0% nice 100% idle 0% iowait 0% irq 0% softirq
CPU0 states: 0% user 0% system 0% nice 100% idle 0% iowait 0% irq 0% softirq
CPU1 states: 0% user 0% system 0% nice 100% idle 0% iowait 0% irq 0% softirq
Memory: 1032988k total, 443536k used (42.9%), 572604k free (55.4%), 16848k
freeable (1.7%)
Average network usage: 18 / 16 kbps in 1 minute, 15 / 14 kbps in 10 minutes,
15 / 13 kbps in 30 minutes
Average sessions: 22 sessions in 1 minute, 17 sessions in 10 minutes, 15
sessions in 30 minutes
Average session setup rate: 0 sessions per second in last 1 minute, 0
sessions per second in last 10 minutes, 0 sessions per second in last 30
minutes
Virus caught: 0 total in 1 minute
IPS attacks blocked: 0 total in 1 minute
Uptime: 6 days,  22 hours,  50 minutes
```

The *get system performance status* command presents a quick snapshot of allocated system-level resources for memory and CPU. It also provides a quick overview of session metrics. To drill down further into sessions, run the following command:

Details on session full-stat command:

https://kb.fortinet.com/kb/viewContent.do?externalId=FD40600&slic eId=1

```
30E-B-231 # diagnose sys session full-stat
session table:          table_size=524288 max_depth=1 used=30
misc info:         session_count=15 setup_rate=0 exp_count=0 clash=0
        memory_tension_drop=0 ephemeral=0/65536 removeable=0
delete=0, flush=1, dev_down=10/6013 ses_walkers=0
TCP sessions:
        1 in ESTABLISHED state
firewall error stat:
error1=00000000
error2=00000000
error3=00000000
error4=00000000
tt=00000000
cont=00000000
ids_recv=00000000
url_recv=00000000
av_recv=00000000
fqdn_count=00000006
fqdn6_count=00000000
```

I've bolded a few important fields. Session clash counter is found here, which points to NAT port exhaustion, meaning FortiOS has no more available ports to allocate new sessions. Also, you see the setup rate, which could hinder FortiGate performance if this value is higher than expected. To obtain an "expected value", you must know your network and generate a known good baseline. The *exp_count* field points to expected session entries created by session helpers. Ephemeral sessions are halfway established TCP sessions or one-way UDP traffic; if this value is high, this could point to a DoS attack. The memory tension drop field is a counter that increments when FortiOS must drop sessions to account for low overall available system memory.

To check details around CPU utilization, run the following CLI command:

```
30E-B-231 # diagnose sys top
top             Show top processes information.
top-summary     Show top aggregated processes information.
```

```
top-fd         Display processes with the most active file descriptors
(default 5 processes).
top-mem        Display processes with the most used memory (default 5
processes).
top-sockmem    Display processes with the most used socket memory (default 5
processes).
```

```
30E-B-231 # diagnose sys top-summary
   CPU [|||||||||||||||||||||||              ] 50.0%
   Mem [|||||||||||||||||||||                ] 45.0%   455M/1008M
   Processes: 20 (running=1 sleeping=103)

   PID      RSS   ^CPU% MEM%   FDS     TIME+   NAME
 * 256       5M    0.0  0.6     10  00:11.86   fsd
   259       6M    0.0  0.6     12  00:00.51   autod
   260       8M    0.0  0.9     18  02:24.63   fcnacd
```

This command comes with a few options:

```
diagnose sys top-summary '-n 5 --sort=mem'
diagnose sys top-summary '-n 5 --sort=cpu_percent'
diagnose sys top-summary '-n 5 --sort=fds'
diagnose sys top-summary '-n 5 --sort=pid'
```

These options can be useful to filter through various daemons running on FortiOS.

1) mem = memory
2) fds = file descriptor
3) pid = process ID

The diagnose sys top-summary command was removed from 6.4 MR

File descriptors are used in programming to keep cached data that the daemon is using to perform its function. Sometimes there are FDS leaks, meaning these files keep growing, which will max out the memory. Note you can also press 'm' or 'p' to sort by memory or CPU utilization, respectively. To see all daemons running on FortiOS run the following command:

```
30E-B-231 # diagnose sys top
<value>    Delay in seconds (default 5).


30E-B-231 # diagnose sys top 5
<Integer>  Maximum lines to display (default 20).
           Show all the running processes if larger than its total number.


30E-B-231 # diagnose sys top 5 99
```

```
<value>    Iterations to run (default unlimited).
```

```
30E-B-231 # diagnose sys top 5 99 10
```

This command states, FortiOS displays up to 99 daemons metrics and refreshes these metrics every five seconds, ten times. Lastly, for 6.4 MR, the *top* options are:

```
FGT-B-232 # diagnose sys top
top            Show top processes information.
top-all        Show top threads information.
top-fd         Display processes with the most active file descriptors
(default 5 processes).
top-mem        Display processes with the most used memory (default 5
processes).
top-sockmem    Display processes with the most used socket memory (default 5
processes).
```

Each daemon can be in one of four states, which are:

1) Sleeping (S)
2) Running (R)
3) Do Not Disturb (D)
4) Zombie (Z)

Note that S and R states are normal, and it is also normal for the daemon to go into the D state for a short period of time. The Z state is not normal, and also, if a daemon stays in the D state for long periods is not normal.

Conserve Mode

FortiOS has a mechanism called conserve mode if memory utilization becomes a problem. The following command displays information around conserve mode:

```
FGT-B-232 # diagnose hardware sysinfo conserve
memory conserve mode:                          off
total RAM:                               1918 MB
memory used:                              668 MB    34% of total RAM
memory freeable:                          310 MB    16% of total RAM
memory used + freeable threshold extreme: 1822 MB    95% of total RAM
memory used threshold red:               1688 MB    88% of total RAM
memory used threshold green:             1573 MB    82% of total RAM
```

These thresholds have changed throughout various Major Releases, but as of 6.4, the output has become more intuitive to understand.

```
30E-B-231 (global) # show ful | grep memory-use
    set memory-use-threshold-extreme 95
    set memory-use-threshold-green 82
```

```
      set memory-use-threshold-red 88
```

If memory utilization reaches 88 percent, then the unit is placed in *red* conserve mode. Features on FortiOS like proxies and daemons like AV and IPS have specific options if conserve mode is triggered. In general, the system begins using many different methods to reduce memory utilization. For example, AV provides the following global options if conserve mode is hit:

```
FGT-B-232 (global) # set av-failopen ?
pass        Bypass the antivirus system when memory is low. Antivirus
scanning resumes when the low memory condition is resolved.
off         Stop accepting new AV sessions when entering conserve mode, but
continue to process current active sessions.
one-shot    Bypass the antivirus system when memory is low.
```

If the 95% memory utilization is hit, then an extreme threshold is triggered, which in addition to red threshold functions, FortiGate will no longer accept new sessions. The green threshold at 82% and is when FortiGate completely exits conserve mode.

Another good command that displays what proxies are in a fail open state is:

```
FGT-B-232 # diag firewall iprope state
av_break=off/off av_conserve=off Alloc: iprope=144 shaper=12 user=0 nodes=3
pol=11
app_src=0 auth_logon=0 auth_info=0
av_service=http   fail open act=off
av_service=imap   fail open act=off
av_service=pop3   fail open act=off
av_service=smtp   fail open act=off
av_service=ftp    fail open act=off
av_service=im     fail open act=off
av_service=p2p    fail open act=off
av_service=nntp   fail open act=off
av_service=https  fail open act=off
av_service=imaps  fail open act=off
av_service=pop3s  fail open act=off
av_service=smtps  fail open act=off
av_service=ftps   fail open act=off
av_service=cifs   fail open act=off
total group number = 13 act=2
00004e20 00000001 00100012 00000003 00100003 00100004 00000005 00000008
0010000a 0010000c 0010000d 0010000e 0010000f
```

The act=off output indicates the related proxy is not operating effected by conserve mode. if *pass* is seen then application proxy is affected by system conserve mode.

If your system ever hits conserve mode, the first thing to do is find out what is using all the memory on the system, which would most likely be either daemons, sessions, or cached information (or all three). If a daemon(s), is the culprit, a workaround would be to restart that daemon by killing it off. To do this, find PID within TOP output and run the following command:

diagnose sys kill <signal> <process id>

diagnose sys kill 11 123

Kill signal 11 generates a crashlog entry that can help development teams investigate issues. Before killing any daemons on FortiGate production devices, I would recommend opening a Fortinet TAC case.

Sessions entries are a common culprit in memory utilization. FortiGate has commands to optimize session table entries ttl, which are:

```
FGT-B-232 (global) # show ful | grep tcp
    set reset-sessionless-tcp disable
    set tcp-halfclose-timer 120
    set tcp-halfopen-timer 10
    set tcp-option enable
    set tcp-timewait-timer 1


FGT-B-232 (global) # show ful | grep udp
    set udp-idle-timer 180
```

To obtain more detailed information around memory used by session entries, run the following command:

```
diagnose hardware sysinfo slab
```

Lastly, cached information could add up over time and cause memory issues. FortiGate has features to limit caching for various features. A few important ones to know about are:

```
FGT-B-232 (dns) # show ful | grep cache
    set dns-cache-limit 5000
    set dns-cache-ttl 1800
..
FGT-B-232 (global) # show ful | grep cache
    set max-route-cache-size 0
..
FGT-B-232 (fortiguard) # show ful | grep cache
    set antispam-cache enable
    set antispam-cache-ttl 1800
    set antispam-cache-mpercent 2
    set outbreak-prevention-cache enable
    set outbreak-prevention-cache-ttl 300
    set outbreak-prevention-cache-mpercent 2
    set webfilter-cache enable
    set webfilter-cache-ttl 3600
```

..

"Memory optimization techniques for FortiOS"

https://kb.fortinet.com/kb/documentLink.do?externalID=FD35126

This section covers CPU and memory on FortiGate. Next, we look at the crashlog.

<u>Crash Logs</u>

FortiOS manages a crashlog file, which contains system-level events, some minor and some major. When your system is acting *weird*, the first place to check is here. When a daemon is found in the crashlog, you will most likely open a case with Fortinet TAC because this is most likely a software defect. Here is what a crashlog entry looks like after you kill a daemon:

```
FGT-B-232 # diagnose sys  top
Run Time:  5 days, 0 hours and 34 minutes
0U, 0N, 0S, 100I, 0WA, 0HI, 0SI, 0ST; 1918T, 955F
        cmdbsvr        131       S        0.0      2.2
       forticron       168       S        0.0      2.0
       ipshelper       214       S <      0.0      1.8
..
FGT-B-232 # diagnose sys kill 11 214
FGT-B-232 # diagnose debug crashlog read
107: 2020-11-16 15:03:14 <00214> *** signal 11 (Segmentation fault) received
***
108: 2020-11-16 15:03:14 <00214> Register dump:
109: 2020-11-16 15:03:14 <00214> R0: fffffffffffffffc   R1: 0000007fc52c5b60
R2: 0000000000000400
110: 2020-11-16 15:03:14 R3: 00000000000000c8
..
117: 2020-11-16 15:03:14 <00214> IP0: 0000007f95f13898    IP1:
0000007f9792d508    PR: 00000000000003cf
118: 2020-11-16 15:03:14  R19: 000000000000000a
119: 2020-11-16 15:03:14 <00214> R20: 00000000000000c8    R21:
0000007fc52c5ac0   R22: 0000007f96045000
120: 2020-11-16 15:03:14   R23: 0000007f968f7f80
121: 2020-11-16 15:03:14 <00214> R24: 0000007fc52c5ad0    R25:
0000007f95f20000   R26: 0000007fc52c5ae0
122: 2020-11-16 15:03:14   R27: 0000007f96045460
123: 2020-11-16 15:03:14 <00214> R28: 0000007f95f9fac0    FP: 0000007fc52c59f0
LR: 0000007f95c8d940
124: 2020-11-16 15:03:14 <00214> fault_address: 0000000000000000   sp:
0000007fc52c59f0
```

```
125: 2020-11-16 15:03:14 <00214> pc: 0000007f9792d36c    pstate:
0000000060000000
126: 2020-11-16 15:03:14 <00214> Backtrace:
..
145: 2020-11-16 15:03:14 [IPS Engine <00214>] base: 0x7f95843000
146: 2020-11-16 15:03:14 [IPS Engine <00214>] Last session info:
147: 2020-11-16 15:03:14 [IPS Engine <00214>]    No session found.
Crash log interval is 3600 seconds
ipsengine 06.002.058 crashed 1 times. The last crash was at 2020-11-16
15:03:14
```

Don't worry; you're not supposed to be able to understand crashlog entries. Developers and TAC use this output information.

FortiGate Disk

Some FortiGate platforms come with HDD, SSD, or compact flash. Some FortiOS features are required to use disk space. To view this, run the following commands:

diagnose hardware deviceinfo disk

```
Disk SYSTEM(boot)              14.9GiB    type: SSD [ATA 16GB SATA Flash]
dev: /dev/sda
   partition         247.0MiB, 188.0MiB free  mounted: N  label:  dev:
/dev/sda1(boot) start: 1
   partition         247.0MiB, 181.0MiB free  mounted: Y  label:  dev:
/dev/sda2(boot) start: 524289
   partition ref:  3  14.2GiB,  14.1GiB free  mounted: Y  label:  dev:
/dev/sda3 start: 1048577


Disk HDD           ref:  16 111.8GiB    type: SSD [ATA D2CSxxxxx-012] dev:
/dev/sdb
   partition ref:  17 110.0GiB, 109.5GiB free  mounted: Y  label:
LOGUSEDX3CEB909F dev: /dev/sdb1 start: 2048


Total available disks: 2
Max SSD disks: 1  Available storage disks: 1
```

diagnose sys flash list

Partition	Image	TotalSize(KB)	Used(KB)
Use%	Active		
1	FGT3HD-6.00-FW-build0163-180725	253871	60668
24%	No		
2	FGT3HD-6.02-FW-build1066-191218	253871	67864
27%	Yes		

```
3         EXDB-1.00000                          14866900     38976
0%  No
Image build at Dec 18 2019 22:05:11 for b1066
```

Sometimes right might be necessary to format disk or flash on FortiGate. To do this the below commands are available:

```
# diagnose sys flash format
# execute formatlogdisk
Formatting this storage will erase all data on it, including
  logs, quarantine files;
  WanOpt caches;
and require the unit to reboot.
Do you want to continue? (y/n)
# execute disk list
Disk HDD              ref:  16 111.8GiB    type: SSD [ATA D2CSTK251M3T-012]
dev: /dev/sdb
  partition ref:  17 110.0GiB, 109.5GiB free  mounted: Y  label:
LOGUSEDX3CEB909F dev: /dev/sdb1 start: 2048
# execute disk format ?
<integer>    partition/device reference number(s), as reported by 'disk list'
query
# execute disk format 17
format requested for:  device=/dev/sdb1 17/HDD status=enable media-
status=enable
Formatting this storage will erase all data on it, including
  logs, quarantine files;
This action requires the unit to reboot.
Do you want to continue? (y/n)
```

Alright, folks, this covers NSE4 system-level troubleshooting. Time to move onto the network interface!

Advanced System-Level Troubleshooting

Let's face it, hardware dies, and even better, it dies at the worse time possible! If you suspect a FortiGate hardware issue, then there are a few commands to run on FortiOS. The first is the HQIP test.

Hardware Quick Inspection Package (HQIP)

```
The HQIP test features on 6.4 FortiOS are available without using the BIOS
menu to load a HQIP image. Here are the 6.4 options:
(global) # diagnose hardware test
bios       Perform BIOS related test.
```

```
system      Perform system related test.
pci         Show PCI device list.
usb         Perform USB related test
button      Perform button related test.
cpu         Perform CPU related test.
memory      Perform memory related test.
network     Perform network related test.
npu         Perform NPU related test.
disk        Perform disk related test.
led         Perform led related test.
wifi        Perform wifi related test.
suite       Run a test suite.
info        Show test parameters etc.
```

```
Hughes_QA1 (global) # diagnose hardware test suite
<all|pcba|rack-burn-in>    Run a test suite.
```

To run all HQIP test on FortiGate issue the follow command:

```
#diagnose hardware test suite all
```

You will entry a interactive CLI menu. The final report snippet will look like:

```
===================== Fortinet Hardware Test Report =========================
...

BIOS
  Check System ID......................................... PASS
  BIOS Image Checksum..................................... PASS
  Check License........................................... PASS
SYSTEM
  CPU Configuration Check................................. PASS
  Memory Configuration Check.............................. PASS
  Storage Configuration Check............................. PASS
  Network Configuration Check............................. PASS

...
```

COMLog Feature

Sometimes software and hardware issues cause random reboots of hardware. In cases like these, to obtain more information around the problem, some FortiGate platforms support a COMLog feature.

For details around feature, see:

https://kb.fortinet.com/kb/documentLink.do?externalID=FD35193

Essentially, when COMLog is enabled, it stores console output into a 4MB file on flash memory and will not be erased during BIOS format or software upgrade. The goal is to catch important debug information to help push investigations forward. If you are working with COMLog, you will most like have a TAC case open. Here are the debug commands to use COMLog:

```
# diagnose debug comlog
info       Get log information.
clear      Clear log.
disable    Disable logging.
enable     Enable logging.
```

Once enabled, to read comlog file issue:

```
#diag debug comlog read
```

non-maskable interrupt (NMI) switch

Non-maskable Interrupt is a hardware interrupt feature used when FortiGate is in a boot-loop. Fortinet is not the only vendor that uses this feature.

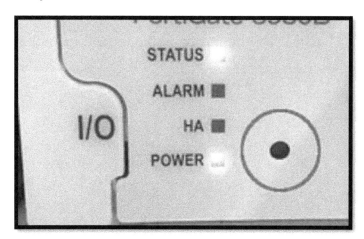

NMI button is located on FortiGate within a small pin-hole, to push the button, it is required to have a paper-clip or small tool to push and hold it down. Once the NMI button is pushed, this causes a software dump of board registers and backtraces to the console; once this data is dumped, the FortiGate restarts. This information could be useful for TAC.

Network Level Troubleshooting

Once the system level troubleshooting clears the next step is to check interfaces for errors which could indicate a NIC or median issue. To check error counters run the follow command:

```
# diagnose hardware deviceinfo nic port1
Description     :FortiASIC NP6 Adapter
Driver Name     :FortiASIC Unified NPU Driver
```

```
Name                 :np6_0
PCI Slot             :0000:01:00.0
irq                  :16
Board                :FGT300d
SN                   :FGT3HD3xxxxx
Major ID             :5
Minor ID             :0
lif id               :0
lif oid              :134
netdev oid           :134
netdev flags         :1003
Current_HWaddr       90:6c:ac:x
Permanent_HWaddr     90:6c:ac:x
phy name             :port1
bank_id              :1
phy_addr             :0x00
lane                 :0
flags                :220
sw_port              :0
sw_np_port           :0
vid_phy[6]           :[0x02][0x00][0x00][0x00][0x00][0x00]
vid_fwd[6]           :[0x00][0x00][0x00][0x00][0x00][0x00]
oid_fwd[6]           :[0x00][0x00][0x00][0x00][0x00][0x00]
========== Link Status ==========
Admin                :up
netdev status        :up
autonego_setting:1
link_setting         :1
link_speed           :1000
link_duplex          :0
Speed                :1000
Duplex               :Full
link_status          :Up
rx_link_status       :1
int_phy_link         :0
local_fault          :0
local_warning        :0
remote_fault         :0
============ Counters ===========
Rx_CRC_Errors        :0
Rx_Frame_Too_Longs:0
rx_undersize         :0
Rx Pkts              :4428122834
Rx Bytes             :5755207512018
Tx Pkts              :2256967201
```

```
Tx Bytes          :417703713352
Host Rx Pkts      :264984715
Host Rx Bytes     :53048667629
Host Tx Pkts      :195770893
Host Tx Bytes     :34388272179
Host Tx dropped   :0
FragTxCreate      :0
FragTxOk          :0
FragTxDrop        :0
```

You will need to obtain many samples of this commands output to see if errors or drop counters are actively incrementing. Once the interface is cleared the next step is to see if ARP entries are seen on the FortiGate:

```
#  get sys arp
Address           Age(min)   Hardware Addr      Interface
10.123.233.2      0          08:5b:0e:xx:xx:xx port2
172.22.220.4      8          a4:11:62:xx:xx:xx port3
192.168.1.1       0          fc:ae:34:xx:xx:xx port1
172.22.220.3      254        00:d9:d1:xx:xx:xx port3
192.168.1.254     1          fc:ae:34:xx:xx:xx port1
```

If the gateway IP is not seen in the ARP cache, then attempt to ping the gateway IP while running a sniffer packet command on the interface:

```
#diag sniffer packet port1 'host 108.253.1.12'
```

Note to see MAC address on sniffer command, and then the interface must be referenced. Once the gateway is confirmed reachable. It is time to check the routing table.

```
# get router info routing-table  all

Routing table for VRF=0
Codes: K - kernel, C - connected, S - static, R - RIP, B - BGP
       O - OSPF, IA - OSPF inter area
       N1 - OSPF NSSA external type 1, N2 - OSPF NSSA external type 2
       E1 - OSPF external type 1, E2 - OSPF external type 2
       i - IS-IS, L1 - IS-IS level-1, L2 - IS-IS level-2, ia - IS-IS inter
area
       * - candidate default

S*     0.0.0.0/0 [5/0] via 192.168.1.1, port1
```

Next is to run the diag flow debug command set to check transit traffic:

```
diag debug dis
diag debug reset
diag debug flow filter clear
```

```
diag debug flow sh con en
diag debug flow sh func en
diag debug console timestamp en
diag debug flow filter addr x.x.x.x // IPv4 address
diag debug flow trace start 5000
diag debug en
```

Once traffic is confirmed to pass through a policy, then this confirms functionality for layers one, two, and three. To test TCP layer-4, Telnet could be used to Telnet to a known good port for the service of interest.

The last point to touch on for network troubleshooting is the FortiGate ASICs. FortiOS provides commands to gather stats like drop counters on NP6 ASIC.

```
FGT3HDxx # diagnose npu np6 dce 0
MACFIL_BASE1    :0000000000000015 [01]   IHP1_PKTCHK    :0000000000018255
[5b]
FGT3HDxx # diagnose npu np6 dce 0
```

Note that the drop counters are cleared for these fields every time you run this NP6 DCE command. This information is useful to Fortinet TAC if drops are indeed occurring. Here are the commands for SoC4 ASIC.

```
FGT-B-232 # diagnose npu np6xlite ?
fastpath          Configure fastpath
ipsec-fragment    Configure ipsec fragmentation type.
dce               Show non-zero subengine drop counters.
anomaly-drop      Show non-zero L3/L4 anomaly check drop counters.
session-stats     Show session offloading statistics counters
port-list         Show port list
sse-stats         Show hardware session statistics counters
session-dump      Dump hardware session summary or session list
mse-dump          Dump MSE session
register          Show NP6XLITE registers.
npu-feature       Show NPU feature and status.
```

Just like before, if ASIC drops occur, then this output could be useful to TAC to ID software defects. Alright, folks, this covers network layer troubleshooting; next, we move onto FortiGuard troubleshooting.

Layer-2 Troubleshooting

A common layer-2 issue in IPv4 networks is when a MAC to IPv4 address mapping has changed within the segment, but the device did not send out a GARP (gratuitous arp); then you may be required to manually clear the ARP cache locally on FortiGate so to re-learn it. To perform this, run the following command:

(root) # execute clear system arp table

FortiGuard Troubleshooting

FortiGate must have access to DNS to resolve FortiGuard FQDN's:

1) update.fortiguard.net
   a. AV and IPS update
2) service.fortiguard.net
   a. web filtering and anti-spam updates.
3) securewf.fortiguard.net
   a. web filtering and anti-spam updates

Next, it is important to know the Ports used for public FortiGuard Servers: udp-8888, udp-53, https-8888, and https-53. Next, if using FortiManager as an FDN, then the ports are udp-8888; udp-53, http-80; https-8888

Next, below are a few FQDN used by the FDN:

- service.fortiguard.net (UDP - World Wide Servers)
- securewf.fortiguard.net (HTTPS - World Wide Servers)
- usservice.fortiguard.net (UDP - USA Based Only Servers)
- ussecurewf.fortiguard.net (HTTPS - USA Based Only Servers)

FortiGate can be configured to use only USA based servers or Worldwide FDN servers; see the following CLI configuration:

```
#config system fortiguard
#set update-server-location [use|any]
#config global
#config system fortiguard
#set update-server-location usa
#end
```

Test DNS resolution by issuing the PING command against the following FQDNs.

```
# execute ping service.fortiguard.net
# execute ping securewf.fortiguard.net
# execute ping usservice.fortiguard.net
# execute ping ussecurewf.fortiguard.net
# diagnose test application dnsproxy 3
```

```
FGT-B-232 # exe ping update.fortiguard.net
PING fds1.fortinet.com (173.243.138.68): 56 data bytes
64 bytes from 173.243.138.68: icmp_seq=0 ttl=41 time=104.3 ms
^C
--- fds1.fortinet.com ping statistics ---
1 packets transmitted, 1 packets received, 0% packet loss
```

```
round-trip min/avg/max = 104.3/104.3/104.3 ms
```

```
FGT-B-232 # exe ping service.fortiguard.net
PING guard.fortinet.net (209.222.147.36): 56 data bytes
```

If FortiOS is having a hard time resolving DNS, then use the following command for insight:

```
#diagnose test application dnsproxy 3
```

This command dumps all DNS settings on the unit. FortiGate also provides the ability to check FDN Web Filtering queries service and reachability by running the following command:

```
FGT-B-232 # diagnose debug rating
Locale        : english

Service       : Web-filter
Status        : Enable
License       : Contract

Service       : Antispam
Status        : Disable

Service       : Virus Outbreak Prevention
Status        : Disable

Num. of servers : 1
Protocol        : https
Port            : 443
Anycast         : Disable
Default servers : Included

-=- Server List (Mon Nov 16 16:13:24 2020) -=-

IP                                          Weight   RTT Flags   TZ
Packets  Curr Lost Total Lost   Updated Time
173.243.138.210                                0       0 DI T     0
4            2          2
```

Once DNS and layer-3 reachbilitiy is confirmed to FortiGuard server force an update and run debug in parallel:

```
#diag debug application update 255
#diag debug end
#exec update-now
installUpdObjRest[700]-Step 7:Validate object
installUpdObjRest[724]-Step 8:Re-initialize using new obj file
```

```
installUpdObjRest[736]-Step 9:Delete backup /tmp/update.backup
upd_install_pkg[1365]-AVEN031 is up-to-date
upd_install_pkg[1365]-AVDB002 is up-to-date
upd_install_pkg[1365]-AVDB007 is up-to-date
upd_install_pkg[1391]-FCNI000 installed successfully
upd_install_pkg[1391]-FDNI000 installed successfully
upd_install_pkg[1391]-FSCI000 installed successfully
upd_install_pkg[1365]-FLEN069 is up-to-date
upd_install_pkg[1365]-FLEN050 is up-to-date
upd_install_pkg[1391]-FLDB002 installed successfully
upd_install_pkg[1365]-NIDS024 is up-to-date
upd_install_pkg[1365]-MUDB001 is up-to-date
upd_install_pkg[1365]-APDB001 is up-to-date
upd_install_pkg[1371]-ISDB001 is unauthorized
upd_install_pkg[1365]-CIDB000 is up-to-date
upd_install_pkg[1365]-IPGO000 is up-to-date
upd_install_pkg[1365]-FFDB003 is up-to-date
upd_install_pkg[1365]-FFDB004 is up-to-date
upd_install_pkg[1365]-UWDB001 is up-to-date
upd_install_pkg[1365]-CRDB000 is up-to-date
upd_install_pkg[1365]-MMDB001 is up-to-date
upd_install_pkg[1365]-DBDB001 is up-to-date
upd_install_pkg[1365]-MCDB001 is up-to-date
upd_install_pkg[1365]-ALCI000 is up-to-date
upd_status_save_status[143]-try to save on status file
upd_status_save_status[209]-Wrote status file
__upd_act_update[353]-Package installed successfully
upd_comm_disconnect_fds[499]-Disconnecting FDS 96.45.33.88:443
```

FortiGuard updates are only applied to UTM modules actively being used in atleast one Firewall Policy Entry

Once an update is successful the following debug command shows local database versions:

```
FGT-B-232 # diagnose autoupdate versions

AV Engine
---------
Version: 6.00154
Contract Expiry Date: Fri Sep 10 2021
Last Updated using manual update on Fri Aug 21 16:28:00 2020
Last Update Attempt: Mon Nov 16 16:13:13 2020
Result: No Updates
```

```
Virus Definitions
---------
Version: 81.00882
Contract Expiry Date: Fri Sep 10 2021
Last Updated using manual update on Mon Nov 16 16:09:26 2020
Last Update Attempt: Mon Nov 16 16:13:13 2020
Result: No Updates
..
FDS Address
---------
96.45.33.88:443
```

Next, sometimes FortiGuard traffic conflicts with other application traffic or is being blocked by upstream ISP. In 6.4, FortiGuard ports can be changed in the CLI by first disabling fortiguard-anycast via:

FGT-B-232 # config system fortiguard

FGT-B-232 (fortiguard) # set fortiguard-anycast disable

```
..
FGT-B-232 (fortiguard) # set port
8888     port 8888 for server communication.
53       port 53 for server communication.
443      port 443 for server communication.
```

The last FortiGuard troubleshooting item to touch on is to be certain that FortiGate has the correct license(s) to receive FortiGuard updates. A common issue with licenses is found with HA clusters. Be certain all FortiGates within an HA cluster have the same entitlements.

This section wraps up FortiGuard troubleshooting. The next topic is IPsec and SSL VPNs!

VPN Troubleshooting

FortiOS provides a few helpful commands when troubleshooting VPNs like IPsec and SSL. IPsec as a real-time debug that presents any issues with the Phase-1 or Phase-2 negotiation the following debugs are available.

```
#diagnose debug application ike 255
#diagnose vpn ike log filter ?
list          Display the current filter.
clear         Erase the current filter.
name          Phase1 name to filter by.
src-addr4     IPv4 source address range to filter by.
msrc-addr4    multiple IPv4 source address to filter by.
```

```
dst-addr4      IPv4 destination address range to filter by.
mdst-addr4     multiple IPv4 destination address to filter by.
src-addr6      IPv6 source address range to filter by.
msrc-addr6     multiple IPv6 source address to filter by.
dst-addr6      IPv6 destination address range to filter by.
mdst-addr6     multiple IPv6 destination addresses to filter by.
src-port       Source port range to filter by.
dst-port       Destination port range to filter by.
vd             Index of virtual domain. -1 matches all.
interface      Interface that IKE connection is negotiated over.
negate         Negate the specified filter parameter.
```

Here is a complete debug list for IPsec for reference:

```
=====IPSEC debugs=======

diag vpn ike log-filter dst-addr4 216.171.247.27
diag debug reset
diag debug enable
diag debug console timestamp enable
diag debug application ike -1


collect:

#diag vpn ike config list
#diag vpn ike gateway list
#diag vpn tunnel list
#get vpn ipsec tunnel details
#diag vpn ike status summary
#diag vpn ike status detailed
#get vpn ipsec tunnel summary
#get vpn ipsec stats tunnel
#diag vpn tunnel stat
#get vpn ipsec stats crypto
#diag vpn ipsec status
#diag vpn ike crypto stats
#get ipsec tunnel list
#diag netlink interface list
#diagnose vpn ike routes list
#diag vpn ike errors
#diagnose vpn ike counts
#diag vpn ike log terminal stats
```

```
#diagnose sys session filter clear
#diag sys session filter src x.x.x.x // source or dst ip
#diag system session list
```

```
...
npu info: flag=0x81/0x81, offload=4/4, ips_offload=0/0, epid=1/23, ipid=23/1,
vlan=32779/0
```

```
Specifically, look at the "offload" field.
offload=(forward_direction)/(reverse_direction)
```

```
#diagnose vpn tunnel list
```

Note it is important to understand the npu_flag field value:

- npu_flag=00 Means that ingress & egress ESP packets are not offloaded
- npu_flag=01 Means only egress ESP packets can be offloaded; ingress ESP packets will be handled by the kernel
- npu_flag=02 Means only ingress ESP packets can be offloaded; egress ESP packets will be handled by the kernel
- npu_flag=03 Means that both ingress & egress ESP packets will be offloaded
- npu_flag=20 Indicates transform set is not supported by NP ASIC.

I know every command here I did not explain, but essentially, these commands are what I use in my day to day job when troubleshooting IPsec. Next, SSL-VPN FortiGate provides a few useful debug commands that might be helpful when SSL-VPNs are not working as expected. For reference:

--- real time debug----

```
#diagnose debug application sslvpn -1
#diagnose debug application fnbamd -1
#diag debug console timestamp enable
#diagnose debug enable
```

```
======SSL debug commands =======
#diag vpn ssl list
#diag vpn ssl mux
#diag vpn ssl statistics
#diag vpn ssl hw-acceleration-status
================================
```

Most of the time, FortiClient is used with FortiGate SSL-VPN. There is a progress percent that is displayed on FortiClient while connecting. From my experience, here are some likely causes of issues at each percentage.

- If Forticlient stops at 10%, this means it's most likely a layer 3 issue with the routing or a mismatch port number.
- If Forticlient stops at 40%, the FortiGate might need to be rebooted, or the SSL Daemon restarted because of system issues. This is also where a certificate warning could appear.
- If Forticlient stops at 80%, this means the username/password is incorrect
- If the Forticlient stops at 98%, this could be an interoperability issue with other software on the system, or this could point to a FortiClient driver install issue.

This section wraps up troubleshooting VPNs. In the next section, I will provide a use case on FTP session helper.

FTP Session Helper

I feel like in the first chapter, I did not provide enough information about how sessions work. So I want to clarify that in this section. We are going to run through an FTP Session Helper use case. The topology is simple; it goes:

FTP-Client------→NAT FortiGate------→ FTP server

FTP can operate in two different modes, Active or Passive; this is because a second TCP connection is utilized for the data transfer. FTP Passive is when the client asks the server what port it should use for the data connection using the PASV command. Once the server opens a local socket for data transfer and communicates this value. The client initiates the data connection to the specified socket. For FTP Active mode, the client opens a data socket locally and sends this value and the PORT command to the server. The server initiates an outbound connection to the client-side specified port number.

This matters because FortiGate is a stateful device and keeps track of TCP ports upon traffic egress, which allows return traffic to be allowed without an explicit Firewall Policy Entry. When working with application layer protocols like FTP that negotiate different port values other than those used in the initial connection (port 21 in this case), FortiGate must dynamically parse these negotiated port values out and create an Expected Session Entry or a pin-hole. Therefore, FortiGate must know if FTP uses the Active or Passive communication method to set up the data ports correctly. This is accomplished through the Session Helper.

In this example, we set up a simple FTP transfer using FortiGate as a NAT device. The FTP client uses IP 192.168.1.110 and is NAT'ed behind 192.168.209.232, and the FTP server is using 192.168.209.101. The first example uses Passive Mode:

```
FTP Server sessions:
[user@cent-1 ~]# netstat -tulna | grep 192.168.209.232
tcp        0      0 192.168.209.101:35789      192.168.209.232:61076
TIME_WAIT
tcp        0      0 192.168.209.101:21         192.168.209.232:64984
ESTABLISHED
```

```
...
Windows PC FTP Client:
PS C:\Users\user> netstat -an | grep 101
   TCP     192.168.1.110:64984     192.168.209.101:21      ESTABLISHED
   TCP     192.168.1.110:64985     192.168.209.101:35789   ESTABLISHED
...
FGT-B-232 # diagnose sys session list

session info: proto=6 proto_state=05 duration=4 expire=0 timeout=3600
flags=00000000 socktype=0 sockport=0 av_idx=0 use=4
origin-shaper=
reply-shaper=
per_ip_shaper=
class_id=0 ha_id=0 policy_dir=0 tunnel=/ vlan_cos=255/255
state=intree
statistic(bytes/packets/allow_err): org=906868/22666/1
reply=261778114/176053/1 tuples=2
tx speed(Bps/kbps): 216954/1735 rx speed(Bps/kbps): 62626343/501010
orgin->sink: org pre->post, reply pre->post dev=25->5/5->25
gwy=192.168.209.101/192.168.1.110
hook=post dir=org act=snat 192.168.1.110:64985-
>192.168.209.101:35789(192.168.209.232:61076)
hook=pre dir=reply act=dnat 192.168.209.101:35789-
>192.168.209.232:61076(192.168.1.110:64985)
pos/(before,after) 0/(0,0), 0/(0,0)
misc=0 policy_id=5 auth_info=0 chk_client_info=0 vd=0
serial=000e6f78 tos=ff/ff app_list=0 app=0 url_cat=0
sdwan_mbr_seq=0 sdwan_service_id=0
rpdb_link_id=00000000 rpdb_svc_id=0 ngfwid=n/a
npu_state=0x000001 no_offload
no_ofld_reason:  disabled-by-policy

session info: proto=6 proto_state=01 duration=13 expire=3599 timeout=3600
flags=00000000 socktype=0 sockport=0 av_idx=0 use=4
origin-shaper=
reply-shaper=
per_ip_shaper=
class_id=0 ha_id=0 policy_dir=0 tunnel=/ helper=ftp vlan_cos=0/255
state=may_dirty
statistic(bytes/packets/allow_err): org=713/14/1 reply=939/13/1 tuples=2
tx speed(Bps/kbps): 51/0 rx speed(Bps/kbps): 68/0
orgin->sink: org pre->post, reply pre->post dev=25->5/5->25
gwy=192.168.209.101/192.168.1.110
hook=post dir=org act=snat 192.168.1.110:64984-
>192.168.209.101:21(192.168.209.232:64984)
```

```
hook=pre dir=reply act=dnat 192.168.209.101:21-
>192.168.209.232:64984(192.168.1.110:64984)
pos/(before,after) 0/(0,0), 0/(0,0)
misc=0 policy_id=5 auth_info=0 chk_client_info=0 vd=0
serial=000e6f78 tos=ff/ff app_list=0 app=0 url_cat=0
sdwan_mbr_seq=0 sdwan_service_id=0
rpdb_link_id=00000000 rpdb_svc_id=0 ngfwid=n/a
npu_state=0x000001 no_offload
no_ofld_reason:  disabled-by-policy
total session 2
```

FGT-B-232 #

Something to note, some versions of FortiOS places a 'complex' flag on a session entry state field to indicate that the sessions were generated from a Session Helper. Lastly, a command to use to see active Expected Sessions is:

`diagnose sys session list expectation`

High Availablity Troubleshooting

FortiOS provides many High Availability (HA) troubleshooting commands. I will review a few of them here. The first item to check when you are looking into an HA problem, be sure the HB (heartbeat) interfaces are not taking errors and also HB packets are seen ingress/egress. The following command captures HB packets.

`# diag sniffer packet port1 "ether proto 0x8890" 4`

Here are all the HA HB frame Ethertypes:

- 0x8890 for NAT/Route Mode Heartbeat
- 0x8891 for Transparent Mode Heartbeat
- 0x8892 for Session Synchronization
- 0x8893 for HA telnet sessions

Next, to debug HA issues, on all members of a cluster run the following debug commands:

On the Master unit:

```
execute ha synchronize stop
diag debug reset
diag debug enable
diagnose debug console timestamp enable
diag debug application hasync -1
diag debug application hatalk -1
```

On Backup Units:

```
dia debug reset
diag debug enable
diag debug application hasync -1
diag debug application hatalk -1
execute ha synchronize start
```

Disable debugging on both the units once the Backup unit is in sync with the Master unit or the capturing of logs is completed:

```
diag debug disable
diag debug reset
```

These debugs provide insight into the problem at hand. Next, if units never sync, run the following HA debug commands on Slave FortiGate(s):

```
# diagnose sys ha hadiff status | grep state
state: get-csum <------ Slave waiting on response from master
```

if hasync or hatalk daemons are not acting as expected, sometimes as a workaround, these daemons can be killed to resume HA functions. Be sure to open a TAC case before killing HA daemons in production environments.

If nothing is working on syncing the cluster, then take a config backup on both units, perform a comparison and see what configuration is not correct.

To fail a HA cluster over, you can reset system uptime if the *override* setting is set to disable:

```
# diagnose sys ha reset-uptime
```

Troubleshoot Logging

Logs are the key resource to troubleshooting most issues, but sometimes the logging daemon itself has issues.

I've worked on a few issues around the miglog daemon not performing correctly or taking up too much memory or CPU. For issues like these, restarting the miglog daemon could serve as a workaround but as always, first, open a TAC case to confirm. FortiOS also provides many functions specific to miglog daemon testing; for your reference, here is the full list as of 6.4 GA.

```
FGT-B-232 # diagnose test application miglogd
1. Show global log setting.
2. Show vdom log setting.
3. Show log buffer sz.
4. Show log statistics
5. Show MAX file descriptor number.
6. Dump statistics.
9. Delete all policy sniffer files.
```

10. Show cid cache.
11. Show UTM traffic cache.
12. Show policy cache.
13. Increase the number of miglog children.
14. Decrease the number of miglog children.
15. Show miglog ID.
16. Show log disk usage.
18. Show network interface cache.
19. Show application cache.
20. Show FortiCloud log state.
24. Show WLAN AP cache.
26. Enable/disable log dumping (per daemon).
27. Show DNS cache.
28. Show miglog shared memory.
30. Show remote queues and items.
31. Show log dumping file content (per daemon).
32. Delete log dumping file (per daemon).
33. List log dumping file name.
34. Backup log dumping file to usb key.
36. Show memory log file lists.
37. Enable/disable dumping FAZ/FDS packets
38. Delete FAZ/FDS dumping file (per daemon).
39. Backup FAZ/FDS dumping files to usb key.
40. Show dropped logs due to log rate limit for all devices.
41. Show remote queues.
42. Show UUID Cache.
43. Show ISDB Cache.
44. Show ISDB Country Cache.
45. Show ISDB Region Cache.
46. Show ISDB City Cache.
47. Show remote sockets.
48. Show publish info.
49. Show publish logs.

101. Vdom-root Show log setting.
102. Vdom-root Show application custom cache.
103. Vdom-root Show application list cache.
104. Vdom-root Show UTM traffic cache.
105. Vdom-root Show reputation traffic cache.
106. Vdom-root Show firewall service cache.

The last set of debugs to provide you are:

```
FGT-B-232 # diagnose debug application miglogd 255
Debug messages will be on for 30 minutes.
FGT-B-232 # diagnose debug enable
```

These debug commands can provide further insight into miglogd issues.

Troubleshoot SDWAN

SD-WAN!! Or should I say dynamic best path application routing over IPsec overlay tunnel technology suite? I guess we should stick to just SD-WAN. Since SD-WAN is a compilation of technologies used together for one purpose, instead of providing specific troubleshooting commands on this topic, I would like to provide a methodology. Once confirmed that IPsec tunnels and routing are all operational. If traffic is not flowing as expected, then ask yourself.

1) Am I performing application routing or just IP routing?
    a. If application routing is being used, then is App. Control and DPI configured on transit policy?
    b. If Application Signature is being used, then has the learning phase occurred yet?
    c. Do you see Policy Route entries?
    d. Are Service Rules using gateway/default enable or disable settings?
2) Are the SLA probes reporting under defined thresholds?
3) Have I had recent link failures?
    a. If so, what are the settings for snat-route-change and preserve-session-route?
4) Has there been any dynamic routing issues?
5) Check Syslog for system-level events.
6) Are any UTM modules being used on transit traffic?

SD-WAN can become complicated, but the technology is still based on the TCP/IP protocol stack. Start your troubleshooting at the system level first, and then work up the stack to isolate the problem.

PING is a very simple program and one of our most used tools when troubleshooting computer networking issues. There are important SD-WAN ping features on FortiOS:

```
(root) # execute ping-options
adaptive-ping      Adaptive ping <enable|disable>.
data-size          Integer value to specify datagram size in bytes.
df-bit             Set DF bit in IP header <yes | no>.
interface          Auto | <outgoing interface>.
interval           Integer value to specify seconds between two pings.
pattern            Hex format of pattern, e.g. 00ffaabb.
repeat-count       Integer value to specify how many times to repeat PING.
reset              Reset settings.
source             Auto | <source interface IP>.
timeout            Integer value to specify timeout in seconds.
tos                IP type-of-service option.
ttl                Integer value to specify time-to-live.
use-sdwan          Use SD-WAN rules to get output interface <yes | no>.
```

```
validate-reply    Validate reply data <yes | no>.
view-settings     View the current settings for PING option.
```

When testing reachability, know what your PING setting is and how SD-WAN Rules affect it. Like I said before, many local-out protocols have options now to use SD-WAN Rules or not to.

This brings us to the end of Chapter 11 and the end of Introduction to FortiGate Part-II. Go ahead and jump into the chapter summary and those end of chapter questions!!

Chapter 11 Summary

Chapter 11 focuses on FortiGate troubleshooting. It is better to learn a troubleshooting methodology than memorize countless commands. When engaging in a troubleshooting issue, it is good practice to check the system-level resources like CPU, memory, and disk because if the system is not healthy, things will not work correctly. More advanced troubleshooting techniques involve the use of HQIP, which is software designed to test hardware components. Also, certain FortiGate platforms have a COMLog feature that log console output to a special file on FortiGate, which could be useful if the system is randomly rebooting or crashing. Next, NMI is a small button on FortiGuard that, if pressed, send debug information to the console and force FortiGate to reboot.

Once the system health is confirmed, then the next area to focus on is the network interface. FortiOS provides commands to check the interfaces for errors and anomalies caused by a bad cable, a bad NIC, or transmission interference. Once the interface health is confirmed, the next item to check is layer-2. For IPv4 networks, ARP entries could be present for the next hope gateway routers.

When troubleshooting FortiGuard related issues, it is critical that DNS works correctly, or else FortiGate won't resolve FDN various FQDN's for services. Once DNS is confirmed next item to check is to make sure FortiGate has a valid license.

VPN's are a big part of the FortiOS feature set. There are many tools on FortiGate to help debug and troubleshoot VPNs. I've place many commands I use in my day to day job in the VPN Troubleshooting section for reference.

Troubleshooting logging usually involves FortiGate generating too many logs that overwhelm FortiOS. When this occurs, limit what is being logs. Sometimes it might be necessary to kill the miglog daemon, but a TAC case should be opened before performing it.

In the last section, we discussed SD-WAN troubleshooting, which involves identifying what SD-WAN features FortiOS is using. Remember that Application Signatures require a learning phase before the correct SD-WAN Rule are used. Also, Application Contol, Web Filtering profile, and DPI are required to be placed on transit policies to steer traffic base on Application Signature or FortiGuard web categories. Be sure the check SLA probe thresholds hold and check SD-WAN logs for events.

Alright, folks! This completes Chapter 11 troubleshooting. The last thing to do is to jump into those end of chapter questions!

Chapter 11 End of Chapter Questions

1) A local site Network administrator reports packet loss on their FortiGate; what is the first thing you will check on the site's local FortiGate?
    a. Check the NIC for CRC errors
    b. Ping gateway IP
    c. **check system-level resources**
    d. Run diagnose flow command set

2) What is conserve mode?
    a. Used to limit bandwidth for users
    b. **Used when FortiGate memory utilization is too high**
    c. Used when FortiGate CPU utilization is too high
    d. Used when FortiGate disk utilization is too high

3) What command will display CPU, memory, and sessions?
    a. diagnose sys top
    b. diagnose sys top-summary
    c. **get system performance status**
    d. get sys top

4) Why would you be unable to specify FortiGuard Ports on FortiOS 6.4?
    a. **As of 6.4, you must disable fortiguard-anycast first**
    b. These values are now hardcoded into FortiOS and cannot be changed.
    c. Because there is no license
    d. As of 6.4, you must register FortiGate to support.fortinet.com first

5) What command will show active processes and related memory and CPU utilization?
    a. get sys top
    b. **diag sys top**
    c. get sys process
    d. diag sys process

6) What command is used to see if certain FortiOS proxies are affected by conserve mode?

    a. get sys proxy
    b. diagnose sys proxy
    c. diagnose firewall iprope state
    d. get firewall state proxy.

7) In 6.4 FortiOS, what percentage of memory utilization will FortiGate enter red conserve mode?
    a. 72%
    b. 82%
    c. 92%
    d. 95%

8) The output of "diagnose sys top", what does fds mean?
    a. free daemon space
    b. FortiOS daemon space
    c. FortiOS denoting service
    d. File Descriptor

9) What command will display global statistics on active FortiGate sessions?
    a. diagnose sys session full-stat
    b. diagnose session full-stat
    c. diagnose debug session full-stat
    d. get sys session full-stat

Note from Author

To all my loyal readers,

Firstly, let me congratulate you on completing the Introduction to FortiGate Part-II. I know it is hard to learn new technologies, and I hope the material in this book has helped you get you where you want to be in your career.

Secondly, I want to thank you for your support, and if I had not received much awesome feedback from Part-I, then this book might not have happened. Thank you for the motivation.

I will work on Part-III in 2021, which starts the security side of the NSE4 topics. My goal is to have it complete sometime in the summer. But as always, keep up the hard work, and I look forward to sharing Part-III with you soon. Please follow me on either LinkedIn, Amazon, or Facebook for updates on my progress.

Best Regards,

Daniel

Appendix A: End of Chapter Answers

Chapter Five End of Chapter Answers

1) **True** - Most session Helpers are enabled by default. A full list of session helpers can be obtained in the CLI via 'show sys session-helper'. For SIP, ALG has been the default setting since 5.2 MR FortiOS, and SIP helper has not been used by default.
2) **False** - SIP ALG provides the same base functions for SIP as the Session Helper module, but SIP ALG provides SIP security features as well
3) **D** - The default management VDOM is root.
4) **C** - The management VDOM is responsible for all system-level local-out traffic, including FortiGuard traffic.
5) **B** - The management VDOM is responsible for all system-level local-out traffic, including DNS queries.
6) **False** - The management VDOM can be explicitly configured to be any VDOM.
7) **False** - Physical Interfaces and related virtual interfaces can be in separate VDOMs.
8) **True** - A Transparent Mode VDOM can only create an inter-vdom link with a NAT Mode VDOM.
9) **False** - It is not required to have IP on an Inter-vdom interface.
10) **False** - VDOM's do share a global pool of resources but are not distributed evenly. The administrator must explicitly define resource limits for each VDOM.
11) **True** - FortiGuard Web Rating queries are only performed by the management VDOM.
12) **B** - diagnose sys vd stats

Chapter Six End of Chapter Answers

1) **D** – The HA vMAC OUI is 00-09-0f-09
2) **C** - The virtual MAC is generated base on the following algorithm: 00-09-0f-09-<group-id>-(<vcluster_integer> + <idx>)
3) **C** – Virtual Clustering is when VDOMs are declared as primary or secondary, and the primary VDOM can be placed on either Master or Slave units to process traffic.
4) **A** – Heartbeat interfaces are used to process heartbeat packets between cluster members used as a keepalive.
5) **B** – Monitored Interfaces are part of the HA configuration that can trigger a HA failover if these interfaces go down.
6) **B** – HA election process when Override is set to <u>enabled</u> is: Monitored Interfaces UP > Priority > Cluster uptime value > Serial Number
7) **A** - HA election process when Override is set to <u>disable</u> is: Monitored Interfaces UP > Cluster uptime value > Priority > Serial Number
8) **True** – SSD failure can trigger cluster failover if configured:

```
config system ha
set ssd-failover enable
end
```

9) **False** - By default, FGCP checks every 60 seconds that the config hash values match for each unit in the cluster.

10) **True** - If a Slave unit becomes out of sync, the hash value is then checked every 15 seconds, and after five checks, a complete re-synchronization is performed.

11) **C** - Master forwards the frame to Slave using the Slaves physical MAC address

12) **A** – Master HA unit will sync FIB routes to Slave units

13) False – Only certain HA settings are synced between cluster members.

14) **C** – Split Brain is when one more than device in a single HA cluster attempts to take the Master role.

15) **B** - session-pickup setting control HA session synchronization.

16) **C** – With Override disabled, the command 'diagnose sys ha reset-uptime' will trigger a HA failover

17) **C** – The command to provide checksum for a cluster is 'diagnose sys ha checksum cluster'

18) **B** – High-level overall HA health can be displayed with 'get sys ha status'

19) **C** – The command to recalculate hash values used by HA is 'diagnose sys ha recalculate.'

20) **D** – Two HA daemons that run on FortiOS are hatalk and hasync

Chapter Seven End of Chapter Answers

1) **C** – The three types of log message generated by FortiOS are, Traffic, Security and Event.

2) **D** – There eight log severity levels:

```
Levels      Details
0 – Emergency - System unstable
1 – Alert - Immediate action required
2 – Critical - Functionality effected
3 – Error - An error exists that can affect functionality
4 – Warning - Functionality could be affected
5 – Notification - Information about normal events
6 – Information - General System information
7 – Debug - Diagnostic information for investigating issues
```

3) **B** – To send VDOM specific logs out VDOM routing table the override command must be used under remote logging settings.

4) **C** – Reliable logging is when syslog data uses TCP as a transport protocol

5) **C** - Optimized Fabric Transfer Protocol over SSL
6) **B** - (OFTPs) is a Fortinet proprietary protocol used between FortiGate and FortiAnalyzer/FortiManager, and the purpose of this protocol is to synchronize information between the devices or carry log transmission.
7) D – FortiGate will cache logs locally if FAZ is unavailable.
8) D - diagnose test application miglogd 6 will display cached logs on FortiOS

```
# diagnose test application miglogd 6
mem=247, disk=0, alert=0, alarm=0, sys=0, faz=2116, faz-cloud=0, webt=0,
fds=594
interface-missed=296
Queues in all miglogds: cur:178  total-so-far:130675
global log dev statistics:
faz 0: sent=2002, failed=0, cached=114, dropped=0 , relayed=433691
Num of REST URLs: 15
```

9) C – The command #exec log fortianalyzer test-connectivity , will test FAZ connectivity
10) False – Threat weight can be changed on FortiOS
11) C -Log rolling is when a flat log file is compressed
12) D - A log message has two major parts, a header and a body
13) C- UTM Extended Logging is a feature to add HTTP header information to the 'rawdata=' field when HTTP traffic is denied.
14) A – The command to provide debug out for local disk is #diagnose sys logdisk usage
15) C – Default port and transport protocol for Syslog traffic is 514 UDP:

```
            (setting) # show ful
            config log syslogd setting
                set status enable
                set server ''
                set mode udp
                set port 514
                set facility local7
                set source-ip ''
                set format default
                set priority default
                set max-log-rate 0
            end
```

Chapter Eight End of Chapter Answers

1) **C** – ESP is assigned protocol numbe 50
2) **C** – ISAKMP is responsible for the exchange of the secret key information between IPsec peers

3) **D** - is responsible for generating the secret keying material to be used in the encryption function of ESP packets

4) **A** - is a framework used to accomplish the overall goal of secure communication between two devices that have never communicated before over the public Internet

5) **D** – ESP stands for Encapsulated Security Payload

6) **C** - The purpose of HMAC within ESP trailer is To Provide authentication and integrity for ESP packets

7) **D** - An Security Association is a common set of security protocols used between IPsec peers for secure communication

8) **D** - the characteristics of Phase-1 Aggressive Mode, Three packets are exchanged, and the Peer ID and Authentication Hash are unencrypted

9) **B** - the characteristics of Phase-1 Main Mode, Six packets are exchanged, and the Peer ID and Authentication Hash are encrypted

10) **True** - ADVPN is where Shortcut messages are passed through Hub to IPsec Spokes

11) **D** – The sequence of events when XAuth and Mode Config is used within the IPsec framework is: Phase-1 -> XAuth -> Mode Config -> Phase-2

12) **A** - command will show IPSec tunnel MTU and if Anti-Replay is being used is #get vpn ipsec tunnel details

13) **D** - The debug command will show XAuth user information is # diagnose vpn ike gateway

14) **D** - The sniffer command will allow you to see ISAKMP traffic with no NAT is #diag sniffer packet any 'port 500

15) **C** - The sniffer command will allow you to see ISAKMP traffic with no NAT is #diag sniffer packet any 'port 4500'

16) **A** – The sniffer command will allow you to see ESP traffic # diag sniffer packet any 'esp'

17) **C** - the Add-Route feature work on FortiOS is the Local IPsec peer performs a reverse route injection for source Quick Mode Selector value received into the local routing table

18) **D** –

```
diag vpn ike log-filter dst-addr4 192.168.1.1
diag debug reset
diag debug enable
diag debug application ike -1
```

19) **True** - the net-device setting enabled, then FortiOS will create virtual interfaces for each IPsec tunnel dynamic peer

20) **D** - IPsec function is responsible for assigning DNS IP information to the remote IPsec peer is Mode Config

Chapter Nine End of Chapter Answers

1) C – The Handshake Protocol is used for the initial TLS client to server communication to set up a secure encrypted channel

2) D – the Change Cipher Spec Message means the client & server agree to put in use the proposed Cipher Suite, and all further communication will be encrypted
3) D – DTLS is TLS using UDP as a transport protocol
4) B – Cipher Suite is a set of cryptographic protocols used by TLS client and server
5) C – SSL-VPN Modes are Web and Tunnel
6) C - Authentication Group being referenced in SSL-VPN Firewall Policy Entry make SSL-VPN live
7) False – It is not required to explicitly add a route to the SSL-VPN interface because host route for remote user is inject into FIB.
8) A – Realms differentiate Web Portals by assigning users to different authentication groups
9) A – The idle-timeout settings controls how long a connected user can be inactive before being disconnected
10) C – The login-time controls how long the initial authentication process can take.
11) B – The auth-timeout setting controls when a connected user is forced to reauthenticate
12) A – Two settings that help SSL-VPN stability are

```
set auth-session-check-source-ip disable    //default enabled
set tunnel-connect-without-reauth enable     // default disable
```

13) B – strong-crypto enforces the use of strong cipher suites
14) B - banned-cipher is used to explicitly ban cipher suites
15) False- SSL-VPN can listen on any port that doesn't conflict with others
16) C – The setting mac-addr-check can restrict what machines can connected to a SSL-VPN
17) C – The command #execute vpn sslvpn del-tunnel 5
18) D – the command # diagnose debug application sslvpn 255, can debug SSL-VPN issues
19) False – It is recommend for businesses to obtain there own custom SSL-VPN certificate
20) A – When building a policy for a SSL-VPN a group or user must be selected in the source field
21) C - 'Destination Address of split tunnel policy is invalid' occurs when the policy destination subnet does not match the specified related Portal split-tunnel subnet.

Chapter Ten End of Chapter Answers

1) False – As of 6.2.3 an 6.4.0 Local out traffic in a SD-WAN environment uses only local routing table and not policy routes or Rules
2) C – Maximum Strategy, SD-WAN Rule Strategy load-balances across all SD-WAN members that meet SLA Health-Check threshold
3) D – Lowest Cost, SD-WAN Rule Strategy steers traffic to SD-WAN member interfaces that meet SLA targets and has the lowest cost value
4) B – Best Quality Strategy, SD-WAN Rule Strategy steers traffic to SD-WAN interface members based on the most desirable health check statistics
5) A – Manual Strategy, SD-WAN Rule Strategy is managed directly by the administrator
6) C - SD-WAN Health Check probes measure Latency, Jitter, and Packet Loss

7) C – There are six queues, 0 -5
8) B – Queue Zero is processed first
9) A – ToS is the 6.4 FortiOS GA default method is used to assigned Global Priority Value
10) A - Once Global Priority is assigned the next function to assign additional priority values are the Firewall Policy Entry or Traffic Shaper
11) C – The Priority packets that match a Traffic Shaper and has a transmission rate below the guaranteed threshold receive priority 0.
12) B - The Global Priority value is added to the Policy Priority value, and the result will be the egress interface queue if the packet matched a Traffic Shaper and is above the Guaranteed threshold but below the maximum threshold
13) True - Source NAT sessions will not be flushed from the routing table by default if route change occurs
14) B - Service Rule with gateway & default settings enabled the FortiGate FortiOS will skip FIB lookup
15) True - By default, if a Route Table update occurs, all sessions without SNAT are marked as dirty
16) B - preserve-session-route enable, the command will prevent sessions from being marked as dirty that do not have SNAT
17) C - requirements to use Application Signatures within SD-WAN Rules are Application Control profile, Deep Packet Inspection Profile within transit Firewall Policy Entry and active FortiGuard license
18) A – A learning phase required when using Application Signatures within SD-WAN Rules because FortiOS needs time to use Machine Learning to identify application and associate protocol, destination IP, and destination Port to the detected application
19) True – Applications learned through Application Control and used in SD-WAN Rule header attributes will be temporarily cached in the ISDB
20) True - Application matched within Traffic Shaper is accounted for separately from other traffic being generated from the same source IP
21) D - BGP encapsulated in IPsec ESP packets are marked with DSCP value CS6

Chapter Eleven End of Chapter Answers

1) C – When engaging on troubleshooting issues it is best to check system level health first like CPU or memory
2) B – Conserve mode is used when FortiGate memory utilization is too high
3) C – get system performance status – displays CPU, memory, and sessions on Fortigate
4) A - As of 6.4, you must disable fortiguard-anycast first before being able to specify FortiGuard Ports
5) B – diagnose sys top will show active processes and related Memory and CPU utilization
6) C – The command diagnose firewall iprope state is used to see if certain proxies are affected by conserve mode
7) B – FortiGate will enter conserve mode at 82%
8) D – fds means File Descriptor
9) A – The command diagnose sys session full-stat is used to display global statistics on active FortiGate sessions